# OECD Sci
# Technology
# and Industry Scoreboard

# 2005

OECD

ORGANISATION FOR ECONOMIC CO-OPERATION AND DEVELOPMENT

## ORGANISATION FOR ECONOMIC CO-OPERATION AND DEVELOPMENT

The OECD is a unique forum where the governments of 30 democracies work together to address the economic, social and environmental challenges of globalisation. The OECD is also at the forefront of efforts to understand and to help governments respond to new developments and concerns, such as corporate governance, the information economy and the challenges of an ageing population. The Organisation provides a setting where governments can compare policy experiences, seek answers to common problems, identify good practice and work to co-ordinate domestic and international policies.

The OECD member countries are: Australia, Austria, Belgium, Canada, the Czech Republic, Denmark, Finland, France, Germany, Greece, Hungary, Iceland, Ireland, Italy, Japan, Korea, Luxembourg, Mexico, the Netherlands, New Zealand, Norway, Poland, Portugal, the Slovak Republic, Spain, Sweden, Switzerland, Turkey, the United Kingdom and the United States. The Commission of the European Communities takes part in the work of the OECD.

OECD Publishing disseminates widely the results of the Organisation's statistics gathering and research on economic, social and environmental issues, as well as the conventions, guidelines and standards agreed by its members.



*Publié en français sous le titre :*
**Science, technique et industrie**
TABLEAU DE BORD DE L'OCDE 2005

# Foreword

*The* OECD Science, Technology and Industry Scoreboard 2005 *brings together the latest internationally comparable data to explore the growing interaction between knowledge and globalisation at the heart of the ongoing transformation of OECD economies. It draws mainly on OECD databases, indicators and methodology developed by the Directorate for Science, Technology and Industry and focuses on:*

- R&D and innovation: *investment in knowledge, the financing and performance of research activities, linkages in innovation systems, science and engineering publications.*
- Human resources in science and technology: *university graduates, R&D personnel, the international mobility of scientists.*
- Patents: *"triadic" patent families, patents in new technological fields, cross-border ownership of inventions.*
- ICT: *resources and infrastructure for the information economy, the diffusion and use of Internet technologies and electronic business, the contribution of the ICT sector to economic activity and international trade.*
- Knowledge flows and the global enterprise: *key channels of economic integration and technology diffusion, including foreign investment, the role of foreign-owned affiliates, as well as the contribution of multinationals to productivity.*
- *The impact of knowledge on productive activities: comparison of OECD economies in terms of income, productivity and industrial performance, the growing importance of technology and knowledge-intensive industries, the interaction between services and manufacturing, and the changing nature of manufacturing.*

*The 2005 edition is the seventh in a biennial series that started over a decade ago and has become a widely used reference for benchmarking the innovative performance of OECD countries. With each edition, a continued effort is made to offer new or improved official measures for international comparisons in key areas of policy interest. The Scoreboard favours using a wide range of indicators to map the complexity of innovative activities, and refrains from producing an overall ranking of countries derived from a unique, synthetic value.*

*This volume was prepared by the Economic Analysis and Statistics Division of the OECD Directorate for Science, Technology and Industry. Vladimir López-Bassols served as overall co-ordinator of the publication, Sandrine Kergroach provided statistical assistance and Julie Branco-Marinho, Beatrice Jeffries and Paula Venditti provided secretarial support. Laudeline Auriol, Frédéric Bourassa, Agnès Cimper, Chiara Criscuolo, Hélène Dernis, Isabelle Desnoyers-James, Mosahid Khan, Laurent Moussiegt, Karsten Olsen, Xavier Reif, Sheridan Roberts, Martin Schaaper, Cristina Serra-Vallejo, Sharon Standish, Brigitte van Beuzekom, Desirée van Welsum, Colin Webb and Alison Young all contributed to the publication. Alessandra Colecchia, Thomas Hatzichronoglou, Sam Paltridge, Dirk Pilat and Andrew Wyckoff offered guidance and commented on the draft. Joseph Loux supervised the publication process.*

# Table of Contents

OECD SCIENCE, TECHNOLOGY AND INDUSTRY SCOREBOARD 2005 – ISBN 92-64-01055-6 – © OECD 2005

ISBN 92-64-01055-6
OECD Science, Technology and Industry Scoreboard 2005


# Executive Summary

The long-term trend towards a knowledge-based economy continues. Science, technology and innovation have become key factors contributing to economic growth in both advanced and developing economies. This seventh edition of the OECD *Science, Technology and Industry Scoreboard* focuses on the growing globalisation of knowledge. This is not a new phenomenon *per se*, but it has become more pervasive, mainly driven by the use of information and communication technology (ICT). In the knowledge economy, information circulates at the international level through trade in goods and services, direct investment and technology flows, and the movement of people. Firms use ICTs to organise transnational networks in response to international competition and the increasing need for strategic interaction. As a result, multinational firms are a primary vehicle of the ever-spreading process of globalisation.

New technologies and their implementation in productive activities are changing the economic structure and contributing to productivity increases in OECD economies. Some examples of recent trends include:

- New channels for knowledge generation, diffusion, protection and application.
- New interactions owing to the increasing importance of networks, linkages, partnerships and mobility.
- New global actors from non-OECD countries.

This publication brings together a wide range of charts and analyses relative to emerging policy issues including the changing nature of research activities, the international mobility of researchers and scientists, the increasing pace of innovation as measured by patenting, the growth of the information economy, the important role of multinational enterprises, and new patterns in trade competitiveness. It also focuses on the emergence of key international players outside the OECD area, notably China. A selection of the most notable facts and figures in each of these areas is presented below:

## *R&D and innovation: creating and diffusing knowledge*

- Investment in knowledge (comprising expenditure on R&D, software and higher education) in the OECD area reached around 5.2% of GDP in 2001, compared to around 6.9% for investment in machinery and equipment.
- In 2003, Sweden had the highest R&D intensity (4% of GDP), followed by Finland, Japan and Iceland (all over 3%).
- China has become the third largest R&D performer behind the United States and Japan (mainly owing to rapid growth in researchers' salaries).
- Small and medium-sized enterprises (fewer than 250 employees) play an important role in innovation but only account for around 30% of total R&D expenditure.

- R&D activities are increasingly internationalised, but the share of foreign affiliates in industrial R&D varies widely, from less than 5% in Japan to over 70% in Hungary and Ireland.
- Government R&D budgets in OECD countries have increased annually by an average of 3.5% (in real terms) since 2000. Three-quarters of the growth in the government R&D budget in the United States between 2001 and 2005 is attributable to defence R&D.
- An increasing number of countries use R&D tax concessions to encourage business R&D expenditure. Today, 18 OECD countries have R&D tax credits in place, 50% more than in 1996. Canada, the Netherlands and Italy focus on small firms, while others do not distinguish by size.
- In 2001, 82% of the world's scientific articles were from the OECD area, two-thirds of which from G7 countries. In terms of relative intensity (articles per population), Sweden, Switzerland and Finland have the highest figures within the OECD.

## *Human resources in science and technology: knowledge and skills*

- Science and engineering (S&E) degrees represent 23% of new degrees awarded in OECD countries, 27% in the EU and 16% in the United States. However, since 1998, these shares have declined in many countries.
- Professional and technical workers represent between 25% and 35% of total employment in most OECD countries, and over 35% in Sweden, Luxembourg, Switzerland and Australia.
- In 2003, China had the world's second largest number of researchers (862 000), behind the United States (1.3 million in 1999), but ahead of Japan (675 000) and the Russian Federation (487 000).
- More women than men have found employment in the rapidly rising professional and technical occupations, but women represent only 25% to 35% of total researchers, mainly in the higher education sector. Their participation is particularly low in industry.
- Migration streams converge towards four main destinations: the United States with over 7.8 million highly skilled expatriates, the European Union (4.7 million), Canada (2 million) and Australia (1.4 million). Over half come from outside the OECD area.
- Foreign students represent more than a third of doctoral enrolments in Switzerland and Belgium and more than a quarter in the United Kingdom and the United States.

## *Patents: protecting and commercialising knowledge*

- More than 442 000 patent applications were filed in Europe and the United States in 2002, compared to around 224 000 a decade earlier.
- Patenting activity is heavily concentrated. In 2001, France, Germany, Japan, the United Kingdom and the United States accounted for 83.6% of all triadic patent families.
- Two technology fields contributed more than the average to the overall surge in patenting: biotechnology and ICT. Between 1991 and 2001, biotechnology and ICT patent applications to the European Patent Office (EPO) increased by 9.1% and 8.3% respectively, compared to 6.0% for all EPO patent applications.

- Non-member countries such as Brazil, China, India and the Russian Federation have a high level of internationalisation compared to large OECD countries. For example, two-thirds of the Russian Federation's EPO patents are owned or co-owned by foreign residents.
- Of the G7 countries, the United Kingdom is the most internationalised according to three measures: foreign ownership of domestic inventions, domestic ownership of inventions made abroad and patents with foreign co-inventors.
- The breakdown of internationalisation indicators by partner country shows that common language, historical links and geographical proximity play an important role in determining partner countries.

### *ICT: an enabler for the knowledge society*

- In 2001, the ICT sector represented 10% of business value added in the OECD area. Its share was highest in Finland (16%), followed by Ireland (13%).
- The ICT sector invests heavily in R&D. In 2002, ICT manufacturing industries accounted for more than a quarter of total business R&D expenditure in most OECD countries.
- In the OECD area on average, a quarter of all businesses use the Internet for purchasing and about one-eighth for selling.
- The share of Internet sales in total sales is increasing across the OECD area, but the level is still quite low. The most commonly reported barrier is that the products are not suitable for Internet sale. Other significant barriers are security and legal concerns.
- By the end of 2004 there were 118 million broadband subscribers in the OECD area, an increase of 34 million from 2003.
- For the first time, the number of fixed telephone lines is falling, with the increasing prevalence of mobile phones and broadband. With the latter, many users are giving up fixed lines previously used for dial-up Internet access.
- Demand for the Internet has largely driven the growth in home computer access. In Iceland in 2004, 86% of households had access to a computer.
- In almost all OECD countries, households with children are more likely to have Internet access at home and men are more likely than women to use the Internet. However, significantly more women than men use the Internet in the United States.

### *Knowledge flows and the global enterprise*

- Over 1999-2003, trade in both goods and services increased but the share of trade in goods was four times that of trade in services. High-technology goods (mainly computers and aircraft industry products) were the most exposed to international trade competition as they had the highest export (exports/production) rates and import penetration rates (imports/domestic demand).
- Over the period 2000-03, direct investment flows showed a marked decline. Among the G7 countries, the decline was largest in the United Kingdom and France for outward investment and in Germany, France and the United Kingdom for inward investment.
- In 2001, the share of the turnover of foreign-controlled affiliates in total manufacturing turnover ranged from 75% in Ireland to less than 3% in Japan.



OECD SCIENCE, TECHNOLOGY AND INDUSTRY SCOREBOARD 2005 – ISBN 92-64-01055-6 – © OECD 2005

- In 2002, the share of the turnover of foreign affiliates was lower in services than in manufacturing industry, except in Norway, Finland and Germany.
- Between 1995 and 2001, the share of foreign affiliates in manufacturing value added increased, particularly in Ireland, Sweden and Norway.
- The contribution of foreign affiliates to labour productivity growth in host countries was largest in the Czech Republic and Sweden.
- As regards trade in technology, between 1993 and 2003, the United States and Japan were largely in surplus while the European Union showed a deficit, mainly due to Germany, Italy, Spain and Ireland.

## *The impact of knowledge on productive activities*

- Investment in ICT accounted for between 0.35 and 0.9 percentage point of growth in GDP over the period 1995-2003. Australia, Sweden, and the United States received the largest boost from ICT capital. In Ireland, Finland and Greece, growth in multi-factor productivity was also an important source of GDP growth.
- In many OECD countries, notably Australia, Greece and the United States, business sector services accounted for the bulk of labour productivity growth in recent years. ICT manufacturing and services were particularly important in Finland and Sweden, whereas other high- and medium-high-technology industries were particularly important in Japan, Sweden and the United States.
- The share of knowledge-based "market" services continues to rise and now accounts for over 20% of OECD value added. The share of high- and medium-high-technology manufacturing fell to about 7.5% of total OECD value added in 2002, compared to about 8.5% in 2000.
- Trade in high technology industries has recovered from a strong downturn in 2000-01. From 1994 to 2003, pharmaceuticals had the highest growth rate in manufacturing trade in the OECD area.
- High-technology industries accounted for over 50% of all manufacturing exports in Ireland, and for over 30% of exports in Switzerland, Korea, the United States, the United Kingdom, Hungary and the Netherlands.
- In 2002, about 40% of all persons employed in the manufacturing sector were employed in occupations that can be considered services-related, *e.g.* management, business, finance and legal professionals.
- OECD countries accounted for just under 80% of worldwide value added in manufacturing in 2002. China accounted for about 8%, slightly above Germany's share. Out of the ten top global manufacturing countries in 2002, nine were OECD members.

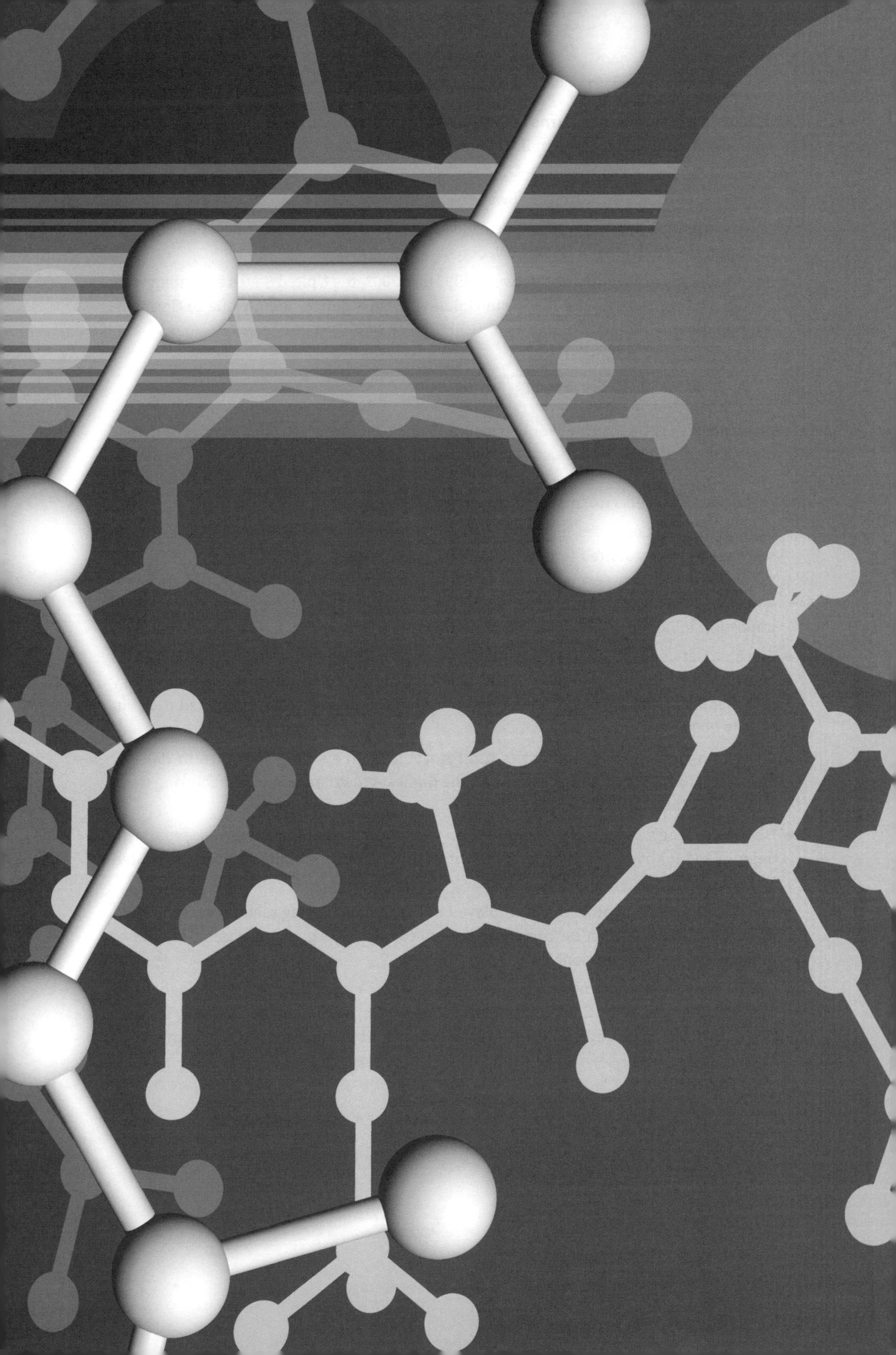

# A. R&D AND INNOVATION: CREATING AND DIFFUSING KNOWLEDGE

## A.1. Investment in knowledge

■ Expenditure on research and development (R&D), higher education and software can be considered as investment in knowledge. Such investment is crucial for economic growth, job creation and improved living standards.

■ In 2002 it amounted to 5.2% of GDP in the OECD area, a share that has increased over time. If expenditure for all levels of education were included, investment in knowledge would be in excess of 9% of GDP for the OECD area.

■ The United States invests most in knowledge (6.6%) followed by Japan (5.0%) and the EU (3.8%). The United States and Japan are also moving more rapidly towards a knowledge-based economy than the EU: since 1994, their investment in knowledge to GDP ratios have grown at a higher rate than that of the EU.

■ The ratio of investment in knowledge to GDP varied from 1.8% to 6.8% across OECD countries. The share was lowest in southern European countries and highest in Nordic countries, Korea and the United States.

■ For all the reported countries, except Ireland, the ratio of investment in knowledge to GDP was higher in 2002 than in 1994. For most countries, increases in software expenditure were the major source of increased investment in knowledge. Notable exceptions are Finland (R&D expenditure was the main source of increase) and Greece (higher education and software were the main sources of increase).

■ In countries with a high ratio of investment in knowledge to GDP, this ratio increased more than the ratio of machinery and equipment to GDP, during 1994-2002.

■ Investment in machinery and equipment accounts for around 6.9% of OECD-wide GDP. The ratio of investment in machinery and equipment to GDP varies from 5.7% (Canada and Finland) to around 10% (Korea and Italy.

### Sources

- OECD, Capital services database, June 2005.
- OECD, Education database, June 2005.
- OECD, National Accounts database, June 2005.
- OECD, Main Science and Technology Indicators database, June 2005.

### For further reading


- Khan, M. (2004), "Estimating the Level of Investment in Knowledge across OECD Countries" in A. Bounfour and L. Edvinsson (eds.), *Intellectual Capital for Communities: Nations, Regions, and Cities.*


### *Measuring investment in knowledge*

Investment in knowledge is defined and calculated as the sum of expenditure on R&D, on total higher education from both public and private sources and on software. Simple summation of the three components would lead to overestimation of the investment in knowledge owing to overlaps (R&D and software, R&D and education, software and education). Therefore, before calculating total investment in knowledge, the data must be reworked to derive figures that meet the definition.

- The R&D component of higher education, which overlaps R&D expenditure, was subtracted from total expenditure on higher education (note that higher education includes both public and private sources).
- The software component of R&D, which overlaps R&D expenditure, was estimated using information from national studies and subtracted from software expenditure.
- Owing to a lack of information, it was not possible to separate the overlap between expenditure on education and on software; however, the available information indicates that this overlap is quite small.

A more complete picture of investment in knowledge would also include parts of expenditure on innovation (expenditure on the design of new goods), expenditure by enterprises on job-related training programmes, investment in organisation (spending on organisational change, etc.), among others. However, owing to the lack of available data, such elements could not be included.

In previous years, the software component of investment in knowledge was estimated from a private data source (International Data Corporation, IDC). However, the OECD has recently developed a capital services database, which includes software investment data. The software data from the OECD database is used to estimate the total investment in knowledge; therefore, the figures reported here differ from those of previous years.

## A.1. Investment in knowledge

### Investment in knowledge

As a percentage of GDP, 2002

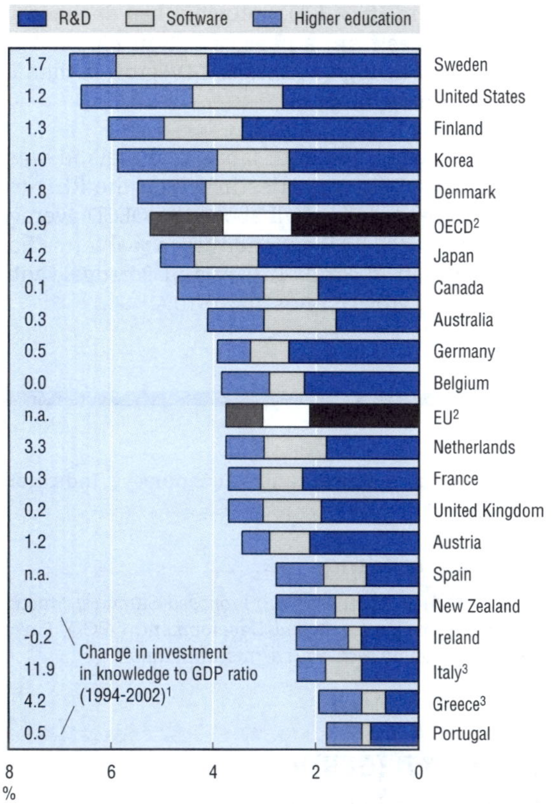


### Investment in machinery and equipment

As a percentage of GDP, 2002

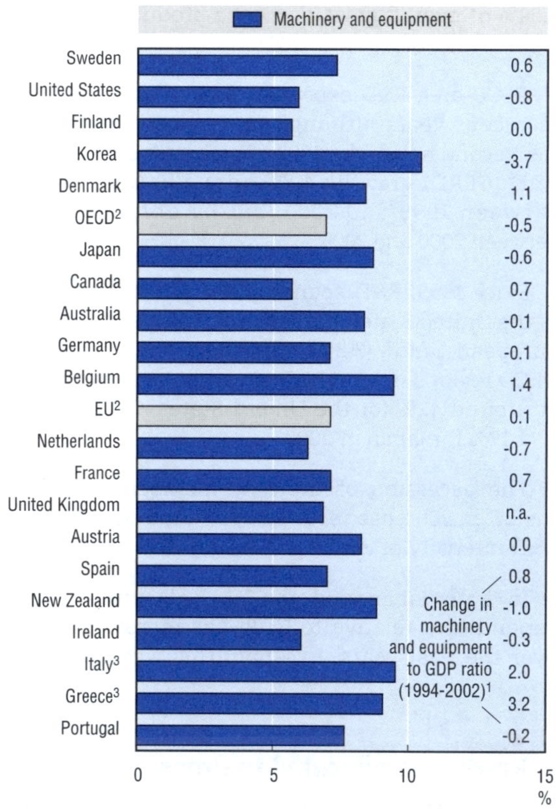


### Contributions to the growth of investment in knowledge, as a percentage of GDP, 1994-2002[1]

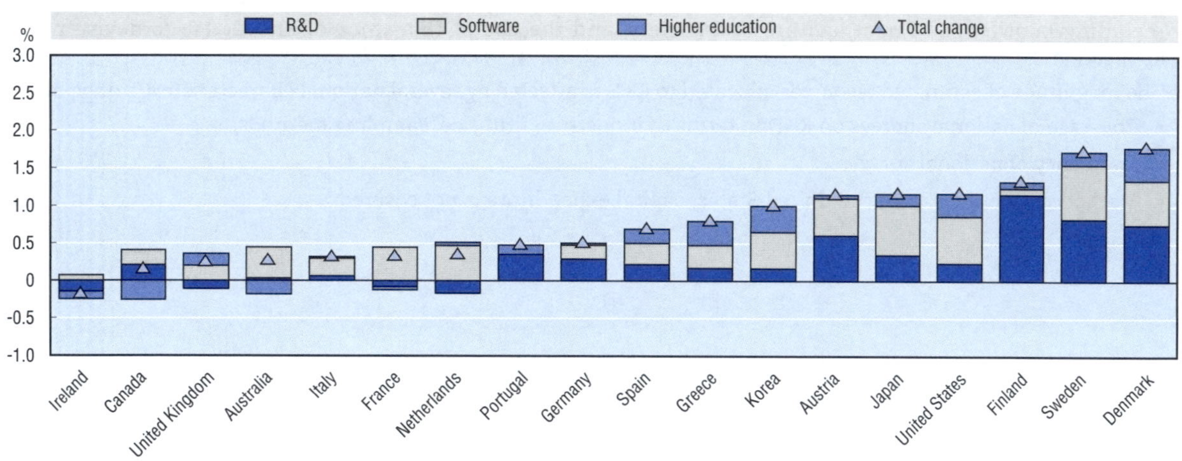


1. 1994-2001 for Greece and Italy. 1995-2002 for Korea. EU figure excludes Belgium, Greece and Italy. OECD figure excludes Belgium, Greece, Italy and New Zealand.
2. Excludes Greece and Italy.
3. 2001 data.

StatLink: *http://dx.doi.org/10.1787/480375180182*

## A.2. Trends in domestic R&D expenditure

■ In 2003, OECD expenditure on research and development (R&D) reached almost USD 680 billion (in current purchasing power parities – PPP), or about 2.24% of overall gross domestic product (GDP), down from a peak of 2.27% in 2001.

■ OECD-area R&D expenditure has increased steadily in recent years although more slowly than during the second half of the 1990s. Total gross expenditure on R&D (GERD) grew by 4.8% annually (in real terms) between 1995 and 2000, but by only 1.8% a year between 2000 and 2003.

■ Since 1995, R&D spending has grown more slowly in the United States and Japan (2.7% a year) than in the European Union (3.3%). The share of the three main OECD regions in total R&D expenditure remains stable at around 42% for the United States, 30% for the EU and 17% for Japan in 2003.

■ The accession of the new member countries to the EU in 2004 has resulted in a small decrease in EU R&D intensity of less than 0.1% of GDP.

■ In both Japan and the EU, R&D intensity (R&D expenditure relative to GDP) has increased steadily over the past years. In Japan, this was due both to stagnation in GDP and to steady increases in R&D expenditure. In 2001, R&D intensity in the EU15 exceeded 1.9% for the first time in a decade and reached 1.95% in 2003. R&D intensity has declined in the United States from a peak of 2.73 in 2001 to 2.60 in 2003, mainly owing to stronger GDP growth than in the other main regions.

■ In 2003, Sweden, Finland, Japan and Iceland were the only four OECD countries in which the R&D-to-GDP ratio exceeded 3%, well above the OECD average of 2.2%. Since 1995, R&D expenditure in real terms has grown fastest in Iceland, Turkey and Portugal, with average annual growth rates above 10%.

### Source

- OECD, Main Science and Technology Indicators database, May 2005.

### For further reading

- OECD (2002), *Frascati Manual: Proposed Standard Practice for Surveys on Research and Development*, OECD, Paris, available at *www.oecd.org/sti/frascatimanual*.

### Resources allocated to gross domestic expenditure on R&D (GERD)

Resources allocated to a country's R&D efforts are measured using two indicators, R&D expenditure and personnel. For R&D expenditure, the main aggregate used for international comparisons is gross domestic expenditure on R&D (GERD), which represents a country's domestic R&D related expenditure for a given year. The R&D data are compiled on the basis of the methodology of the *Frascati Manual 2002* (OECD, Paris, 2002) which defines R&D as "creative work undertaken on a systematic basis in order to increase the stock of knowledge, including knowledge of man, culture and society, and the use of this stock of knowledge to devise new applications".

The magnitude of estimated resources allocated to R&D is affected by several national characteristics, principally:

- Coverage of national surveys on R&D in terms of industries, firm size, sampling methods.
- Frequency of national surveys.
- Methodology used, *e.g.* for the United States, capital expenditure is not covered.



OECD SCIENCE, TECHNOLOGY AND INDUSTRY SCOREBOARD 2005 – ISBN 92-64-01055-6 – © OECD 2005

## A.2. Trends in domestic R&D expenditure

### R&D intensity,[1] 2003

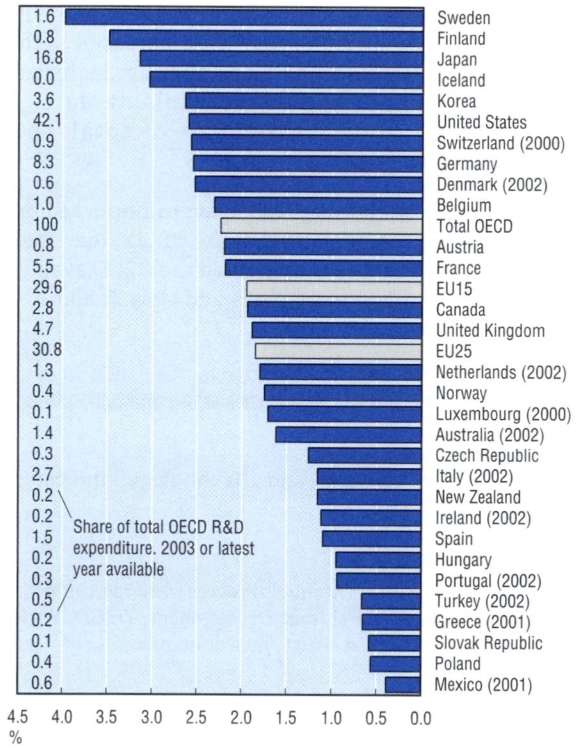


### Evolution of gross domestic expenditure on R&D, 1995-2003

Average annual growth rate

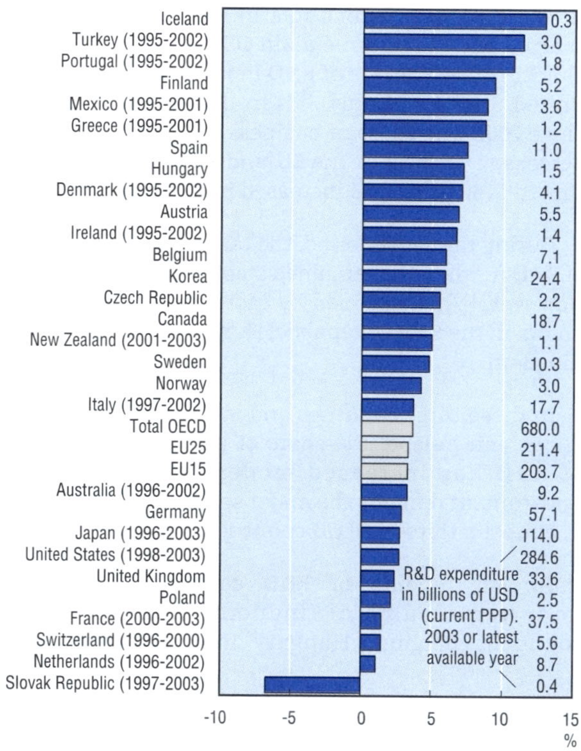


### Trends in R&D intensity[1] by area, 1991-2003

As a percentage of GDP

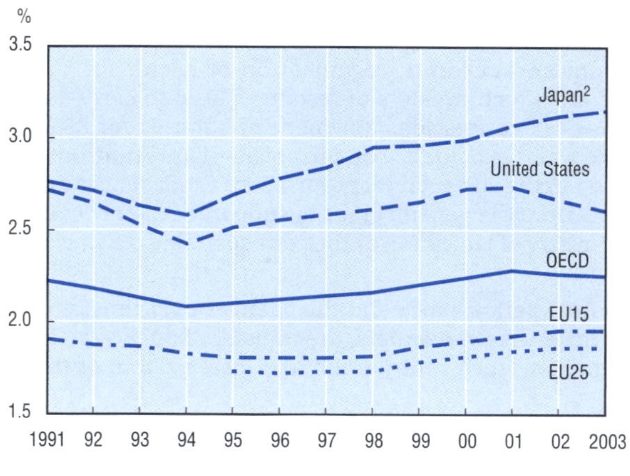


### Gross domestic expenditure on R&D by area, 1991-2003

Billions of USD PPP (2000)[4]

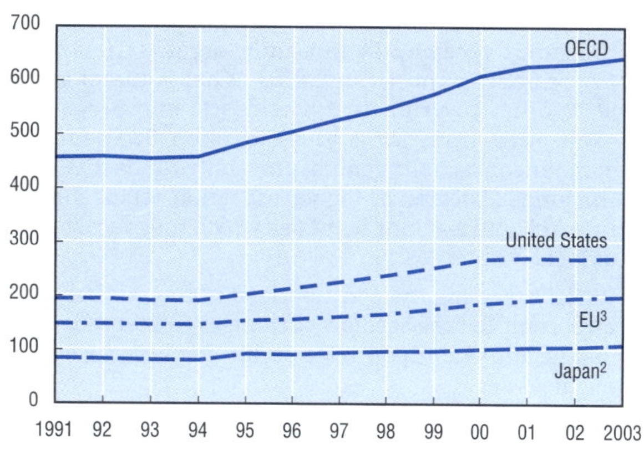


1. Gross domestic expenditure on R&D as a percentage of GDP.
2. Data are adjusted up to 1995.
3. Data are EU15 to 1994 and EU25 from 1995.
4. USD of 2000 in purchasing power parities (PPP).

StatLink: *http://dx.doi.org/10.1787/117388751182*

## A.3. R&D financing and performance

■ The business sector continues to be the major source of financing of domestic R&D. It accounted for almost 62% of funding in OECD countries in 2003.

■ The business sector's role in R&D funding differs sharply across the three main OECD regions. It funds almost three-quarters of R&D in Japan and 63% in the United States, but only 55% in the European Union. Since 2000, the share of business funding of R&D has decreased slightly in the EU and significantly in the United States, but has increased moderately in Japan.

■ During the same period, the business sector's share of R&D funding has remained stable in most countries. However, it has declined by more than 4 percentage points in the Slovak Republic, Hungary and the United Kingdom.

■ In these three countries and in Canada, the United States and Ireland, the share of government funding of R&D has increased moderately since 2000. Government remains the major source of R&D funding in almost a third of OECD countries.

■ Foreign funding of R&D continues to be an important source of financing in many OECD countries. Belgium, Hungary and the Netherlands receive more than 10% of their R&D funding from abroad. Austria, Greece, Iceland and the United Kingdom receive more than 15%.

■ The business sector also performs most R&D. Its contribution to the overall R&D effort increased in the second half of the 1990s and has slightly decreased since. According to the latest available data, it accounted for about two-thirds of total R&D expenditure in the OECD area in 2003.

■ The higher education and government sectors perform almost 30% of all R&D in the OECD area. Their combined share is more than double the OECD average in Poland, Turkey, Mexico, Greece and New Zealand.

### Source

- OECD, Main Science and Technology Indicators database, May 2005.

### For further reading

- OECD (2002), *Frascati Manual: Proposed Standard Practice for Surveys on Research and Development*, OECD, Paris, available at *www.oecd.org/sti/frascatimanual*.

### *R&D performance and funding*

The R&D effort (expenditure and personnel) is usually broken down among four sectors of performance: business enterprise, higher education, government and private non-profit institutions serving households (PNP). This breakdown is largely based on the System of National Accounts, but higher education is viewed as a special sector, owing to the important role played by universities and similar institutions in the performance of R&D.

R&D has various sources of financing. Five are generally taken into account: the four R&D-performing sectors mentioned above and funds from "abroad". Flows of funds are measured using performance-based reporting on the funds received by one unit, organisation or sector from another unit, organisation or sector for the performance of intramural R&D. What is therefore measured are direct transfers of resources used to carry out R&D; other government provisions to encourage R&D, such as tax concessions, payment of bonuses for R&D, exemption from taxes and tariffs on R&D equipment, etc., are excluded. For purposes of international comparisons, public general university funds (GUF) are included in the sub-total for government funds. These are the funds allocated by higher education establishments to R&D from the general grant in support of their overall research and teaching activities which they receive from the Ministry of Education or the corresponding provincial or local authorities.

When assessing the contributions of the different sectors to R&D performance and the changes over time, it is important to take account of changes in methods and breaks in series. For example, the transfer of public-sector organisations to the private sector would reduce the government sector's contribution and increase that of the business sector.


OECD SCIENCE, TECHNOLOGY AND INDUSTRY SCOREBOARD 2005 – ISBN 92-64-01055-6 – © OECD 2005

## A.3. R&D financing and performance

### R&D expenditure by source of financing, 2003

As a percentage of the national total

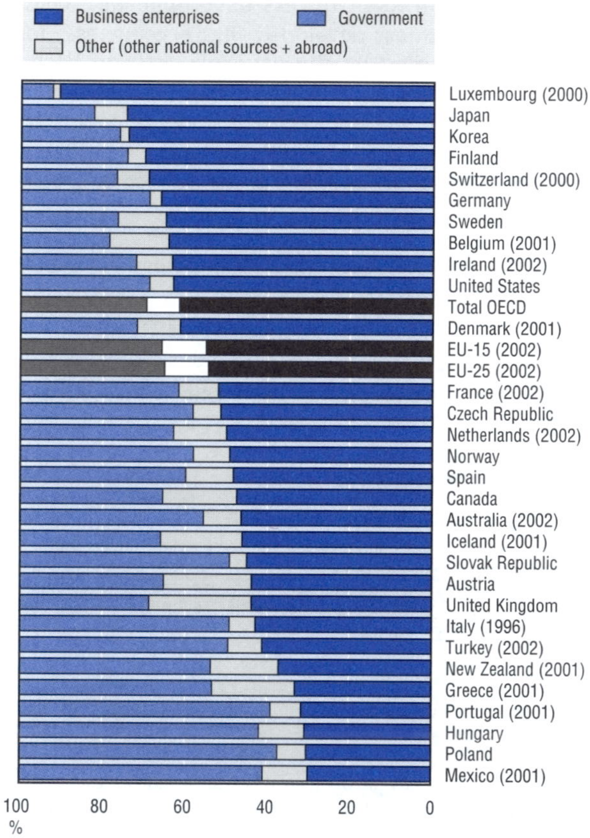


### R&D expenditure by performing sector, 2003

As a percentage of the national total

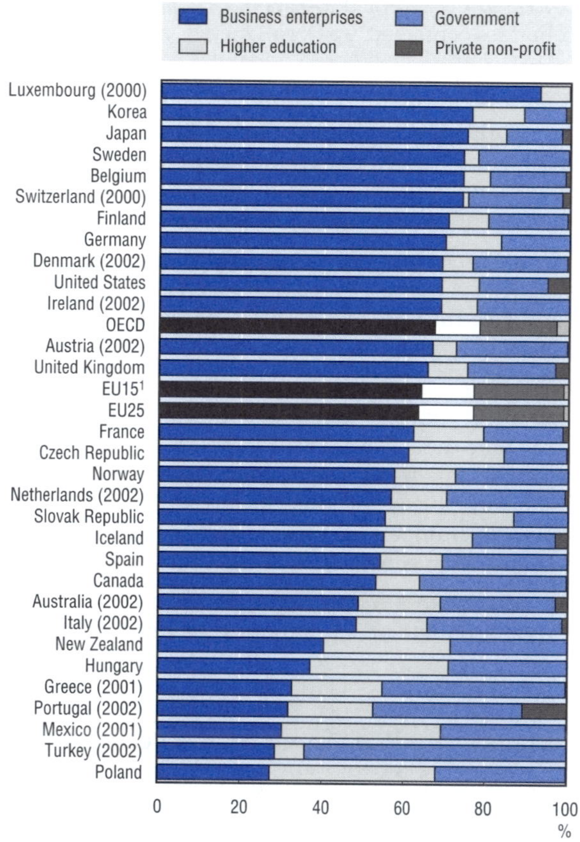


### R&D expenditure by source of financing, 1991-2003

As a percentage of GDP

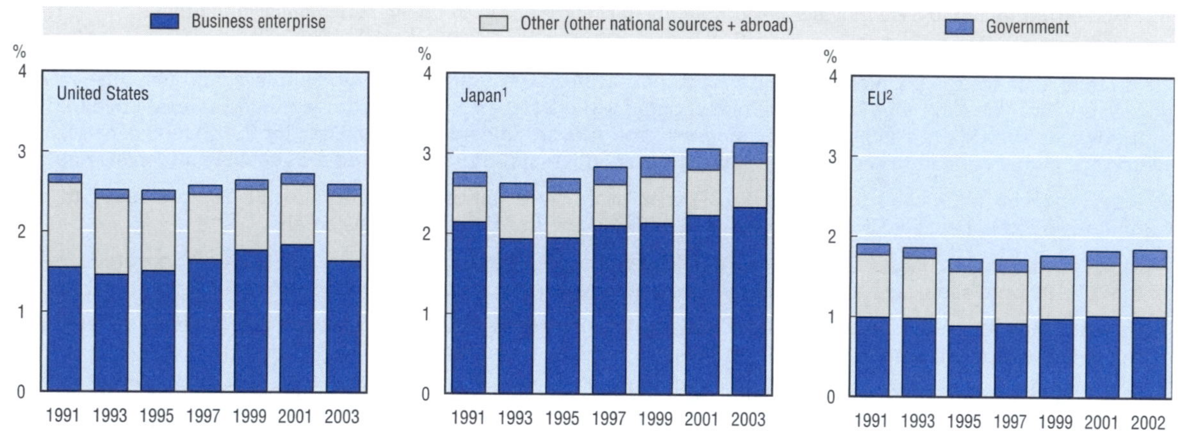


1. Data are adjusted up to 1995.
2. Data are EU15 up to 1994 and EU25 from 1995.

StatLink: *http://dx.doi.org/10.1787/563002707732*

## A.4. R&D in non-OECD economies

■ Non-OECD economies account for a growing share of the world's R&D. In 2003, the non-OECD countries included here accounted for 20% of the R&D expenditure (expressed in current USD PPP) of OECD and non-OECD economies combined, up from 17% two years earlier.

■ China made by far the largest contribution, accounting for half of the non-OECD share. It ranked third worldwide, behind the United States and Japan, but ahead of individual EU member states. However, the conversion from national currency into USD PPP may overestimate China's R&D effort.

■ In 2003, Israel had the world's highest R&D intensity, spending 4.9% of GDP on civilian R&D, more than twice the OECD average. Chinese Taipei was the only other non-OECD economy with an R&D intensity above the OECD average.

■ In most of the non-OECD economies covered, recent growth rates were well above the OECD average. For China, this was largely due to researcher salaries, which have risen very fast in recent years. Indeed, growth in numbers of researchers was much more moderate than growth in R&D expenditure (see B.10).

■ Industrial R&D is very closely linked to the creation of new products and production techniques and is therefore an important driver of economic growth. In the Asian countries and the Russian Federation, the business enterprise sector carries out most of the expenditure on R&D. In less developed non-OECD countries, as in less developed OECD countries, most R&D is performed by the government and higher education sectors.

### Sources

- OECD, Main Science and Technology Indicators database, May 2005.
- Eurostat, NewCronos database, May 2005.
- World Bank, World Development Indicators.
- Data for some countries have been compiled from national sources.

### For further reading


- OECD (2002), *Frascati Manual 2002: Proposed Standard Practice for Surveys on Research and Experimental Development*, OECD, Paris, available at *www.oecd.org/sti/frascatimanual*.
- OECD (2005), *Main Science and Technology Indicators 2005/1*, OECD, Paris.


### Measuring R&D in non-OECD economies

R&D data for Argentina, China, Israel, Romania, the Russian Federation, Singapore, South Africa, Slovenia and Chinese Taipei are included in the OECD database and are published in the OECD's Main Science and Technology Indicators (MSTI). Data for Bulgaria, Croatia, Cyprus, Estonia, Latvia and Lithuania are from Eurostat's NewCronos database. Data for Brazil, Chile, Hong Kong (China) and India are from national S&T ministries (or equivalent) or the central statistical office.

The R&D data for non-OECD countries that are included in the MSTI database largely comply with the recommended methodology of the *Frascati Manual*, and the same can be said for the data from Eurostat's database. Data for the other countries included here may not be completely in accordance with the *Frascati Manual* guidelines.

When examining the data, the following should be kept in mind.

- In Brazil, data for the business enterprise sector are collected through innovation surveys, and response rates are very low. The estimated totals only reflect data for the 1 100 enterprises that responded at least once to the innovation survey since 1993. Hence business sector data are underestimated. Data for the government sector and the higher education sector are estimated using budgetary information and are probably underestimated.
- For China, the rates used to convert R&D expenditure from national currency to USD PPP are likely to be underestimated, hence R&D data expressed in USD PPP are likely to be overestimated.
- In India, the higher education sector and the small-scale industry sector are only partially covered. Data for 2000-01 were estimated by applying sector-wise growth rates for the period 1994-95 to 1998-99.
- In Israel and Lithuania, defence R&D is not covered. In Israel, humanities and law are only partially covered in the higher education sector.
- In Latvia, the business enterprise sector is not fully covered, hence the data are underestimated.
- In Romania and the Russian Federation, much R&D is traditionally performed by public enterprises, which are classified in the business enterprise sector.
- Due to the lack of a comprehensive business register for South Africa, R&D expenditure may be underestimated by 10% to 15%.

## A.4. R&D in non-OECD economies

### R&D in the OECD and non-OECD area, 2003.

GERD as a percentage of GDP and researchers per 1 000 employees

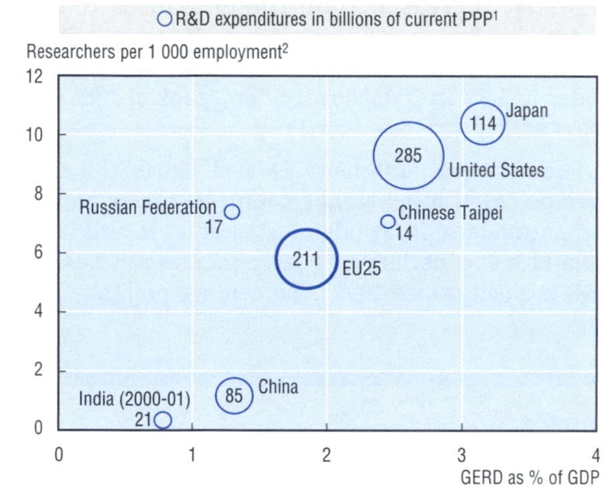


### Intensity of gross expenditure on R&D (GERD), 2003

As a percentage of GDP

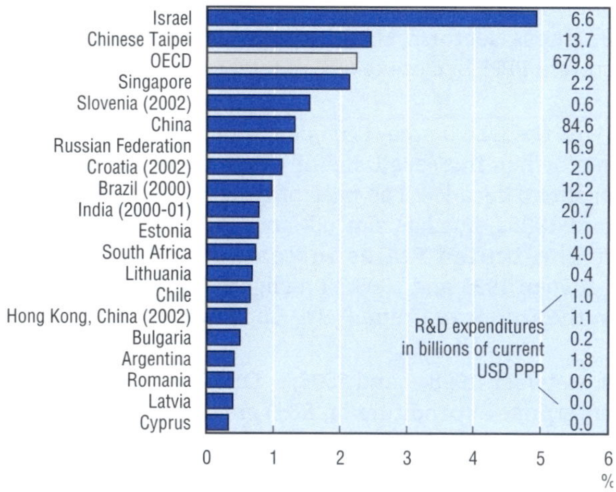


### Evolution of GERD, 2000-2003

Annual average growth rate[3]

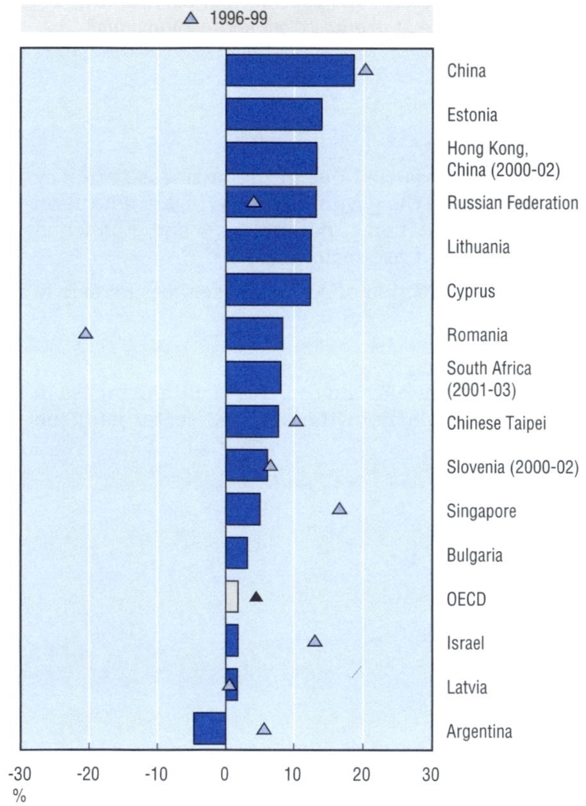


### R&D expenditures by performing sector, 2003

As a percentage of the national total

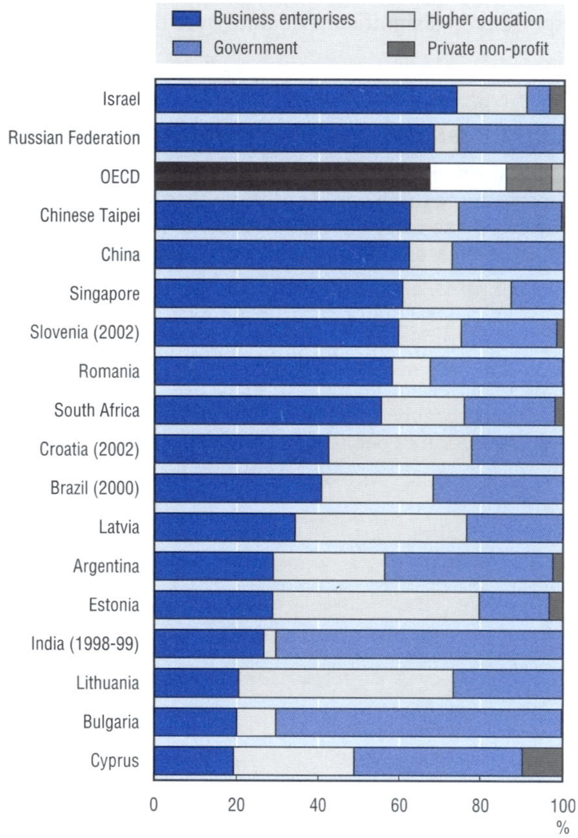


1. The size of the bubble represents R&D expenditure in billions of current USD in purchasing power parities (PPP).
2. For researchers per 1 000 persons employed: EU25, 2002; United States, 1999; and India, 1998.
3. Based on data in constant 2000 prices.

StatLink: *http://dx.doi.org/10.1787/083778005723*

## A.5. Business R&D

■ Business enterprise R&D accounts for the bulk of R&D activity in OECD countries in terms of both performance and funding (see A.3). In 2003, R&D performed by the business sector reached almost USD 458 billion (in current PPP), or close to 68% of total R&D.

■ In the OECD area, R&D performed by the business sector has increased steadily in real terms over the past two decades. The pace of growth picked up in the mid-1990s, but has slowed since 2001. Business R&D in the United States increased by 3.2% a year between 1995 and 2003, at a slightly slower pace than in the European Union (3.7%) and Japan (3.5%).

■ Between 1998 and 2003, OECD-area business enterprise expenditure on R&D grew by USD 55 billion (in PPP of 2000). EU15 accounted for around 40% of this growth, and the United States for less than a fifth.

■ Since 1995, annual average growth rates for business enterprise R&D were highest in Iceland, Portugal, Mexico and Turkey. Only the Slovak Republic experienced a significant decline over the period.

■ In the three main OECD regions, business R&D intensity (expenditure relative to domestic product of industry) increased from the mid-1990s to 2000. Growth has continued since in both Japan and the EU, but business R&D intensity dropped in the United States to 2.6% in 2003, down from a peak of 2.9% three years earlier.

■ Business R&D intensity is well above the OECD average (2.1%) in all Nordic countries except Norway, but particularly in Sweden (4.7%) and Finland (3.7%). Iceland has experienced a large increase in business R&D intensity since 1995 (2 percentage points).

### Source

- OECD, Main Science and Technology Indicators database, May 2005.

### For further reading

- OECD (2002), *Frascati Manual: Proposed Standard Practice for Surveys on Research and Experimental Development*, OECD, Paris, available at *www.oecd.org/sti/frascatimanual*.

### Business enterprise expenditure on R&D

Business enterprise expenditure on R&D (BERD) covers R&D activities carried out in the business sector by performing firms and institutes, regardless of the origin of funding. While the government and higher education sectors also carry out R&D, industrial R&D is most closely linked to the creation of new products and production techniques, as well as to a country's innovation efforts. The business enterprise sector includes:

- All firms, organisations and institutions whose primary activity is production of goods and services for sale to the general public at an economically significant price.
- The private and non-profit institutes mainly serving them.

When assessing changes in BERD over time, it is necessary to take account of changes in methods and breaks in series, notably concerning the extension of survey coverage, particularly in the services sector, and the privatisation of publicly owned firms.

## A.5. Business R&D

### Business R&D intensity,[1] 2003

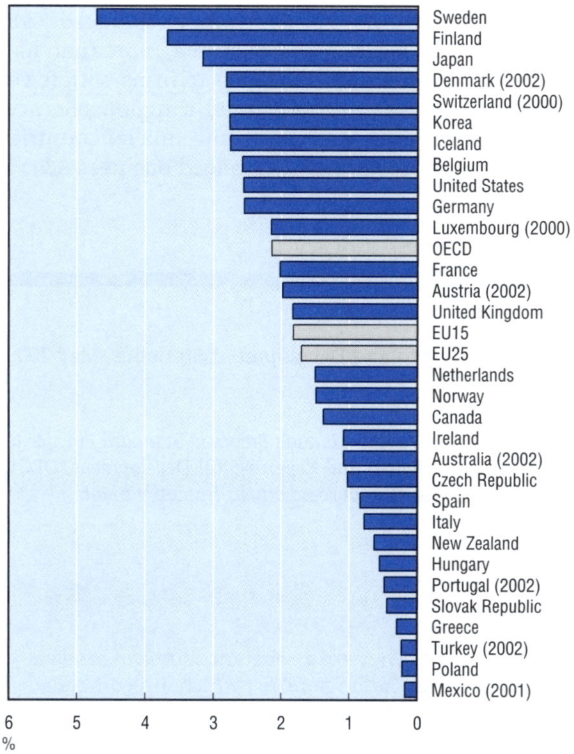


### Growth of business R&D, 1995-2003

Annual average growth rate, USD PPP of 2000[2]

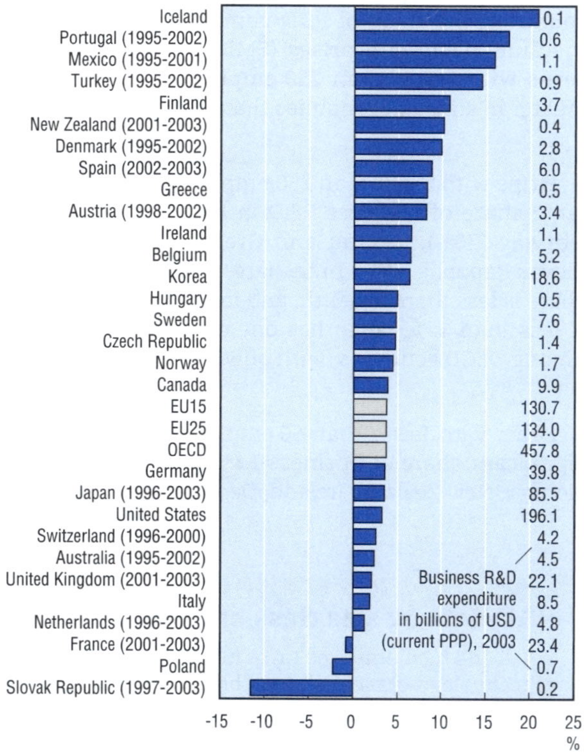


### Evolution of business R&D intensity,[1] 1991-2003

As a percentage of value added in industry

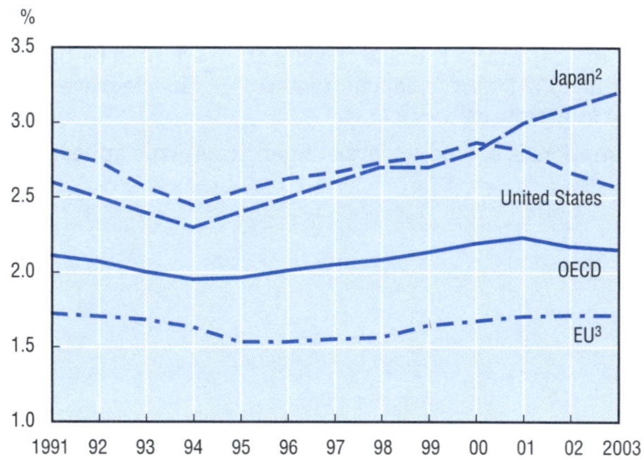


### Evolution of business R&D, 1991-2003

Billions of USD PPP (2000)[2]

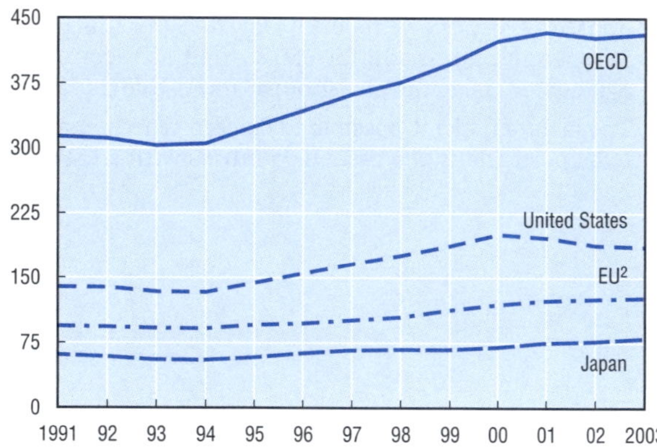


1. Business enterprise sector R&D expenditure as a percentage of value added in industry.
2. USD of 2000 in purchasing power parities (PPP).
3. Data are EU15 up to 1994 and EU25 from 1995.

StatLink: *http://dx.doi.org/10.1787/868030534350*

## A.6. Business R&D by size classes of firms

Both small and large firms play an important role in countries' innovative performance, but their relative importance for business R&D varies. In OECD countries, the share of R&D performed by small and medium-sized enterprises (SMEs) (defined here as firms with fewer than 250 employees) is generally greater in smaller economies than in larger ones.

Firms with fewer than 250 employees account for a large share of business R&D in New Zealand (72%), Norway (70%), Ireland and Greece (49%), and the Slovak Republic (46%). In the larger EU countries, their share is less than one-fifth, and in the United States it is less than 15%. Japan has one of the lowest shares among OECD countries, with only 9%.

Firms with fewer than 50 employees account for a significant share of business R&D (over one-fifth) in Norway, New Zealand, Ireland, Denmark and Australia.

OECD countries also differ greatly in terms of government financing of business R&D by size class. In Ireland, New Zealand and Australia, SMEs receive three-quarters or more of government-financed R&D. In Ireland, New Zealand and Australia, more than half of government-financed R&D goes to firms with fewer than 50 employees. In the United Kingdom, France, the United States, as well as in some smaller countries such as Turkey, government-financed business R&D is mainly directed to large firms.

### Source

- OECD, Research and Development Statistics, May 2005.

### For further reading

- OECD (2002), *Frascati Manual: Proposed Standard Practice for Surveys on Research and Experimental Development*, OECD, Paris, available at *www.oecd.org/sti/frascatimanual*.

### R&D data by size class of firms

Small and medium-sized firms (SMEs) play an important role in innovation. They are a constant source of renewal of technology, of technological breakthroughs and of competitive pressures for large firms, which are compelled to innovate to maintain their technological edge. However, SMEs face specific problems for innovating and for adopting new technologies (access to funds, markets and skilled labour). Moreover, it is often argued that public policies are biased against SMEs and that this might justify corrective action in their favour.

On the other hand, the role of large firms should not be ignored: they play a leading role in structuring markets, carrying out large-scale innovations and even in co-ordinating smaller firms. The respective and complementary roles of small and large firms may vary across industries and across countries. The relevance of various types of policy tools may vary with the size profile of the target population of firms.

Data in this section are based on a mini questionnaire launched in 1997. The data have subsequently been updated every two years until May 2005 (for this publication). To conform to the size classification adopted by the European Commission for SMEs – and as recommended in the 2002 *Frascati Manual* (para. 183) – the data were aggregated using the size groups "fewer than 50" and "50 to 249 employees".

These data make it possible to discern whether government support is biased towards larger firms. This appears to be particularly the case in countries with large defence budgets.



OECD SCIENCE, TECHNOLOGY AND INDUSTRY SCOREBOARD 2005 – ISBN 92-64-01055-6 – © OECD 2005

## A.6. Business R&D by size classes of firms

**Share of business R&D by size class of firms,[1] 2003** | **Share of government-financed business R&D by size class of firms, 2003**

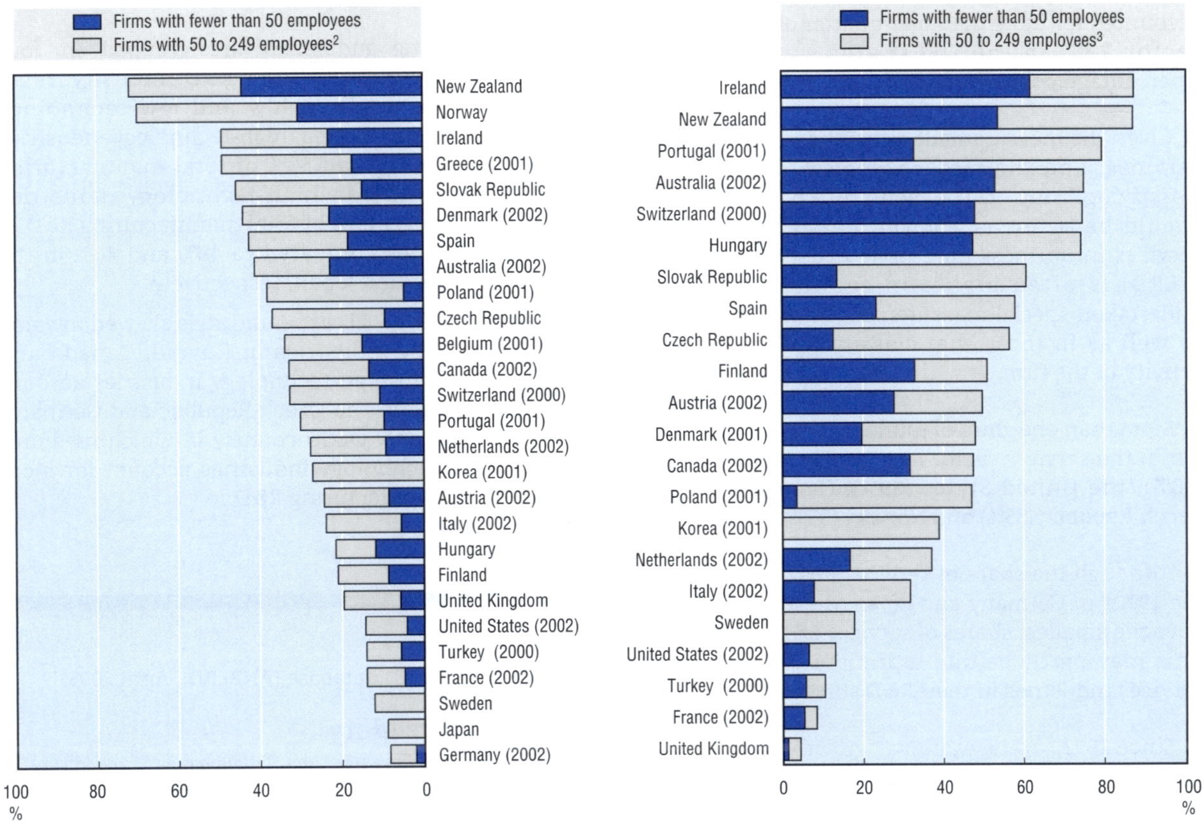


1. For the United States, federally funded research and development centers (FFRDCs) are excluded. German data excludes co-operative research institutes.
2. For Japan and Korea, fewer than 299 employees.
3. For Korea, fewer than 299 employees.

StatLink: *http://dx.doi.org/10.1787/430048678578*

## A.7. Business R&D by industry

■ While the economic structure of OECD countries has moved towards services, these still represent a much smaller share of R&D than of GDP. In 2002, they accounted for more than one-quarter of total business sector R&D in the OECD area, an increase of 8 percentage points from 1993.

■ Given the measurement difficulties associated with services, and the methodological differences in classifying firms' R&D expenditure by industry, this should be taken as a lower bound. The share of services in business enterprise expenditure on R&D (BERD) is often higher in countries that have undertaken special measurement efforts in this area, as well as in those that classify R&D by principal activity of the firm.

■ More than one-third of total business R&D is carried out in the services sector in Australia (42%), Denmark (40%), the United States (39%), Canada (36%), the Czech Republic (35%) and Norway (33%).

■ Although the share of services R&D increased over the 1990s in Germany and Japan, these countries still have the smallest shares of services R&D at under 10%. This may partly be due to limited coverage of the services industries in their R&D surveys.

■ Since 1993, average annual growth rates for R&D were higher in services than in manufacturing for all countries except Finland, the Czech Republic and Poland. Ireland had the most notable difference in R&D growth rates for the two sectors: between 1993 and 2001, Irish R&D increased by 27% in services (mainly driven by growth in computer services) and by 7% in manufacturing.

■ Manufacturing industries are grouped in four categories according to their R&D intensity: high, medium-high, medium-low and low technology (see F.5). In the OECD area, high-technology industries account for more than 53% of total manufacturing R&D. In 2002, R&D in high-technology industries accounted for over 60% of total manufacturing R&D in the United States compared to 48% and 46% in the European Union and Japan, respectively.

■ Manufacturing R&D expenditure is skewed towards high-technology industries in Ireland, Canada and Finland. Medium-high-technology industries account for 50% or more in the Czech Republic and Germany. Norway is the only OECD country in which medium-low and low-technology industries account for more than 40% of manufacturing R&D.

### Source

- OECD, STAN R&D database (ANBERD), April 2005.

### For further reading

- OECD (2005), *Research and Development Expenditure in Industry*, available at *www.oecd.org/sti/anberd/*.
- OECD (2002), *Frascati Manual: Proposed Standard Practice for Surveys on Research and Experimental Development*, OECD, Paris, available at *www.oecd.org/sti/frascatimanual*.

### Business R&D by industry

National statistical authorities recognise the need to improve R&D data for services, and R&D surveys are being extended to this end. However, certain methodological issues that have arisen need to be resolved. One is the way in which a firm's R&D is assigned to an industry, in particular for firms conducting heterogeneous research activities. Some countries follow a "principal activity" approach in which all of a firm's R&D is assigned to that firm's principal industrial activity code. Others break R&D down by "product field", *i.e.* the R&D is assigned to the industries of final use. Many countries follow a combination of these approaches. The *Frascati Manual* (2002) recommends distributing R&D by product field for all industry groups and as a minimum for the R&D industry (ISIC Rev. 3 Division 73), but not all countries follow this method.

The Analytical Business Enterprise R&D (ANBERD) database was constructed to create a data set that is as consistent as possible in order to overcome problems of international comparability and temporal discontinuities associated with official data on business enterprise expenditure on R&D (BERD). The current ANBERD database covers 19 OECD member countries and 58 sectors and has greater coverage of services. The data, from 1987, are based on ISIC, Rev. 3. ANBERD data are estimated by the OECD from official data supplied by national statistical authorities. Therefore, while efforts are made to adjust the data, it is important to exercise caution when using them.


OECD SCIENCE, TECHNOLOGY AND INDUSTRY SCOREBOARD 2005 – ISBN 92-64-01055-6 – © OECD 2005

## A.7. Business R&D by industry

### Share of services in business R&D,[1] 2003

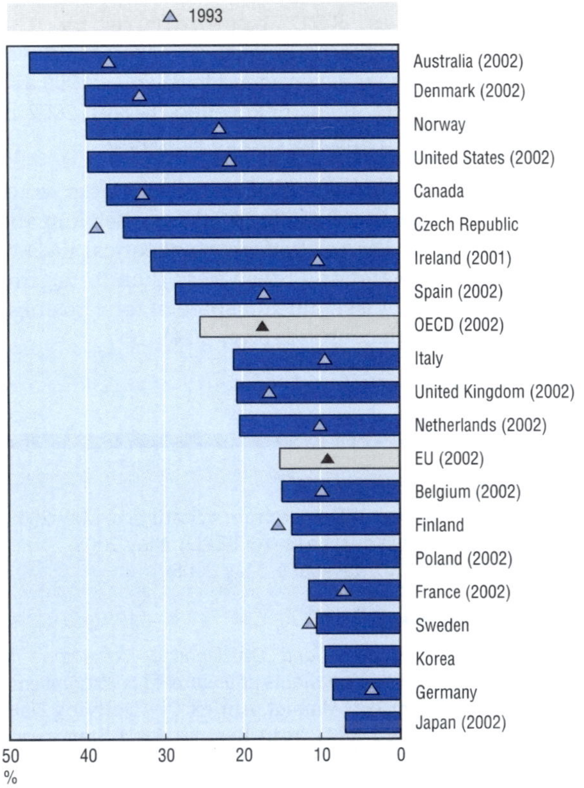


### R&D in selected services industries and manufacturing sector, 1993-2002

Average annual growth rate

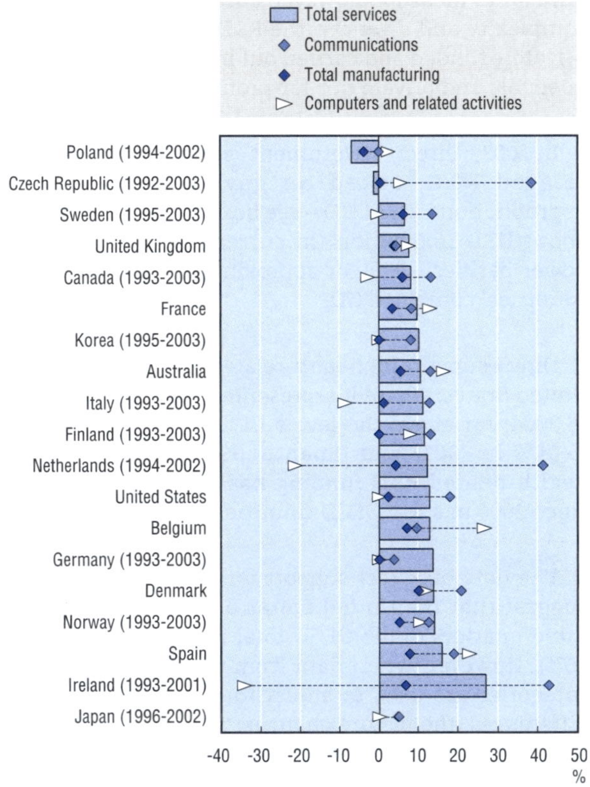


### Share of business R&D in the manufacturing sector by technological intensity, 2002

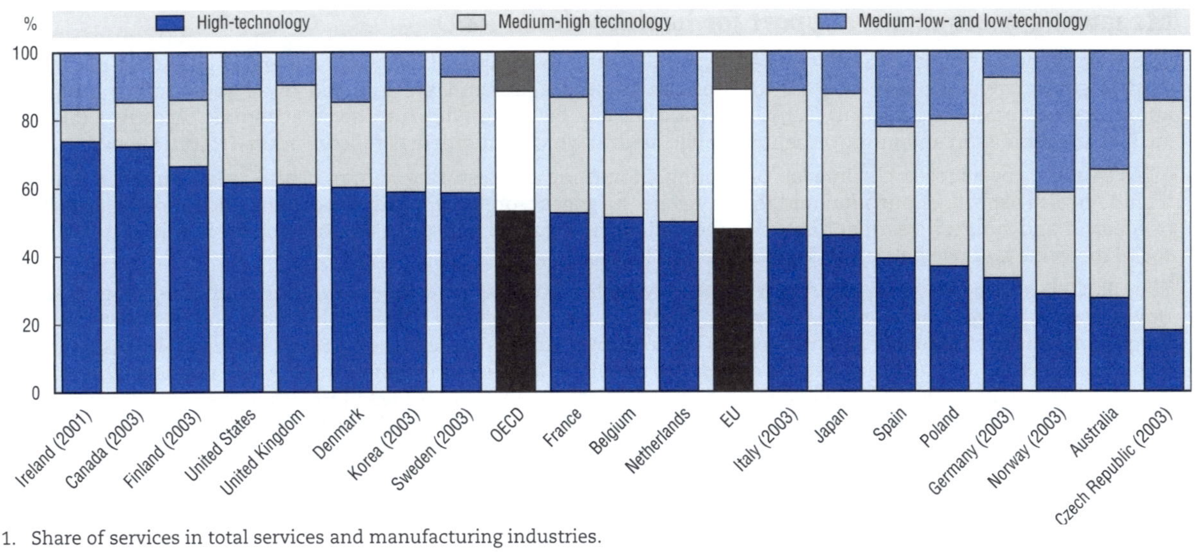


1. Share of services in total services and manufacturing industries.

StatLink: *http://dx.doi.org/10.1787/414837170815*

## A.8. Health-related R&D

R&D expenditures for health are of great interest because of the sector's size and expected growth as the population ages in many OECD countries. They are difficult to measure, however, because of institutional complexity and diversity (the R&D may be publicly or privately funded and carried out in firms, universities, hospitals and private not-for-profit institutions).

In 2003, direct government support for health-related R&D, based on government budget appropriations (GBAORD – see box for definition), was about USD 36.6 billion (in current USD purchasing power parities – PPP), or approximately 0.1% of OECD countries' combined GDP.

Direct support for health-related R&D is high in the United States, where it represented over 0.25% of GDP in 2004, far above the levels in the European Union (0.04% in 2001) and Japan (0.03% in 2003). Direct health-related R&D funding has actually decreased since 2000 in a few OECD countries.

The data on direct support for health-related R&D suggest that the United States accounts for around three-quarters of the OECD total (and the EU for only 16%). However, when data from additional GBAORD categories are used to adjust for some institutional differences, the picture changes. The United States is no longer an outlier: relative to GDP, health-related R&D budgets approach that of the United States in a number of countries. Sweden, with one of the smallest direct government budgets for health-related R&D as a percentage of GDP, is a case in point.

An indicator often used as a component of health-related R&D is R&D expenditure by the pharmaceutical industry. In 2003, it represented over 0.6% of GDP in Sweden, compared to 0.47% in 1999 and only 0.25% in 1991. It also exceeded 0.3% in 2002 in Denmark, Belgium and the United Kingdom.

The share of pharmaceutical R&D in business sector R&D is above 20% in the United Kingdom, Belgium and Denmark. While the ratio of pharmaceutical R&D to GDP is low in Poland and Spain (less than 0.1%), this sector accounts for a significant share of total business sector R&D in both countries (over 10%).

### Sources

- OECD, Research and Development Statistics, May 2005.
- OECD, STAN R&D database (ANBERD), May 2005.
- Eurostat, GBAORD database, May 2005.

### For further reading


- OECD (2005), *Research and Development Expenditure in Industry*, OECD, Paris, available at *www.oecd.org/sti/anberd/*.
- OECD (2002), *Frascati Manual*, Annex 4 – "Deriving Data on Health-related R&D from Regular R&D Statistics", available at *www.oecd.org/sti/frascatimanual*.
- OECD (2001), *Measuring Expenditure on Health-related R&D*, OECD, Paris.


### Measuring government support for health-related R&D

One way of measuring health-related R&D expenditure is to compile data from funders of R&D. The data on central government support for R&D are derived from budgets and are referred to as government budget appropriations or outlays for R&D (GBAORD). GBAORD can be broken down by socio economic objectives (SEO), such as the protection and improvement of public health, which is defined as follows in the *Frascati Manual*:

"This category covers research aimed at protecting, promoting and restoring human health broadly interpreted to include health aspects of nutrition and food hygiene. It ranges from preventative medicine, including all aspects of medical and surgical treatment both for individuals and groups and provision of hospital and home care to social medicine and paediatric and geriatric research."

The GBAORD health category is used here as a proxy for total central government funding of health-related R&D. However, it only covers programmes for which health is the primary objective. Furthermore, the classification of programme and institutional funding depends on how governments present their R&D priorities as well as on the formal mandate of the institutions concerned. For example, long-term research may be the responsibility of a medical research body classified in health objectives (*e.g.* the National Institutes of Health in the United States) or of a general research council whose funds are mainly awarded for non-oriented research (*e.g.* the National Council for Scientific Research in France). Arrangements for funding of R&D in hospitals also vary.

To address some of the limitations and to provide a more complete picture of health-related R&D, funding of medical sciences via non-oriented research and general university funds (GUF) is included when available, as are other relevant funds, notably general support for R&D in hospitals.



OECD SCIENCE, TECHNOLOGY AND INDUSTRY SCOREBOARD 2005 – ISBN 92-64-01055-6 – © OECD 2005

# A.8. Health-related R&D

## Health-related R&D in government budgets (GBAORD[1]), 2004

As a percentage of GDP

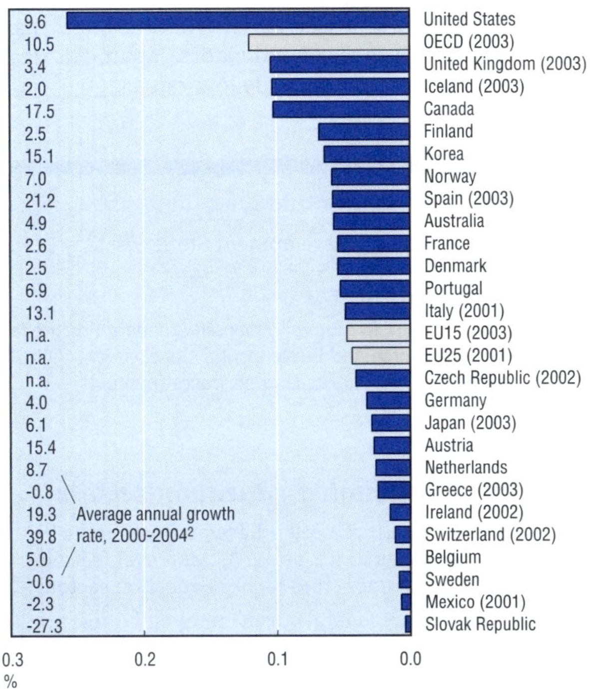


## Effect of including other health-related NABS[3] categories in health-related GBAORD, 2004

As a percentage of GDP

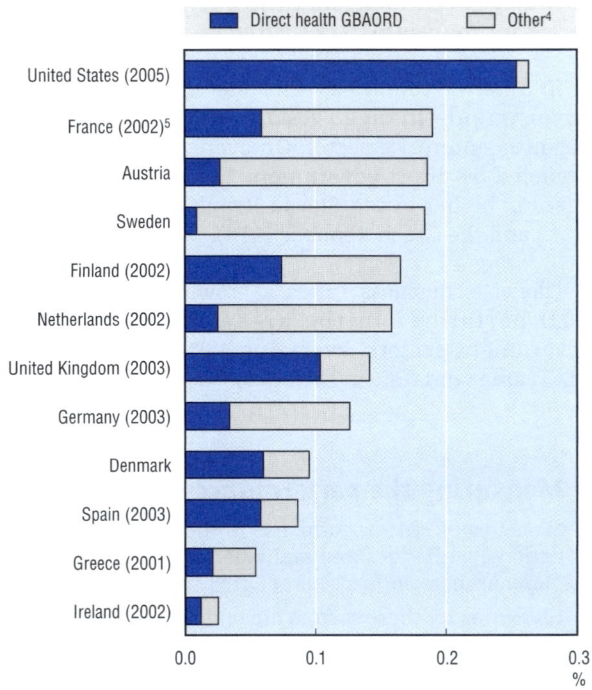


## R&D expenditure in the pharmaceutical industry, 2002

As a percentage of GDP and BERD[6]

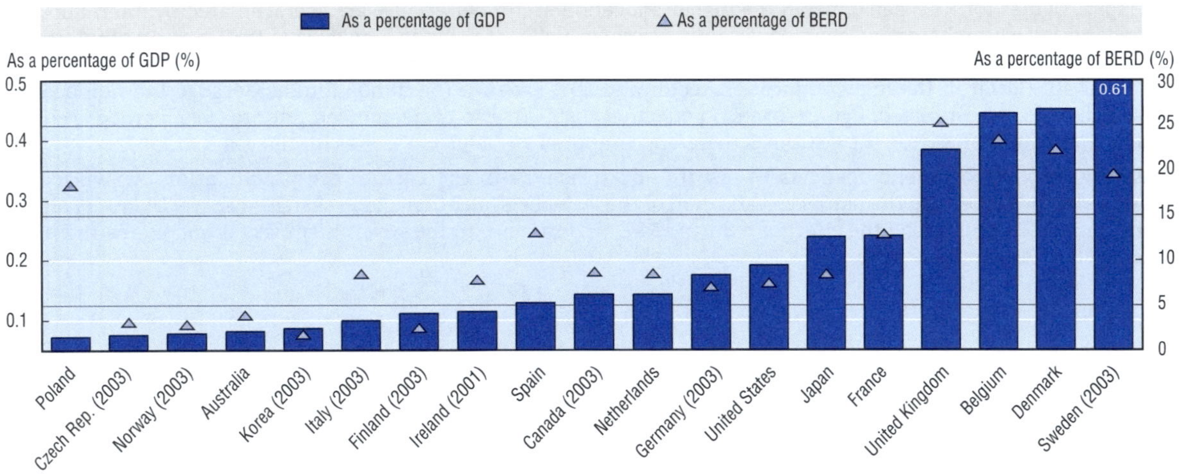


1. Government budget appropriations or outlays for R&D.
2. Growth rate period is 2000-03 for Greece, Iceland, Japan, Spain, Sweden, the United Kingdom and Total OECD; 2001-04 for Denmark; 2000-02 for Ireland and Switzerland; 2000-01 for Italy and Mexico.
3. Nomenclature for the analysis of science budgets.
4. Comprises non-oriented R&D, general university funds (GUF) and other relevant national and international categories.
5. Includes some other life sciences research.
6. Business enterprise expenditure on R&D.

StatLink: *http://dx.doi.org/10.1787/318784332420*

## A.9. R&D linkages

■ Co-operation among actors in science and innovation systems takes many forms and is often difficult to quantify. Direct financial flows for R&D between government and the business enterprise sector are one way to track such cross-sectoral linkages.

■ In many countries, an increasing share of government-financed R&D is performed in the business enterprise sector. On average, around 7% is financed by direct government funds, although the share is higher in the Slovak Republic (22%), Poland (15%) and the Czech Republic (12%).

■ Likewise, business funds a growing share of the R&D performed in the higher education and government sectors, averaging 4.9% in 2002 in the OECD area (and 6.3% in the EU25).

■ In spite of increases in many countries, these flows still represent less than 7% in most large OECD economies.

■ Poland (and to a lesser extent New Zealand) has high values for both these indicators. Japan, Portugal and Denmark all have relatively low values.

### Source

- OECD, Research and Development Statistics, May 2005.

### For further reading

- OECD (2002), *Frascati Manual: Proposed Standard Practice for Surveys on Research and Experimental Development*, OECD, Paris, available at *www.oecd.org/sti/frascatimanual*.

### *Measuring the performance of R&D in the government and higher education sectors*

Measures of R&D performance in the higher education sector and its evolution are often based on estimates by national authorities and evaluation methods are periodically revised (see boxes in A.2 and A.3). Moreover, certain national characteristics may strongly influence R&D performance by the government and higher education sectors:

US figures for these sectors are underestimated. Public-sector R&D covers only federal government activities, not those of individual state and local governments; and since 1985 figures for researchers exclude military personnel in the government sector. In the higher education sector, R&D in the humanities is not included, and since 1991 capital expenditures have been excluded. In Sweden, too, the government sector, which includes only the central administrative units, is seriously underestimated; inclusion of county and local units might double the figures. Finally, in Korea, the higher education sector is probably greatly underestimated owing to the exclusion of R&D in the social sciences and humanities (SSH).

In Japan, figures for R&D personnel in the higher education sector before 1996 are overestimated by international standards, as researchers were counted according to the number of persons employed in R&D instead of full-time equivalent (FTE) staff. According to studies conducted by some Japanese authorities, the number of FTE researchers is about 40% lower in the higher education sector and 30% lower in the national total. Because the number of researchers is overestimated, figures for R&D personnel costs are also overestimated prior to 1996, particularly for the higher education sector; the OECD has therefore computed an "adjusted" series for the years to 1995.

Certain transfers of public agencies to private enterprise, as in the case of the privatisation of Swisscom (Switzerland) in 1998, and the partial privatisation of the Defence Evaluation and Research Agency – DERA – (United Kingdom) in 2001, have had the effect of reducing R&D performance in the government sector and increasing it in the business enterprise sector.

 OECD SCIENCE, TECHNOLOGY AND INDUSTRY SCOREBOARD 2005 – ISBN 92-64-01055-6 – © OECD 2005

## A.9. R&D linkages

### Share of government-financed business R&D, 2003

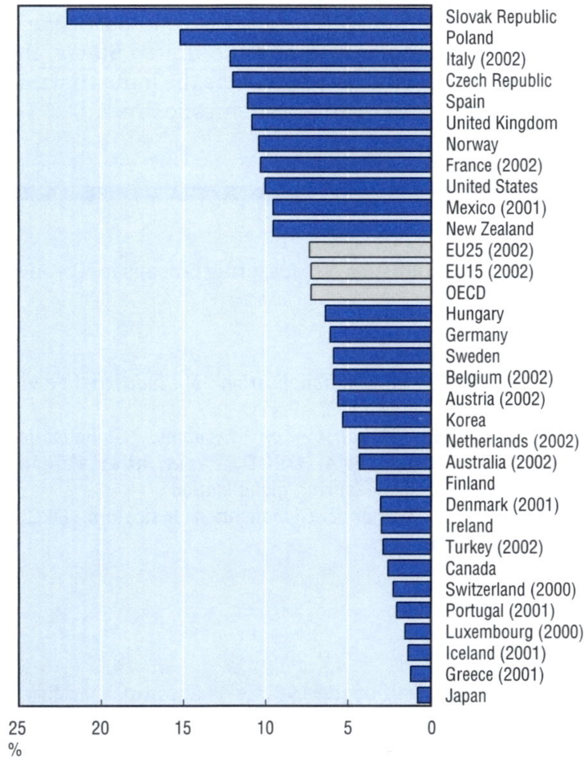


1. Higher education sector only.
2. Government sector only.

### Business-funded R&D in the higher education and government sectors, 2003

As a percentage of R&D performed in these sectors (combined)

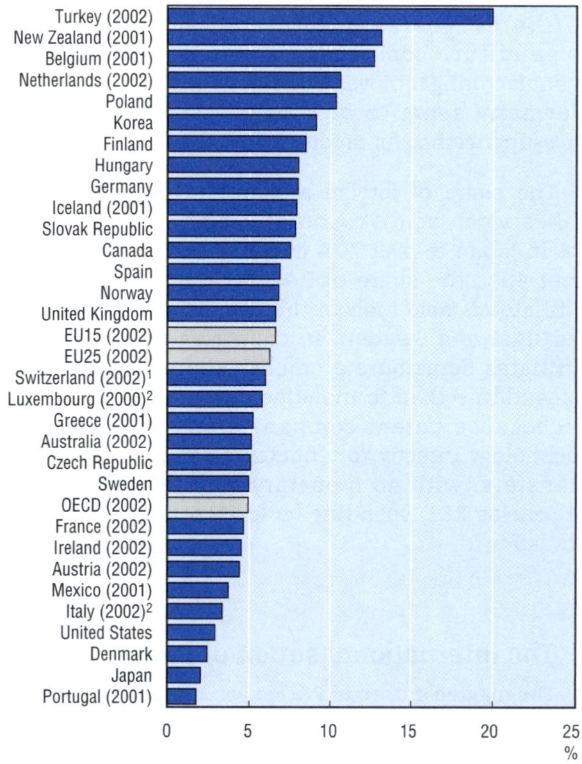


StatLink: *http://dx.doi.org/10.1787/184805617807*

## A.10. Internationalisation of manufacturing R&D

More multinationals are setting up offshore R&D laboratories, and many R&D activities have become more internationalised and more closely linked to production abroad. Still, there are differences in foreign affiliates' shares in total R&D manufacturing expenditure compared to their shares in total manufacturing turnover. Countries such as Portugal and Germany seem to be more attractive for R&D investments than for production activities and *vice versa*.

The share of foreign affiliates in industrial R&D varies widely across countries, ranging from less than 5% in Japan to over 70% in Hungary and Ireland. At over 40%, the share of R&D conducted by foreign affiliates is also high in the Czech Republic, Spain, Portugal and Sweden. In countries where foreign affiliates contribute a smaller share to total R&D expenditure than to manufacturing turnover, it may be because parent companies prefer to transfer technology directly to affiliates. Such intra-company transfers, with no monetary counterpart, do not appear as R&D spending by foreign affiliates in the statistics.

The share of foreign affiliates in R&D also reflects the size of their R&D effort relative to that of domestic firms. In Hungary and Ireland, for example, foreign affiliates carry out relatively more R&D than national firms. In most other OECD countries, and particularly in Japan, Sweden, Finland and the United States, the opposite is true. This largely reflects the industrial mix of foreign affiliates relative to domestic firms.

### Source

- OECD, OECD Statistics on Measuring Globalisation – AFA, March 2005.

### For further reading

- OECD (1998), *Internationalisation of Industrial R&D: Patterns and Trends*, OECD, Paris.
- OECD (2005), *Handbook on Economic Globalisation Indicators*, Chapter 4, OECD, Paris, available at *www.oecd.org/sti/measuring-globalisation*.
- OECD (2005), *Economic Globalisation Indicators*, OECD, Paris, forthcoming.

### *The internationalisation of industrial R&D*

The marked growth in R&D expenditures in OECD countries from the first half of the 1980s was accompanied by two major trends:

- First, the growing internationalisation of R&D activities of multinational firms linked to an increase in the number of R&D laboratories located abroad.
- Second, the emergence and development of international networks of co-operation agreements or alliances either between firms or between firms and government or university R&D bodies.

While the first of these trends is restricted to multinationals, the second characterises all innovation-intensive firms. Decentralisation of the R&D activities of multinational firms, *i.e.* the establishment of laboratories outside the home country of the parent company, is by no means a new phenomenon. Decentralised R&D facilities have been used for some time to serve and support overseas production units. Until recently, owing to the absence of data on the R&D activities of multinationals, internationalisation of R&D was thought to be fairly marginal to the general process of economic globalisation. The OECD data, which cover more fully the activities of foreign affiliates (affiliates under foreign control) in OECD countries and of affiliates of parent companies abroad (AFA database), show that R&D performed abroad and by foreign affiliates represents on average well over 16% of total expenditure on industrial R&D in the OECD area. In most OECD countries, the share of foreign affiliates in industrial R&D is increasing. In the United Kingdom, Canada and Ireland, it currently exceeds 35%.

## A.10. Internationalisation of manufacturing R&D

### Share of R&D expenditure and turnover of affiliates under foreign control in total manufacturing R&D and turnover, 2002

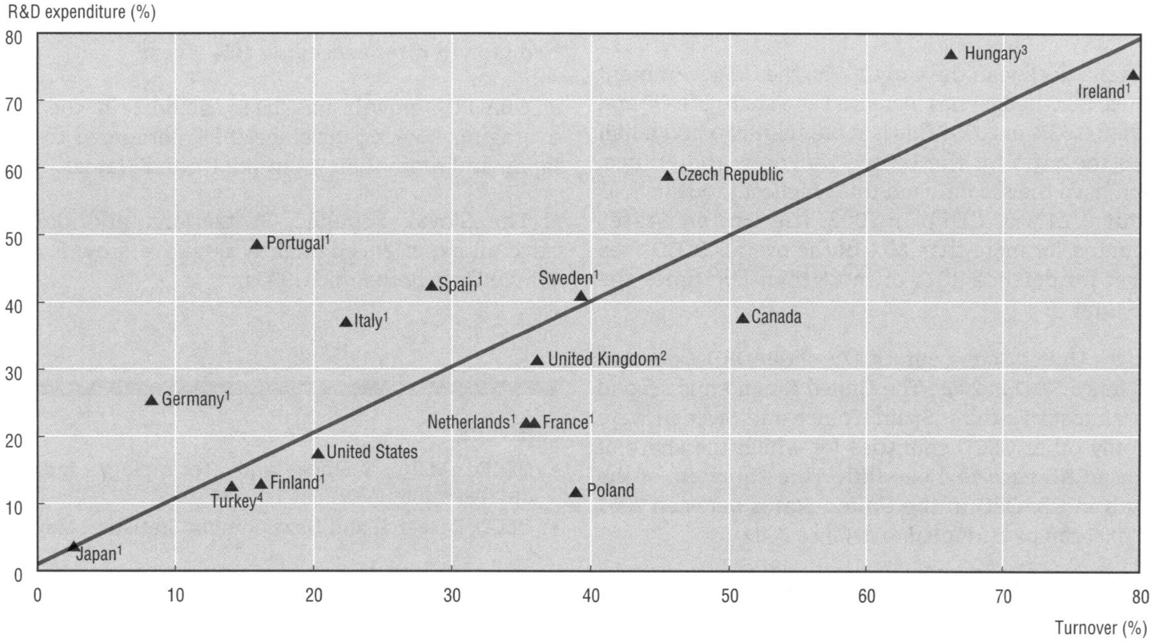


### R&D intensity[5] of affiliates under foreign control and firms controlled by the compiling countries, 2002

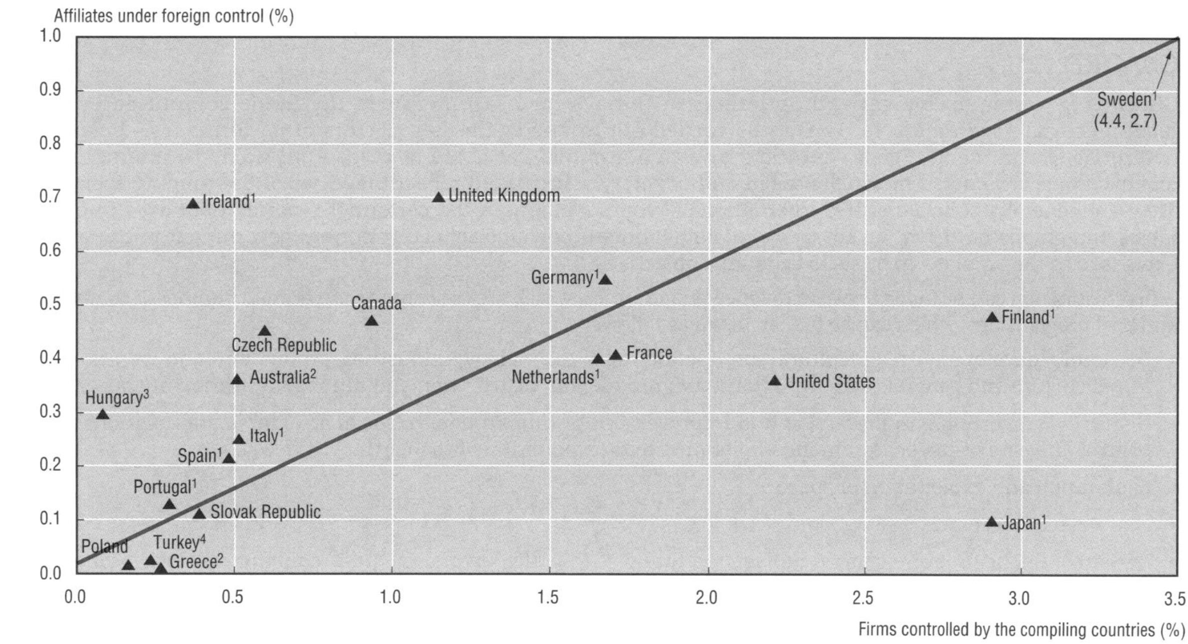


1. 2001.
2. 1999.
3. 1998.
4. 2000.
5. R&D expenditures as a share of value added in industry.

StatLink: *http://dx.doi.org/10.1787/334034710484*

## A.11. Government R&D budgets

■ Data on GBAORD (see box for definition) provide an indication of the relative importance of various socio-economic objectives, such as defence, health and the environment, in public R&D spending.

■ After a decline in the early 1990s, the US government defence R&D budget has increased as a share of GDP and reached 0.63% in 2005. This is more than two and a half times the ratio for the United Kingdom and France, which have the second- and third-highest ratios in 2003 (about 0.24% of GDP). In 2003, the United States accounted for more than 80% of the overall OECD-area budget for defence R&D, or more than five times the EU15 total.

■ In the United States, almost 57% of GBAORD is devoted to defence R&D in 2005. The United Kingdom is second with almost one-third. Spain, France and Sweden were the only other OECD countries for which the share of defence R&D exceeded one-fifth. Three-quarters of the growth in GBAORD in the United States between 2001 and 2005 can be attributed to defence R&D.

■ In 2003, Iceland has the highest figure in the OECD area for GBAORD as a percentage of GDP, at 1.2%. Finland is the only other OECD country in which civil GBAORD exceeds 1% of GDP, which is twice the OECD average.

■ Since 2000, government R&D budgets have grown on average by 3.5% (in real terms) in the OECD area. Luxembourg grew fastest at more than 20% annually between 2000 and 2005. Spain, Korea and Ireland all had growth rates exceeding 10% a year.

■ GBAORD growth has been modest in the EU25, averaging 1.5% a year since 1995, compared to 6% in Japan and more than 7% in the United States.

■ The Slovak Republic, Switzerland and Germany have all experienced slightly negative growth in real GBAORD since the mid-1990s.

### Sources

- OECD, Main Science and Technology Indicators database, May 2005.
- OECD, Research and Development Statistics, May 2005.

### For further reading

- OECD (2002), *Frascati Manual: Proposed Standard Practice for Surveys on Research and Experimental Development*, OECD, Paris, available at *www.oecd.org/sti/frascatimanual*.

### GBAORD

GBAORD (government budget appropriations or outlays for R&D) measures the funds committed by the federal/central government for R&D to be carried out in one of the four sectors of performance – business enterprise, government, higher education, private non-profit – at home or abroad (including by international organisations). The data are usually based on budgetary sources and reflect the views of the funding agencies. They are generally considered less internationally comparable than the performer-reported data used in other tables and graphs but have the advantage of being more timely and reflecting current government priorities, as expressed in the breakdown by socio economic objectives.

A first distinction can be made between defence programmes, which are concentrated in a small number of countries, and civil programmes, which can be broken down as follows:

- Economic development: agricultural production and technology; industrial production and technology; infrastructure and general planning of land use; production, distribution and rational utilisation of energy.
- Health and environment: protection and improvement of human health, social structures and relationships, control and care of the environment, exploration and exploitation of the Earth.
- Exploration and exploitation of space.
- Non-oriented research.
- Research financed from general university funds (GUF): the estimated R&D content of block grants to universities.

It should be noted that the series for Japan excludes the R&D content of military procurement. In the United States, general support for universities is the responsibility of state governments so that GUF is not included in total GBAORD. In France, a change in the method of evaluating defence R&D resulted in a reduction in the defence objective as from 1997.

## A.11. Government R&D budgets

### Defence and civil R&D budgets (GBAORD), 2005

As a percentage of GDP

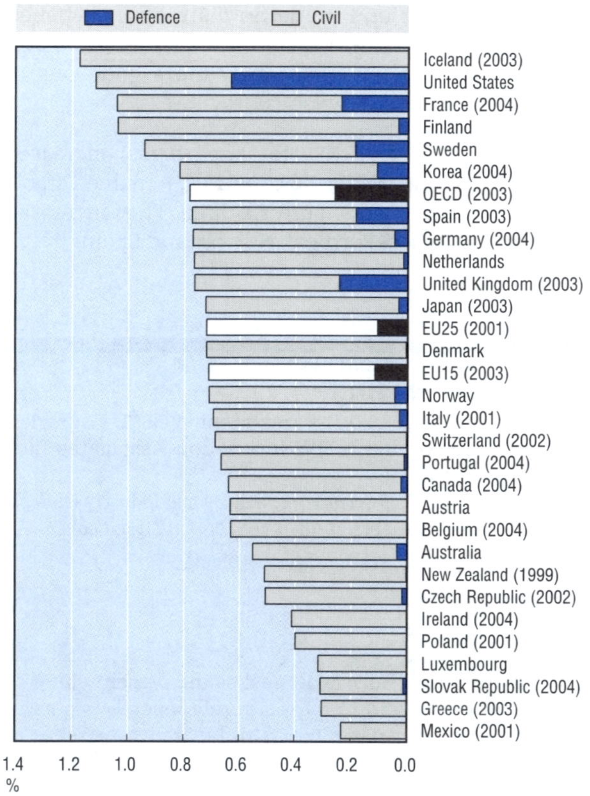


### Growth in government R&D budgets (GBAORD), 1995-2005

Average annual growth rate (%)

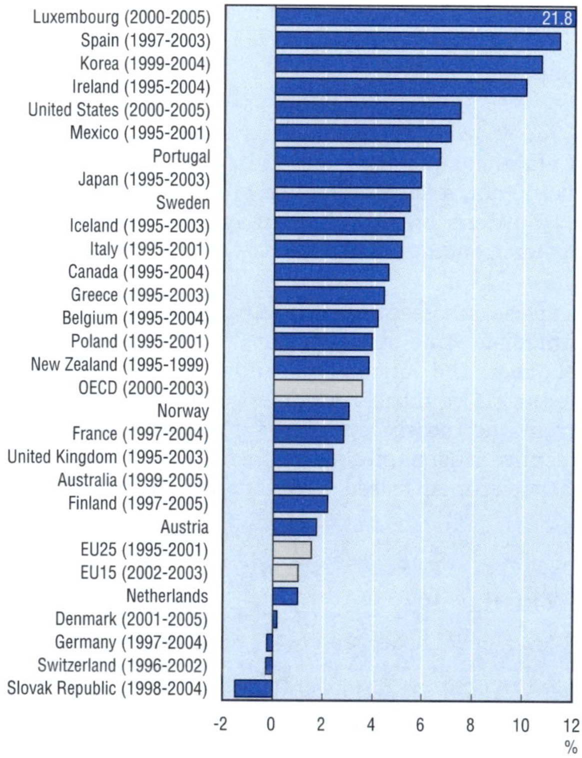


StatLink: *http://dx.doi.org/10.1787/622450141656*

## A.12. Tax treatment of R&D

R&D tax concessions are extensively used by OECD countries as an indirect way of encouraging business R&D expenditures. Recent years have seen the introduction of new tax incentive schemes, as well as changes in existing schemes to make them more generous and more targeted towards certain types of beneficiaries (*e.g.* small firms, firms in specific industries, etc.).

Today, 18 OECD countries have R&D tax incentives in place, compared to only 12 in 1996. Even in those that do not, reduced corporate tax rates have lowered tax burdens on firms and may have encouraged greater spending on R&D.

Special tax treatment for R&D expenditures includes immediate write-off of current R&D expenditures (all countries) and various types of tax relief such as tax credits (12 countries in 2004) or allowances against taxable income (six countries). While many existing tax incentive programmes reward incremental increases in R&D investment (based on various formulas), a number of new incentives are based on the level of R&D spending in a given year.

In 2004, Spain, Mexico and Portugal provided the largest subsidies and made no distinction between large and small firms. Canada, the Netherlands and especially Italy are significantly more generous to small firms than to large ones.

Tax subsidies for R&D (for large firms) increased between 1995 and 2004 in 16 countries, remained stable in five and decreased slightly in three. They increased the most in Mexico, Portugal, Norway and Spain.

### For further reading


- Warda, J. (2004), "R&D Tax Treatment in OECD Countries: A 2003-2004 Update", JPW Innovation Associates Inc., mimeo, August.
- OECD (2004), *OECD Science, Technology and Industry Outlook*, OECD, Paris, available at *www.oecd.org/sti/sti-outlook*.


### The B index

The amount of tax subsidy to R&D is calculated as 1 minus the *B index*. The *B index* is defined as the present value of before-tax income necessary to cover the initial cost of R&D investment and to pay corporate income tax, so that it becomes profitable to perform research activities. Algebraically, the *B index* is equal to the after-tax cost of an expenditure of USD 1 on R&D divided by one minus the corporate income tax rate. The after-tax cost is the net cost of investing in R&D, taking into account all the available tax incentives.

$$B\ index = \frac{(1-A)}{(1-\tau)}$$

where A = the net present discounted value of depreciation allowances, tax credits and special allowances on R&D assets; and $\tau$ = the statutory corporate income tax rate (CITR). In a country with full write-off of current R&D expenditure and no R&D tax incentive scheme, $A = \tau$, and consequently B = 1. The more favourable a country's tax treatment of R&D, the lower its *B index*.

The *B index* is a unique tool for comparing the generosity of the tax treatment of R&D in different countries. However, its computation requires some simplifying assumptions. It should therefore be examined together with a set of other relevant policy indicators. Furthermore, its "synthetic" nature does not allow for distinguishing the relative importance of the various policy tools it takes into account (*e.g.* depreciation allowances, special R&D allowances, tax credit, CITR).

*B indexes* have been calculated under the assumption that the "representative firm" is taxable, so that it may enjoy the full benefit of the tax allowance or credit. For incremental tax credits, calculation of the *B index* implicitly assumes that R&D investment is fully eligible for the credit and does not exceed the ceiling if there is one. Some detailed features of R&D tax schemes (*e.g.* refunding, carry-back and carry-forward of unused tax credit, or flow-through mechanisms) are therefore not taken into account.

The effective impact of the R&D tax allowance or credit on the after-tax cost of R&D is influenced by the level of the CITR. An increase in the CITR reduces the *B index* only in those countries with the most generous R&D tax treatment. If tax credits are taxable, the effect of the CITR on the *B index* depends only on the level of the depreciation allowance. If the latter is over 100% for the total R&D expenditure, an increase in the CITR will reduce the *B index*. For countries with less generous R&D tax treatment, the *B index* is positively related to the CITR.



OECD SCIENCE, TECHNOLOGY AND INDUSTRY SCOREBOARD 2005 – ISBN 92-64-01055-6 – © OECD 2005

## A.12. Tax treatment of R&D

### Rate of tax subsidies for USD 1 of R&D,[1] large firms and SMEs, 2004

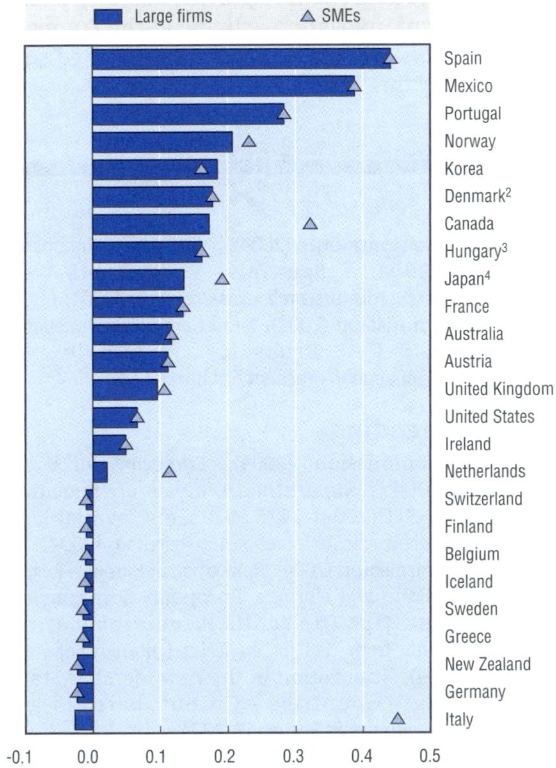


### Change in the rate of tax subsidies for USD 1 of R&D, large firms, between 1995-2004

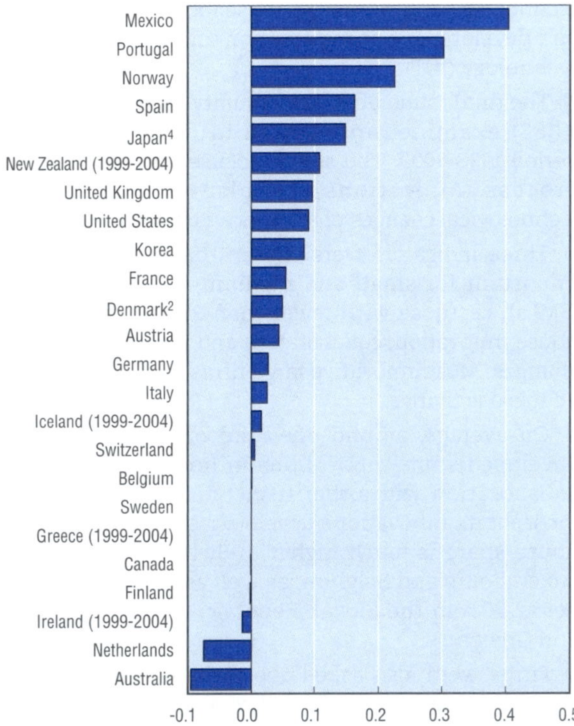


1. Tax subsidies are calculated as 1 minus the *B index*. For example, in Spain, 1 unit of R&D expenditure by large firms results in 0.44 unit of tax relief.
2. The 2004 calculation for Denmark applies to the 150% allowance on collaborative research at universities or public research institutions. Without this incentive, the *B index* is 1.015.
3. The *B index* for Hungary is based on the 100% R&D tax allowance for research and technology development (which also applies to subcontracted R&D if the partner is a public or non-profit research organisation). A 300% allowance is available if the company's R&D laboratory is located at a university or public research site; the *B index* in this situation equals 0.666.
4. The 2004 *B index* for large firms in Japan applies to firms with a ratio of R&D to sales of less than 10%. The *B index* for large firms with a R&D-to-sales ratio above 10% is 0.831. The *B index* for research conducted in collaboration with universities is 0.782.

StatLink: *http://dx.doi.org/10.1787/235300054825*

## A.13. Innovation in small and medium-sized firms

■ Innovation surveys are carried out in a growing number of OECD and developing countries. They attempt to capture aspects of the innovation process that fall outside the scope of other science and technology surveys such as those focusing on research and development or information and communication technology (ICT).

■ The third round of the Community Innovation Survey (CIS3) examined innovation in firms during the period 1998-2000. The survey focused on product and process innovations, but also examined non-technological changes of relevance to innovation.

■ Three indicators were chosen that are particularly important for small and medium-sized enterprises (SMEs), *i.e.* those with fewer than 250 employees: in-house innovation, collaboration and non-technological changes. Most innovative large firms tend to engage in all these activities.

■ On average, around one-third of SMEs in Europe developed some innovations in house (including in collaboration with other firms) and did not simply incorporate innovations developed elsewhere. The in-house share is much higher in Switzerland, Iceland, Luxembourg and Belgium, as well as in Germany. It is below 20% in the Slovak Republic, Poland, Denmark and Greece.

■ Firms were also asked about the extent to which they co-operated with other firms or public bodies in the context of their innovation activities. The average for Europe was around 7% of all SMEs, but the figure was much higher in the Nordic countries, ranging from 12% in Iceland to 20% in Finland. Co-operation was much less frequent in certain eastern and southern European countries.

■ Non-technological changes provide useful evidence on other types of innovation activity: at the European level, close to one out of two SMEs implemented such changes during this period.

### Sources


- European Commission (2004), *European Innovation Scoreboard 2004*, Brussels, available at *http://trendchart.cordis.lu/scoreboards/scoreboard2004.*
- European Commission (2004), *Third Community Innovation Survey (CIS-3)*, Brussels, available at *www.cordis.lu/innovation-smes/src/cis.htm.*


### For further reading


- European Commission (2004), *European Innovation Scoreboard 2004: Comparative Analysis of Innovation Performance*, SEC(2004) 1475, Brussels, available at *http://trendchart.cordis.lu/scoreboards/scoreboard2004.*
- European Commission (2004), *Innovation in Europe – Results for the EU, Iceland and Norway*, European Commission, available at *ftp://ftp.cordis.lu/pub/innovation-smes/docs/results_from_cis3_for_eu_iceland_norway.pdf.*
- Eurostat (2004), "Innovation in the new Member States and Candidate Countries – Output, barriers and protection", *Statistics in Focus*, 13/2004.
- OECD/Eurostat (2005), *Oslo Manual – Proposed Guidelines for Collecting and Interpreting Innovation Data*, OECD, Paris, forthcoming, available at *www.oecd.org/sti/oslomanual.*
- OECD (2004), *OECD Science, Technology and Industry Outlook 2004*, OECD, Paris.


### The Community Innovation Survey (CIS)

The Community Innovation Survey aims to gather information on business innovation across the EU area. It attempts to capture the nature of innovation activities, the characteristics of innovative firms and the factors that hamper innovation. For the third round (CIS3), responses refer to the period 1998-2000 (1999-2001 for the Czech Republic, Hungary and the Slovak Republic) and come from 488 000 respondent firms in the manufacturing, market services and other industry sectors.

The CIS3 survey was based on the second edition of the *Oslo Manual* and defined an innovation as "a new or significantly improved product (goods or service) introduced to the market or the introduction within the enterprise of a new or significantly improved process". Innovation is based on the results of new technological developments, new combinations of existing knowledge or utilisation of other knowledge acquired by the enterprise. Product innovation is defined as a good or service which is either new or significantly improved with respect to its fundamental characteristics, technical specifications, incorporated software or other immaterial components, intended uses or user friendliness. Process innovation includes new and significantly improved production technology and new and significantly improved methods of supplying services and of delivering products. The outcome should be significant with respect to the level of output, quality of products (goods/services) or cost of production and distribution. The innovation should be new to the enterprise; but it is not necessarily new to the market. The enterprise is not necessarily the first to introduce this process. It does not matter whether the innovation was developed by the enterprise or by another enterprise. Changes of solely an aesthetic nature, resale of inventions wholly produced and developed by other enterprises are not counted.

Results of the CIS3 survey can be analysed to compare responses by country, industry and size class, but care must be taken in interpreting the results. Aggregate indicators are influenced by the structural characteristics of the set of responding firms, which differ from those of the total firm population. For example, the CIS does not cover several services sectors for which innovation is thought to be infrequent, nor does it include firms with fewer than ten employees.

## A.13. Innovation in small and medium-sized firms

### SMEs innovating in house, 1998-2000

As a percentage of all SMEs

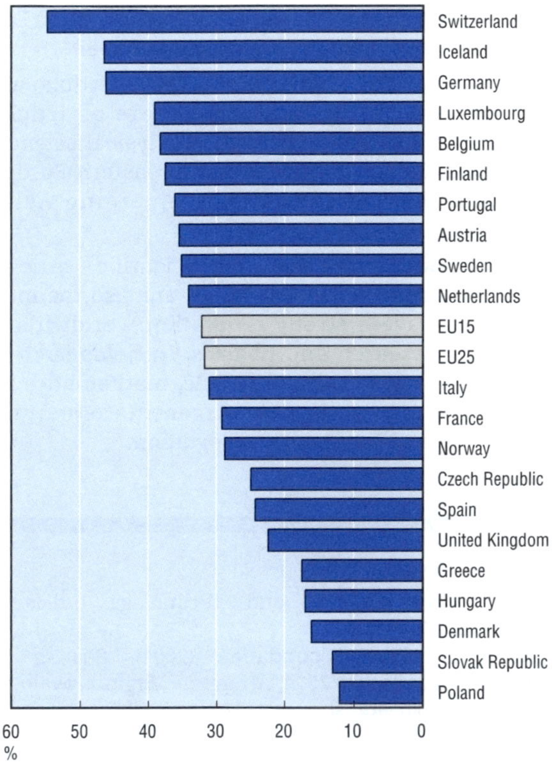


### SMEs involved in innovation co-operation, 1998-2000

As a percentage of all SMEs

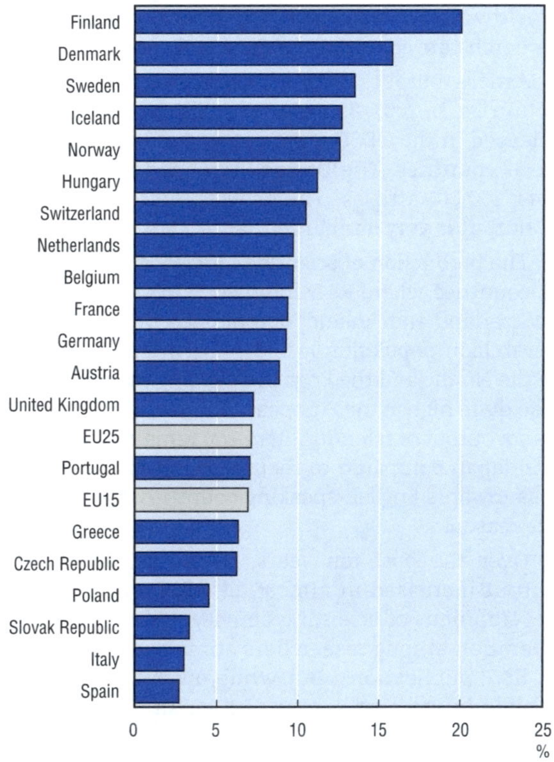


### SMEs using non-technological change,[1] 1998-2000

As a % of all SMEs

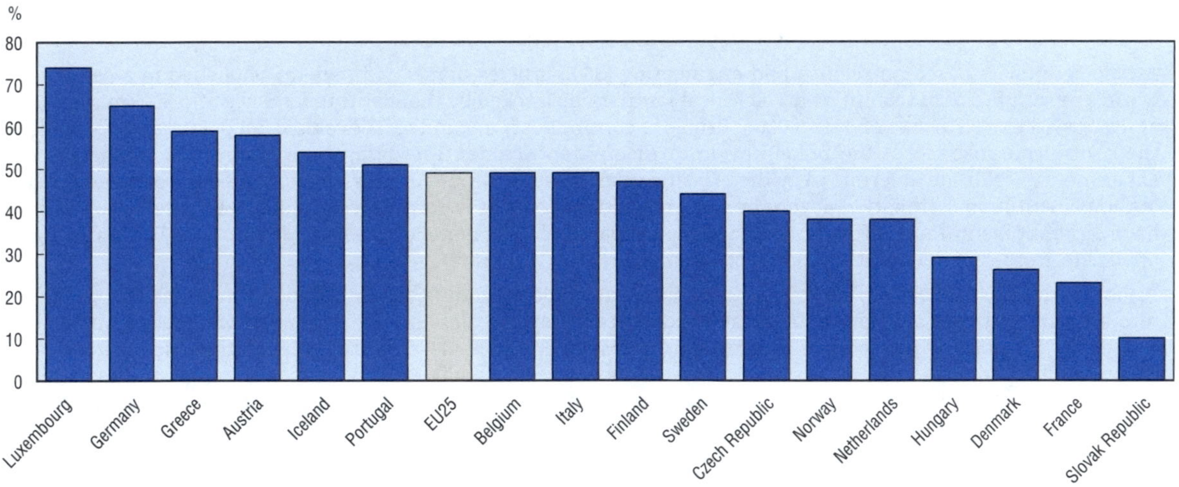


1. This includes implementing "advanced management techniques", "new or significantly changed organisational structures", or "significant changes in the aesthetic appearance or design in at least one product".

StatLink: *http://dx.doi.org/10.1787/720416244570*

## A.14. Scientific articles

■ Volume of articles published is a key indicator of the output of scientific research. About 650 000 new articles in science and engineering were reported worldwide in 2001, most of which resulted from research carried out by the academic sector.

■ Article output is highly concentrated in a few countries. In 2001, 82% of world scientific articles were released in the OECD area, nearly two-thirds of which in G7 countries. The United States is the leader, with over 200 000 articles. The geographical concentration of output is very similar to that of R&D expenditures.

■ The production of scientific articles is usually greater in countries where R&D intensity is higher (see A.2). In Switzerland and Finland, output exceeded 1 100 articles per million population in 2001. The intensity is highest in the Nordic and the English-speaking countries, and is also quite high in the European Union (557). On the other hand, output of scientific literature remains low in Korea and Japan compared to their R&D efforts. A statistical bias towards English-speaking countries may be part of the reason.

■ Over the past ten years, the intensity of article output increased in almost all OECD countries. The development of scientific activity and increasing co-operation among researchers stimulated the increase in S&T publications. But while output kept growing rapidly in western Europe and Japan, the number of articles stabilised in the United States and even started declining in the United Kingdom and Canada. In addition, distribution worldwide shifted slightly from high-income S&T-based economies, towards East Asia (China, Korea, Singapore, Chinese Taipei).

■ Life sciences still dominate the OECD portfolio and account for a particularly large share of articles published in the Nordic countries. Physical sciences are the main field of publication in eastern Europe, Korea and Portugal, as in the emerging Asian economies.

■ The major producers of scientific articles, Switzerland and the United States, are also the most cited. Both have a strong reputation worldwide in biomedical research and physics. In fields such as Earth and space sciences for Chile, mathematics for Slovenia or psychology for Argentina, emerging countries also achieve world recognition.

### Sources

- OECD, Main Science and Technology Indicators database, May 2005.
- National Science Foundation (2004), *Science and Engineering Indicators 2004*, Arlington, Virginia, available at *www.nsf.gov/statistics/seind04*.

### *Article counts: issues and data*

Output from research includes trained personnel (see B.1), advances in knowledge (new products, methods), patents (see section C) and scientific publications. The volume of articles published worldwide is a key indicator since publication is the main means of disseminating and validating research results. In most scientific fields, articles are also crucial for researchers' career advancement (the "publish or perish" rule).

Article counts are based on science and engineering (S&E) articles, notes and reviews published in a set of the world's most influential scientific and technical journals, as tracked by the Institute for Scientific Information (ISI at *www.isinet.com*). This set of over 5 000 journals is continuously expanded. It excludes all documents for which the central purpose is not the presentation or discussion of scientific data, theory, methods, apparatus or experiments. Fields are determined by the classification of each journal. Articles are attributed to countries by the author's institutional affiliation at the time of publication. A paper is considered co-authored only if its authors have different institutional affiliations or are from separate departments of the same institution. The same logic applies to cross-sectoral or international collaboration.

Although the ISI indexes provide good international coverage, including of electronic journals, they do not take into account journals of regional or local importance. They are also English-language-biased. Moreover the propensity to publish differs across countries and across scientific fields, distorting the relationship between real output and publication-based indicators. Lastly, the incentive to publish raises a question of quality. The volume of articles can thus be weighted by the frequency of citations. Citations also attest to the productivity and influence of scientific literature. International citations highlight the visibility of scientific research beyond national boundaries. The relative prominence of S&E literature is measured by comparing a country's share of cited literature with its world share of S&E articles. A country's citation of its own literature is excluded.

Life sciences include clinical medicine, biomedical research and biology. Physical sciences include chemistry, physics and Earth and space sciences. Social and behavioural sciences include social sciences, psychology, health sciences and professional fields. Computer sciences are included in engineering and technology.

## A.14. Scientific articles

### Scientific articles per million population, 2001

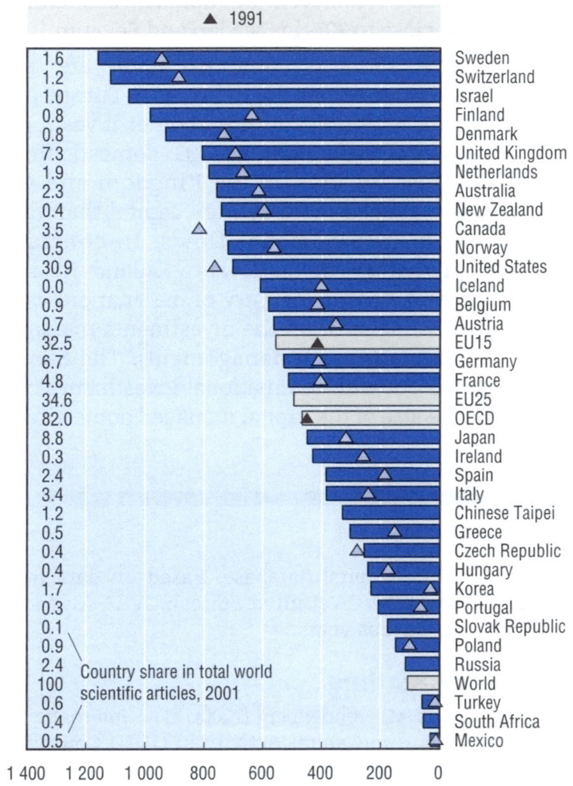


### Relative prominence of cited scientific literature, 2001

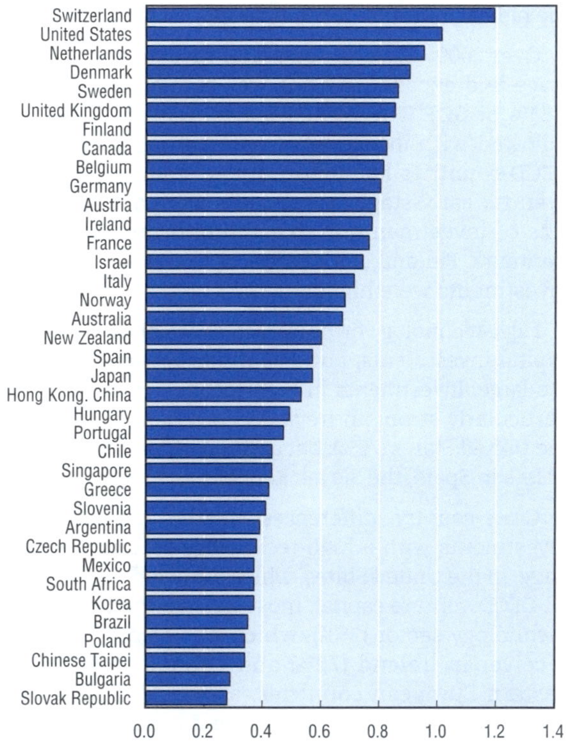


### Growth of scientific articles by area, 1992-2001

Index 1992 = 100

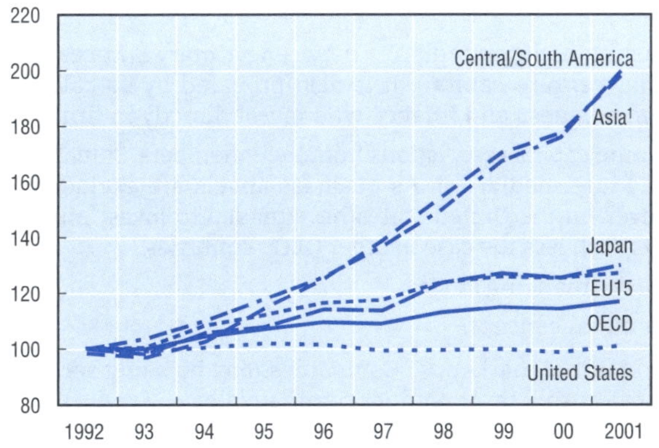


### Distribution of scientific articles by field, 2001

As a percentage of total scientific articles

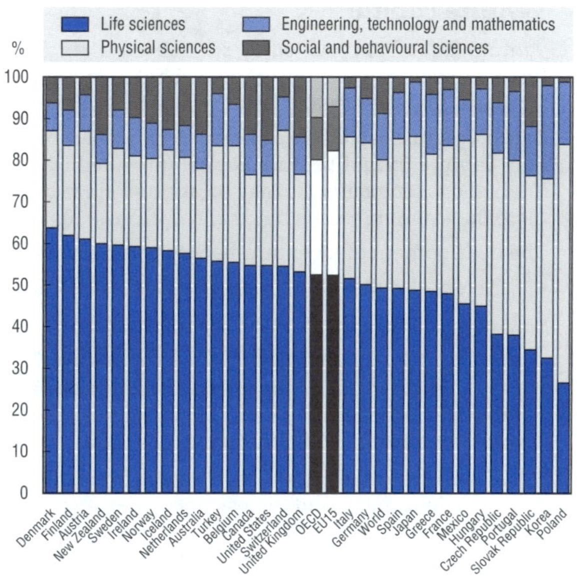


1. Excluding Japan and Korea.

StatLink: *http://dx.doi.org/10.1787/067233471835*

## A.15. Venture capital

Venture capital investment is quite small relative to GDP, although it is a major source of funding for new technology-based firms. It plays a crucial role in promoting the radical innovations often developed by such firms.

Over 2000-03, venture capital investment in early-stage and expanding firms was highest in Iceland at 0.51% of GDP. The United States, Canada and Korea followed with investment shares above 0.25%; other OECD countries had substantially smaller shares. On average, early-stage investments were about half the size of investments in expanding firms. In Canada, Denmark, Finland, and Germany, however, early-stage investments were higher.

High-technology firms attracted 60% of OECD venture capital investments, but disparities between countries are large. Investments in high-technology sectors were particularly strong in Ireland (93%), Canada (85%) and the United States (75%), but accounted for only a quarter or less in Spain, the Slovak Republic and Portugal.

Cross-country differences in the distribution of investments within high-technology sectors were also large. In the United States, which attracted nearly 60% of all OECD venture capital, most went to the information technology sector (35%), which was also the primary receiver in Ireland (72%) and Canada (44%). In the eastern European countries, as well as in Italy, the United Kingdom, New Zealand and Australia, firms in the communications sector attracted most of the investments. Health and biotechnology firms accounted for more than 28% of total venture capital investments in Denmark and close to 20% in Sweden and Belgium.

International flows of venture capital are also important. US firms increasingly invest in Europe and Asia, and there is significant cross-border investment within Europe and Asia. Over 2000-03, domestic firms in Iceland, Sweden, the United Kingdom and the Netherlands managed more venture capital than they received from international flows. In contrast, international venture capital flows to Finland, Ireland, Switzerland and Austria (country of destination) were more than 30% higher than the investments managed domestically (country of management). The Slovak Republic stood out with international investment flows eight times the size of the capital managed domestically.

### Source

- OECD, Venture Capital database. Based on data from EVCA (Europe); NVCA (United States); CVCA (Canada); AVCJ (Asia); various years.

### For further reading

- G. Baygan and M. Freudenberg (2000), "The Internationalisation of Venture Capital Activity in OECD Countries: Implications for Measurement and Policy", *STI Working Paper 2000/7*, available at *www.oecd.org/sti/working-papers*.

### *Venture capital*

Venture capital is provided by specialised financial firms acting as intermediaries between primary sources of finance (such as pension funds or banks) and firms (formal venture capital). It is also provided by so-called "business angels" (usually wealthy individuals experienced in business and finance who invest directly in firms).

Data on venture capital are collected by national or regional venture capital associations from their members. Statistics only capture formal venture capital (provided by specialised intermediaries). As business angels are excluded, international comparisons may be affected since business angels in the United States have tended to invest much more than venture capital funds in new firms. This is probably much less the case in other OECD countries.

The development of a venture-backed company has three basic financing stages:

- *Seed capital* is provided to research, assess and develop an initial concept.
- *Start-up* financing is provided for product development and initial marketing. Companies may be being set up or may have been in business for a short time, but have not yet sold their product commercially.
- *Expansion* financing is provided for the growth and expansion of a company that is breaking even or trading profitably. Capital may be used to finance increased production capacity, market or product development and/or to provide additional working capital.

Not all funds managed by a venture capital firm operating in a given country are from investors in that country. In fact, there are substantial and increasingly important cross-border flows of funds, both inflows and outflows. Venture capital data can be collected using two different approaches: country of management and country of destination. The former refers to the geographic location of the venture capital firms that raise and invest these funds. The latter indicates the geographic destination of investments made by firms. This distinction between country of management and country of destination is important as investment in a country may matter more than investment by a country.

## A.15. Venture capital

### Venture capital investment, 2000-2003

As a percentage of GDP

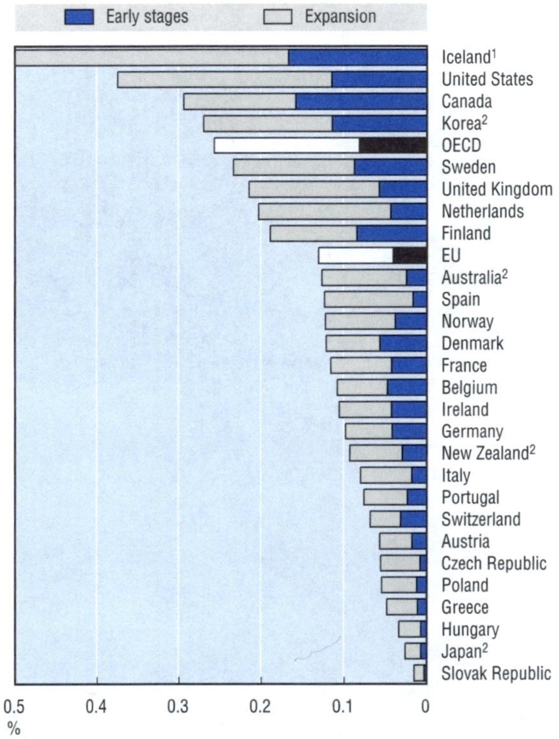


### Share of high-technology sectors in total venture capital, 2000-2003

As a percentage of total venture capital investment[3]

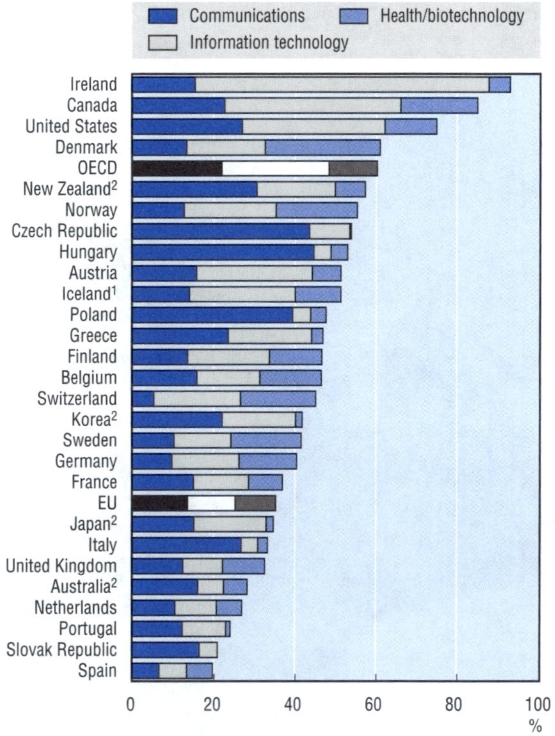


### Total venture capital investment by country of management and destination,[3] 2000-2003

As a percentage of GDP

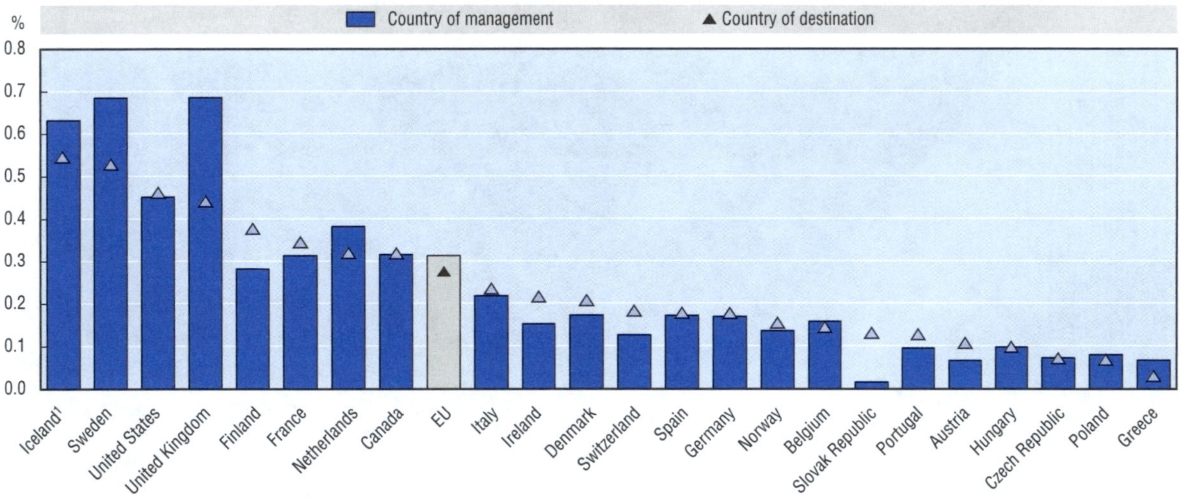


1. Data from 2000-02.
2. Data from 1998-2001.
3. Total venture capital investment includes investments in early stages, expansion, buy-out and others. For the United States and Canada, country of destination equals domestic investment plus European capital invested in the respective country.

StatLink: *http://dx.doi.org/10.1787/687468817165*

# B. HUMAN RESOURCES IN SCIENCE AND TECHNOLOGY: KNOWLEDGE AND SKILLS

## B.1. Flows of university graduates

■ Flows of university graduates are an indicator of a country's potential for assimilating, developing and diffusing advanced knowledge and supplying the labour market with highly skilled workers.

■ In 2002, OECD universities awarded some 5.9 million degrees at university level, of which 156 000 doctorates. In other words, fewer than one person in three at the typical age of graduation completed a university degree, while one out of 100 received a doctoral degree. Finland and Australia had the highest graduation rates at university level (over 45% of the population), and Sweden and Switzerland the highest rates at doctorate level with 2.8 and 2.5 doctorates per 100 at the age of graduation, respectively.

■ Close to one-third of university graduates obtain a degree in the social sciences, business or law. Science-related studies (excluding health and welfare) are the second most popular field of study, with one OECD graduate in four obtaining a science and engineering (S&E) degree. In Korea, S&E degrees account for about 40% of all new degrees. However, since 1998 there are fewer S&E degrees delivered in most countries leading to policy concerns about a falling interest in scientific studies.

■ While US and EU outflows of university graduates represent some 32% and 39%, of total OECD university degrees respectively, EU higher education systems deliver more advanced research and S&E diplomas. In 2002, European universities granted 532 000 S&E university degrees, or 42% of total OECD university degrees awarded in these fields, compared to only 23% for the United States. The gap widens for doctoral degrees: European universities awarded 55% of all S&E doctorates.

■ In two out of three OECD countries, universities deliver more engineering degrees than science degrees; in Finland, Japan, Korea and Sweden the number of engineering degrees awarded exceeds by far that of science degrees. The reverse is true in Ireland, Iceland, New Zealand, Australia and the United Kingdom.

■ OECD governments are concerned about the low level of participation of women in scientific studies and careers. Women account on average for more than two-thirds of OECD degrees granted in humanities, arts, education, health and welfare, but for less than one-third in mathematics and computer science, and less than one-fifth in engineering, manufacturing and construction. Moreover, there are few women in advanced research programmes and scientific careers. They are less likely to graduate at doctoral level (except in Italy); in Japan and Korea, they receive less than a quarter of all doctorates awarded. They are also less likely to obtain university degrees in S&E; 80% of S&E university degrees awarded in Japan, the Netherlands or Switzerland are delivered to men.

### Source

- OECD, Education database, 2005.

### For further reading


- OECD (2004), *Education at a Glance: OECD Indicators 2004*, OECD, Paris, available at *www.oecd.org/edu/eag2004*.
- OECD and Eurostat (1995), *Manual on the Measurement of Human Resources Devoted to S&T – Canberra Manual*, OECD, Paris.


### Higher education outflows and stocks of human resources in science and technology

The higher education system is the main source of human resources in science and technology (HRST). Its output, graduates, is complemented by immigration of highly skilled workers and internal mobility.

Outflows of university graduates include all new degrees delivered at the first and second stage of tertiary education, *i.e.* levels 5A and 6 of the 1997 International Standard Classification of Education (ISCED 1997). Doctoral students are enrolled in the advanced research programmes at ISCED level 6. Doctoral students and doctorate holders are a sub-population of HRST; they have their own labour force characteristics and face specific policy challenges.

Science degrees are delivered in the following fields: life sciences, physical sciences, mathematics and statistics, and computing. Engineering degrees are delivered in engineering and engineering trades, manufacturing and processing and architecture and building.

Graduation rates for advanced research programmes are the number of persons receiving a doctorate level degree as a percentage of the population at the typical age of graduation. Figures refer to net graduation rates, which are calculated by summing graduation rates at each year of age. However, the net graduation rate is unavailable for a few countries and the gross graduation rate is used instead. Gross rates are calculated as the percentage of graduates (the graduates themselves may be of any age) in the population at the typical age of graduation.

## B.1. Flows of university graduates

### Graduation rates at doctoral level, 2002

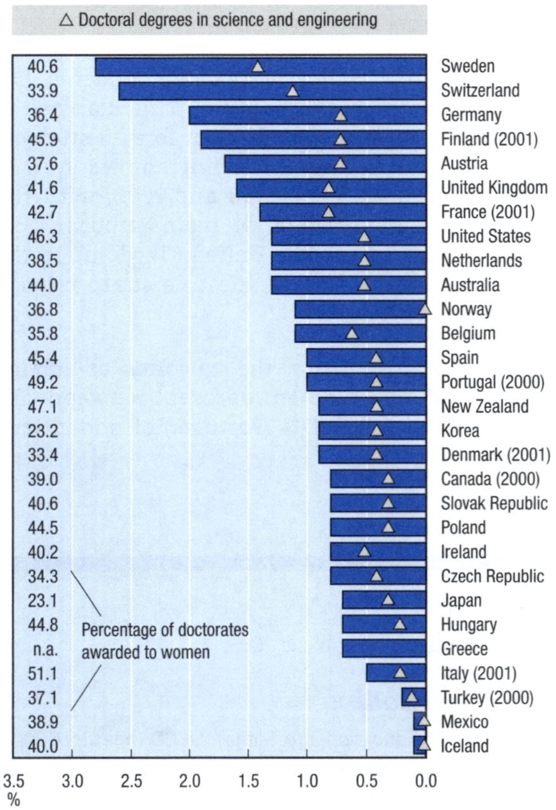


### Science and engineering degrees, 2002

As a percentage of total new degrees

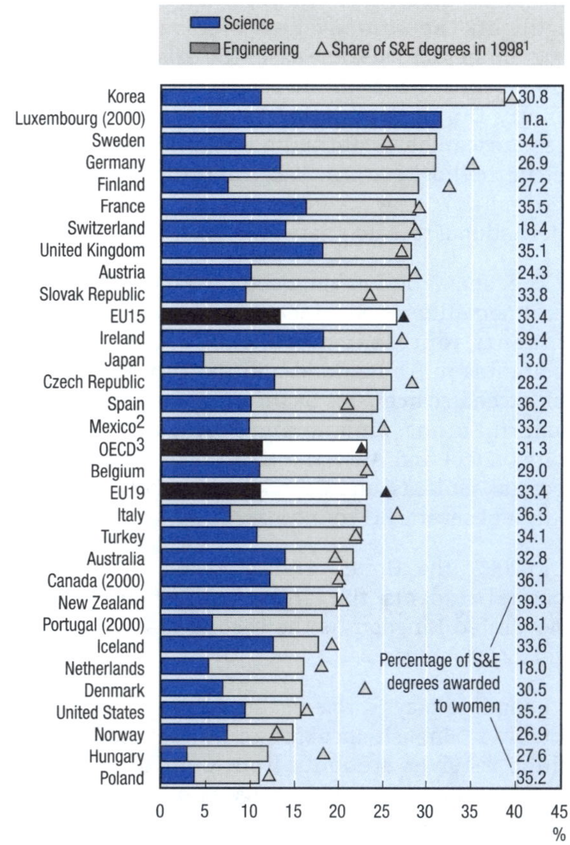


### OECD output of university and doctoral degrees by main region of graduation and field of study, 2002

Percentage of all OECD graduates receiving their degrees by region

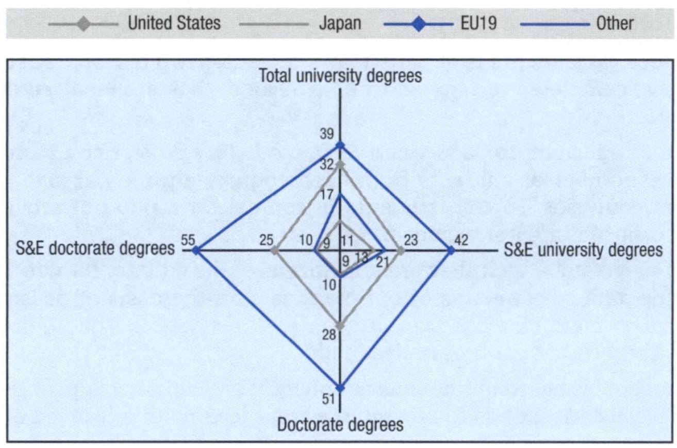


1. 1999 instead of 1998 for the Slovak Republic and Denmark.
2. Excludes tertiary-type A second degree programmes.
3. Average for countries available. Excludes Canada, Portugal and Luxembourg.

StatLink: *http://dx.doi.org/10.1787/621817251270*

## B.2. International mobility of doctoral students

■ International mobility of doctoral students is an indicator of the internationalisation of both the higher education sector and the research system. It also highlights the attractiveness of advanced research programmes and in some cases the existence of career opportunities for junior researchers in the host country. During their doctoral studies and afterwards, these researchers contribute to the research carried out in the host country. When returning home, they bring back new competencies and links to international research networks.

■ The share of foreign doctoral students in total enrolment differs widely across countries. Non-citizen students represent more than a quarter of all doctorates in Switzerland and the United Kingdom, but exceed scarcely 5% of the doctoral population in eastern Europe, Finland and Portugal. The United States (26%) and Australia (24%) have many foreign doctoral students, and Canada's share (17%) is similar to that of several EU countries.

■ In 2002, the United States hosted 79 000 foreign doctoral students, the largest number in the OECD. The United Kingdom is the second major host with over 22 000 students.

■ Language plays a role in the choice of destination, notably in English-speaking countries and in Spain, which receives students from Central and South America. However, a wide range of other factors also matter: geographical proximity, cultural and historical links, exchange programmes (*e.g.* Erasmus) or scholarships, as well as immigration policies. Asian students (in particular from China, Chinese Taipei, India and Korea) represent the bulk of foreign doctorates in the United States, whereas European universities enrol a large share of doctoral students from other European countries.

■ International mobility of doctoral students has increased over the past five years, particularly so in Norway and in Spain. The share of foreign students enrolled in advanced research programmes grew in most countries between 1998 and 2002, with the notable exception of two of the main European host countries (Belgium and the United Kingdom). In the United Kingdom, this was due to a sharp change from 2001 to 2002.

■ Men still account for the majority of foreign doctoral students. Women represent between 23% (Slovak Republic) and 47% (Portugal) of non-citizen doctorates.

### Source

- OECD, Education database, 2005.

### For further reading

- OECD (2004), *Education at a Glance: OECD Indicators 2004*, OECD, Paris, available at *www.oecd.org/edu/eag2004*.
- "Student Mobility Between and Towards OECD Countries: A Comparative Analysis" in OECD (2002), *International Mobility of the Highly Skilled*, OECD, Paris.

### Foreign doctoral students

International mobility of doctoral students is of particular interest for two reasons. First, they are an important subset of HRST, as they have completed tertiary education. Second, they are involved in R&D activities abroad while preparing their degree.

The data used are from the Indicators for Education Systems (INES) project conducted jointly by the OECD, UNESCO and Eurostat. The number of students from each country enrolled abroad is measured from data available in OECD member countries. Foreign students in countries that do not provide these data or those migrating to non-member countries are not included.

Students are classified as foreign students if they are not citizens of the country for which the data are collected. Countries unable to provide data or estimates of non-nationals on the basis of passports were requested to substitute data on the basis of alternative criteria (*e.g.* country of residence). The number of students studying abroad is obtained from the reports of countries of destination.

The educational level of students is based on the International Classification of Education developed by UNESCO (ISCED 1997). ISCED 1997 level 6 corresponds to programmes that lead to an advanced or research qualification, equivalent to a doctorate.

## B.2. International mobility of doctoral students

### Share of foreign doctoral students,[1] 2002

As a percentage of total doctoral enrolment in host country

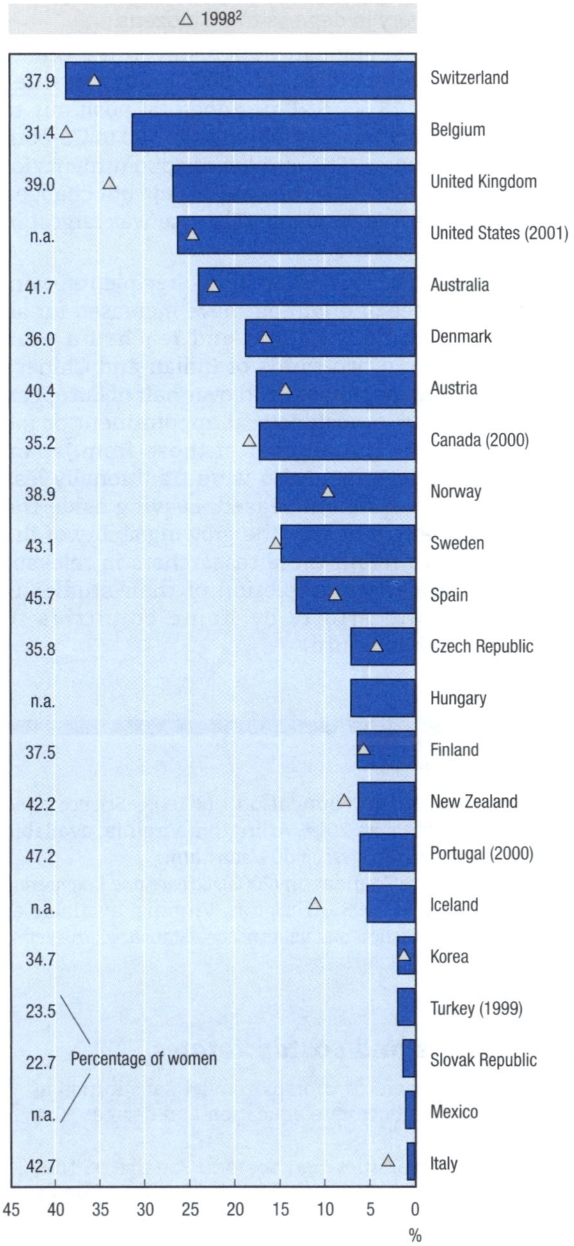


### Number of foreign doctoral students,[1] 2002

By host country

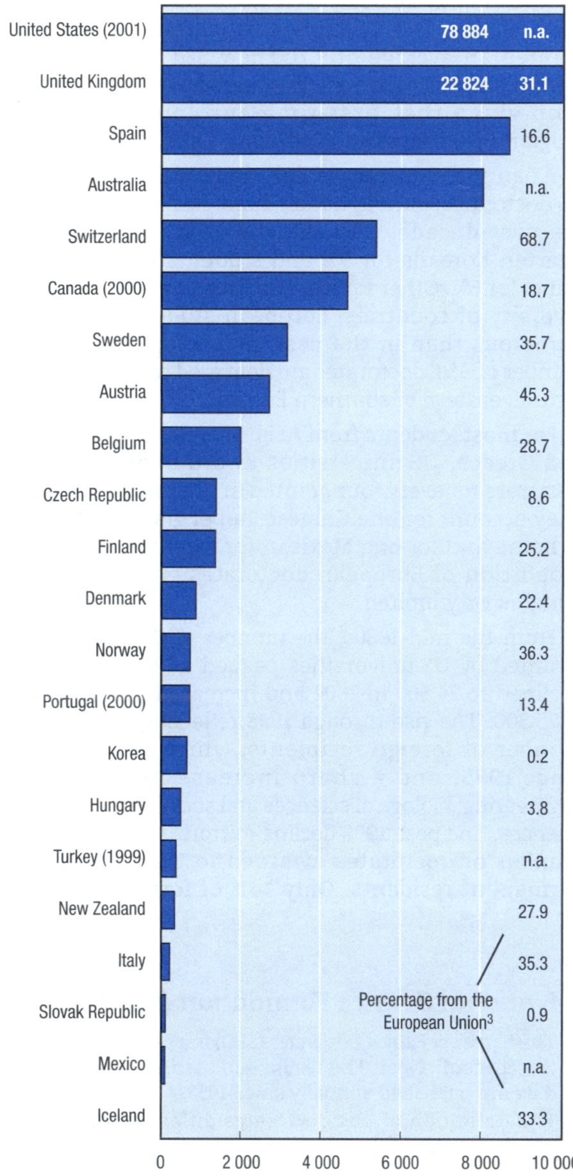


1. Including foreign students from non-OECD countries.
2. 1999 for Belgium and 2000 for Iceland instead of 1998.
3. 1999 for New Zealand and 2000 for Iceland.

StatLink: http://dx.doi.org/10.1787/861232114650

## B.3. S&E doctorates and postdoctorates to foreign citizens in the United States

■ The United States, like France and the United Kingdom, educates large numbers of foreign students. Of the 40 700 doctorates awarded in 2003, two-thirds were in science and engineering (S&E) and 35% of new graduates in these fields were not US citizens. Over the past decade, the US higher education system has granted an average of 9 700 new S&E doctorates to foreign citizens each year, but there is a risk of a future drop given that first-time enrolments in such programmes declined in 2002.

■ Asian students represent the bulk of these new non-US doctorates, although their share has decreased over the past decade. Chinese students account for a quarter, Koreans for 9% and students from Chinese Taipei for 6%. Other foreign students come from a wide diversity of countries. European students are more numerous than in the past, and a rapidly growing number of S&E doctorates are delivered to citizens from central, eastern or southern Europe.

■ For most students from Asia, as well as from Turkey and Greece, US universities award about one S&E doctorate for every four granted in their home country. They account for one Chinese Taipei graduate for two at home and for one Mexican for three at home. The proportion of European doctorates granted abroad remains very limited.

■ From the mid-1980s, the number of S&E doctorates awarded by US universities peaked at 27 300 in 1998, declined to 24 600 in 2002 and increased again in 2003 to 25 300. The rise through 1998 reflects growth in the number of foreign recipients, which had doubled since 1985, and a sharp increase in fields like engineering, biological sciences and social and computer sciences. The post-1998 decline mirrors decreases in the number of doctorates awarded to US citizens and permanent residents. Only 14% of foreign students receiving doctorates in 2003 held resident status or a "green card". The 2003 upsurge was due to growth in the number of degrees granted to foreigners with temporary visas and a recovery in degrees to US citizens.

■ Foreign doctoral graduates often stay in the United States after their studies. In 2002, US universities awarded almost 18 600 S&E postdoctoral positions to temporary visa holders, compared to 13 500 to US-born or resident graduates. The number of appointments for foreigners grew markedly over the decade but changed little for citizens and residents. The rise was largest in biosciences and physics.

■ Stay rates for new doctorate recipients vary according to place of origin but have increased for all citizenships during the 1990s and reached a peak in 2001. More than two-thirds of Indian and Chinese recipients of S&E doctorates and over half of European recipients receive a postdoctoral appointment or job after graduation. The number of those from Japan, Korea or Chinese Taipei, who were traditionally less likely to stay, has also increased. Leaving aside the issue of their length of stay, the growing ability of the United States to retain these researchers in relevant S&T fields just after completion of their studies is evident, despite efforts by home countries to encourage them to return.

### Sources

- National Science Foundation (2004), *Science and Engineering Indicators 2004*, Arlington, Virginia, available at *www.nsf.gov/sbe/srs/seind04/start.htm*.
- National Science Foundation (2003), *Science and Engineering Doctorate Awards 2003*, Arlington, Virginia, available at *www.nsf.gov/statistics/ and www.nsf.gov/statistics/survey.cfm*.

### *National Science Foundation (NSF) data on US doctorates and postdoctorates*

The *Survey of Earned Doctorates* (SED) is a census of all individuals receiving a research doctorate from a US institution in the academic year. The results are used to assess characteristics and trends in doctorate education and degrees. The data are published annually since 1958.

The definition of postdoctorates differs among academic disciplines, universities and sectors. For the US NSF, postdoctorates include "individuals with science and engineering Ph.D.'s, M.D.'s, D.D.S.'s, or D.V.M.'s (including foreign degrees equivalent to US doctorates) who devote their primary effort to their own research training through research activities or study in the department under temporary appointments carrying no academic rank". Postdoctorates may contribute to the academic programme through seminars, lectures or working with graduate students. They may have different titles at different institutions, *e.g.*"Postdoctoral Scholar", "Research Associate", "Postdoctoral Fellow", or "Postgraduate Researcher".

S&E fields include the natural sciences (*e.g.* physical, biological, Earth, atmospheric and ocean sciences), mathematics/computer sciences, agricultural sciences, social/behavioural sciences, engineering, medical/other life sciences.

Stay rates compare new graduates with stated firm plans with total foreign new graduates. They have firm plans when they receive a postdoctoral research appointment or academic, industrial or other firm employment in the United States at receipt of doctorate. Stay rates indicate how much the United States relies on inflows of doctorate holders and whether working in the United States is an attractive option for foreign students who obtain US doctorates.

 OECD SCIENCE, TECHNOLOGY AND INDUSTRY SCOREBOARD 2005 – ISBN 92-64-01055-6 – 

## B.3. S&E doctorates and postdoctorates to foreign citizens in the United States

### S&E doctorates awarded to foreign citizens in the United States, by citizenship or origin

Total number, 2003

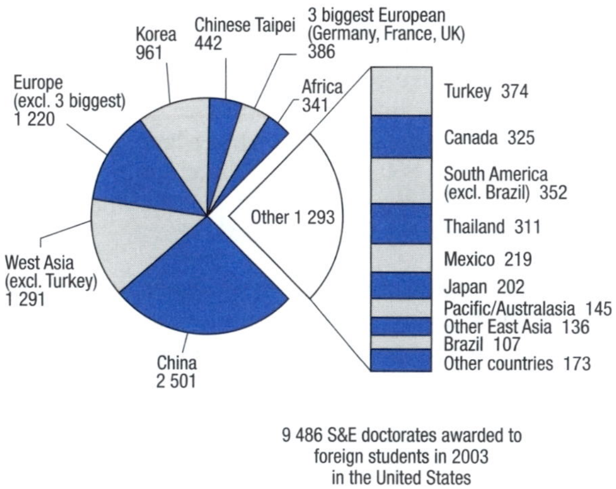


Changes by main geographical area, 1994-2003

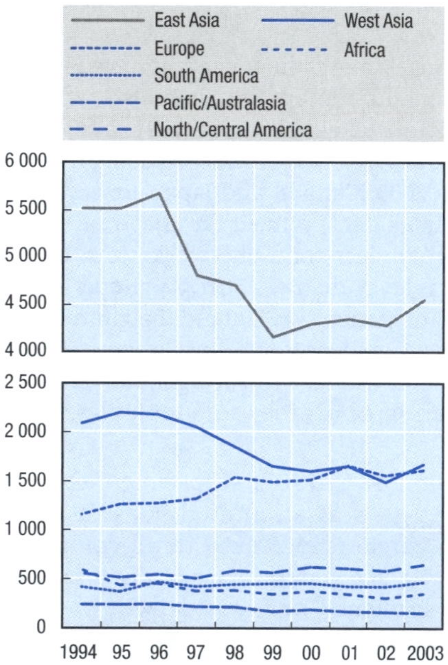


### S&E doctorates and postdoctoral appointments in the United States, by citizenship and type of visa, 1994-2003

Total number

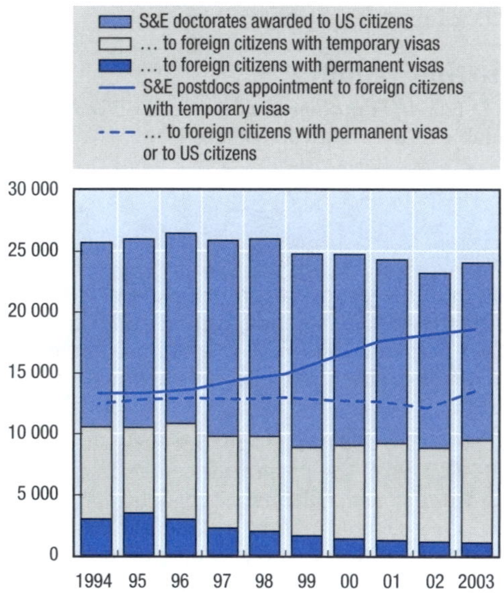


### Stay rates of foreign S&E graduates at doctorate level, 1998-2001

As a percentage of total foreign S&E doctorate recipients

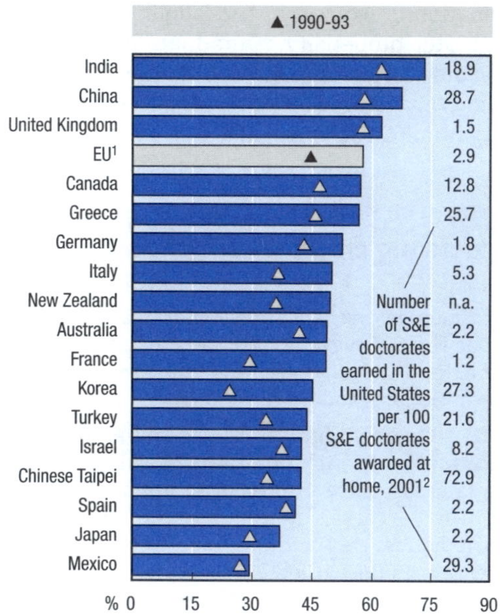


1. Includes all European countries.
2. OECD estimates based on NSF data. The ratio compares the number of new foreign citizens graduating at doctoral level in S&E fields in the United States to the number of earned S&E doctoral degrees in the country of origin. New S&E doctorates refer to 1997 for India, 2001 for China, the United Kingdom, Chinese Taipei and Japan, and 2000 for other countries.

StatLink: *http://dx.doi.org/10.1787/414522285160*

## B.4. Employment of tertiary-level graduates

■ Employment of tertiary-level graduates is an indicator of the labour market's innovative potential and displays a general trend towards upskilling.

■ Large investments in education have led to a rise in educational attainment which is also reflected in the composition of employment. On average, 28% of persons employed in the OECD area had a tertiary-level degree in 2003. Canada and Japan (over 40%) and the United States (38%) ranked far ahead of the European Union, where less than one worker out of four holds a tertiary-level degree. Europe shows large cross-countries disparities. In Finland, Belgium and Sweden, tertiary-level graduates account for more than a third of employment, whereas in Portugal, Italy and the Czech and Slovak Republics they account for less than 15%.

■ Between 1998 and 2003, employment of tertiary-level graduates grew at an annual pace of about 4% in the OECD area. It increased in all countries except Luxembourg, and grew on average four times faster than total employment. The fastest growth was recorded in Spain (8.2%), Iceland (7.5%) and Turkey (7.2%); the lowest in Germany (0.6%), Norway (1.4%) and Finland (2.4%). In countries where levels of tertiary-level graduates were already high (United States, Japan), employment continued to grow at over 2.5% a year.

■ This growth has been sustained by increased participation of women in the labour market. Despite their greater propensity to graduate at tertiary level, women are still less numerous than men in work. They represent on average 45% of tertiary-level employment, ranging from 61% in Portugal to 31% in Switzerland.

■ The population of tertiary-level workers is aging. In 2002, one OECD worker with a tertiary-level degree out of three was over 45 years of age. Those aged 45-64 accounted for more than 40% of tertiary-level employment in Germany, Sweden, Denmark and the Czech Republic. In a span of only five years, their share has increased in almost all countries. The share of those aged 25-34 years with tertiary-level degrees is higher in France, Poland, Portugal and Spain. In Korea and Turkey this group accounted for 43% and 45% of tertiary-level employment, respectively.

■ University graduates are less likely to remain unemployed except in Turkey and Mexico. Turkey's unemployment rate among university graduates is especially high (11.1%). The rates are also high in Spain (8.8) and France (7.7). Women with a university degree are less likely to be unemployed than women without one, yet their unemployment rate is higher than that of men with the same level of education. Their unemployment is significantly higher in countries where overall unemployment at tertiary level is high (Turkey, Spain, Greece, France, Poland and Italy). The largest gender gap is in Italy and Greece, where unemployment rates are twice as high for women than for men.

### Source

- OECD, Educational database, May 2005.

### For further reading

- OECD, (2004), *Education at a Glance: OECD Indicators 2004*, available at *www.oecd.org/eag2004*.

### *Measuring employment of tertiary-level graduates*

The OECD Educational Attainment Database provides data on population at different levels of education distributed by sex, age and work status (employed, unemployed, inactive). It is compiled from member countries' labour force surveys and/or the European labour force survey. Adjustments are made to ensure comparability across countries, notably concerning national levels of education, which are recoded according to the International Standard Classification of Education 1997 (ISCED 1997).

Tertiary-level graduates are defined as holders of degrees at the ISCED 1997 levels 5B, 5A and 6. University graduates only include graduates at ISCED levels 5A and 6. ISCED level 5A programmes are long-stream programmes, since they have a minimum cumulative duration of three years' full-time equivalent and typically are of four years or more. They are largely theoretically based or research preparatory (history, philosophy, mathematics, etc.) and intended to provide sufficient qualifications for gaining entry into advanced research programmes (ISCED level 6) or professions with high skills requirement (medicine, dentistry, architecture, etc.). The short streams (ISCED 5B) are more practically oriented.

## B.4. Employment of tertiary-level graduates

### Employment growth of tertiary-level graduates, 1998-2003

Average annual growth rate

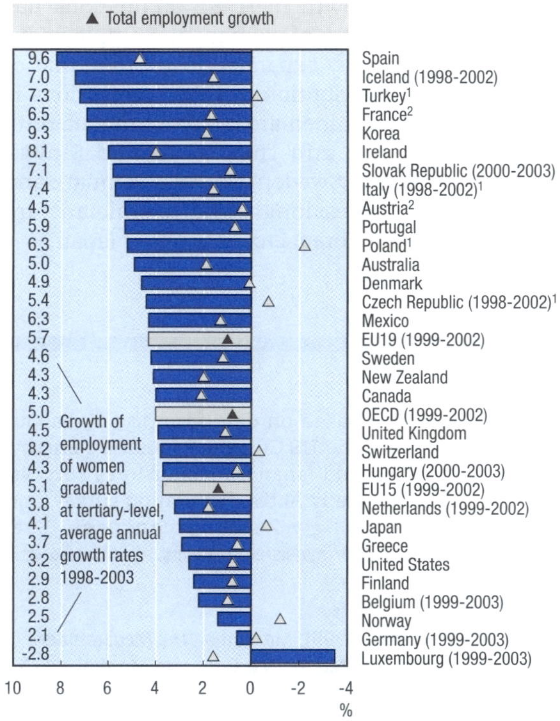


### Tertiary-level graduates, 2003

As a percentage of total employment

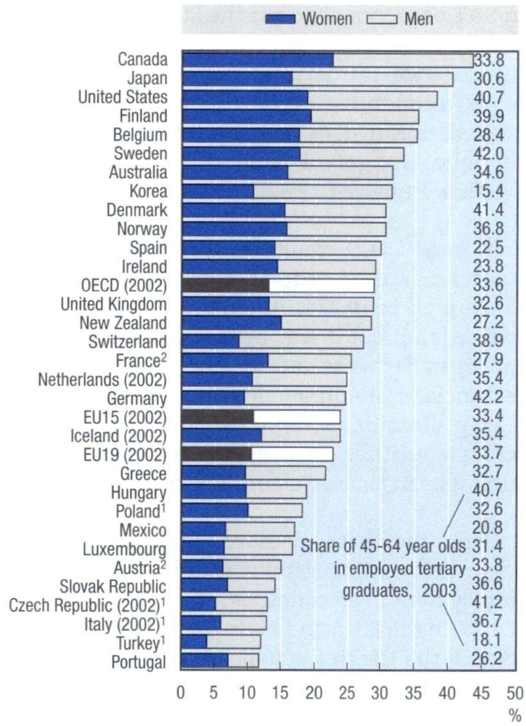


### Unemployment rates of university graduates, 2003

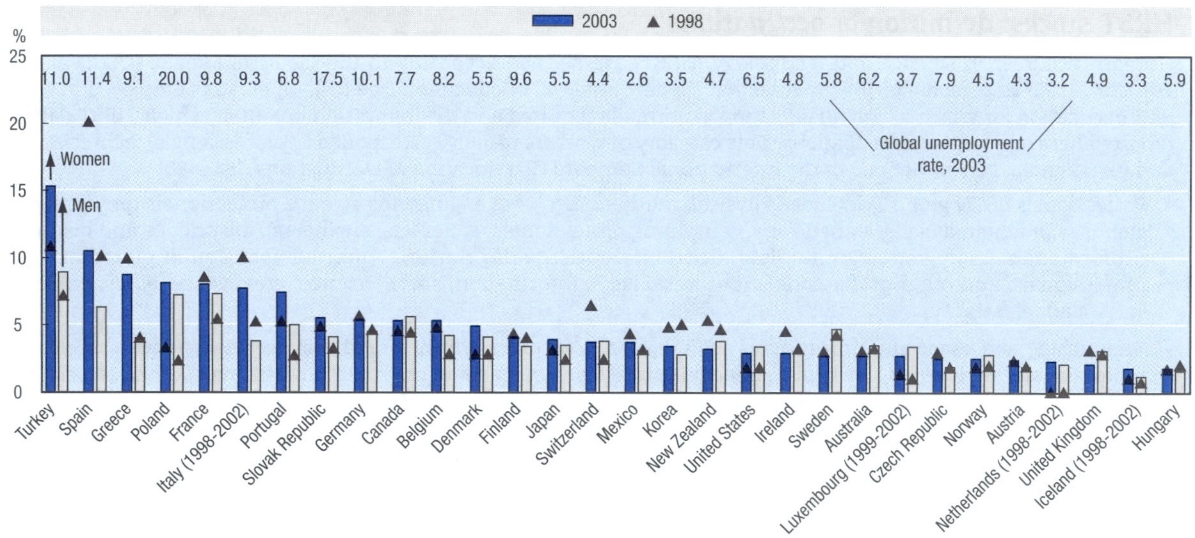


1. Do not include graduates at ISCED level 5B.
2. Do not include graduates at ISCED level 6.

StatLink: *http://dx.doi.org/10.1787/456738663043*

## B.5. Human resources in science and technology

■ Workers in professional and technical occupations (see box) are actively involved in the creation and diffusion of knowledge and technological innovation. In 2004, almost 54 million persons were employed in an S&T occupation, across the EU25, almost 42 million in the United States and about 10 million in Japan. In Europe, two-thirds were concentrated in the four largest economies, *i.e.* Germany (23%), France (14%), the United Kingdom (13%) and Italy (12%). The Czech Republic, Hungary, Poland and the Slovak Republic together employed 12%.

■ In most OECD countries, S&T workers represent a quarter to a third of total employment. In 2004, their share was over 37% in Sweden, Luxembourg and Switzerland, but it was below 20% in Portugal, Korea and Japan (Japanese data are probably underestimated). Technicians are on average slightly more numerous than professionals, although the breakdown varies across countries. Professionals are relatively more numerous in Japan, Ireland, Belgium and Greece.

■ Over the past decade, employment in HRST occupations has grown much faster than total employment in all countries, at an average annual rate of 2.7% in the EU15 and 2% in the United States. Even in Poland, the Czech Republic and the Slovak Republic, where overall employment declined during the period, HRST employment has grown. Some countries with low shares of professionals and technicians (Spain, Ireland, Greece), have been catching up. Luxembourg, Norway and the Netherlands, with already high shares, have maintained strong growth in S&T employment.

■ In many cases, growth in HRST occupations has been driven by the entry of women, and employment of women has generally expanded faster than that of men. The gender distribution in HRST professions is quite balanced, and women are in fact in the majority in Hungary, Poland and the Czech and Slovak Republics as well as in Sweden, Norway, Denmark and Finland. Female professionals and technicians are underrepresented in Korea, Luxembourg or Japan.

### Source

- OECD calculations, based on data from the EU Labour Force Survey; from the US Current Population Survey; from the Canadian and Japanese labour force surveys, the Korean Economically Active Population survey, and the Australia and New Zealand censuses. See: *http://forum.europa.eu.int/irc/dsis/employment/info/data/eu_lfs.*

### For further reading

- OECD and Eurostat (1995), *Manual on the Measurement of Human Resources Devoted to S&T: Canberra Manual*, OECD, Paris.
- OECD (2001), *Innovative People: Mobility of Skilled Personnel in National Innovation Systems*, OECD, Paris.

### HRST stocks: *definition of occupations*

Human resources in science and technology (HRST) are defined according to the *Canberra Manual* (OECD and Eurostat, 1995) as persons having graduated at the tertiary level of education (see B.4), or, persons employed in an S&T occupation for which a high qualification is normally required and the innovation potential is high. HRST data reported here only concern occupations. This category of workers usually corresponds to professionals, technicians and certain managers as defined in the International Standard Classification of Occupations (ISCO-88).

- Professionals (ISCO group 2) includes Physical, mathematical and engineering science professionals (physicists, chemists, mathematicians, statisticians, computing professionals, architects, engineers), life science and health professionals (biologists, agronomists, doctors, dentist, veterinarians, pharmacists, nursing), teaching professionals, and other professionals (business, legal, information, social science, creative, religious, public service administrative).
- Technicians and associate professionals (ISCO group 3) includes: Physical and engineering science associate professionals, life science and health associate professionals, teaching associate professionals, other associate professionals (finance, sales, business services, trade brokers, administrative, government, police inspectors, social work, artistic entertainment and sport, religious).
- Managers includes: directors and chief executives (ISCO group 121), production and operations managers (ISCO group 122) and managers of small enterprises (ISCO group 131).

Persons employed in managerial occupations (ISCO 121, 122, 131) are not included because of the quality of the data and problems of international comparability.

 OECD SCIENCE, TECHNOLOGY AND INDUSTRY SCOREBOARD 2005 – ISBN 92-64-01055-6 – © OECD 2005

## B.5. Human resources in science and technology

### HRST occupations, 2004

As a percentage of total employment

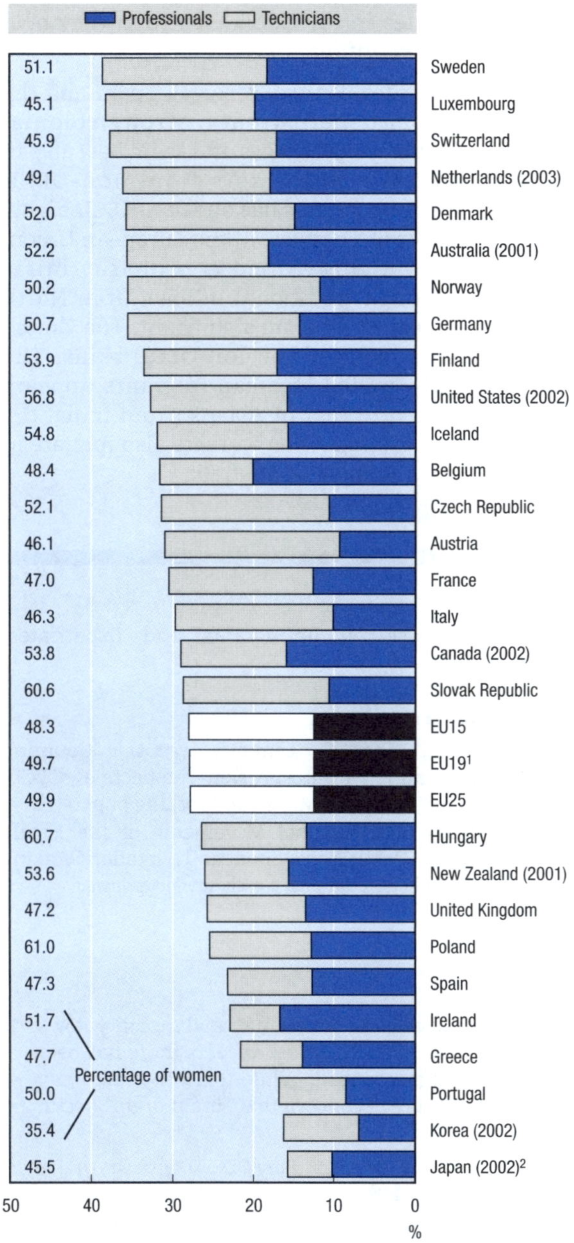


### Growth of HRST occupations, 1995-2004

Average annual growth rate (%)

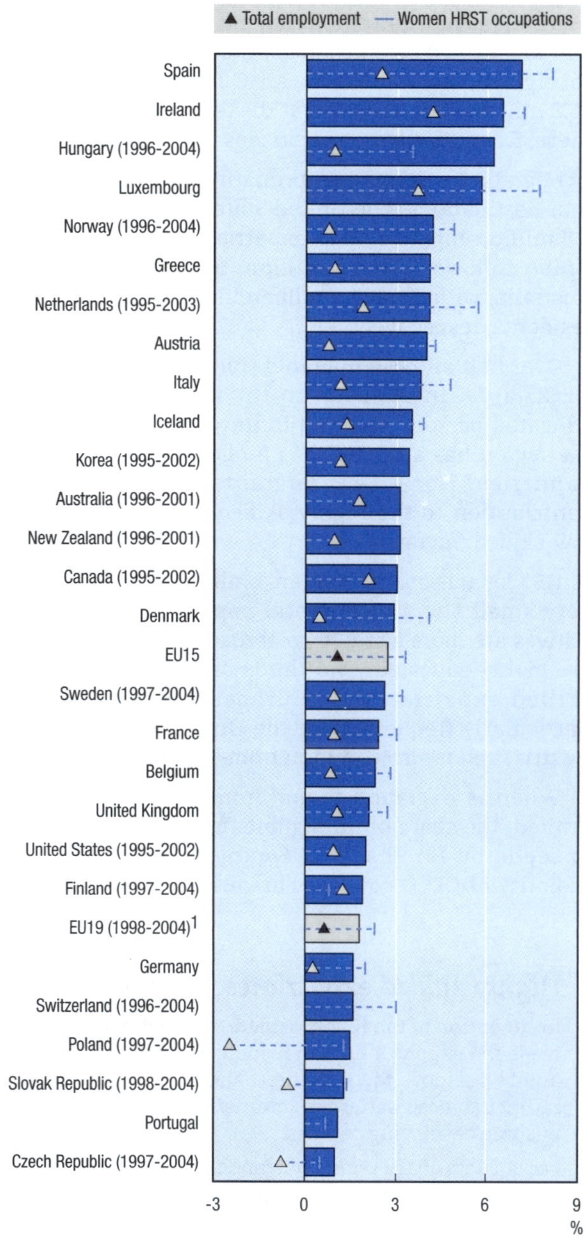


1. OECD estimates.
2. National estimates.

StatLink: *http://dx.doi.org/10.1787/265183674780*

## B.6. International mobility of the highly skilled

■ Modern economies rely on human expertise and compete in attracting the best competencies. Migration of the highly skilled remains limited, however, as most international migrants are medium- and low-skilled persons; in 2001, out of the 67 million foreign-born residing in an OECD country, only 16.8 million were educated at the tertiary level. Among these, 5.7 million were not citizens of the host country.

■ Migration streams are primarily directed towards four destinations. The United States is first, with over 7.8 million highly skilled expatriates. The European Union follows with 4.7 million, before Canada and Australia, with 2 and 1.4 million highly skilled foreign residents, respectively.

■ Over half of these migrants come from outside the OECD area. In addition to the 6.7 million highly educated persons involved in intra-OECD skill flows, the region has attracted 10.1 million from non-OECD countries. Non-OECD migrants make a greater contribution to the highly skilled than medium- or low-skilled migrants.

■ US, Japanese and Korean emigrants represent a very small share of the total population. European natives are more likely to go abroad, especially if they are highly educated. Two-thirds of OECD-area highly skilled expatriates are European. Emigration is particularly frequent from the United Kingdom and Austria, and is also common from eastern Europe.

■ Whereas migration to and from Japan or Korea is limited, the share of immigrants to the United States exceeds by far that of US expatriates. The vast majority of OECD countries are also net beneficiaries of highly skilled migration when immigration from non-OECD countries is taken into account. However, a number of European countries have more highly skilled expatriates in the OECD area than they host from non-OECD countries.

■ The United States, France, Portugal, Spain and the United Kingdom benefit from a strong colonial heritage or linguistic advantages and seem best able to attract highly skilled workers from non-OECD countries. The United States has one non-OECD highly skilled person for ten natives. In the European Union, mobility of the highly skilled is primarily intra-European, although traditional inflows from North Africa and eastern Europe are significant. The United States captures over half of non-OECD skills. The share of highly skilled Mexican migrants appears limited compared to that of Asians (from India, the Philippines and China). Asian workers also migrate in large numbers to Canada or Australia.

### *Source*

- OECD, Database on Immigrants and Expatriates, April 2005.

### *For further reading*


- Dumont, J.C. and G. Lemaître (2004), "Counting Immigrants and Expatriates: A New Perspective", OECD, Social, Employment and Migration Working papers.
- Salt, J. (1997), "International Movements of the Highly Skilled", OECD, Social, Employment and Migration Working papers, available at *www.oecd.org/els/workingpapers*.


### *Highly skilled expatriates: definition and data issues*

Immigration of the highly skilled, together with new higher education graduates and intra-national mobility flows, feeds the supply of human resources in science and technology (HRST) (see Box B.5). In recent years there has been a growing move towards international recruitment and mobility of the highly skilled. While there seems to be a rather balanced pattern of international mobility among OECD countries, there is concern that "brain drain" occurs in some developing countries.

Lack of data on the permanent and temporary flows of migrants according to skill levels in many OECD countries makes international comparisons difficult. Nevertheless, several data sources can be used to gauge the stocks and flows of highly skilled migrants in receiving OECD countries. Censuses are one, and the OECD has developed a new database on immigrants and expatriates based on census data. Most censuses in member countries were conducted around 2000, and the results are currently available for almost all. Several countries, however, do not have a population census, so that data from population registers or from large sample surveys have been used. Census data were used for 23 of the 29 participating countries and other sources for six; Iceland does not participate. The database currently includes data on the foreign-born in OECD countries by place of birth, nationality and educational attainment (three levels).

This is the first internationally comparable data set with detailed information on the foreign-born population for almost all member countries. Expatriates in the OECD area are defined as residents in any OECD country born in another OECD country or in a non-OECD country, whether naturalised or not. The information in the database therefore reflects the cumulative effect of movements within and to the OECD area over the past decades. Highly educated persons are identified as those having a tertiary level of education.

 OECD SCIENCE, TECHNOLOGY AND INDUSTRY SCOREBOARD 2005 – ISBN 92-64-01055-6 – © OECD 2005

## B.6. International mobility of the highly skilled

### Highly skilled migrants from OECD and non-OECD countries, by OECD country of residence, 2001[1]

As a percentage of highly skilled natives in the country of residence

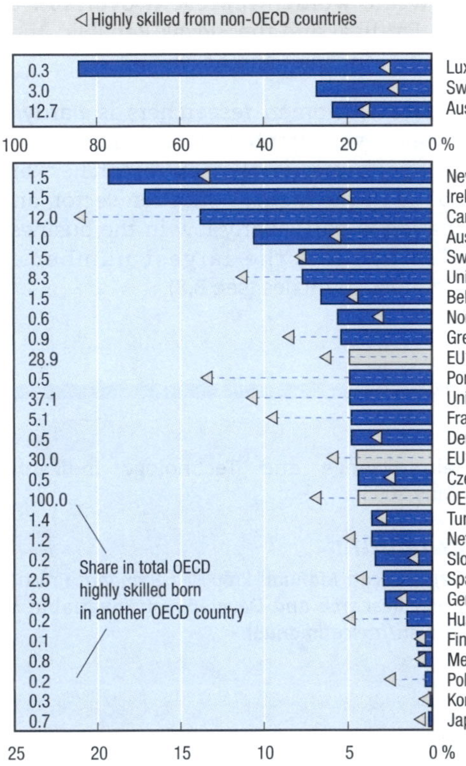


### Highly skilled migrants to the OECD countries, by country of birth, 2001[1]

As a percentage of highly skilled natives in the country of birth

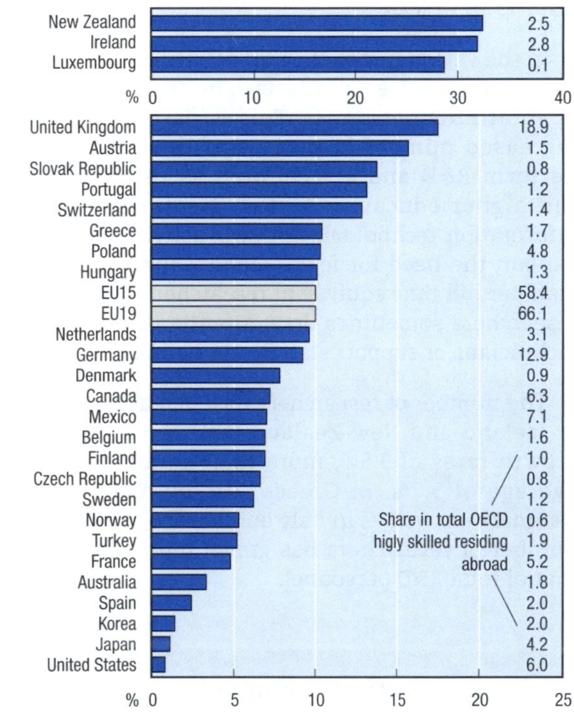


### Main destinations of the highly skilled migrants, 2001[1]

Percentage shares of the 5 top OECD and of the 5 top non-OECD places of birth

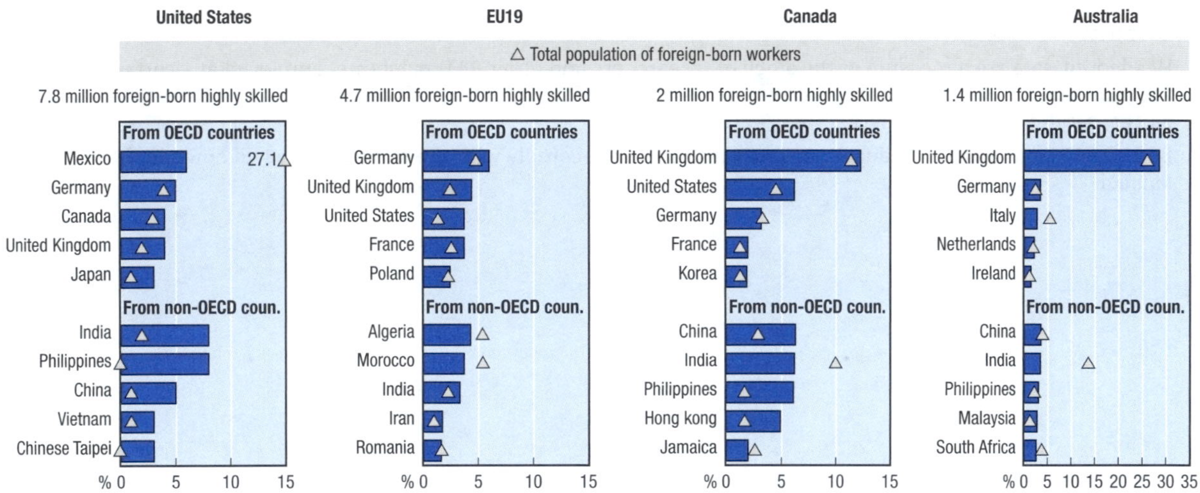


1. 2003 for Norway and Sweden; 2002 for Denmark and Ireland; 2000 for Finland, Japan, Korea, Mexico, Switzerland, Turkey and the United States; 1999 for France; 1999-2002 for Germany: 2001 for other countries.

StatLink: *http://dx.doi.org/10.1787/424837025473*

## B.7. R&D personnel

■ The number of personnel engaged in R&D in OECD economies is directly linked to their R&D effort. In Finland, Sweden and Denmark, over 15 R&D personnel per 1 000 employees contribute to R&D activities, well above the EU25 average of 10.2 per 1 000. Japan also employs a higher than average ratio of R&D personnel (over 13 per 1 000).

■ In the vast majority of OECD countries, the number of researchers rises at a faster rate than the number of total R&D personnel. This is partly due to the increased number of postgraduate students who perform R&D and are counted as researchers in the higher education sector. Greater use of new information technologies in R&D activities may also explain the need for fewer technicians and support staff per full time equivalent researcher. Nevertheless, researchers sometimes draw attention to the lack of technicians or support staff in laboratories.

■ The number of researchers has increased the most in Iceland and New Zealand, with average annual growth rates of 9.5%, more than double the OECD average of 3.7%. In Greece, Turkey, Belgium and Denmark, as well as in Italy and Mexico, however, the number of researchers has grown more slowly than that of total R&D personnel.

■ The under-representation of women in R&D activities is increasingly gaining the attention of policy makers. In most countries for which data are available, women represent between 25% and 35% of total researchers. While women represent over 40% of researchers in Portugal and the Slovak Republic, they represent only 11% in Japan and Korea.

■ The low share of women researchers is partly a reflection of the uneven distribution of women among sectors of R&D performance. Women researchers are principally found in the higher education sector, and their participation is particularly low in the business sector, which attracts the largest number of researchers in most countries (see B.8).

### Source

- OECD, Main Science and Technology Indicators database, May 2005.

### For further reading

- OECD (2002), *Frascati Manual: Proposed Standard Practice for Surveys on Research and Development*, available at *www.oecd.org/sti/frascatimanual*.

### Measuring R&D personnel

Research and development personnel includes all persons employed directly in R&D activities and therefore covers technicians and support staff in addition to researchers.

R&D personnel can be expressed both in full-time equivalents (FTE) on R&D and in headcounts.

A person working half-time on R&D is counted as 0.5 person-year in FTE. FTE includes staff engaged in R&D during the course of a particular year. FTE data are a true measure of the volume of personnel and give an indication of countries' research effort.

Headcount data are a measure of the stock of researchers and other R&D personnel employed at a certain date in the year, and are the most appropriate measure for collecting additional information about R&D personnel, such as age, gender or national origin.

Both the FTE on R&D and headcounts data presented here comply with the methodology laid down in the *Frascati Manual*.

## B.7. R&D personnel

### R&D personnel, 2003

Per thousand employment

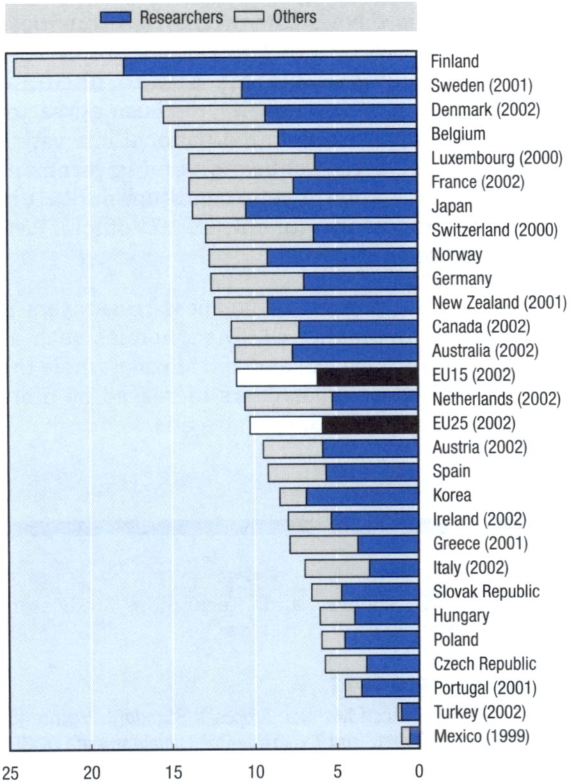


### Growth of R&D personnel, 1995-2003

Average annual growth rate

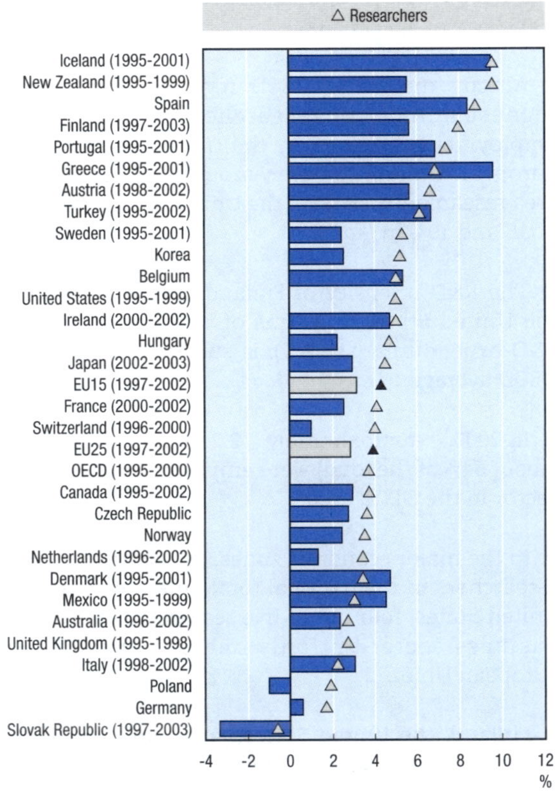


### Women researchers by sector of employment, 2003

As a percentage of total researchers

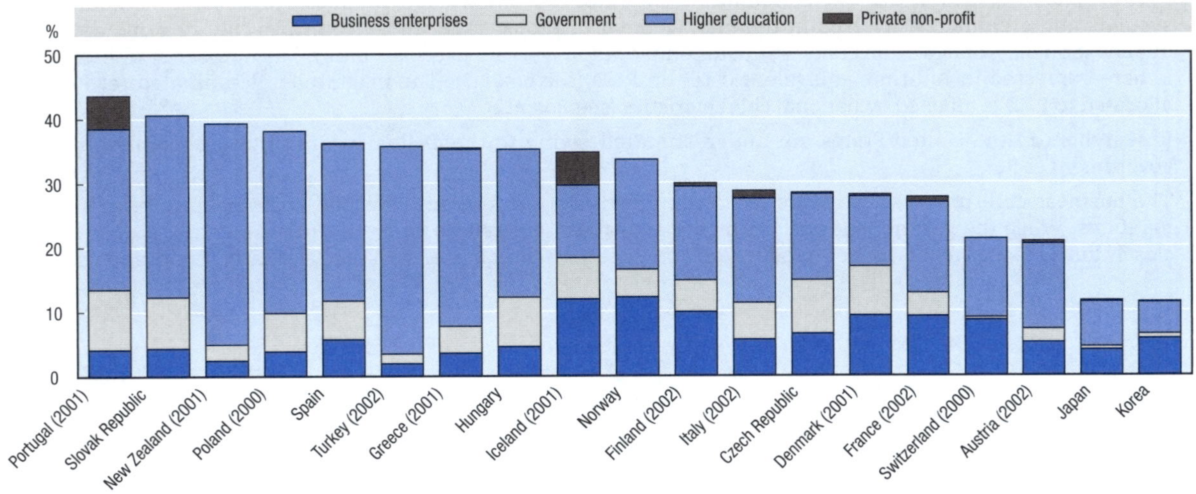


StatLink: *http://dx.doi.org/10.1787/075710471758*

## B.8. Researchers

■ In 2000, approximately 3.4 million researchers were engaged in research and development (R&D) in the OECD area. This corresponds to about 6.6 researchers per 1 000 employees, a significant increase from the 1995 level of 5.6 per 1 000.

■ Among the major OECD regions, Japan has the highest number of researchers relative to total employment, followed by the United States and the European Union. However, around 38% of all OECD-area researchers reside in the United States, 29% in the EU15 and 19% in Japan.

■ The R&D intensity of Finland, Sweden, Japan and the United States, in terms of both researchers and R&D expenditure (see A.2), is substantially above the OECD average.

■ In 2000, approximately 2.2 million researchers (about 64% of the total) were employed by the business sector in the OECD area.

■ In the major economic zones, the share of business researchers in the national total differs widely. In the United States, four out of five researchers work in the business sector but only one out of two in the European Union.

■ Finland, the United States, Japan and Sweden are the only countries where business researchers exceed 6 per 1 000 employees; in the large European economies, they are only 3 or 4 per 1 000.

■ Mexico, Turkey, Portugal, Greece, Poland and the Slovak Republic have a low intensity of business researchers (fewer than 1 per 1 000 employees in industry). This is mainly due to national characteristics; in these countries, the business sector plays a much smaller role in the national innovation system than the higher education and government sectors. Business enterprise expenditure on R&D in these countries accounts for only 25-35% of total R&D expenditure (see A.3).

■ Growth in the number of business researchers is most dynamic in smaller OECD economies such as New Zealand, Portugal, Iceland and Mexico, where the number of business researchers increased by more than 15% annually over the past decade.

### Source

- OECD, Main Science and Technology Indicators database, May 2005.

### For further reading

- OECD (2002), *Frascati Manual: Proposed Standard Practice for Surveys on Research and Experimental Development*, OECD, Paris, available at *www.oecd.org/sti/frascatimanual*.

### Researchers

Researchers are viewed as the central element of the research and development system. They are defined as professionals engaged in the conception and creation of new knowledge, products, processes, methods and systems and are directly involved in the management of projects. For those countries that compile data by qualification only, data on university graduates employed in R&D are used as a proxy. The number of researchers is here expressed in full-time equivalent (FTE) on R&D (see Box B.7). The magnitude of estimated resources allocated to R&D is affected by national characteristics (see Box A.2).

Researchers in the United States are underestimated owing to the exclusion of military personnel in the government sector.

The business enterprise sector covers researchers carrying out R&D in firms and business enterprise sector institutes. While the government and the higher education sectors also carry out R&D, industrial R&D is more closely linked to the creation of new products and production techniques, as well as to a country's innovation effort.



OECD SCIENCE, TECHNOLOGY AND INDUSTRY SCOREBOARD 2005 – ISBN 92-64-01055-6 – © OECD 2005

## B.8. Researchers

### Researchers, 2003

Per 1 000 total employment

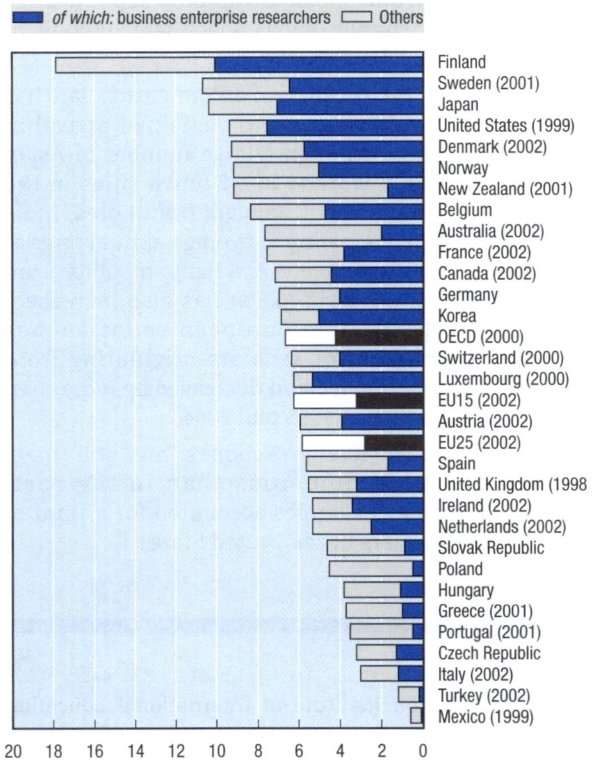


### Growth of business researchers, 1995-2003

Average annual growth rate

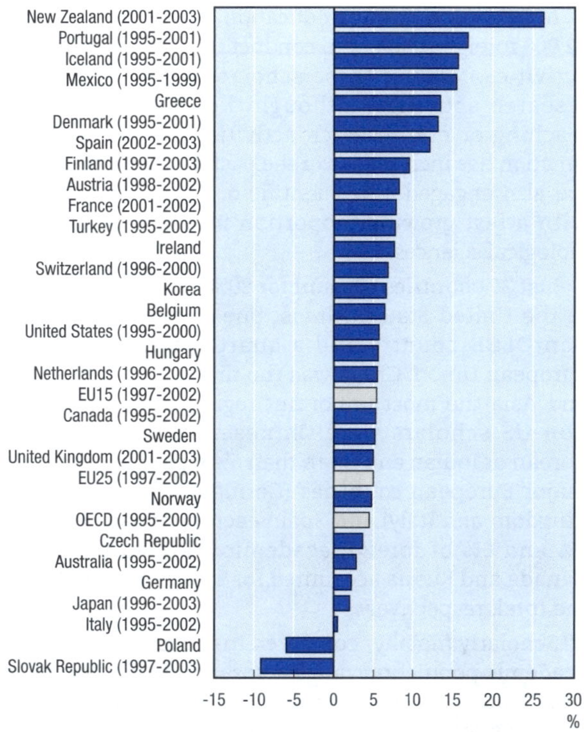


### Researchers by area, 1985-2003

Per 1 000 total employment

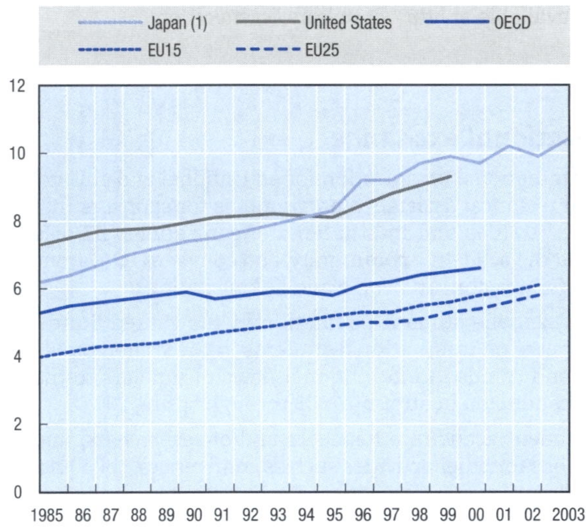


### Business researchers by area, 1985-2003

Per 1 000 employment in industry

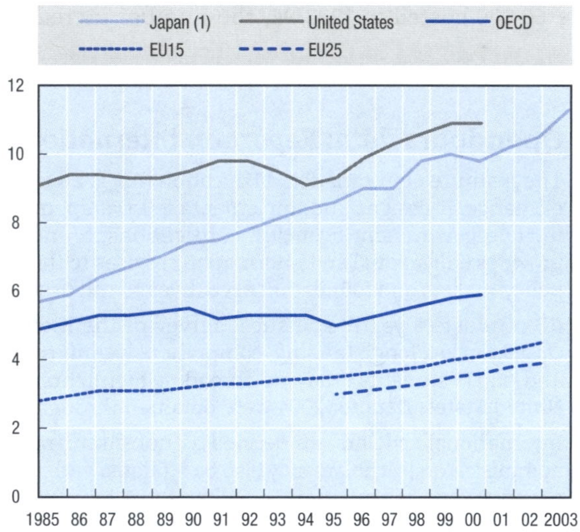


1. Data are adjusted up to 1995.

StatLink: *http://dx.doi.org/10.1787/374361301766*

## B.9. Foreign scholars in the United States

■ The presence of foreign scholars in US higher education institutions is an indicator of the international attractiveness of the country's universities and of opportunities for researchers in the United States.

■ In 2003/04 US higher education institutions hosted 82 900 foreign scholars to conduct teaching or research activities. Most of these scholars were engaged in research activities, although the share for whom teaching or non-research activities are the primary function has increased over the past decade. Two-thirds are also engaged into scientific or engineering fields, with a fast-growing proportion involved in life and biological sciences.

■ Just 20 countries account for 80% of foreign scholars in the United States. Almost one in two was from a non-OECD country and a quarter came from the European Union. China was the first country of origin and Asia the most important region. Around 18% of non-US scholars were Chinese, around 8% were Korean or Indian and more than 6% Japanese. The four major European countries (Germany, France, United Kingdom and Italy) and Spain each provided between 2% and 6% of foreign academic staff. In addition, Canada and Russia accounted for 5% and almost 3% of the total, respectively.

■ Scholarly mobility compared to the size of the local academic population varies across countries. For most OECD countries, two to four scholars hold positions in US universities per 100 working at home. Academic mobility is most significant from Korea (13), Russia (8) and Chinese Taipei (6).

■ The population of foreign scholars working in the United States has grown over the past decade. From the 60 000 hosted in 1993/94, the number increased to 86 000 in 2001/02. The academic year 2003/04 is the second consecutive year of decline, with a decrease of 1.6%. One important factor is the post-September 11 security-related change in visa policy, which modified access to the US labour market.

■ Expansion of the population of foreign scholars has been driven by a massive and sustained arrival of Asian academics. Although a large number of Asian academics already worked in US universities in the mid-1990s, the number of scholars from Korea, India and China has kept growing at average annual rates of 9%, 6% and 4%, respectively. Academic mobility from Turkey (7.7%) and Russia (6.6%) has also increased. However, mobility from European countries has slowed. The number of scholars originating from Finland, Hungary and Iceland decreased by more than 2.5% annually between 1995 and 2004.

■ Although most foreign scholars are still men, women are more numerous than in the past; in 2003/04 female academics accounted for a third of total foreign scholars in the United States.

### Sources

- OECD, based on Institute of International Education (IIE), April 2005.
- OECD, Main Science and Technology Indicators Database, May 2005.

### For further reading


- Institute of International Education (2004), *Opendoors: Report on International Educational Exchange*, New York, available at *http://opendoors.iienetwork.org/*.


### Opendoors *data: Report on international educational exchange*

The Institute of International Education (IIE) is a non-profit international organisation for educational and cultural exchange. It designs and implements fellowship, training and technical assistance programmes for sponsors that include government agencies, corporations, foundations, universities and international organisations. IIE also provides educational and information services to the public and the academic community, and convenes educators, policy makers and foundation executives to discuss strategies for investing in people and linking nations.

IIE conducts a yearly statistical survey of the internationally mobile student population in the United States. *Opendoors* is a long-standing, comprehensive information resource on international students in the United States and on US students studying abroad. It highlights key facts and trends in international flows of scholars to the United States. Data for 2004 were obtained through a survey conducted in autumn 2003 through spring 2004.

International scholars are defined as non-immigrant, non-student academics (teachers and/or researchers, and administrators). Scholars may also be affiliated with US institutions for other activities such as conferences, colloquia, observations, consultations or other short-term professional development activities. The survey was limited to doctoral degree-granting institutions and captured scholar-related information for the period beginning July 2003 and ending June 2004.

Sciences include life and biological sciences, health sciences and physical sciences.

## B.9. Foreign scholars in the United States

### Top 20 places of origin of foreign scholars in the United States, 2003/04

Headcounts

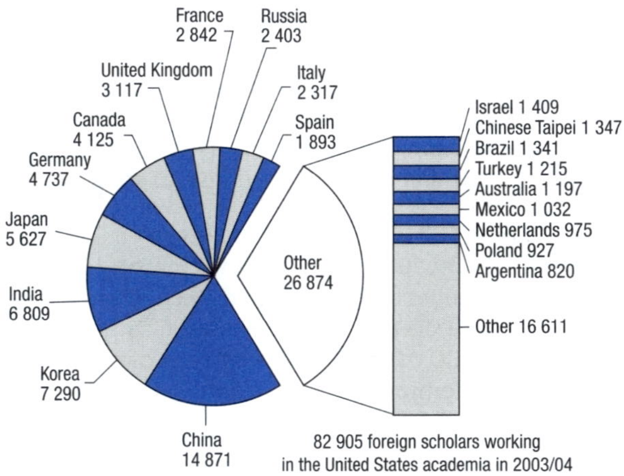


### Growth of foreign US scholars, by gender and activity, 1993/94-2003/04

Headcounts and as a percentage of total foreign US population

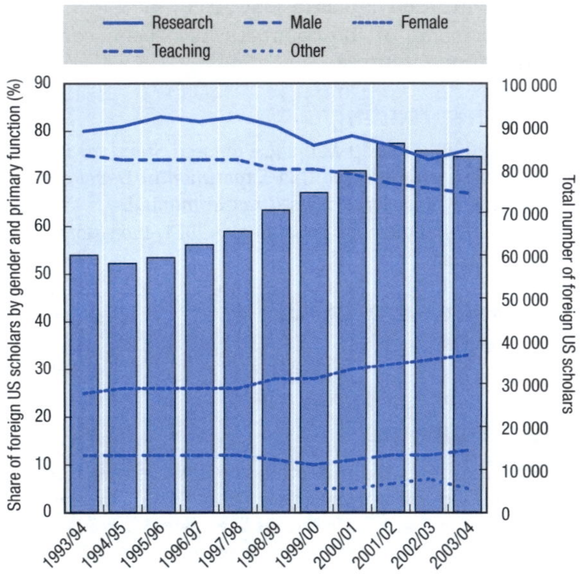


### Growth in foreign scholars, by country of origin, 1995-2004

Average annual growth rate

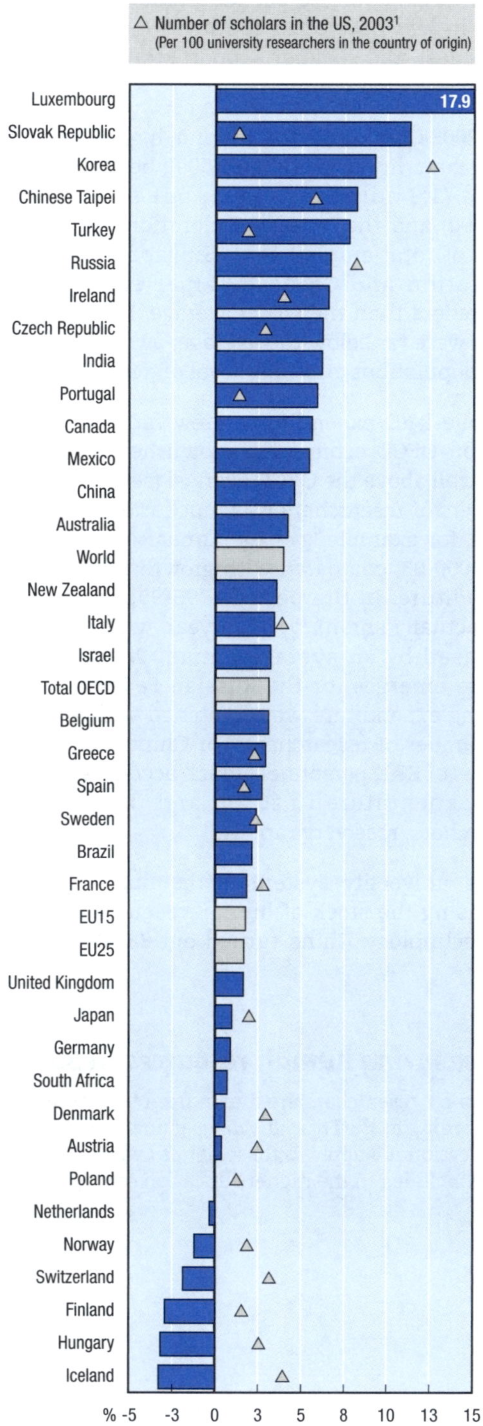


1. 2003 for Russia and Norway; 1999 for Greece, Iceland, Portugal and Sweden; 2002 for other countries.

StatLink: *http://dx.doi.org/10.1787/248585825175*

## B.10. Human resources in S&T in non-OECD economies

■ Non-OECD countries account for one-third of the combined total of OECD and non-OECD researchers, much more than their share in R&D expenditure (see A.4). Expenditure per researcher is considerably lower in less developed countries (because of lower wages, less and cheaper support staff, less expensive equipment, etc.).

■ In 2003 China had the second highest number of researchers in the world (862 000), behind the United States (1.3 million in 1999), but ahead of Japan (675 000) and the Russian Federation (487 000). As a share of total employment, Singapore, the Russian Federation and Chinese Taipei employed more researchers than the OECD average. India, Brazil and China were far below the average, owing to the size of their populations and their level of development.

■ While R&D expenditures grew rapidly in many of the non-OECD economies shown here, with growth rates well above the OECD average (see A.4), growth in numbers of researchers was much more moderate. In China, for example, average annual growth was 7.4% over 2000-03, compared with growth of 18.6% in R&D expenditure. In the period 1996-99, the researcher base actually shrank by 1% a year, while expenditure increased by an average annual 20.4%. A similar picture emerges for the Russian Federation, where growing expenditure was combined with a decline in the number of researchers. For China, it may be that salaries of R&D personnel (which accounted for 23% of R&D expenditure in 2000), and in particular of researchers, rose very rapidly.

■ The university system is the main channel for increasing the stock of human resources for science and technology. China turned out 885 000 university graduates in 2002. Almost 15 000 (1.7%) of these graduates were awarded a PhD degree, a number that rose to 19 000 in 2003. Russia and Brazil awarded fewer university degrees than China (635 000 and 396 000, respectively), but more doctorates.

■ China also experienced the largest university enrolment among non-OECD economies in 2002, with more than 2 million new students, ahead of the Russian Federation (1.5 million) and Brazil (almost 1 million).

■ In addition, 152 000 Chinese students were enrolled abroad in OECD countries in 2002, accounting for 10% of the total number of foreigners enrolled in university education in OECD countries. In total, 62% of foreign students in OECD countries were citizens of non-OECD countries, predominantly from Asian economies.

### Sources

- OECD, Main Science and Technology Indicators database, May 2005.
- Eurostat, NewCronos database, May 2005.
- OECD, Education database, May 2005.
- Data for some of the countries have been compiled from national sources.

### For further reading


- OECD (2002), *Frascati Manual: Proposed Standard Practice for Surveys on Research and Experimental Development*, available at *www.oecd.org/sti/frascatimanual*.
- OECD (2004), *Education at a Glance; OECD Indicators 2004*, OECD, Paris.
- OECD (2005), *Main Science and Technology Indicators 2005/1*, OECD, Paris.


### *Measuring human resources in S&T in non-OECD economies*

Data for researchers are drawn from the same sources as the R&D data presented in section A.4 and are measured according to the *Frascati Manual* guidelines. Researcher data are expressed in full-time equivalents (FTE). The notes in section A.4 apply to these data as well. In addition, in Chinese Taipei, postgraduate students engaged in R&D are not included in the higher education sector. Moreover, researchers must have a university degree or above.



OECD SCIENCE, TECHNOLOGY AND INDUSTRY SCOREBOARD 2005 – ISBN 92-64-01055-6 – © OECD 2005

# B.10. Human resources in S&T in non-OECD economies

### Researchers in non-OECD economies, 2003

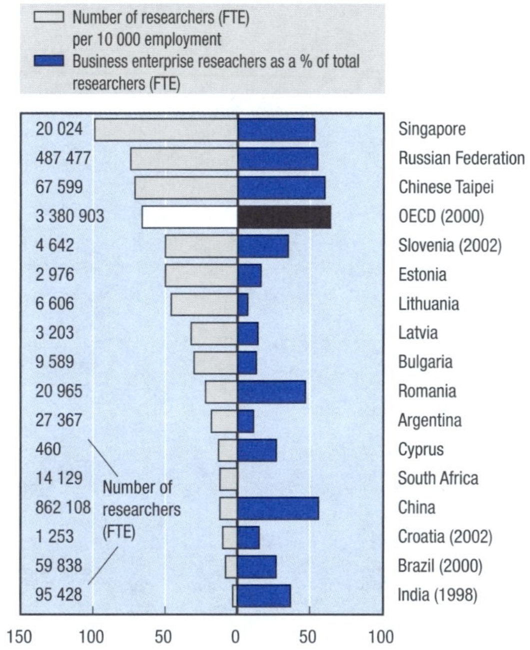


### Evolution of researchers in non-OECD economies, 2000-2003

Average annual growth rate

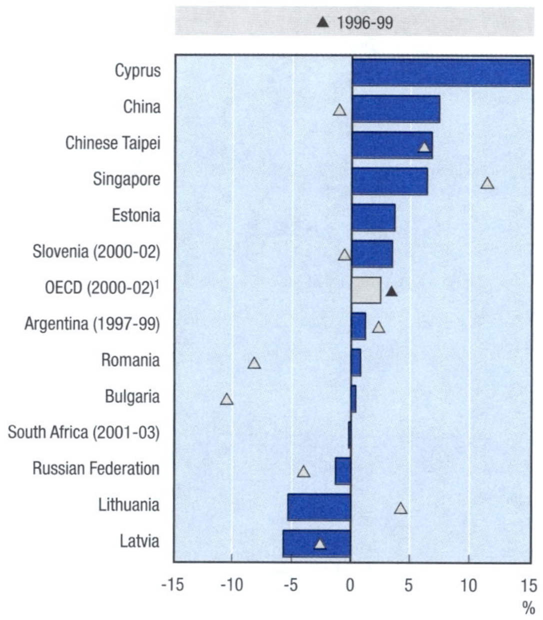


### University entrants and graduates in non-OECD economies, 2002

Thousands

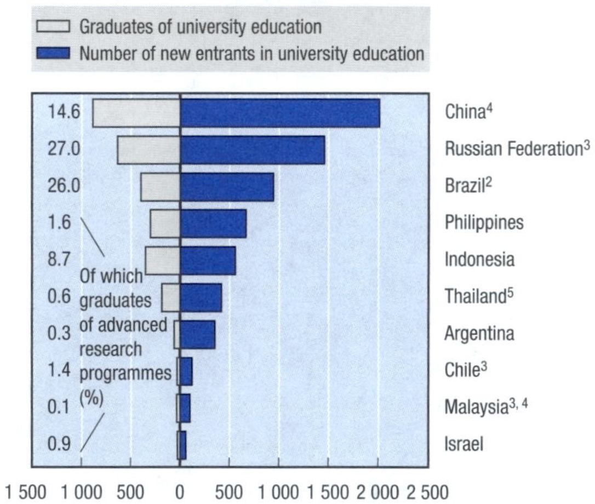


### Students from non-OECD economies enrolled in universities in OECD countries,[6] 2002

By country of citizenship

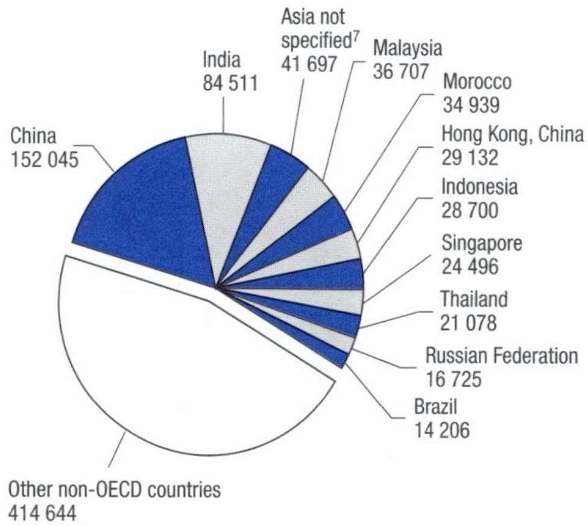


1. The growth rate for the OECD for 2000-02 covers only 17 countries. These account for half the number of researchers in the OECD area.
2. The data on graduates for Brazil include non-university tertiary education.
3. The data on graduates for Chile, Malaysia and the Russian Federation are for 2001.
4. The data on graduates for China and Malaysia do not include private institutions.
5. The number of new entrants for Thailand is for bachelor's degrees only.
6. Not including Canada and Portugal as host countries.
7. Asia not specified includes Chinese Taipei.

StatLink: *http://dx.doi.org/10.1787/644648120157*

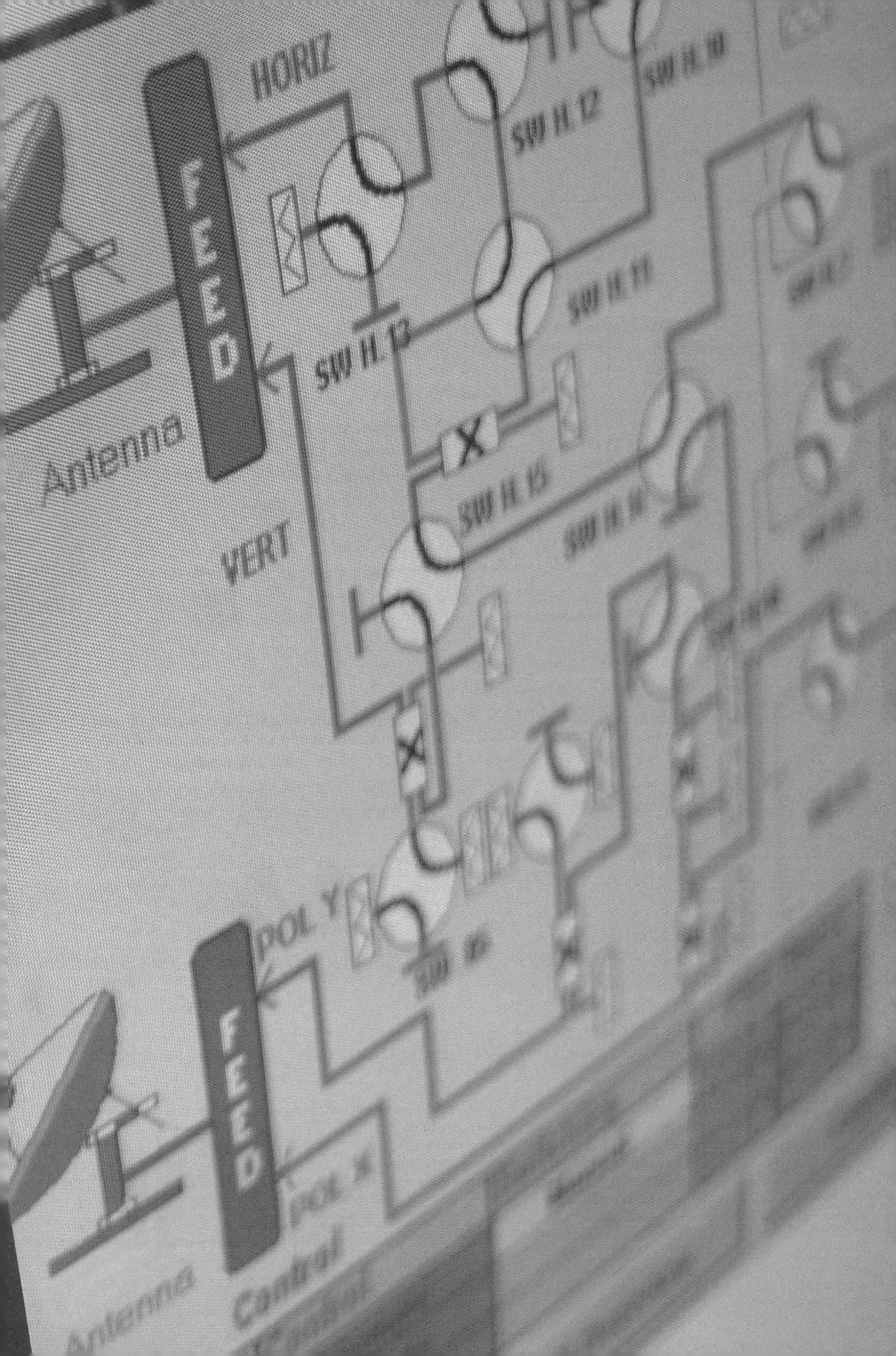
HORIZ
FEED
Antenna
VERT
POL Y
FEED
POL X
Antenna
Control

# C. PATENTS: PROTECTING AND COMMERCIALISING KNOWLEDGE

## C.1. Triadic patent families

■ To improve the quality and international comparability of patent-based indicators, the OECD has developed indicators of triadic patent families (see box for definition). Triadic patent families eliminate the "home advantage" bias and generally represent patents of high value.

■ Between 1985 and 2001, the total number of triadic patent families grew by 4.8% a year, and by 2001 the total number of triadic patent families was estimated to be around 48 200 (OECD countries accounted for the 97.9% of the total). Most of the growth in triadic patent families occurred in 1985-89 and 1993-96. Although triadic patent families show an upward trend, the total number of triadic patent families decreased considerably between 1989 and 1991, both overall and in countries with a large number of triadic patent families.

■ In 2001, the European Union (34.2%) and the United States (34.1%) accounted for a similar share of total triadic patent families, and Japan accounted for 24.4% of the total. During the 1990s, the European Union's share of triadic patents converged towards that of the United States, while that of Japan declined.

■ To normalise patent counts for country size, triadic patent families are expressed relative to population. In contrast to its ranking in absolute numbers of triadic patent families, Japan has a high patent-to-population ratio compared to the European Union and the United States. In 2001, Switzerland had the highest patent-to-population ratio (119), followed by Finland (99), Japan (92), Sweden (92) and Germany (91). India, Turkey and China had a very low patent-to-population ratio.

■ For all reported countries except Poland, patent-to-population ratios increased between 1991 and 2001, particularly in Finland, Germany and Sweden.

### Source

- OECD, Patent database, March 2005.

### For further reading


- Dernis, H. and M. Khan (2004), "Triadic Patent Families Methodology", *STI Working Paper* 2004/2, OECD, Paris, available at: *www.oecd.org/sti/ipr-statistics*.


### Triadic patent families

Patent indicators are commonly constructed on the basis of information from a single patent office. While patents filed at a given patent office are a source of rich data, these data have certain weaknesses (such as "home advantage" and highly heterogeneous value) as indicators of technological performance.

The OECD has developed a set of indicators based on "triadic" patent families to reduce the major weaknesses of traditional patent indicators. Triadic patent families are defined as a set of patents taken at the European Patent Office (EPO), the Japanese Patent Office (JPO) and the US Patent & Trademark Office (USPTO) that share one or more priorities (see Dernis and Khan, 2004).

Triadic patent families have advantages for statistical analysis. First, they improve the international comparability of patent-based indicators, because only patents applied for in the same set of countries are included in the "family"; they therefore eliminate home advantage and the influence of geographical location. Second, patents in the family typically have high value, because patentees only take on the additional costs and delays of extending protection to other countries if they deem it worthwhile.

The criteria for counting the triadic patent families are the earliest priority date, the inventor's country of residence and fractional counts (see C.3). Owing to the time lag between priority date and the availability of information, 1998 is the latest year for which complete triadic patent family data are available. (USPTO patents refer to the grant date, because prior to the change in rules regarding the publication of patent applications at the USPTO, patents were only published after the patent had been granted.) Data for 1999-2001 are OECD estimates. Patent indicators are frequently reported according to the grant date. Drawing conclusions about innovative activity based on grant date can be extremely misleading, however, because the number of patents granted is not only a function of the flow of patent applications, but also depends on the administrative process of the patent office (its budget, number of examiners, etc.). It is therefore preferable, when measuring innovative activity, to use data by priority date rather than grant date, because the priority date is close to the date of invention and the data are not affected by the administrative process of the patent office or the procedure used to file the patent application.

## C.1. Triadic patent families

### Trends in triadic patent families:[1] total and main OECD regions

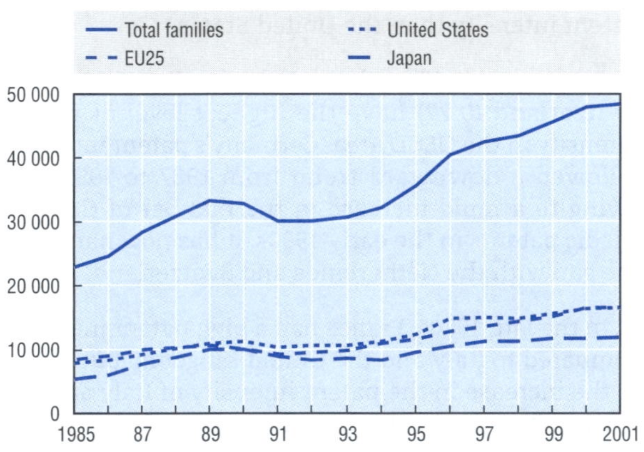


### Trends in triadic patent families:[1] leading patenting countries

### Share of countries in triadic patent families, 2001

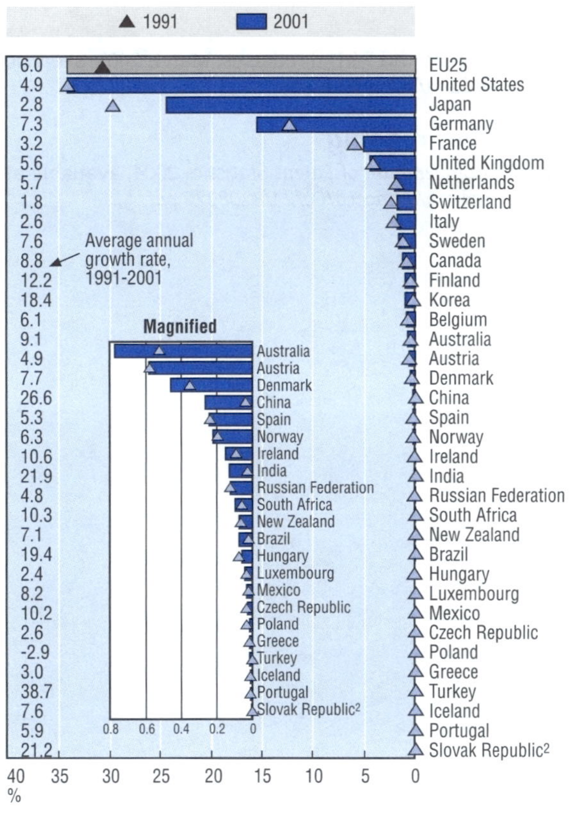


### Triadic patent families per million population, 2001

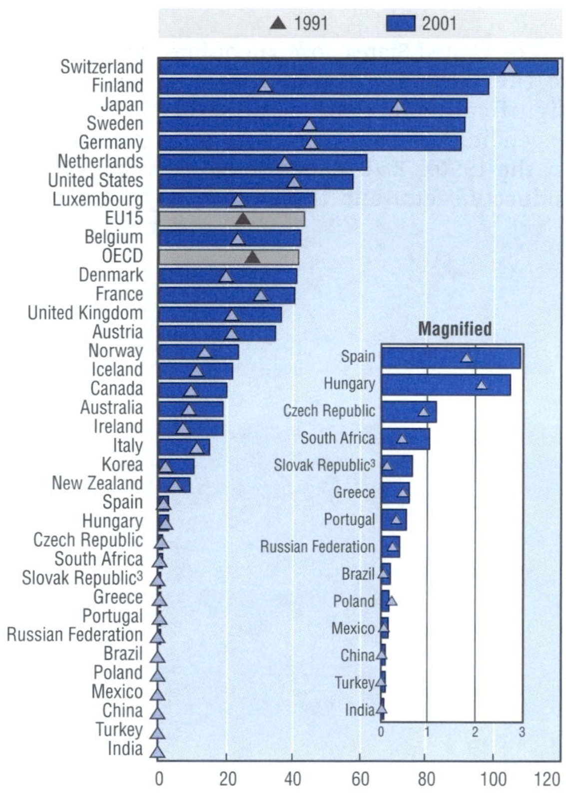


*Note:* Patent counts are based on the inventor's country of residence, the earliest priority date and fractional counts. 1999-2001 data are OECD estimates.

1. Patents filed at the European Patent Office (EPO), the US Patent & Trademark Office (USPTO) and the Japanese Patent Office (JPO) that protect the same invention.
2. 1992-2001 growth rate.
3. Data for 1992 and 2001.

StatLink: *http://dx.doi.org/10.1787/511321017431*

## C.2. Patent intensity

■ There is a strong positive correlation between the number of triadic patent families and industry-financed research and development (R&D) expenditures ($R^2 = 0.98$). Countries with a high level of industry-financed R&D expenditures (such as the United States, Japan, Germany and France) also have large numbers of triadic patent families. In contrast, countries with a low level of industry-financed R&D expenditures (such as Iceland, Greece, Portugal and the Slovak Republic) have small numbers of triadic patent families.

■ The patent intensity (triadic patent families divided by industry-financed R&D) of the main OECD regions has followed similar patterns and appears to be cyclical: it decreased during the late 1980s and early 1990s and increased in the mid-1990s. Patent intensity is similar in the European Union and Japan and above the OECD average. In contrast, it is low in the United States and has decreased continuously since 1996.

■ The United States' low patent intensity (compared to the European Union and Japan) is due to a significant increase in industry-financed R&D expenditure and a modest increase in triadic patents. In the 1990s, R&D expenditures financed by the industry sector and the number of triadic patent families remained stable in Japan, while both increased at a similar rate in the European Union. As a result, the European Union and Japan have a higher patent intensity than the United States.

■ Germany (0.19), the Netherlands (0.22) and Switzerland (0.22) have the highest level of patent intensity in the OECD area. Germany's patent intensity followed a downward trend from 1987 to 1992, but owing to a rapid increase in the number of German triadic patents in the early 1990s, it has now narrowed the gap with the Netherlands and Switzerland.

■ In the late 1980s, France had a high patent intensity compared to Italy and the United Kingdom, but owing to the increase in the patent intensity of Italy and the United Kingdom during the early 1990s, these countries now have a similar level of patent intensity.

### *Source*

- OECD, Patent and R&D databases, March 2005, see also: *www.oecd.ord/sti/ipr-statistics.*

### *For further reading*

- OECD, *Compendium of Patent Statistics 2004*, available at: *www.oecd.org/dataoecd/60/24/8208325.pdf.*


OECD SCIENCE, TECHNOLOGY AND INDUSTRY SCOREBOARD 2005 – ISBN 92-64-01055-6 – © OECD 2005

## C.2. Patent intensity

### Triadic patent families[1] and industry-financed R&D,[2] 1991-2001 average

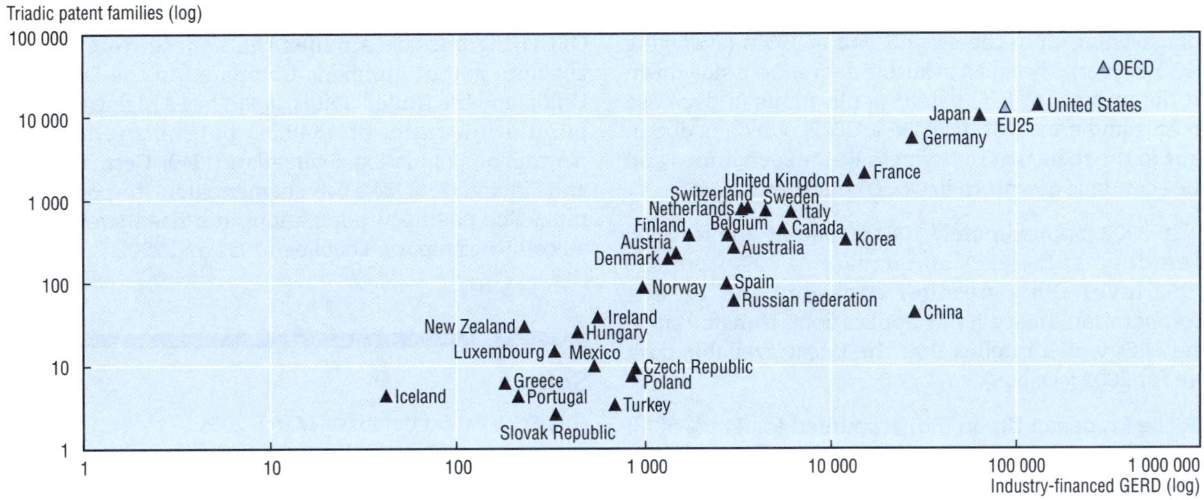


### Ratio of triadic patents families[1] to industry-financed R&D:[2] main OECD regions, 1985-2001

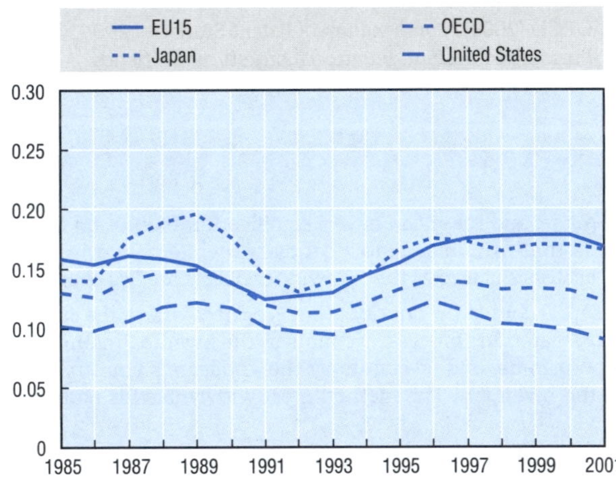


### Ratio of triadic patent families[1] to industry-financed R&D:[2] selected countries, 1985-2001

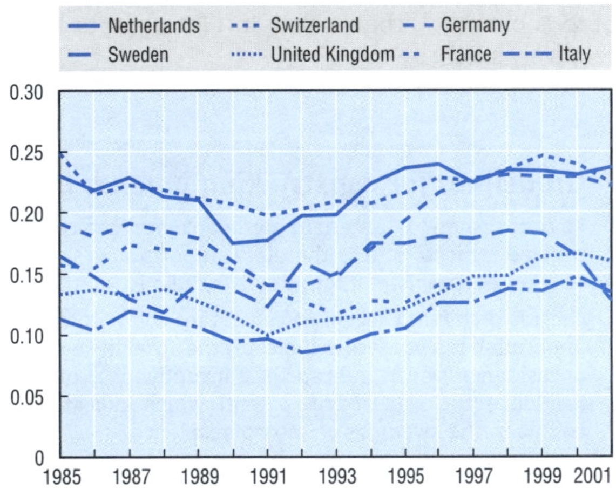


*Note:* Patent counts are based on the inventor's country of residence, the earliest priority date and fractional counts. Data for 1999-2001 on triadic patent families are OECD estimates.

1. Patents filed at the European Patent Office (EPO), the US Patent & Trademark Office (USPTO) and the Japanese Patent Office (JPO) that protect the same invention.
2. Gross domestic expenditure on R&D (GERD) financed by industry, millions of USD (2000) using purchasing power parities, lagged by one year. A 1996-2000 average has been used for the EU25 industry-financed R&D aggregate.

StatLink: *http://dx.doi.org/10.1787/016374211324*

## C.3. Patent applications to the European Patent Office

■ Patent applications to the European Patent Office (EPO) grew relatively rapidly during the second half of the 1980s, stagnated in the first half of the 1990s and increased again in the second half of 1990s (averaging 10% per year). The latest available data show a slowdown in the number of EPO patent applications (a decrease in 2001 and a modest increase in 2002), which is due in part to the reduction in business R&D expenditures and the economic downturn in OECD countries.

■ In 2002, approximately 108 000 patent applications were filed at the EPO, an increase of 80% from the 1991 level. This number includes the Patent Co-operation Treaty (PCT) applications transferred to the EPO, which implies that the latest available data are for 2002 (see box).

■ The European Union (EU) accounted for 44.9% of all EPO patents, a share far above that of the United States (26.3%) and Japan (18.2%). This somewhat overstates the EU's inventive performance, as patents taken at the EPO primarily reflect EU countries' domestic market ("home advantage"). Although patent applications from China, India and Korea increased sharply over the 1990s (annual growth rates of 25% or more), their share in EPO patents is still relatively small.

■ To standardise for country size, EPO patent applications are expressed relative to population. Differences in the propensity to patent of the three main OECD regions are smaller than the differences in absolute patent numbers. Compared to the European Union and the United States, Japan has a high patent-to-population ratio, of 154 EPO patent applications per million population. Switzerland (349), Germany (253) and Finland (226) have even higher patent-to-population ratio. The patent-to-population ratio has increased for all countries reported between 1991 and 2002.

### Source

- OECD, Patent database, March 2005.

### For further reading


- Khan, M. and H. Dernis (2005), "Impact of Patent Cooperation Treaty Data on EPO Patent Statistics and Improving the Timeliness of EPO Indicators", STI Working Paper 2005/2, OECD, Paris, available at: *www.oecd.org/sti/ipr-statistics*.
- OECD (2004), *Compendium of Patent Statistics 2004*, OECD, Paris, available at: *www.oecd.org/sti/ipr-statistics*.


### Guidelines for constructing patents indicators

To count patent data, certain methodological choices have to be made, and these can have a significant influence on the derived indicators. It is therefore important to rely on methods that minimise statistical biases while conveying a maximum amount of information. In order to interpret patent indicators accurately, the following concepts are important.

*Geographical distribution of patents*. Three main criteria can be used: *i)* counts by priority office (country where the first application is filed), which indicates the attractiveness of a country's patenting process; *ii)* counts by the inventor's country of residence, which indicates the inventiveness of the local labour force; and *iii)* counts by the applicant's country of residence (the owner of the patent), which indicates control of the invention. The method most widely used is patent counts by the inventor's country of residence.

*Patents with multiple inventors from different countries*. Such patents can either be attributed fractionally to each country mentioned or fully attributed to every relevant country (this generates multiple counting). Standard practice is to use fractional counting procedures.

*Reference date*. The choice of a date, among the set of dates included in patent documents, is important. The priority date (first filing worldwide) is the earliest date and therefore closest to the invention date. Counts by application date introduce a bias owing to a one-year lag between residents and foreigners: the latter usually first file a patent application at their domestic office (the priority office) and later in other countries. The lag increases up to 31 months for Patent Co-operation Treaty (PCT) applications. To measure inventive activity, patent data should be computed with respect to the priority date. Patent indicators based on priority date are frequently criticised as being outdated. However, the "delay" is largely a question of the labelling of the published statistics. While patent statistics based on counts by the year of grant may appear to be more up to date, in fact they are not, as the label (year) corresponds to the grant date and not to the date when the invention was made (OECD, 2004).

*Increasing use of the PCT procedure*. The PCT procedure makes it possible to seek patent rights in a large number of countries by filing a single application. PCT application data should be included when calculating the total number of EPO patent applications, because applicants increasingly use the PCT procedure for EPO patent applications. However, only the PCT applications that proceed to the EPO regional phase should be included in EPO statistics. This procedure enhances the comparability of patent statistics and limits overestimation of EPO patent statistics (Khan and Dernis, 2005).

 OECD SCIENCE, TECHNOLOGY AND INDUSTRY SCOREBOARD 2005 – ISBN 92-64-01055-6 – © OECD 2005

## C.3. Patent applications to the European Patent Office

### Annual growth rate of patent applications to the EPO,[1] 1985 to 2002

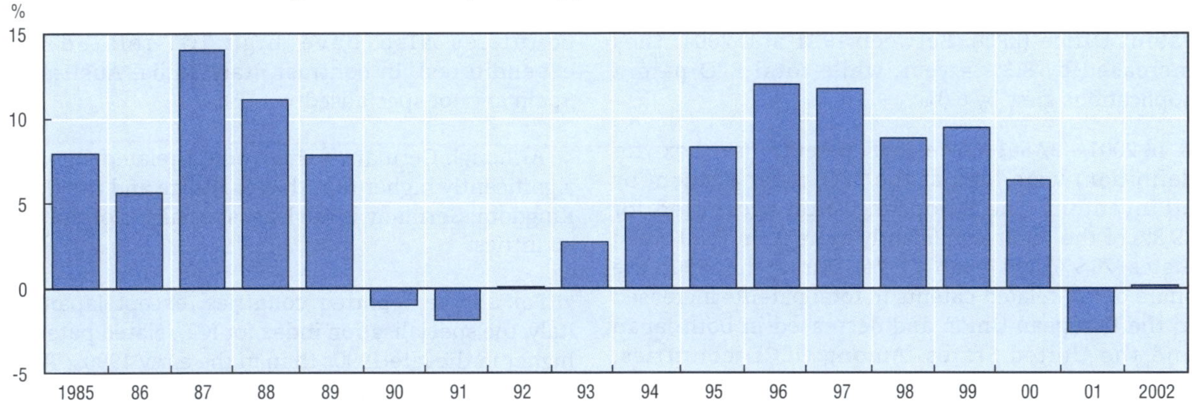


### Share of countries in EPO[1] patent applications, 2002

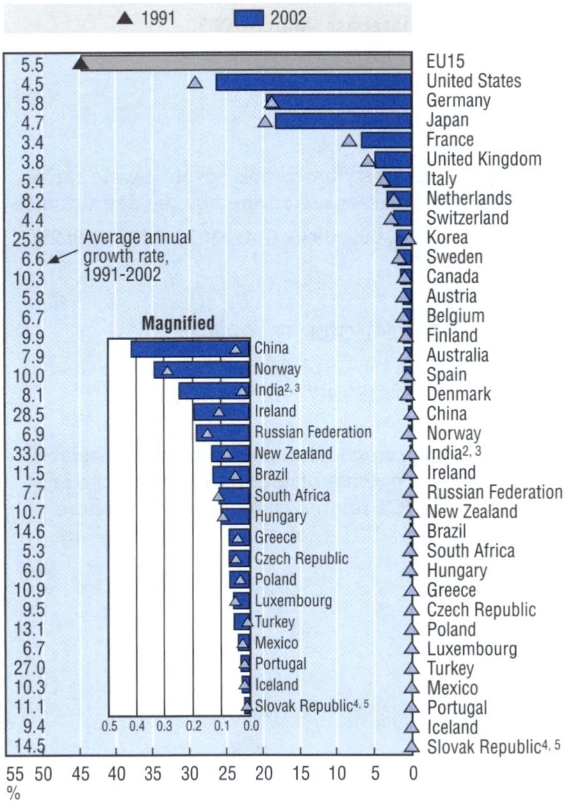


### Number of EPO[1] patent applications per million population, 2002

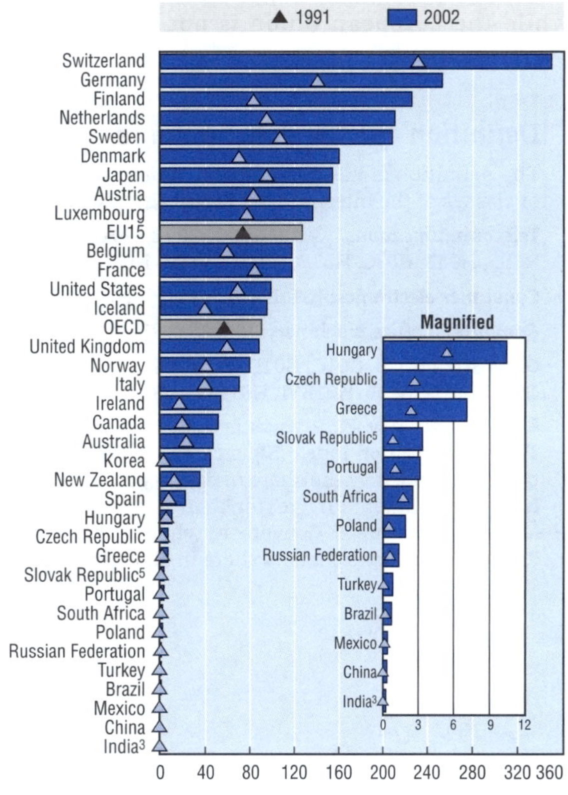


*Note:* Patent counts are based on the inventor's country of residence, the earliest priority date and fractional counts. Data for 2002 are OECD estimates.

1. European Patent Office.
2. 1991-2001 growth rate.
3. Data for 1991 and 2001.
4. 1992-2002 growth rate.
5. Data for 1992 and 2002.

StatLink: *http://dx.doi.org/10.1787/684652764278*

## C.4. ICT-related patents

■ ICT-related patents have grown much more rapidly than overall patent applications at the European Patent Office (EPO). Between 1991 and 2001, they increased by 8.3% a year, while total EPO patent applications grew by 6.0%.

■ In 2001, 37 501 ICT-related patents (see box for definition) were filed at the EPO, most of them by EU inventors. The European Union accounted for 39.8% of the total, significantly more than the United States (28.9%) and Japan (21.8%). During the 1990s, the share of ICT-related patents in total patents increased in the European Union and decreased in both Japan and the United States. Among OECD countries, Germany, France, the Netherlands and the United Kingdom have a high share of ICT-related patents.

■ To measure a country's level of specialisation in ICT-related patents, country shares can be expressed in terms of a specialisation index (see box). By this measure, Japan and the United States are specialised, while the European Union is not. Among OECD countries, Finland, Korea and the Netherlands are the most specialised in ICT-related patents (these countries also have high ICT-related R&D expenditures). In contrast, Italy, India, Austria and Spain are not specialised.

■ Although Germany's share of ICT-related patents is significantly higher that that of France and the United Kingdom, Germany is the least specialised of the three countries.

■ For all the reported countries, except Japan and Italy, the specialisation index for ICT-related patents is higher in the late 1990s than in the early 1990s. This is most notably the case for Iceland, Finland and China.

### Source

- OECD, Patent database, March 2005.

### *Definition of ICT-related patents*

The definition of ICT-related patents used to calculate ICT-related patents is very broad and covers a wide range of classes of the International Patent Classification (IPC). The following IPC classes are covered by the definition:

***Telecommunications:*** [G01S, G08C, G09C, H01P, H01Q, H01S3/(025, 043, 063, 067, 085, 0933, 0941, 103, 133, 18, 19, 25), H1S5, H03B, H03C, H03D, H03H, H03M, H04B, H04J, H04K, H04L, H04M, H04Q].

***Consumer electronics:*** [G11B, H03F, H03G, H03J, H04H, H04N, H04R, H04S].

***Computers, office machinery:*** [B07C, B41J, B41K, G02F, G03G, G05F, G06, G07, G09G, G10L, G11C, H03K, H03L].

***Other ICT:*** [G01B, G01C, G01D, G01F, G01G, G01H, G01J, G01K, G01L, G01M, G01N, G01P, G01R, G01V, G01W, G02B6, G05B, G08G, G09B, H01B11, H01J(11/, 13/, 15/, 17/, 19/, 21/, 23/, 25/, 27/, 29/, 31/, 33/, 40/, 41/, 43/, 45/), H01L].

For further details on the IPC classes, see *www.wipo.int/classifications/fulltext/new_ipc/index.htm.*

The specialisation index (SI) is calculated as the share of country A in a specific technology area (*i.e.* ICT-related patents) divided by the share of country A in all technology areas (total EPO patents of country A). When the SI of ICT-related patents is greater than 1, the country has a higher share in ICT-related patents than its share in all technology areas. Conversely, when the SI of ICT-related patents is below 1, the country has a lower share in ICT-related patents than its share in all technology areas.

## C.4. ICT-related patents

### Share of countries in ICT-related patents filed at the EPO,[1] 2001

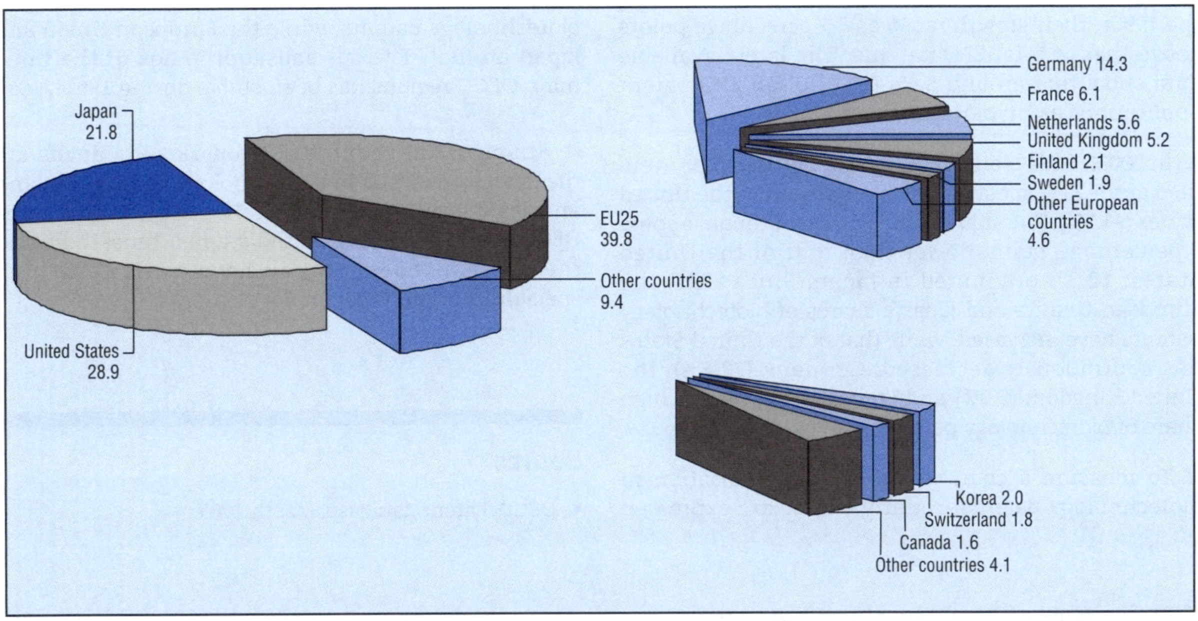


### Specialisation index of ICT-related patents filed at the EPO,[1] 1996-2001

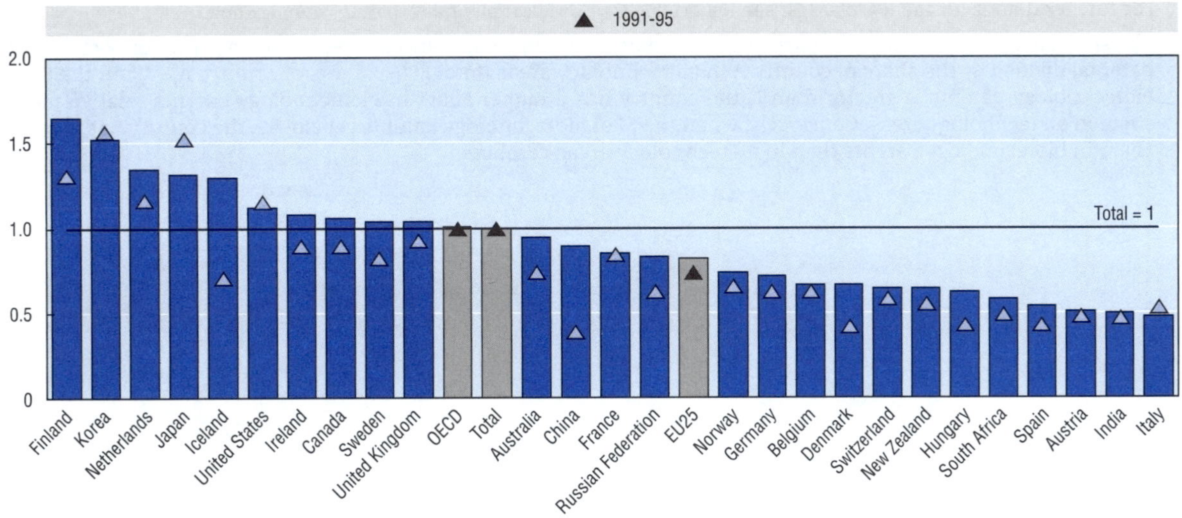


*Note:* Patent counts are based on the inventor's country of residence, the priority date and fractional counting. The graph only covers countries with, on average, more than ten ICT-related patents over the 1996-2001 period.

1. European Patent Office.

StatLink: *http://dx.doi.org/10.1787/247043035688*

## C.5. Biotechnology patents

■ Biotechnology patents have grown more rapidly than overall EPO patent applications. During the 1990s, their growth rate was 3.1 percentage points above that of total EPO patents. The latest available data show that around 5.4% (2001) of all EPO patent applications are in biotechnology.

■ In 2001, 5 834 biotechnology patents (see box) were filed at the EPO, most of which originated in the United States (41.5%). The share of the European Union is some 7 percentage points lower than that of the United States; 12.3% originated in Japan. Since 1997, the European Union's and Japan's shares of biotechnology patents have increased, while that of the United States has continuously decreased. Germany (12.8%), the United Kingdom (5.9%) and France (5.3%) have a high share of biotechnology patents.

■ To measure a country's level of specialisation in biotechnology patents, country shares are expressed in terms of a specialisation index (see box). By this measure, the United States is highly specialised in biotechnology patents, while the European Union and Japan are not. The specialisation index of the three main OECD regions has been stable during 1991-2001.

■ Among OECD countries, Denmark and Canada are the most specialised in biotechnology patents. Finland and Italy are the least specialised. The three non-OECD countries shown on the graph (China, India and the Russian Federation) all have a relatively high specialisation in biotechnology patents.

### Source

- OECD, Patent database, March 2005.

### *Definition of biotechnology patents*

The definition of biotechnology patents covers the following IPC classes: A01H1/00, A01H4/00, A61K38/00, A61K39/00, A61K48/00, C02F3/34, C07G(11/00, 13/00, 15/00), C07K(4/00, 14/00, 16/00, 17/00, 19/00), C12M, C12N, C12P, C12Q, C12S, G01N27/327, G01N33/(53*, 54*, 55*, 57*, 68, 74, 76, 78, 88, 92).

For further details on the IPC classes, see *www.wipo.int/classifications/fulltext/new_ipc/index.htm*.

The specialisation index (SI) is calculated as the share of country A in a specific technology area (*i.e.* biotechnology patents) divided by the share of country A in all technology areas (total EPO patents of country A). When the SI of biotechnology patents is greater than 1, the country has a higher share in biotechnology patents relative to its share in all technology areas. Conversely, when the SI of biotechnology patents is below 1, the country has a lower share in biotechnology patents than in all technology areas combined.

## C.5. Biotechnology patents

### Share of countries in biotechnology patents filed at the EPO,[1] 2001

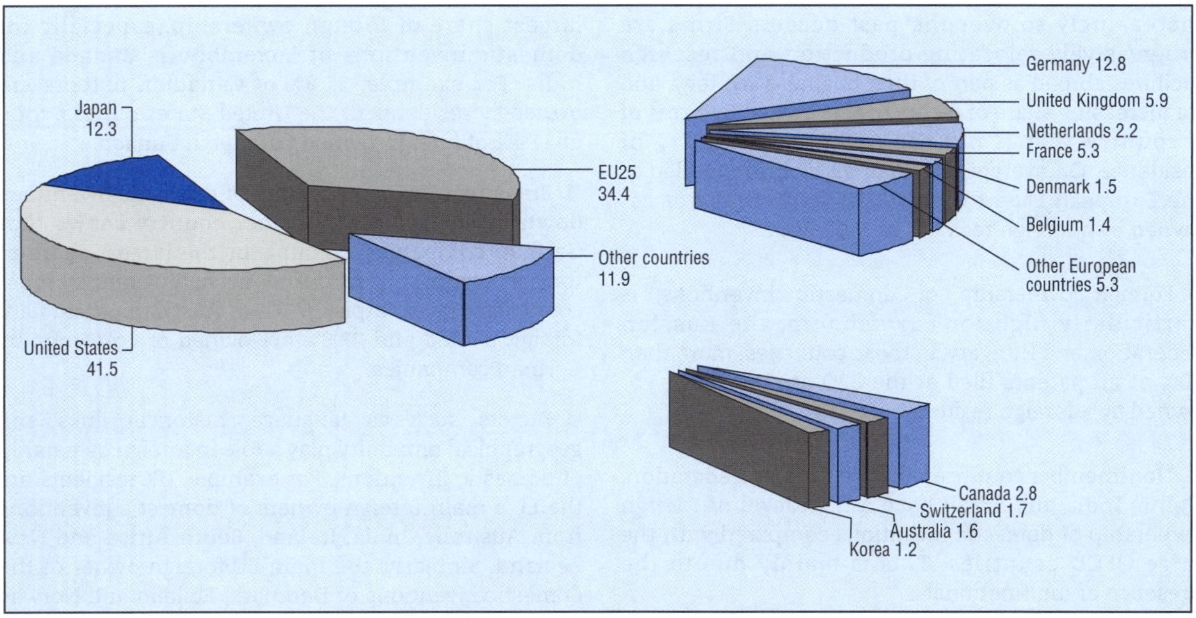


### Specialisation index of biotechnology patents filed at the EPO,[1] 1996-2001

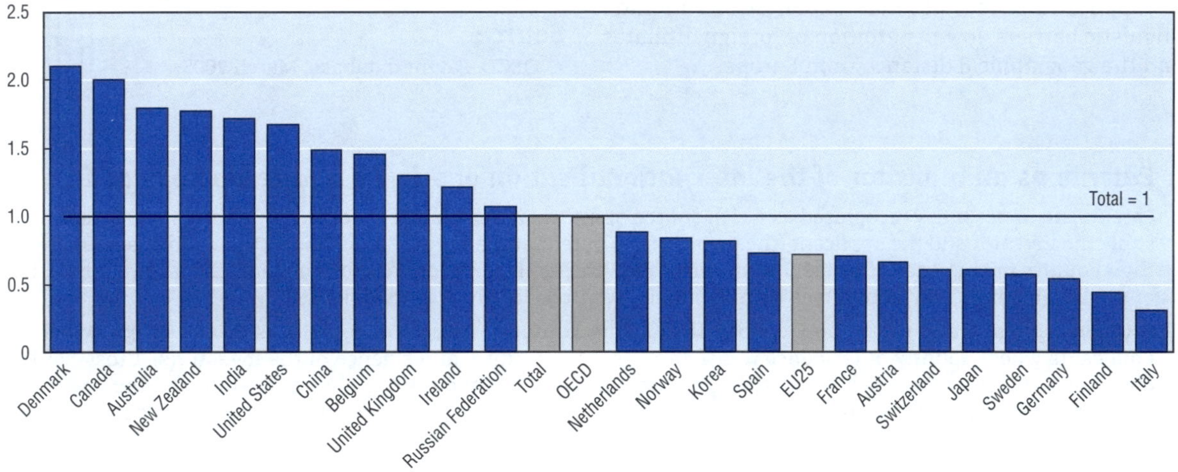


*Note:* Patent counts are based on the inventor's country of residence, the priority date and fractional counting. Only countries with, on average, more than ten biotechnology patents during 1996-2001 are included in the graph.

1. European Patent Office.

StatLink: *http://dx.doi.org/10.1787/817865227014*

## C.6. Foreign ownership of domestic inventions

■ Although R&D activities are less internationalised than trade and production, they have become increasingly so over the past decade. Firms are progressively relocating production and research facilities abroad as part of their business strategy, and an increasing share of technology is owned by firms of a country that is not the inventor's country of residence. On average, 15.4% of all inventions filed at the European Patent Office (EPO) were owned or co-owned by a foreign resident in 1999-2001.

■ Foreign ownership of domestic inventions is particularly high for Luxembourg, the Russian Federation and Hungary. In these countries, more than 50% of all patents filed at the EPO are owned or co-owned by a foreign resident.

■ Non-member countries like the Russian Federation, China, India and Brazil have a high level of foreign ownership of domestic inventions compared with the large OECD countries. This is mainly due to the presence of multinationals.

■ Japan, Korea and Finland, on the other hand, are much less internationalised; less than 10% of their patents filed at the EPO are foreign-owned. In the case of Japan and Korea, possible explanations include linguistic barriers, low penetration of foreign affiliates and the geographical distance from Europe.

■ Foreign ownership by partner country shows that for most countries, US companies account for the largest share of foreign ownership, especially for domestic inventions of Luxembourg, Canada and India. For example, 21.9% of Canadian patents are owned by residents of the United States out of a total of 34.4% of foreign-owned patents in Canada.

■ Breaking foreign ownership of domestic inventions down by the main EU partner country shows that German companies account for the largest share of foreign ownership of domestic inventions in most countries. For example, 37.8% of Austrian patents are foreign-owned and 23.8% are owned or co-owned by German companies.

■ Factors such as language, historical links and geographical proximity play a role in foreign ownership of domestic inventions. For example, UK residents are the EU's main foreign owners of domestic inventions from Australia, India, Ireland, South Africa and New Zealand. Similarly, the main EU foreign owner of the domestic inventions of Denmark, Finland and Norway is another Nordic country.

### Source

- OECD, Patent database, March 2005.

### *Patents as an indicator of the internationalisation of science and technology activities*

Patents are increasingly recognised as a rich source of information about technological performance. Patent files show the inventor and the applicant (the owner of the patent at the time of application), their addresses and thus their country or countries of residence. In most cases, the applicant is an institution (generally a firm, university or public laboratory), but sometimes an individual. Inventors are always individuals.

An increasing share of patent applications filed at the European Patent Office (EPO) is owned or co-owned by applicants whose country of residence is different from the country of residence of the inventor(s). Cross-border ownership is mainly the result of activities of multinationals; the applicant is a conglomerate and the inventors are employees of a foreign subsidiary. Patent data thus make it possible to trace the international circulation of knowledge from "inventor" countries to "applicant" countries.

The internationalisation measure (of science and technology activities) presented here relates to foreign ownership of domestic inventions. It evaluates the extent to which foreign firms control domestic inventions by dividing the number of domestic inventions controlled by a foreign resident by the total number of domestic inventions.

The analysis is based on the database of patent applications to the EPO. Patents granted by the United States Patent & Trademark Office (USPTO) show similar internationalisation trends.

The ownership of a patent is attributed to a country based on the address of the applicant at the time of application.



OECD SCIENCE, TECHNOLOGY AND INDUSTRY SCOREBOARD 2005 – ISBN 92-64-01055-6 – © OECD 2005

## C.6. Foreign ownership of domestic inventions

### Foreign ownership of domestic inventions[1] by partner country, 1999-2001

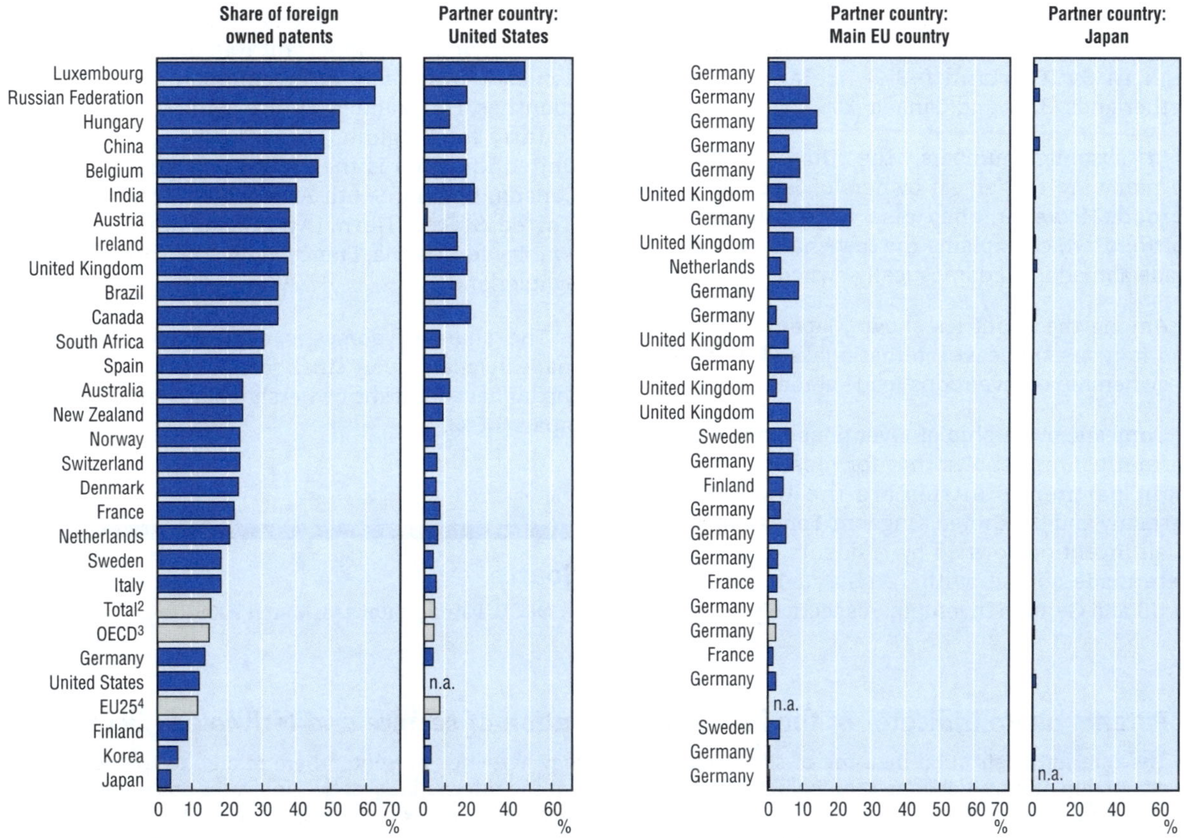


*Note:* Patent counts are based on the inventor's country of residence and the priority date.

1. Patent applications filed at the European Patent Office.
2. All EPO patents that involve international co-operation.
3. Patents of OECD residents that involve international co-operation.
4. The EU is treated as one country; intra-EU co-operation has been netted out.

StatLink: *http://dx.doi.org/10.1787/285308278247*

## C.7. Domestic ownership of inventions made abroad

■ Domestic ownership of inventions made abroad is high in small, open countries. For example, close to 80% of all inventions owned by residents of Luxembourg were made abroad. This share is also high in Switzerland (48%), Ireland (41%), the Netherlands (31%) and Canada (30%).

■ In absolute numbers, the United States and Germany are the largest owners of inventions made abroad. However, they also have a large patent portfolio, which explains the low share of inventions made abroad in all domestically owned inventions.

■ Among the countries shown, Japan, Korea, Spain and Italy are the least internationalised with respect to ownership of inventions made abroad.

■ Domestic ownership of inventions made abroad by partner country shows that for most countries, the main partner countries are the United States, Germany and the United Kingdom. For example, 47.8% of all inventions owned by residents of Switzerland were made abroad, with 12.1% and 16.5% invented by US and German inventors, respectively.

■ The breakdown of ownership of inventions made abroad by main EU partner country shows that common language, historical links and geographical proximity play an important role in determining the domestic ownership of inventions made by partner countries. For example, France is the main EU partner country for Belgium, Luxembourg and Spain. The United Kingdom is the main EU partner country for Canada, Ireland, South Africa, New Zealand and the United States. Germany is the main EU partner country for Austria, France, Italy, the Netherlands and Switzerland.

■ The share of domestic ownership of inventions made in Japan is very small for all countries. China has the highest domestic ownership of inventions made in Japan (1.6%).

### Source

- OECD, Patent database, March 2005.

### *Patents as an indicator of the internationalisation of science and technology activities*

The internationalisation measure of science and technology activities presented here relates to the domestic ownership of inventions made abroad. It is a mirror image of the internationalisation indicator presented in C.6. Domestic ownership of inventions made abroad indicator evaluates the extent to which domestic firms control inventions made by residents of other countries. The number of foreign inventions controlled by resident applicants is divided by the total number of domestic applications. For example, a multinational from country A may have research facilities in both country A and country B. This indicator provides the share of patents from its facilities in country B in the total number of patents in country A.

The analysis is based on the database of patent applications to the EPO. Patents granted by the United States Patent & Trademark Office (USPTO) show similar internationalisation trends.

The ownership of a patent is attributed to a country based on the address of the applicant at the time of application.

## C.7. Domestic ownership of inventions made abroad

### Domestic ownership of inventions made abroad[1] by partner country, 1999-2001

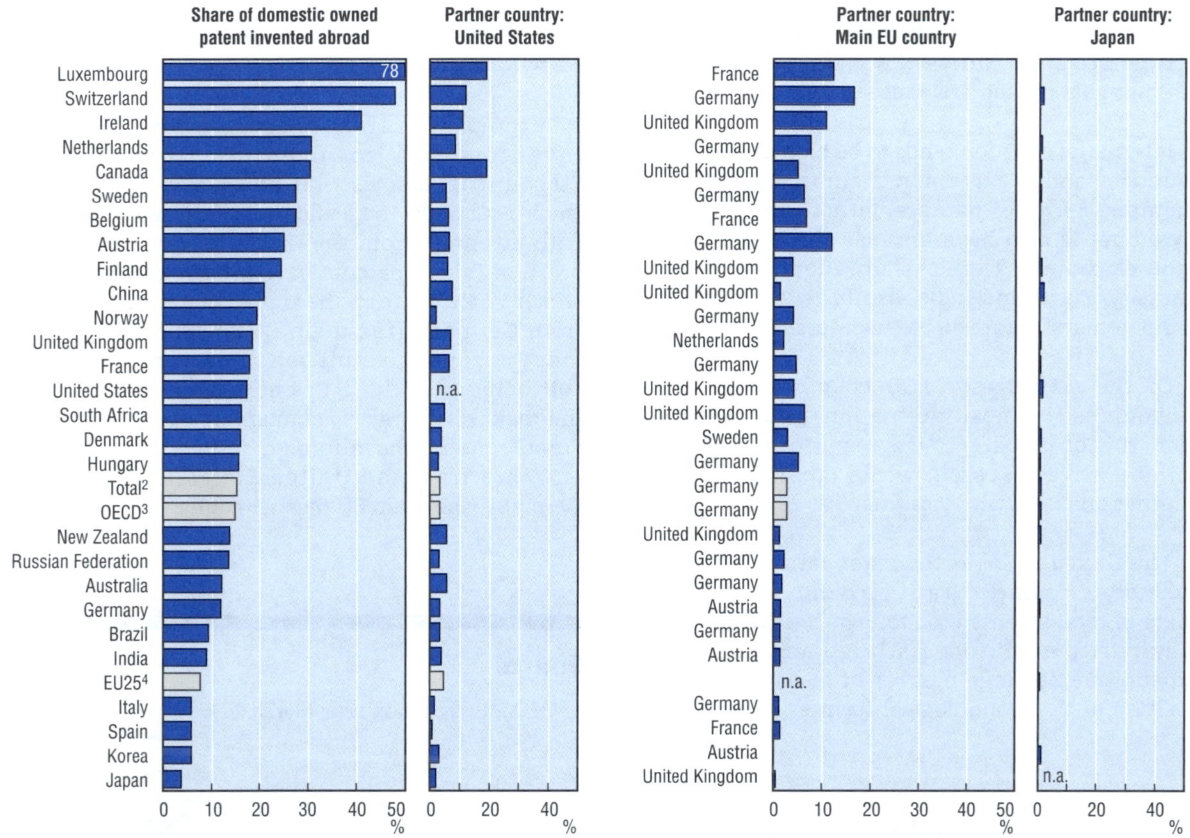


*Note:* Patent counts are based on the inventor's country of residence and the priority date.

1. Patent applications filed at the European Patent Office.
2. All EPO patents that involve international co-operation.
3. Patents of OECD residents that involve international co-operation.
4. The EU is treated as one country; intra-EU co-operation has been netted out.

StatLink: *http://dx.doi.org/10.1787/267150665256*

## C.8. International co-operation in patenting activity

■ Co-invention of patents provides an indication of the internationalisation of science and technology activities. In 1999-2001, 6.7% of all patents filed at the European Patent Office (EPO) were the result of international collaborative research.

■ Internationalisation tends to be high in small OECD countries and in large non-member countries. For example, 53.2% of patents with an inventor from Luxembourg also have at least one inventor from another country. The Russian Federation, Belgium, Hungary, China and India also have a high share of EPO patents with foreign co-inventors.

■ Of the six largest OECD countries, the United Kingdom is the most internationalised, with more than 20% of its patents the result of international collaborative research, while Japan is the least internationalised, with less than 3%.

■ The United States is the main partner country for most other countries (*i.e.* it accounts for the largest share of total patents with foreign co-inventors). This may partly be due to its large amount of R&D expenditure, its large number of researchers and its position at the technological frontier. This makes it easier for inventors to find US researchers working in a similar area and provides an opportunity to collaborate on the latest technological developments with US researchers.

■ A comparison of the share of patents with US co-inventors and co-inventors from the main EU countries shows that non-European countries (such as Canada, India and China) typically collaborate with inventors from the United States. For example, 32.4% of Indian patents have foreign co-inventors, of which 19.4% are from the United States and only 5.0% from Germany (the main EU partner country). For most European countries, however, the level of collaboration with US inventors and inventors from the main EU country is similar. For example, 15.0% of French patents have foreign co-inventors, of which 4.3% are from the United States and 4.1% from Germany (the main EU partner country).

### Source

- OECD, Patent database, March 2005.

### *Indicators of international co-operation*

Patent data include the name and address of all inventors (individuals). An increasing share of European Patent Office (EPO) patents involves inventors with different countries of residence (an indication of the increasing level of internationalisation of science and technology). International collaboration by researchers can take place either within a multinational corporation (research facilities in several countries) or through a research joint venture among several firms.

The propensity to collaborate internationally can be derived from the address of the inventors listed in the patent file. Here, it is approximated as the ratio of the number of inventions involving a country's residents and at least one inventor with foreign residence to the total number of inventions involving a country's residents. An increasing share of patents involves inventors with residences in more than two countries.

## C.8. International co-operation in patenting activity

### Share of patents[1] with foreign co-inventors by partner country, 1999-2001

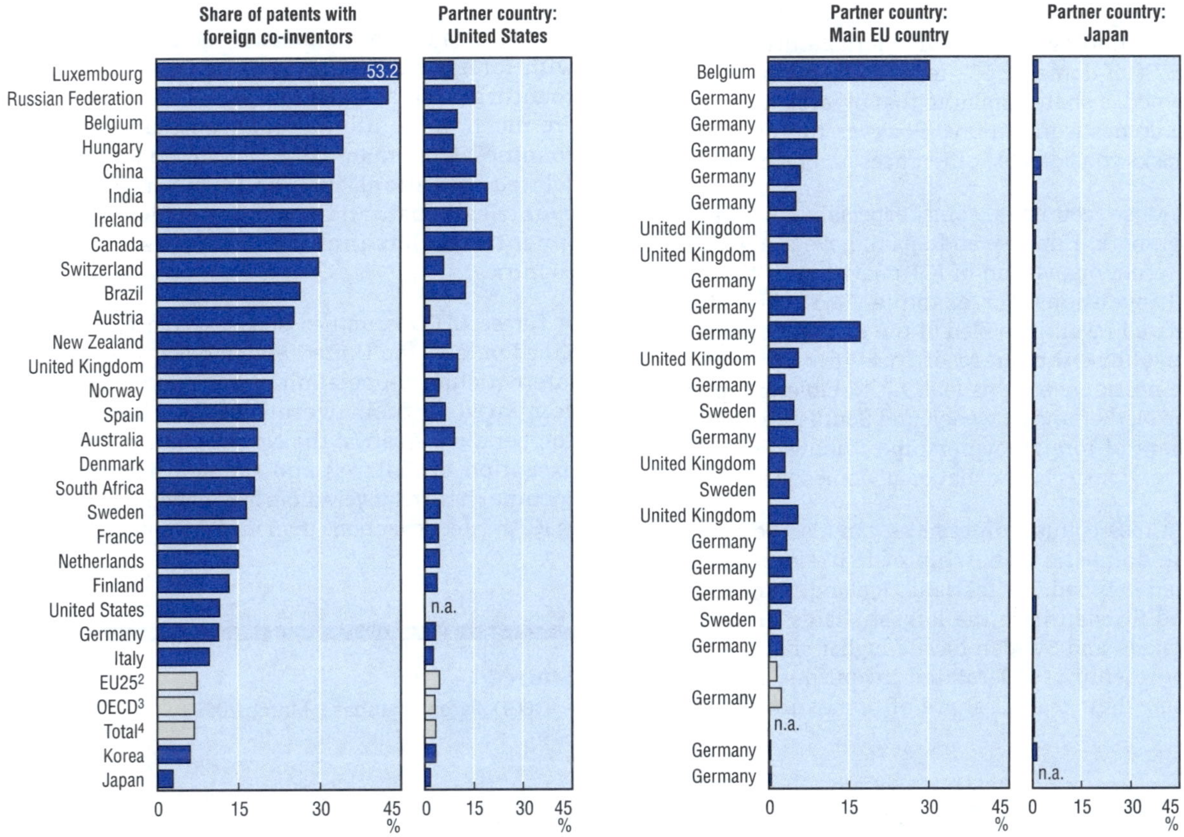


*Note:* Patent counts are based on the inventor's country of residence and the priority date.

1. Patent applications filed at the European Patent Office.
2. The EU is treated as one country; intra-EU co-operation has been netted out.
3. Patents of OECD residents that involve international co-operation.
4. All EPO patents that involve international co-operation.

StatLink: *http://dx.doi.org/10.1787/622567751004*

## C.9. Internationalisation of ICT-related inventions

■ Not all technology areas are equally internationalised. Indicators of internationalisation for key areas of patenting, such as ICT and biotechnology, show considerable diversity. About 15.7% of domestic ICT-related inventions are foreign-owned, a share similar to that of foreign ownership of all domestic inventions. However, this overall average masks considerable differences among countries.

■ Most countries, and especially Austria, India, Denmark, Hungary and Spain, have a higher level of internationalisation of ICT-related inventions than of all inventions. For example, 74.5% of Indian ICT-related inventions filed at the EPO are foreign-owned, far above the share of foreign ownership in all domestic inventions (40.1%). Notable exceptions are the Netherlands, Sweden and South Africa, where the share of foreign ownership of domestic ICT-related inventions is below that of all domestic inventions.

■ Cross-country differences can also be observed in the domestic ownership of ICT-related inventions made abroad. Switzerland, Iceland, Canada, Ireland and Sweden have the largest shares. However, only Canada and Sweden have a higher share of domestic ownership of ICT-related inventions made abroad than their overall share of domestic ownership of inventions made abroad, while the opposite is true for Ireland and Switzerland.

■ Measures of internationalisation based on patents with foreign co-inventors show that non-member countries, such as India and the Russian Federation, are much more internationalised than large OECD countries. More than half of Indian and Russian ICT-related inventions include inventors from other countries. Japan and Korea have few ICT-related inventions that include inventors form other countries.

■ Larger OECD countries such as France, the United Kingdom and the United States have relatively little international co-operation in ICT-related inventions, compared to their overall level of international co-operation. Austria, the Nordic countries (with the exception of Finland) and the southern European countries have relatively more international co-operation in ICT-related inventions than in all inventions.

### Source

- OECD, Patent database, March 2005.

## C.9. Internationalisation of ICT-related inventions

### Foreign ownership of domestic ICT-related inventions,[1] 1999-2001

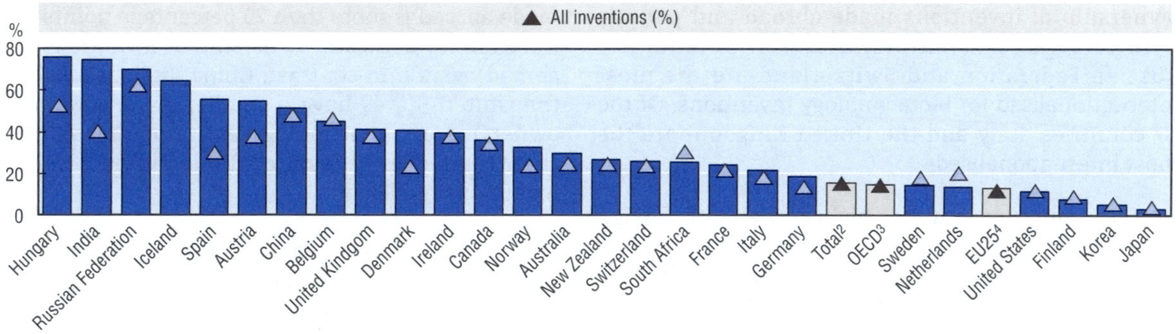


### Domestic ownership of ICT-related inventions[1] made abroad, 1999-2001

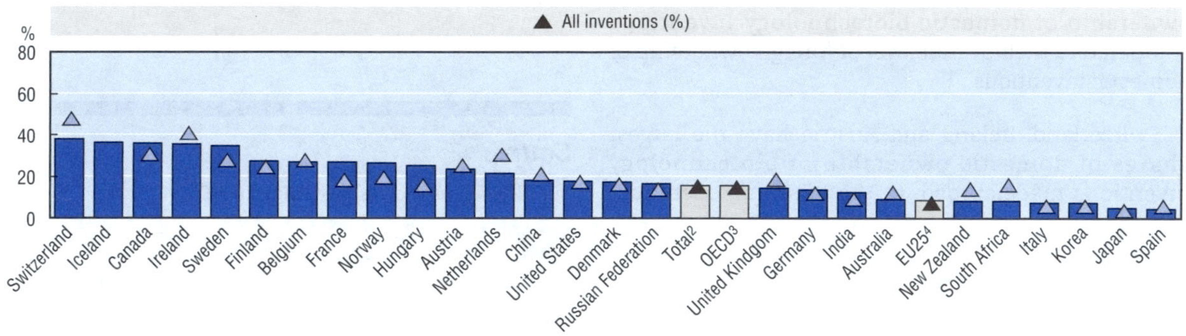


### Share of ICT-related inventions[1] with foreign co-inventors, 1999-2001

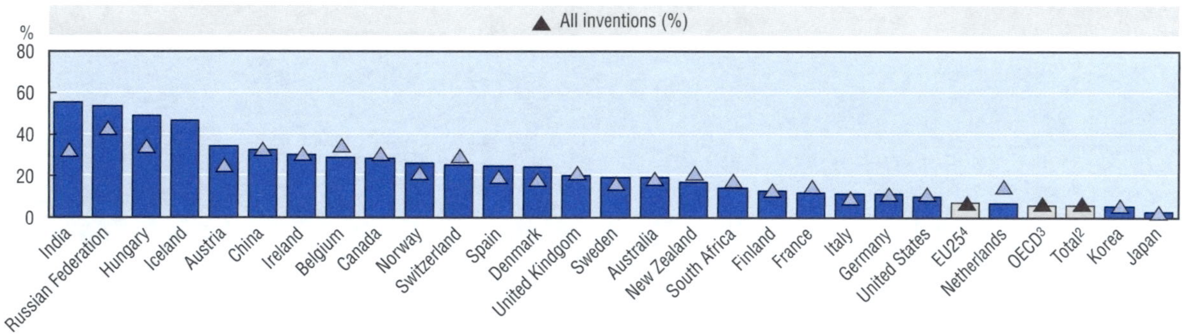


*Note:* Patent counts are based on the inventor's country of residence and the priority date. The graph only covers countries with, on average, more than ten ICT-related patents over the 1999-2001 period (see C.4).

1. Patent applications filed at the European Patent Office.
2. All EPO patents that involve international co-operation.
3. Patents of OECD residents that involve international co-operation.
4. The EU is treated as one country; intra-EU co-operation has been netted out.

StatLink: *http://dx.doi.org/10.1787/713343061636*

## C.10. Internationalisation of biotechnology inventions

■ On all three measures of internationalisation (foreign ownership of domestic inventions, domestic ownership of inventions made abroad and patents with foreign co-inventors), Austria, Ireland, the Russian Federation and Switzerland are the most internationalised for biotechnology inventions. Of the G7 countries, Italy and the United Kingdom are the most internationalised.

■ Most countries have a higher share of foreign ownership of domestic biotechnology inventions than of all domestic inventions. This is most notably the case for Spain, Finland, Switzerland, Ireland, Italy and the Russian Federation, where the share of foreign ownership is more than 20 percentage points above the overall share of foreign ownership of domestic inventions. In contrast, Belgium, Canada and the United Kingdom have a smaller share of foreign ownership of domestic biotechnology inventions compared to their overall level of foreign ownership of domestic inventions.

■ Switzerland, Ireland and Austria have the largest shares of domestic ownership of biotechnology inventions made abroad. In the Russian Federation, Switzerland, Austria and New Zealand, the share of domestic ownership of biotechnology inventions made abroad is more than 20 percentage points above the share of domestic ownership of inventions made abroad overall. In contrast, China, India, Canada and the United States have a smaller share of domestic ownership of biotechnology inventions made abroad than their overall level of domestic ownership of inventions made abroad.

■ In all reported countries, except Belgium and India, the level of international co-operation is higher for biotechnology inventions than for international co-operation overall. This is most true for Switzerland, Spain, Italy, Ireland and Sweden, where the level of international co-operation on biotechnology inventions is more than 26 percentage points above that of international co-operation overall.

### Source

- OECD, Patent database, March 2005.



OECD SCIENCE, TECHNOLOGY AND INDUSTRY SCOREBOARD 2005 – ISBN 92-64-01055-6 – © OECD 2005

## C.10. Internationalisation of biotechnology inventions

### Foreign ownership of domestic biotechnology inventions,[1] 1999-2001

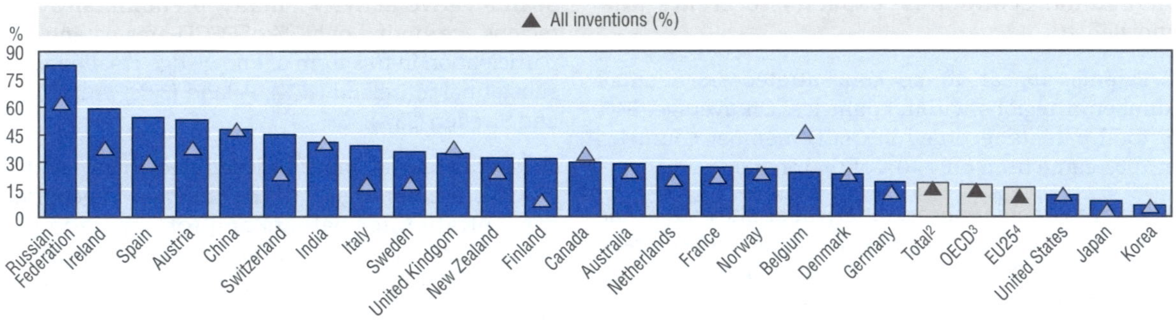


### Domestic ownership of biotechnology inventions[1] made abroad, 1999-2001

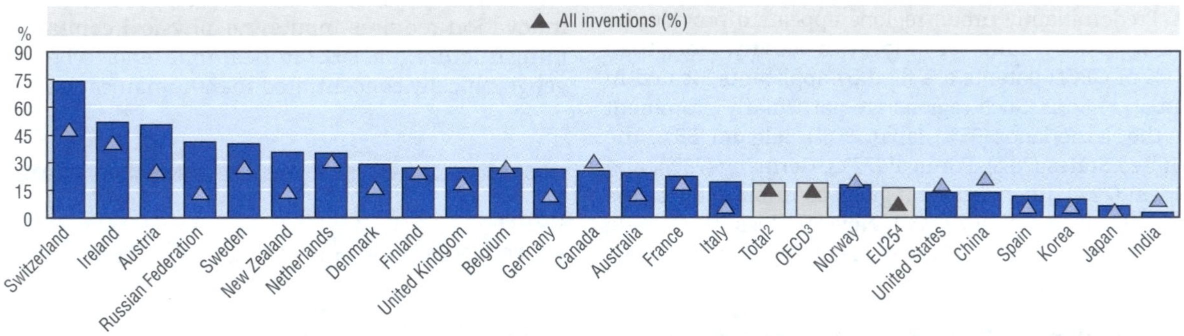


### Share of biotechnology inventions[1] with foreign co-inventors, 1999-2001

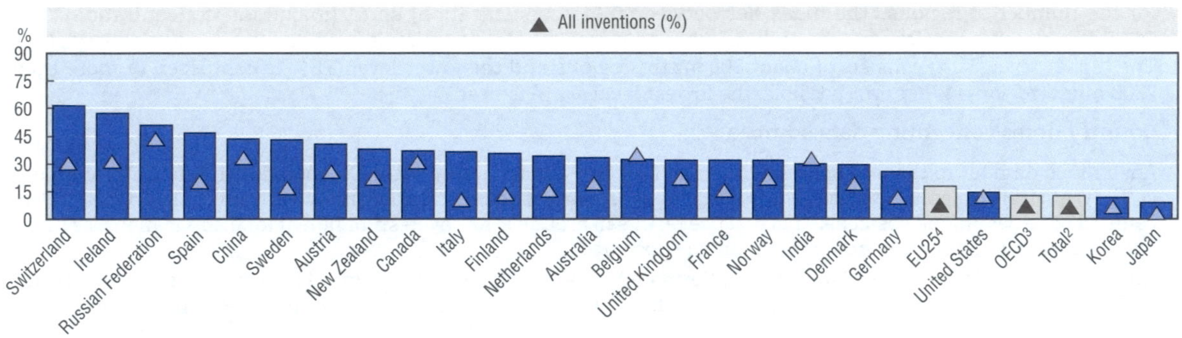


*Note:* Patent counts are based on the inventor's country of residence and the priority date. The graph only covers countries with, on average, more than ten biotechnology patents over the 1999-2001 period (see C.5).

1. Patent applications filed at the European Patent Office.
2. All EPO patents that involve international co-operation.
3. Patents of OECD residents that involve international co-operation.
4. The EU is treated as one country; intra-EU co-operation has been netted out.

StatLink: *http://dx.doi.org/10.1787/423578407066*

## C.11. Geographic concentration of patents

■ The geographic distribution of patents is indicative of regional economies' capacity to create new knowledge.

■ Patents appear to be concentrated in a small number of regions within countries. On average, 54% of total patents recorded in OECD member countries in 2001 came from only 10% of their regions.

■ The geographic concentration index shows that the concentration of patents was the highest in Australia (0.89), Japan (0.79), Portugal (0.73) and Korea (0.72), followed closely by Spain (0.66), Sweden (0.65), Finland (0.64), the United States (0.63) and Greece (0.61). The geographic concentration of patents is lowest in Poland (0.35), Belgium (0.39), the Netherlands (0.42) and Germany (0.43).

■ Predominantly urban regions appear to provide the most fertile ground for innovative activity. More than 81% of OECD patents are filed by applicants located in urban regions. Such regions are particularly prominent in the Netherlands (95%), Japan (90%), Belgium (88%), the United States (78%), Portugal (77%), Germany (73%), and Spain (72%). Intermediate regions contribute much less to patenting activity (14%). Nevertheless, in Canada (96%), Poland (55%), Norway (48%) and Austria (39%), intermediate regions are responsible for the largest part of innovative activity. Finally, predominantly rural regions account for only 5% of OECD-area patents. Their participation in this form of knowledge creation is more substantial in Ireland (42%), Poland (37%), Austria (33%) and Sweden (33%).

■ Patents are far more concentrated than population or GDP. A comparison of the indexes of geographic concentration for patents and for population with tertiary education shows that in most countries the highly skilled population is less concentrated than patents. Only in the United Kingdom does the level of concentration of skilled population exceed that of patents.

■ Thus, the geographic pattern of knowledge creation and skilled population is not necessarily the same. Innovation requires inputs (*e.g.* physical capital) and infrastructure (*e.g.* laboratories) that tend to be more geographically concentrated than human capital.

### Source

- OECD (2005), *Regions at a Glance*, OECD, Paris.

### Measuring the geographic concentration of patents

The geographic concentration index of patents is defined as: $\sum_{i=1}^{N} |p_i - a_i|$

where $p_i$ is the patents' share of region i, $a_i$ is the area of region i as a percentage of the country area, and N stands for the number of regions. The index lies between 0 (no concentration) and 1 (maximum concentration). The OECD has classified regions within each member country. The classification is based on two territorial levels (TL). The higher level (TL 2) consists of about 300 macro-regions and the lower level (TL 3) is composed of more than 2300 micro-regions. Whenever possible, the lowest level (TL 3) is used.

**Country notes concerning data sources**

Australia: data refer to the number of all Australian patent applications (Patent Co-operation Treaty [PCT] and non-PCT) by Australian applicants filed with Intellectual Property Australia. Applications with multiple applicants are counted once per unique postcode. This practice results in around a 10% overestimation of total applications, as many applications have applicants from more than one postcode.

Austria, Belgium, Denmark, Finland, France, Germany, Greece, Iceland, Ireland, Italy, Luxembourg, the Netherlands, Norway, Portugal, Spain, Sweden and the United Kingdom: data refer to the number of patent applications to the European Patent Office (EPO), directly filed under the European Patent Convention or to applications filed under the Patent Co-operation Treaty and designating the EPO (Euro-PCT). The regional distribution of patent applications is assigned according to the inventor's region of residence. If an application has more than one inventor, the application is divided equally among all to avoid double counting.

Canada: data refer to the number of total patent filings (PCT and non-PCT) with the Canadian Intellectual Property Office.

Japan, Korea: data refer to the number of patent applications made by national applicants to the national Patent Office.

Poland: Data refer to the number of patent applications filed with the Patent Office of the Republic of Poland.

United States: data refer to the number of utility patents awarded to inventors in each US county, by grant date. The distribution of patents by county is, to a large extent, based on inventor city and state data. Fractional patent counts may occur for some counties when a patent is associated with multiple counties within a state. All fractional patent counts are rounded to the nearest whole number.

## C.11. Geographic concentration of patents

### Share of total patents concentrated in the top 10% of patenting regions, 2001

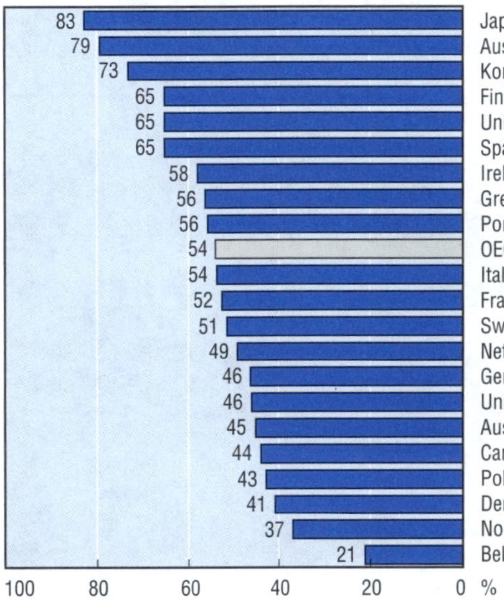


### Geographic concentration index of patents, 2001

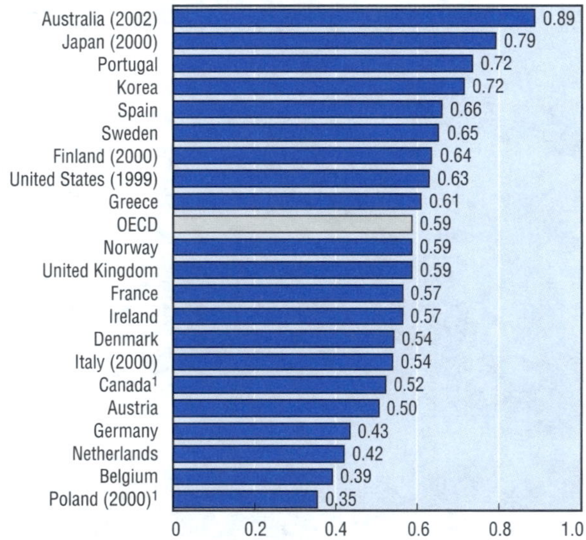


### Distribution of patents by type of region, 2001

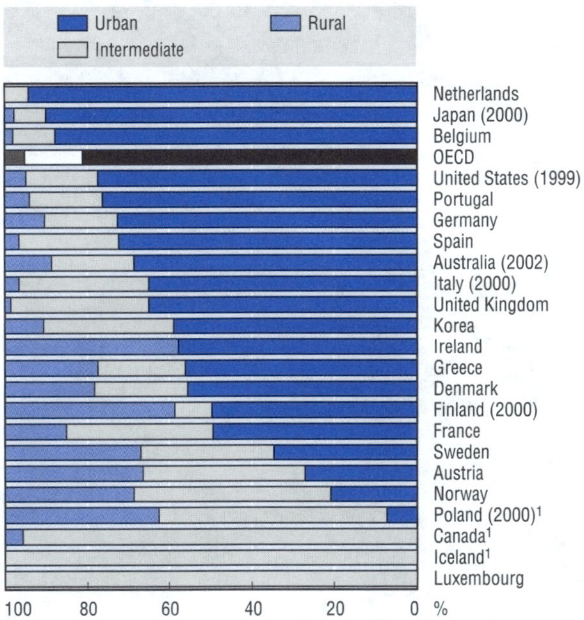


### Concentration index for patents and population at tertiary education level, 2001

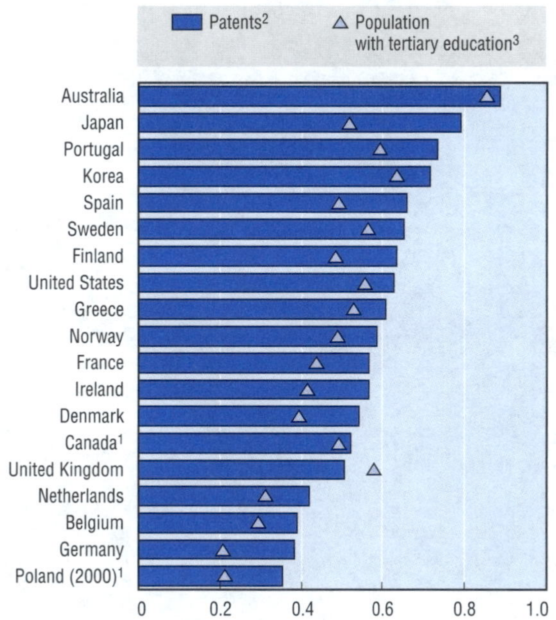


1. TL 2.
2. 2000 for Poland, Finland and Japan; 2002 for Australia; 1999 for the United States.
3. 2002 for Poland, Denmark and Ireland;. 2000 for Finland, Japan, the United States and Korea; 1999 for France.

StatLink: *http://dx.doi.org/10.1787/378365116716*

Scroll Lock
Pause Break
Backspace
Home

# D. ICT: AN ENABLER FOR THE KNOWLEDGE SOCIETY

## D.1. Investment in ICT equipment and software

■ Investment in physical capital is a way to expand and renew the capital stock and enable new technologies to enter the production process and is therefore important for growth. Information and communication technology (ICT) has been the most dynamic component of investment in recent years.

■ In several OECD countries, ICT's share in total non-residential investment doubled and in some cases quadrupled between 1985 and 2003. In 2003, its share was particularly high in Finland, Sweden and the United States.

■ ICT investment also accounts for a considerable share of GDP. In 2003, its share in GDP was over 4% in Australia, Korea and the United States, but under 2% in France, Germany, Ireland and Portugal.

■ Software has been the fastest-growing component of ICT investment. In many countries, its share in non-residential investment increased strongly between 1985 and 2003. In 2003, software's share in total investment was highest in Denmark, Sweden and the United States.

■ By 2003, software accounted for 50% or more of total ICT investment in Denmark, Japan, the Netherlands and Sweden. Communications equipment was the major component of ICT investment in Greece, Italy, Portugal, New Zealand and Spain. IT equipment was the major component in Belgium, Ireland and Norway.

■ Data on investment in ICT for 2003 and 2004 are currently only available for certain OECD countries. The available data indicate that ICT's share in total investment declined from 2000 to 2001 and has subsequently deteriorated further. In Korea, it declined from 20.8% of investment in 2000, to 15.5% in 2004. While the share of IT hardware in total investment has declined in most countries, that of investment in software has grown in several countries.

### Sources

- OECD, database on Capital Services, July 2005.
- OECD, productivity database, June 2005, available at *www.oecd.org/statistics/productivity.*
- Groningen Growth and Development Centre, June 2005.

### For further reading


- Lequiller, F., N. Ahmad, S. Varjonen, W. Cave and K.H. Ahn (2003), "Report of the OECD Task Force on Software Measurement in the National Accounts", *OECD Statistics Working Paper 2003/1*, OECD, Paris.
- Ahmad, N. (2003), "Measuring Investment in Software", *STI Working Paper* 2003/6, OECD, Paris, available at *www.oecd.org/sti/working-papers.*
- Schreyer, P., P.E. Bignon and J. Dupont (2003), "OECD Capital Services Estimates: Methodology and a First Set of Results", *OECD Statistics Working Paper,* 2003/6, OECD, Paris.


### Measuring investment in ICT

Correct measurement of investment in ICT in both nominal and volume terms is crucial for estimating its contribution to economic growth and performance. Data availability and measurement of investment in ICT based on national accounts (SNA93) vary considerably across OECD countries, especially as regards measurement of investment in software, deflators applied, breakdown by institutional sector and temporal coverage. In the national accounts, expenditure on ICT products is considered as investment only if the products can be physically isolated (*i.e.* ICT embodied in equipment is considered not as investment but as intermediate consumption). This means that investment in ICT may be underestimated and the order of magnitude of the underestimation may differ depending on how intermediate consumption and investment are treated in each country's accounts.

In particular, expenditure on software has only very recently been treated as capital expenditure in the national accounts, and methodologies still vary considerably across countries. Difficulties for measuring software investment are also linked to the ways in which software can be acquired, *e.g. via* rental and licences or embedded in hardware. Moreover, software is often developed on own account. To tackle the specific problems relating to software in the context of the SNA93 revision of the national accounts, a joint OECD-EU Task Force on the Measurement of Software in the National Accounts has developed recommendations concerning the capitalisation of software. These are now being implemented by OECD member countries.

## D.1. Investment in ICT equipment and software

### Investment in ICT,[1] 1985-2003[2]

As a percentage of gross fixed capital formation

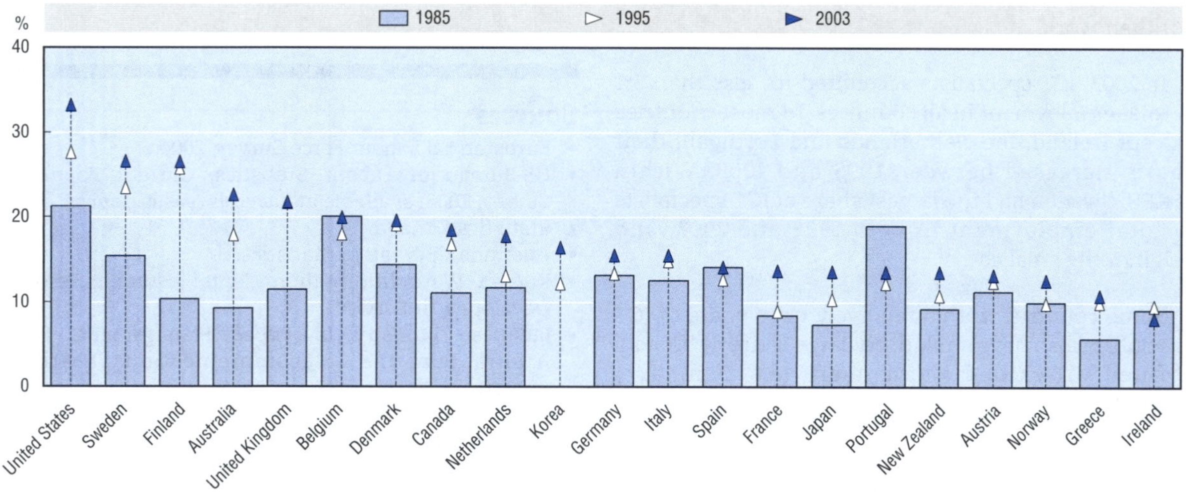


### ICT investment by asset[1] in OECD countries, 2003

As a percentage of non-residential gross fixed capital formation, total economy

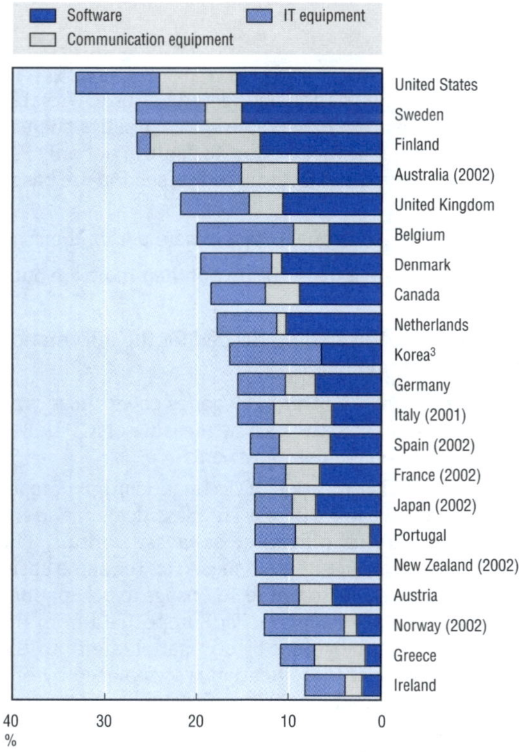


### Software investment[1] in OECD countries, 1980-2003[2]

As a percentage of non-residential gross fixed capital formation, total economy

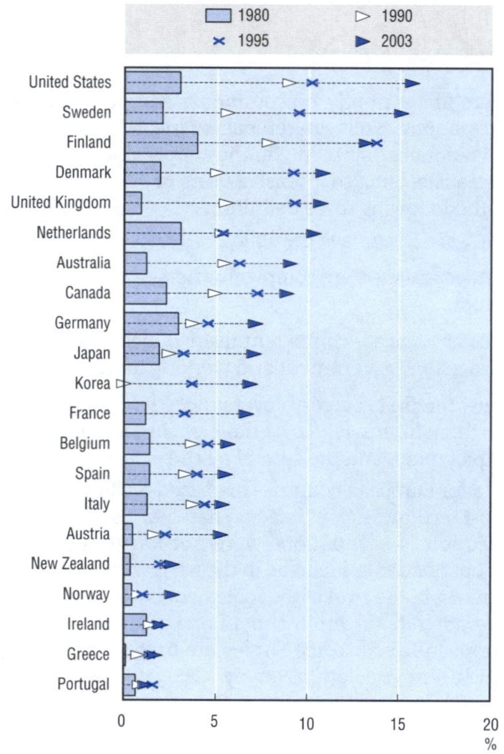


1. ICT equipment is defined as computer and office equipment and communication equipment; software includes both purchased and own account software. In Japan, investment in software is likely to be underestimated, owing to methodological differences.
2. 2002 for Australia, France, Japan, New Zealand, Norway and Spain, and 2001 for Italy.
3. Communication and IT equipment for Korea.

StatLink: *http://dx.doi.org/10.1787/133011685100*

## D.2. ICT occupations and skills

■ Two occupation indicators assess the use of ICTs in the economy: one for ICT specialists and one for basic and advanced ICT users who rely on ICTs in carrying out their work.

■ In 2003, ICT specialists accounted for less than 5% of total employment in all countries. In most countries (except Ireland, the Netherlands and Portugal), their share increased between 1995 and 2003. Within the EU, Sweden had the largest share of ICT specialists in total employment in both 1995 and 2003, and Belgium the smallest.

■ Some countries with a relatively large share of ICT specialists also have a relatively large share of broadly defined ICT-skilled employment (*e.g.* Denmark, Finland, Sweden and the United Kingdom).

■ In 2003, ICT specialists and ICT users combined generally accounted for 20-30% of total employment. In most countries (except Portugal, the United States and Canada), the share of broadly defined ICT-skilled employment increased. Within the EU, the United Kingdom had the largest share of broadly defined ICT-skilled employment in both 1995 and 2003, and Greece the lowest.

### Sources

- Eurostat, EU Labour Force Survey, 2004.
- US Bureau of Labour Statistics, Current Population Survey, 2003, available at *www.bls.census.gov/cps*.
- Statistics Canada.
- Australian Bureau of Statistics.
- Korean Work Information Center, Human Resource Development Service.
- Japanese Ministry of Public Management, Home Affairs, Post and Telecommunications, Statistics Bureau.

### For further reading


- OECD (2004), *OECD Information Technology Outlook 2004*, Paris, available at *www.oecd.org/sti/ito*.
- Van Welsum, D. and G. Vickery (2005), "New Perspectives on ICT Skills and Employment", Information Economy working paper DSTI/ICCP/IE(2004)10/FINAL, OECD, available at *www.oecd.org/dataoecd/26/35/34769393.pdf*.


### ICT-related skills

There are currently no commonly adopted definition of ICT skills and no internationally agreed list of ICT-related occupations. Skills are difficult to measure, and proxies are often used to capture observable characteristics such as educational attainment, on the supply side, and occupations, on the demand side. In an effort to capture not only ICT specialists, but also intensive users of ICTs at various levels of skill complexity, the indicators in this section are based on the following three definitions:

- *ICT specialists* have the ability to develop, operate and maintain ICT systems. ICTs constitute the main part of their job.
- *Advanced users* are competent users of advanced, often sector-specific, software tools. ICTs are not their main job but a tool.
- *Basic users* are competent users of generic tools (*e.g.* Word, Excel, Outlook, PowerPoint) needed for the information society, e-government and working life. Here too, ICTs are a tool, not the main job.

Thus, the first category covers those who supply the ICT tools, and the second and third categories cover those who use them intensively to do their job. In this section, the first category corresponds to the narrow measure of ICT-skilled employment, and the sum of all three categories to the broad measure of ICT-skilled employment.

Data for European countries are based on ISCO 88 (the International Standard Classification of Occupations), but data for non-EU countries are based on national classification systems which tend to give more detail. The classification and the selection of occupations were not harmonised internationally as there are no official cross-classifications. The occupations to be included in the narrow and broad definition of ICT-skilled employment were chosen on the same basis. As a result, the level of the indicators is not directly comparable across countries. Furthermore, ICT usage in occupations may differ, both within and among countries, even when based on the same classification. For Europe, data from the European Labour Force Survey are based on three-digit ISCO 88. US data on employment by occupation are from the US Current Population Survey (CPS). However, as the 1990 Census Occupational Classification was replaced by one derived from the US Standard Occupational Classification (SOC) in January 2003, data for 2003 were estimated. Statistics Canada provided the labour force data for Canada based on SOC91-Canada. The data for Australia are based on four-digit ASCO (Australian Standard Classification of Occupations) provided by the Australian Bureau of Statistics. Data for Korea are provided by the Human Resource Development Services of the Korean Work Information Center, and are based on a new classification system, which is currently being revised. Finally, labour force survey data for Japan were provided by the Statistics Bureau of the Japanese Ministry of Public Management, Home Affairs, Post and Telecommunications. These data distinguish a small number of occupations compared to the detail available for other countries.

 OECD SCIENCE, TECHNOLOGY AND INDUSTRY SCOREBOARD 2005 – ISBN 92-64-01055-6 – 

## D.2. ICT occupations and skills

### ICT-related occupations, 2003

As a percentage of total employment

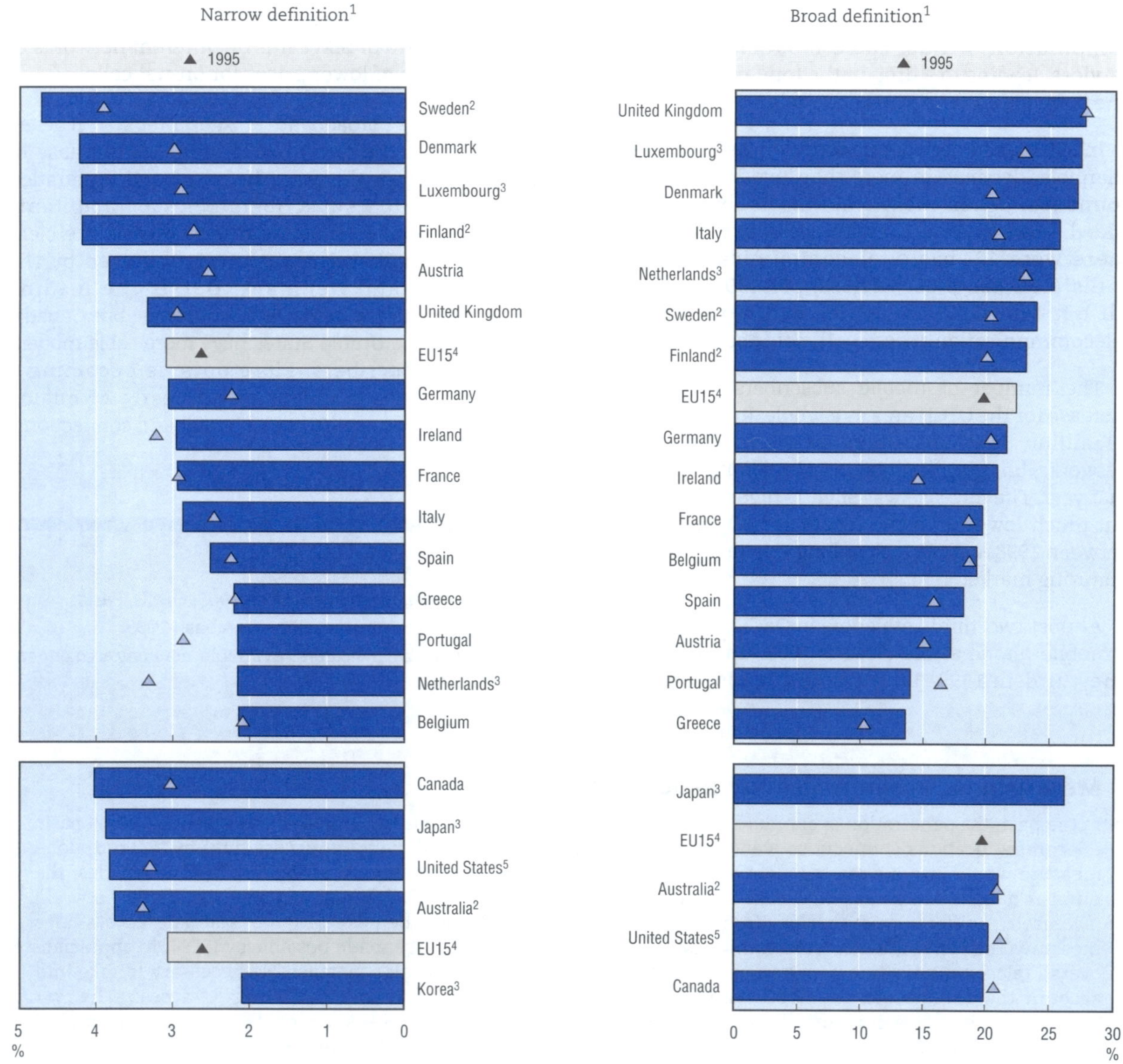


1. Narrow and broad definitions based on methodology described in Chapter 6 of the *Information Technology Outlook 2004*. See also D. van Welsum and G. Vickery (2005), "New Perspectives on ICT Skills and Employment", Information Economy Working Paper DSTI/ICCP/IE(2004)10/FINAL, OECD. Calculations based on EULFS; US Current Population Survey; Statistics Canada; Australian Bureau of Statistics; the Korean Work Information Center, Human Resource Development Service; Japanese Ministry of Public Management, Home Affairs, Post and Telecommunications, Statistics Bureau.
2. 1997 instead of 1995.
3. 2002 instead of 2003.
4. Includes estimates where a full dataset was not available.
5. OECD estimates for 2003.

StatLink: *http://dx.doi.org/10.1787/400455884165*

## D.3. Telecommunications networks

■ For the first time, the number of fixed telephone lines has begun to decline in the OECD area. First, standard analogue lines gradually gave way to ISDN, and ISDN is itself now being replaced by a combination of DSL, cable modems and mobile services, leading to a drop in the total number of fixed line connections and ISDN channels.

■ In 2003, fixed network penetration, as measured by channels, declined in more than two-thirds of OECD countries. When mobile cellular subscribers are added, however, access continues to expand. In 2003, there were 124 basic telecommunication access paths (*i.e.* fixed plus wireless) per 100 inhabitants. All but four OECD countries had more than one telecommunication access path per inhabitant.

■ The number of mobile subscribers continues to increase for the OECD area as a whole. In 2003, just over 69 million new subscribers were added to cellular networks, bringing the total to 741 million at the end of that year. The increase was slightly higher than in 2002 but much lower than the record growth experienced between 1998 and 2001, signalling levelling growth in a maturing market.

■ Almost two-thirds of people in OECD countries had a mobile phone at the close of 2003, up from around one-third in 1999. Luxembourg leads with more mobile telephones than inhabitants. The likely explanation is that users who reside in surrounding countries have a separate mobile for use in Luxembourg. In some countries, users have more than one prepaid card or SIM cards on different networks to take advantage of lower prices for on-net calls.

■ OECD-area broadband subscribers reached 118 million at the end of 2004, with an increase of 34.1 million during the year. The broadband penetration rate reached 10.2 subscribers per 100 inhabitants in 2004, up from 7.3 a year earlier. Korea is the clear leader in broadband penetration, followed by the Netherlands and Denmark. DSL is the leading broadband platform in 27 OECD countries, but Canada, Portugal and the United States have more cable modem than DSL subscribers. Fibre optic is becoming a significant platform in Japan with nearly 2.5 million subscribers, or nearly 12% of all broadband connections.

### Sources

- OECD, *Communications Outlook 2005*, OECD, Paris.
- OECD, Telecommunications database 2005.
- OECD, *ICT Key Indicators*, available at *www.oecd.org/sti/ICTindicators*.

### *Measuring telecommunication network access*

In the past, the penetration of standard access lines provided a reasonable indication of the extent to which basic telecommunications connections were available to users. Today, use of standard access lines as a stand-alone measure would give a distorted view of network development, since in more than half of OECD countries, the number of standard access lines began to decrease as the take-up of ISDN (integrated services digital network) increased. A different methodology from the one traditionally used for the penetration of standard access lines measures the penetration of telecommunication channels, including those made possible by ISDN. To appreciate overall telecommunication penetration rates across the OECD area, it is also increasingly necessary to take into account the development of mobile communication networks and of "broadband" Internet access. The two leading technologies currently used to provide high-speed Internet access are cable modems and digital subscriber lines (DSL). Other broadband connections include satellite broadband Internet access, fibre-to-home Internet access, Ethernet LANs, and fixed wireless access. The data for broadband subscribers includes business and residential connections.

## D.3. Telecommunications networks

### Access paths,[1] 2003

Per 100 inhabitants

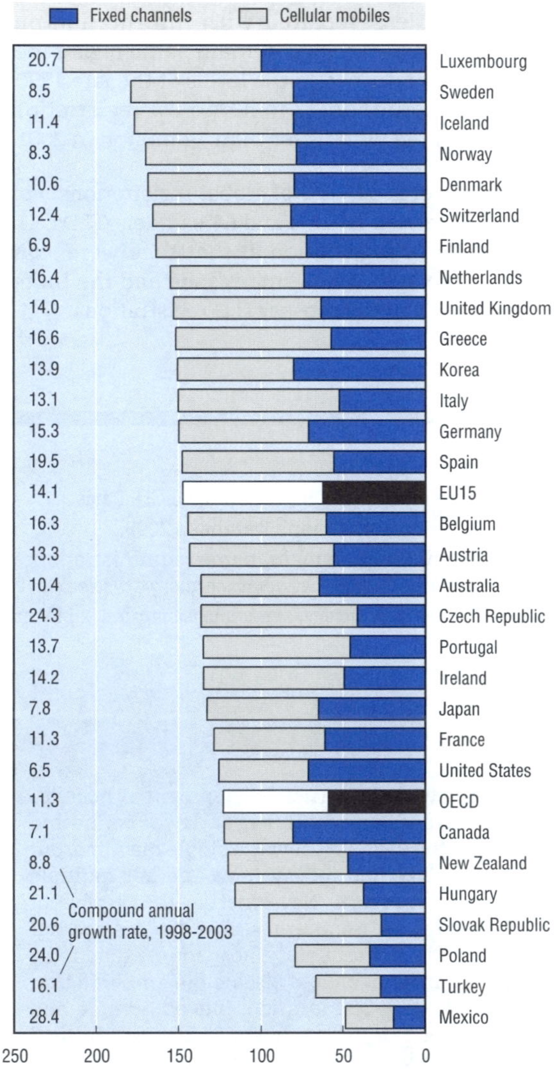


### Broadband subscribers by technology, December 2004

Per 100 inhabitants

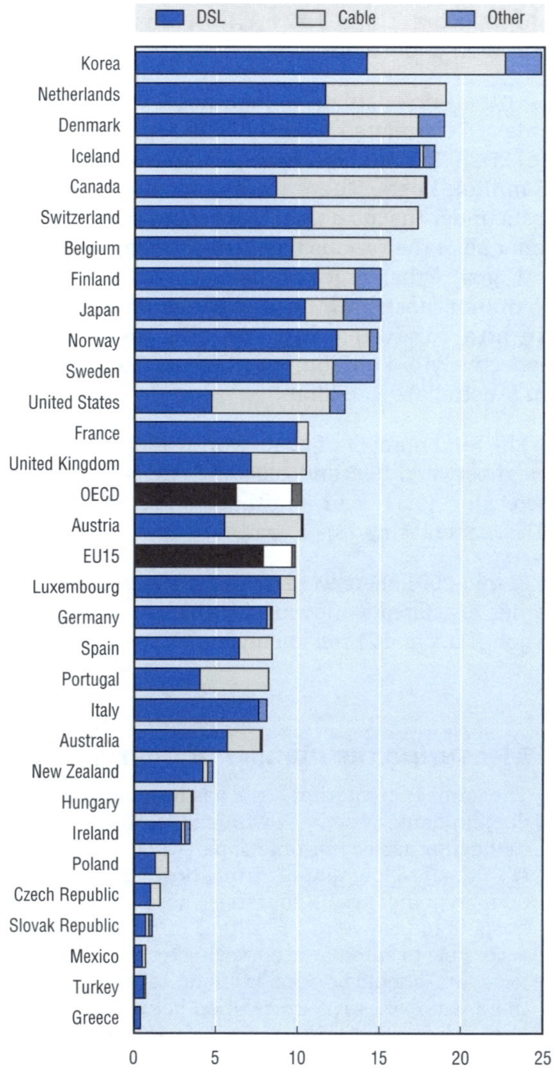


1. Access paths include fixed access channels, cellular mobile subscriptions and xDSL connections.

StatLink: *http://dx.doi.org/10.1787/815450835088*

## D.4. Internet hosts and domain names

■ In January 2004, there were 233 million hosts connected to the Internet worldwide, up from less than 30 million in January 1998. More than 150 million were under generic top level domains (gTLDs), of which more than 100 million under **.net** and 49 million under **.com**.

■ At the same date, 64 million hosts were connected under OECD-related country code top level domains (ccTLDs). The largest was **.jp** (Japan) with almost 13 million hosts. There were just under 1.8 million hosts under the **.us** domain, but more than 11 million under all of the various US-related domains (**.us**, **.edu**, **.mil**, **.gov**). Other large ccTLDs included: **.it** (Italy), with 5.5 million hosts; **.uk** (United Kingdom), 3.7 million; **.de** and **.nl** (Germany and the Netherlands, respectively) 3.4 million; **.ca** (Canada) 3.2 million; and **.au** (Australia) 2.8 million.

■ The total number of hosts worldwide increased 41% a year between 1998 and 2004, with those under gTLDs increasing 49% a year and those under OECD-related ccTLDs increasing 28% a year.

■ In mid-2004, there were more than 64 million domain names registered worldwide, of which 40 million under major gTLDs and 21 million under OECD-related ccTLDs.

■ Since mid-2000, the number of registered domain names has increased by around 19% a year, with faster growth in OECD-related ccTLD registrations than gTLD registrations. After slowing during the bursting of the financial bubble associated with information and communication technology, domain name registration rates have now returned to the levels of the late 1990s. There were more than 17 million new registrations in 2003 compared with fewer than 14 million in 2001.

■ In September 2004, 33% of global registrations were under OECD-related ccTLDs and 64% under gTLDs. The largest gTLDs by registration at that time were **.com**, **.net**, **.org**, **.info** and **.biz**. Germany's **.de** and the United Kingdom's **.uk** had the most ccTLD registrations.

### *Sources*

- OECD, *Communications Outlook 2005*, OECD, Paris.
- OECD, Telecommunications Database 2005.
- OECD, "Comparing domain name administration in OECD countries", 2004, see *www.oecd.org/sti/telecom*.
- *ISC Internet Domain Survey*, see *www.isc.org/index.pl?/ops/ds/*.

### *Measuring the number of Internet hosts*

The number of Internet hosts has been one of the commonly used indicators of Internet development. A host is a domain name associated with an IP (Internet protocol) address. This includes any computer or device connected to the Internet *via* full-time or part-time, direct or dial-up connection. In the past, a host was a single machine, but with the development of virtual hosting, in which a single machine acts like multiple systems and has multiple domain names and IP addresses, hosts are no longer necessarily individual devices. Nevertheless, the number of hosts is indicative of the extent of the growth in Internet hosting activities. Sometimes host devices are not accessible to automated surveying techniques because of security firewalls. Consequently, host counts tend to be lower and should be seen as an indicator of the minimum size of the Internet. It should also be remembered that there is no necessary correlation between a host's domain name and its physical location. Indeed, remote and virtual hosting are increasingly breaking the link between country code domains, hosts and their physical location. The ISC (Internet Systems Consortium) and Network Wizards undertake the longest-running and most comprehensive survey of Internet hosts.

## D.4. Internet hosts and domain names

### Internet hosts, January 2004

Per 1 000 inhabitants

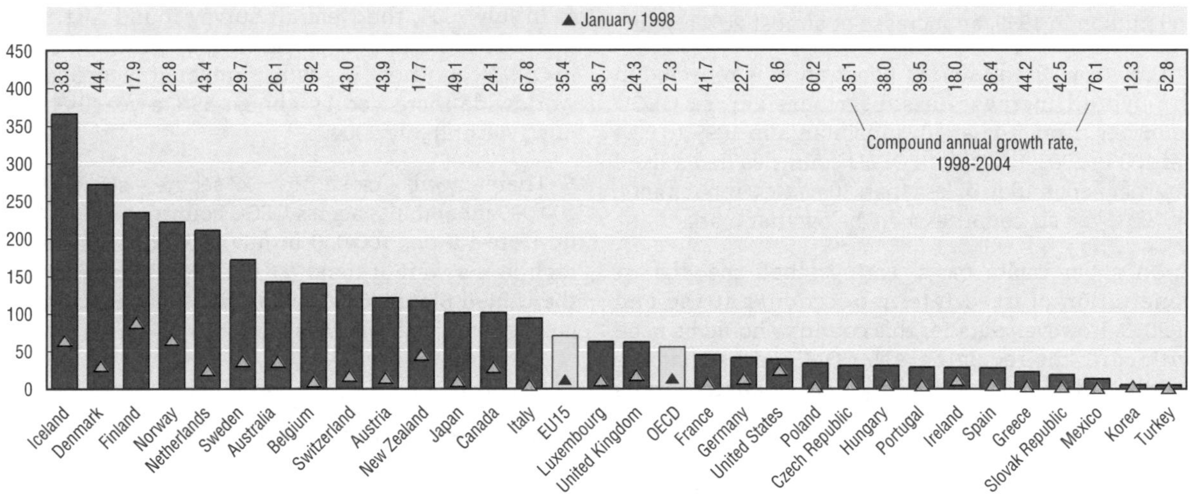


### Domain name registrations under top level domains, 2004

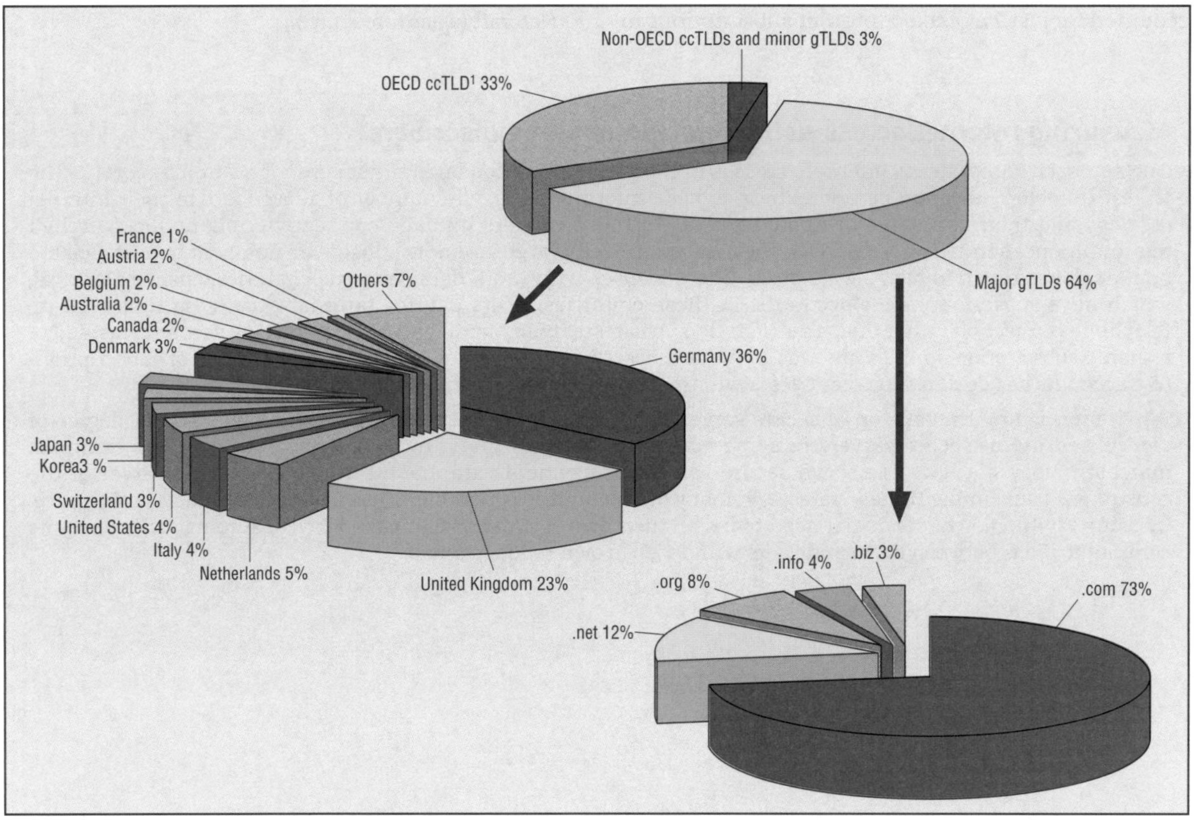


1. Excludes United States.

StatLink: *http://dx.doi.org/10.1787/466332371364*

## D.5. Internet subscribers and secure servers

At the end of 2003, there were around 259 million active Internet subscribers with fixed Internet connections in OECD countries, up from around 106 million in 1999, an increase of almost 26% a year.

Growth in fixed Internet penetration is reflected in the overall increase in subscribers across OECD countries, from 9.4 per 100 inhabitants in 1999 to 22.4 per 100 in 2003. In 1999, 18 OECD countries had a fixed Internet penetration of less than 10 per 100 inhabitants. By 2003, just six countries were below that mark.

On a per capita basis, Portugal had the highest penetration of fixed Internet accounts at the end of 2003. However, data for this country should be used with care: the regulator, ANACOM, warns that the number of individual dial-up access customers is overstated, as some users have more than one ISP and more than one "free" dial-up account.

Dial-up subscribers accounted for 96% of all fixed-line Internet subscribers in 1999 (102 million). By the end of 2003, dial-up subscribers accounted for just 68% but numbered 175 million. Dial-up subscribers accounted for just 2% of fixed Internet subscriptions in Korea at the end of 2003, compared with more than 95% in Greece and the Czech Republic.

In July 2004, the Netcraft survey found just under 325 000 secure servers worldwide, of which 94% were in OECD countries. The total number of secure servers worldwide increased by almost 59% a year between July 1998 and July 2004.

There were close to 27 secure servers per 100 000 inhabitants across OECD countries in July 2004, up from 1.8 per 100 000 in July 1998. Countries with high levels were Iceland (86 per 100 000 inhabitants), the United States (68), Canada (48), New Zealand (41), Luxembourg and Australia (40).

### Sources

- OECD, *Communications Outlook 2005*, OECD, Paris.
- OECD, Telecommunications database 2005.
- OECD, *ICT Key Indicators*, 2005, available at *www.oecd.org/sti/ICTindicators*.
- Netcraft (*www.netcraft.com*).

### *Measuring Internet access using information on subscribers*

One approach to measuring Internet access is to compile information on Internet subscribers from reports by the largest telecommunication carriers. These provide information on the number of subscribers to their Internet services and their estimates of market share. As these carriers manage connectivity *via* public switched telecommunication networks (PSTN), they are often well placed to know subscriber numbers and associated market shares on an industry-wide basis. One drawback with these data concerns countries, such as Portugal, which have subscription-free accounts. In these countries, users pay for Internet access via their dial-up telephone connection rather than a subscription. As a result many families have multiple ISP accounts instead of a shared subscription, in the same way that many users have multiple e-mail accounts. The use of subscription-free accounts has declined in recent years with the increasing use of broadband access.

When interpreting the take-up of secure servers, it is important to remember that there is a higher degree of centralised use of secure servers in some countries than in others. In the Nordic countries, for example, merchants may not have their own secure server but payments are made through the secure server of the consumer's bank. In the United States, and many other countries, merchants use PayPal to conduct e-commerce. By using PayPal, merchants do not need to install their own secure server. Instead PayPal automatically encrypts communications between them and users with PayPal's own secure servers.

## D.5. Internet subscribers and secure servers

### Internet subscribers, 2003

Per 100 inhabitants

1. Data for Portugal include subscription-free ISP accounts.

### Secure servers, 2004

Per 100 000 inhabitants

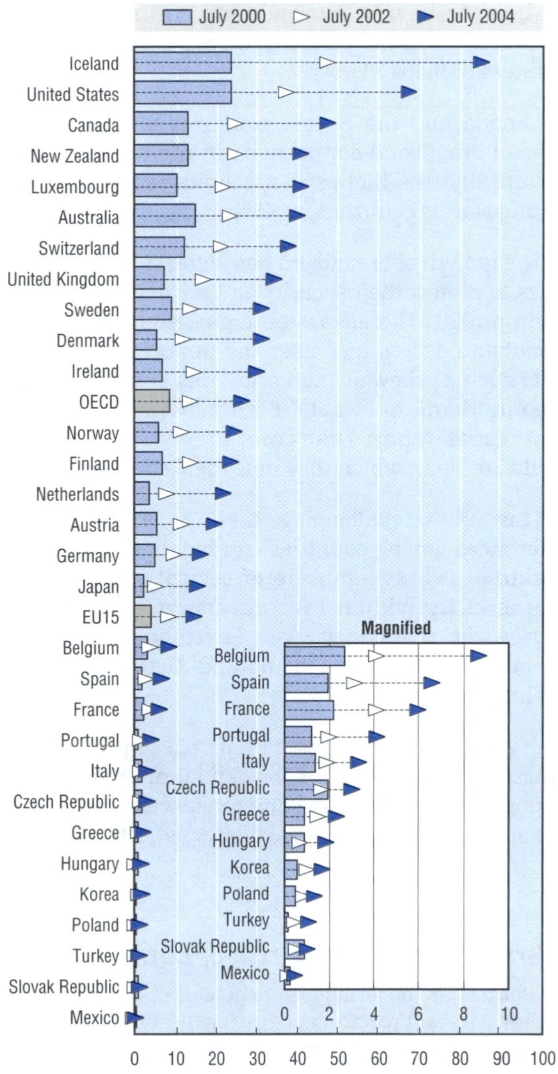


StatLink: *http://dx.doi.org/10.1787/872336322187*

 

## D.6. Broadband and security

Household and business use of broadband Internet access is growing rapidly in the OECD area. In 2004, Korea led, with 86% of households and 92% of businesses having a broadband connection *via* a computer or mobile phone (see D.9 for information on business broadband use).

Canada and the Nordic countries also have high rates of broadband connectivity in the home. In 2004, Iceland had the highest household penetration rate among Nordic countries, at 45%.

The growth of broadband has increased the need for users to protect their security and privacy in the online environment. The always-on connectivity enabled by broadband access increases the importance of using tools such as firewalls and anti-virus software, and of keeping them up to date. Both individual users and businesses report that computer viruses are the "malware" with which they must deal the most.

This is a challenging area to measure, but differences among countries can highlight progress in working towards a culture of security. The highest shares of individual Internet users encountering viruses were reported in Spain, Luxembourg and Korea. For businesses, Japan, Finland and Australia reported the highest shares.

In 2004, few businesses reported incidences of "unauthorised access" or "blackmail or threats", but respondents may be unwilling to answer questions on this subject. So-called "denial of service" attacks against businesses are likely to be a type of incident common to this category.

A threat that has emerged with the rise in the number of broadband connections involves networks of compromised computers acting together without their owners' knowledge or control. Symantec, a private security firm, tracks "bot-infected computers" by country. The most likely explanation for the level of infection is how actively users employ security precautions and install "patches".

The Symantec data can be correlated with the number of broadband connections to see the relative scale of infection across countries. In the second half of 2004, Japan, Belgium and Korea had the lowest proportion of bot-infected computers. The United Kingdom, Portugal, Greece, Spain and Sweden had the highest rates of infection.

### Sources

- OECD, ICT database and Eurostat, Community Survey on ICT usage in households and by individuals, May 2005.
- Symantec, "Internet Threat Security Report", March 2005.

### For further reading

- OECD, *Information Technology Outlook*, 2004.
- OECD, *Communications Outlook*, 2005.

### Broadband and the rise of botnets

"Botnets" is the term given to machines connected to the Internet that have been compromised in such a way that they can be directed to act in concert by an external party without the owners' knowledge or authority. Botnets may be used, by the party that has commandeered the machines, to mount denial of service attacks against particular sites on the Internet or to retransmit spam, phishing and so forth. Symantec's "Internet Security Report Threat Report" for the second half of 2004 contained a new botnet indicator, the percentage of "bot-infected" computers by country.

Symantec gathers data on bot-infected computers by monitoring 20 000 sensors located in networks in over 180 countries. Attacks by infected computers are recorded and matched against other databases such as those for malicious code and those enabling the assessment of originating addresses. Significantly, the data are not specific to Symantec customers, as are some of the company's other indicators, so there should not be a geographical bias. As the capture of computers is believed to be opportunistic rather than targeted toward any particular country, this indicator may be useful as an international benchmark of security awareness and action by Internet users.

## D.6. Broadband and security

### Households with broadband access, 2000-2004[1]

As a percentage of all households

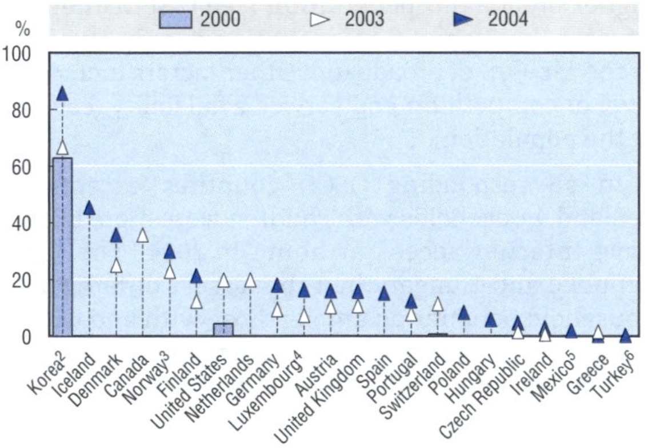


### Individuals who have encountered a computer virus by using the Internet, 2004[1, 7]

As a percentage of individuals using the Internet

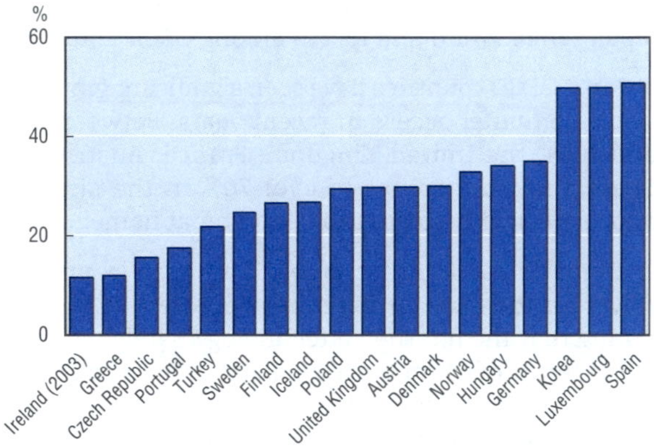


### Businesses that have encountered IT security problems, 2004[8]

As a percentage of businesses with 10 or more employees using the Internet

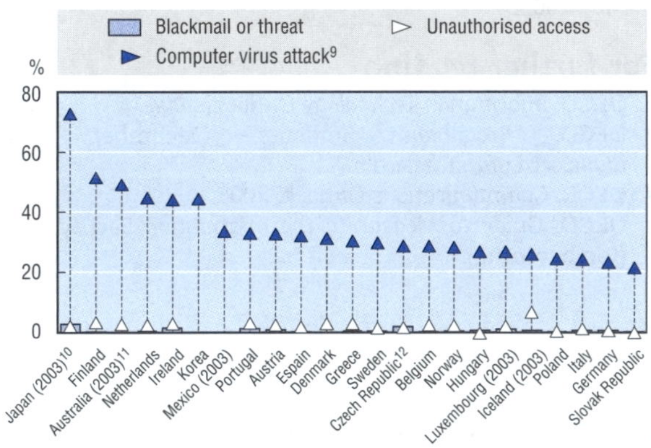


### Bot-infected computers, 2004

Per 100 broadband subscribers

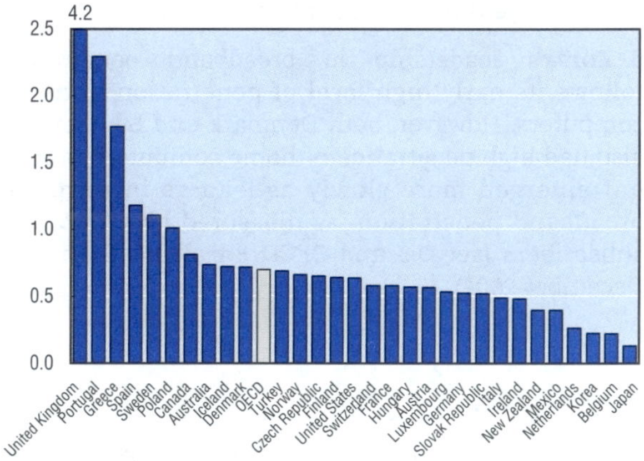


1. Data from the EU Community Survey on household use of ICT, which covers EU countries plus Iceland, Norway and Turkey, generally relate to the first quarter of the reference year. For the Czech Republic, data relate to the fourth quarter of the reference year.
2. For 2000-03, data include broadband access modes such as xDSL, cable and other fixed and wireless broadband *via* computers. For 2004, data also include mobile phone access. 2004 data for xDSL and cable only is 69.4%.
3. For 2003, data include LAN (wireless or cable).
4. For 2004, data include wireless access.
5. For 2001 and 2002, households with Internet access *via* cable. For 2004, households with Internet access *via* cable, ADSL or fixed wireless.
6. Households in urban areas only.
7. Resulting in loss of information or time.
8. For European countries, enterprises in the following industries are included: Manufacturing, Construction, Wholesale and retail, Hotels and restaurants (part), Transport, storage and communication, Real estate, renting and business activities and Other community, social and personal service activities (part). For Australia, the following industries are excluded: Agriculture, forestry and fishing, Education and Religious organisations. For Japan, data refer to enterprises with 100 or more employees and exclude: Agriculture, forestry, fisheries and Mining. Korea includes the following industries: Agriculture and Fisheries, Light Industry, Heavy Industry, Petrochemicals, Construction, Distribution, Finance and Insurance, and Other services. For Mexico, data refer to enterprises with 50 or more employees and include: Manufacturing, Services and Construction.
9. Resulting in loss of information or time. It is likely that some countries also include other threats such as trojans and worms in this category.
10. Defamation, libel, etc., on the Web instead of blackmail or threat.
11. Computer virus attack consists of just viruses.
12. Blackmail or threat covers other security problems.

StatLink: *http://dx.doi.org/10.1787/710631727706*

## D.7. ICT access by households

■ Access to computers in households has increased significantly in recent years. Iceland and Denmark led the way in 2004, with 86% and 79% of households, respectively, having access to a computer. Korea and Japan ranked third and fourth among OECD countries.

■ Most OECD countries have seen significant growth in home computer access in recent years. Between 2000 and 2004, the United Kingdom, France, Austria and Spain saw an increase of over 70% in the share of households with access to a computer at home.

■ Demand for Internet access has been a primary driver for the increase in home computers. It is worth noting that the Internet, a technology barely a decade old in terms of commercial availability to the public, is now used in at least half of households in 15 out of the 28 OECD countries collecting this information.

■ In 2004, penetration of household Internet access was highest in Korea (86%), followed by Iceland, Denmark and Switzerland. Between 2000 and 2004, home Internet access grew fastest in Germany, Portugal, the United Kingdom and Austria.

■ Korea's leadership in broadband penetration follows its early high level of penetration of home computers. However, both Denmark and Switzerland also had high penetration of home computers in 2000 but emerged more slowly as leaders in terms of broadband penetration, as measured by number of subscribers (see D.3 and *OECD Broadband Statistics*, December 2004).

■ Canada and Australia have closely tracked each other in terms of penetration of household computer and Internet access, but in 2004 Canada had much higher broadband penetration (see D.3). It therefore appears that computer penetration is only one factor in the take-up of broadband. Other factors include the level of competition and service availability (coverage of the population).

■ In all responding OECD countries except New Zealand, households with children were more likely to have Internet access at home in 2004. The Czech Republic and Hungary had the largest differences in household penetration among those with and without children; the rate of Internet access for households with dependent children was almost three times that of households without.

### Sources

- OECD, ICT database and Eurostat, Community Survey on ICT usage in households and by individuals, May 2005.

### For further reading

- OECD, *Information Technology Outlook*, 2004.
- OECD, *Broadband Statistics*, December 2004, *www.oecd.org/sti/telecom*.
- OECD, *Communications Outlook*, 2005.
- OECD, *Guide to Measuring the Information Society*, 2005 (forthcoming).

### ICT use in households and by individuals – OECD model survey

In late 2002, the OECD finalised a model survey on ICT usage in households and by individuals. The questionnaire in the model is composed of self-contained modules which can be used either in their totality or as separate modules in specific national surveys. The model survey is intended to provide guidance for measuring ICT usage (including Internet use and Internet commerce) and barriers to ICT use by households and individuals. Participating countries are encouraged to use it as a core part of survey development in order to improve the international comparability of information collected and compiled on this topic.

The OECD's model survey on ICT usage in households and by individuals is being revised during 2005.

## D.7. ICT access by households

### Households with access to a home computer,[1] 2000-2004

As a percentage of all households

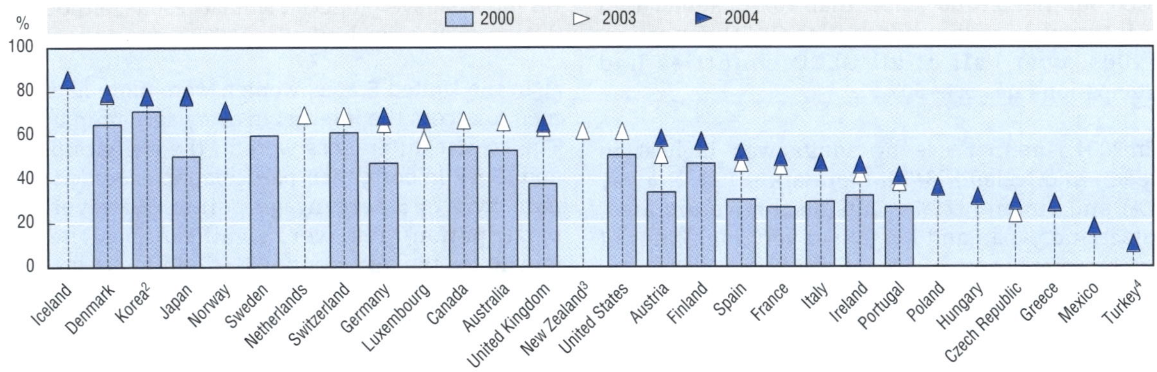


### Households with access to the Internet,[1, 5] 2000-2004

As a percentage of all households

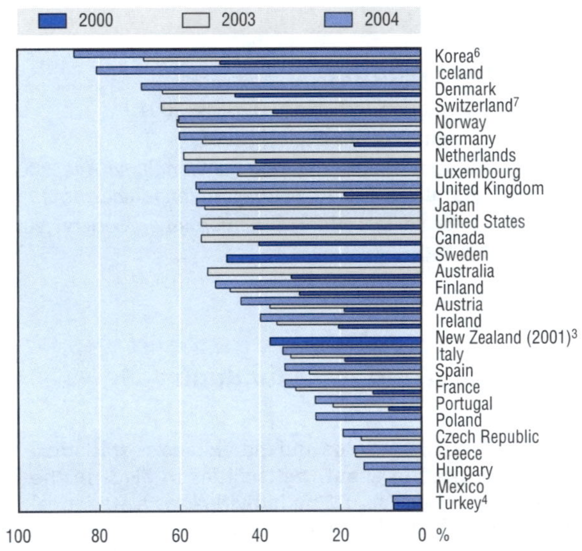


### Household Internet access by household type,[1] 2004

As a percentage of all households

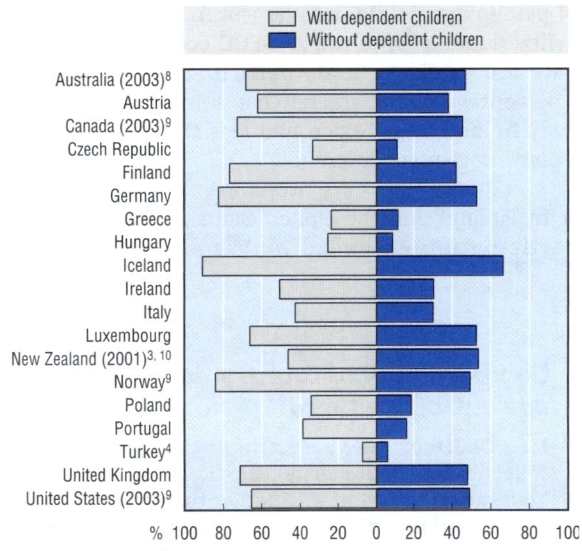


1. Data from the EU Community Survey on household use of ICT, which covers EU countries plus Iceland, Norway and Turkey, generally relate to the first quarter of the reference year. For the Czech Republic, data relate to the fourth quarter of the reference year.
2. Previously, data for Korea were based on the Computer and Internet Use Survey conducted by the Korean National Statistical Office. Certain items of that survey are no longer collected and data are now sourced from the Survey on Computer and Internet Usage conducted by the National Internet Development Agency (NIDA) of Korea. The NIDA series shows higher shares than the earlier survey.
3. The information is based on households in private occupied dwellings with access to the Internet. Visitor-only dwellings, such as hotels, are excluded.
4. Households in urban areas only.
5. Internet access is *via* any device (desktop computer, portable computer, TV, mobile phone, etc.).
6. For 2000-03, data include Internet access only *via* computer. In the 2004 survey, Internet access through mobile phone is also included. The value for 2004 excluding mobile phone access is 72.2%.
7. Figures refer to a sample based on individuals and are private data from *Arbeitsgruppe für Werbemedienforschung* (WEMF AG).
8. Data provided relate to households with or without children under 15 years.
9. Households with dependent children are defined as households with children under the age of 18.
10. Household child dependency status does not include households where there is a child whose dependency status is not known.

StatLink: *http://dx.doi.org/10.1787/575882356433*

## D.8. Use of the Internet by individuals

■ Internet use by adults at home, work or another location is reaching high levels in a growing number of OECD countries. In 2000, more than 50% of adults used the Internet in only a handful of OECD countries. By 2004, over half of all OECD countries had participation rates over 50%.

■ In 2004, Internet use by adults was highest in Sweden and Iceland (84%), Denmark (81%), Norway (78%) and Finland (72%). Outside the Nordic area, Switzerland, Japan and Korea had very high rates of adult Internet use.

■ Between 2000 and 2004, growth rates in Internet use by adults exceeded 60% in Austria, Italy and Turkey. High growth in penetration has also occurred in the United Kingdom, Korea, Switzerland and Japan.

■ In 2004, men were more likely than women to access the Internet in most OECD countries. The gap, in terms of percentage points, was largest in Luxembourg and Switzerland. In 14 of the 23 OECD countries for which data are available, male participation was at least 5 percentage points greater than female participation. Only Ireland and Mexico had less than or equal to a 1 percentage point difference.

■ In Finland and the United States, however, female participation exceeded male participation. The difference was slight in Finland, but in the United States, it was higher by 2.8 percentage points. Previous US surveys have produced similar results, although the difference was much smaller in 2000.

■ In the United States, women were more likely than men to access the Internet in every age group up to 65. The largest differences were in the age groups 16-24 and 25-44. In both, their participation exceeded that of men by 4 to 5 percentage points. However, male participation rates were significantly higher than female for the age groups 65-74 and for 75 years and over.

### Sources

- OECD, ICT database and Eurostat, Community Survey on ICT usage in households and by individuals, May 2005.

### For further reading

- OECD, *Information Technology Outlook*, 2004.
- OECD, *Communications Outlook*, 2005.
- NTIA, *A Nation Online: Entering the Broadband Age*, 2004, available at *www.ntia.doc.gov/reports/anol/index.html*.
- OECD, *Guide to Measuring the Information Society*, 2005 (forthcoming).

### Comparability of country data on ICT use in households and by individuals: age cut-off and recall period

Most OECD countries collect information on this topic and most use both households and individuals as statistical collection units. In general, the household unit is used to elicit information about the facilities in place in the household (for example, whether there is a TV, computer or Internet connection). The individual as a statistical unit is used to provide information on use of these facilities by individuals (both in and away from the home) and, most importantly, the intensity of use (for instance, frequency and range of activities undertaken). In terms of comparability across countries, the greatest differences are probably in the age scope used for individuals. The OECD currently recommends including all individuals aged 16 and over in the survey. Eurostat provides data to the OECD on the age grouping 16-74 (some individual European countries collect data for people over 74). Other OECD countries have a variety of age cut-offs which are usually constrained by the survey vehicle used to collect the data (for instance, countries using labour force surveys are likely to collect information for the relevant age group). The differences can be important as use of information technology is very age-dependent. In particular, younger people are generally more likely to use ICT than older people. In order to improve comparability, OECD has collected data for the age group 16-74 wherever possible. Information on country variations regarding age is given in notes to the relevant figures.

Another issue for cross-country comparability concerns the recall period used for questions on ICT use by individuals. OECD recommends use of a 12-month recall period for such questions although not all countries follow the recommendation (many European countries use 12 months for some items and three months for others). Increasingly, for OECD countries, the differences are minor for data on ICT use as most people who use ICT have done so in the last three months. More information on the recall periods used by different countries for different items can be found in notes to the relevant figures.

## D.8. Use of the Internet by individuals

### Individuals[1, 2] using the Internet from any location, 2001-2004

As a percentage of all adults

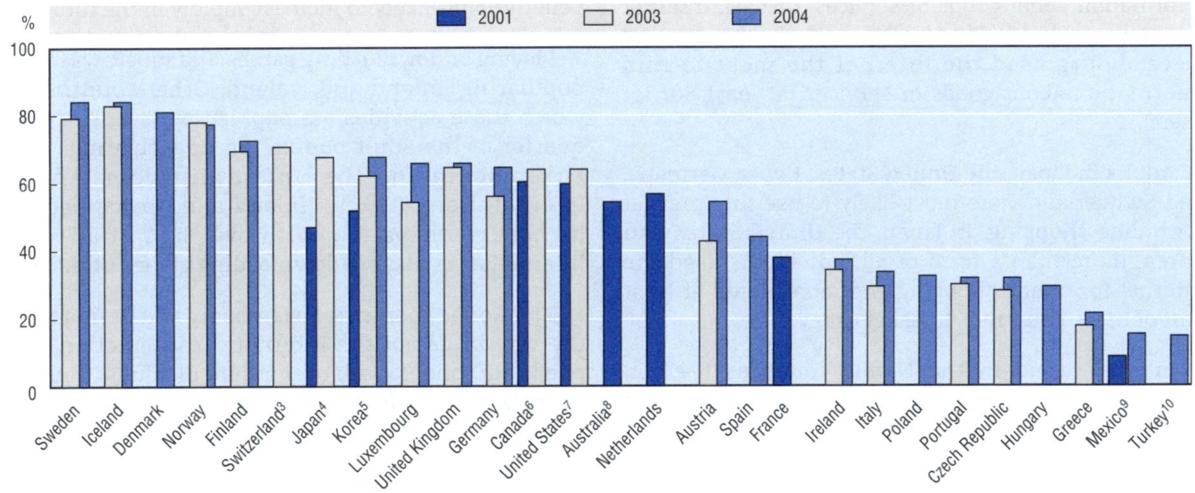


### Individuals[1, 2] using the Internet from any location by gender, 2004

As a percentage of adults, by gender

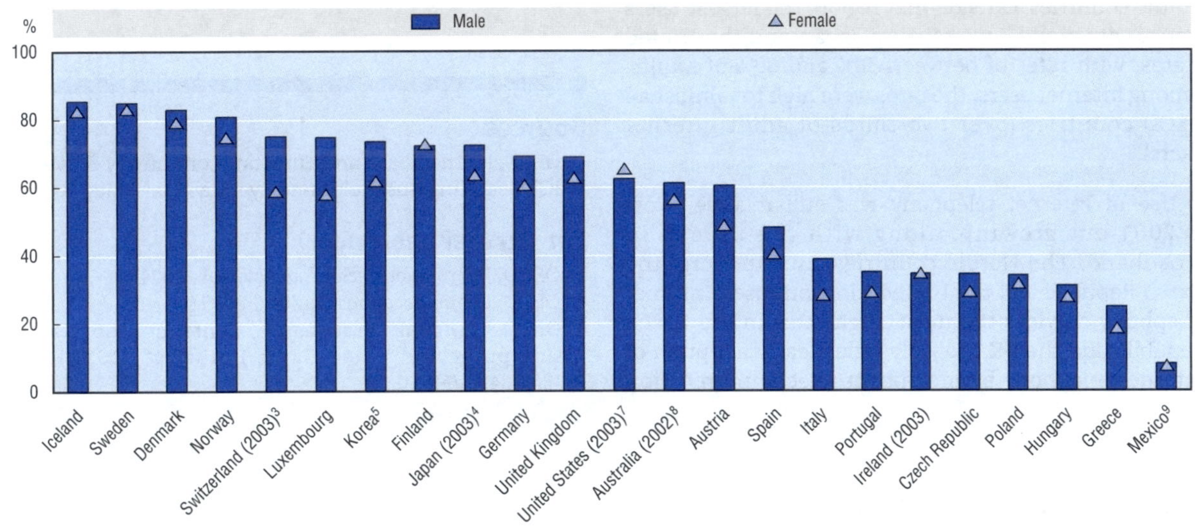


1. Data from the EU Community Survey on household use of ICT, which covers EU countries plus Iceland, Norway and Turkey generally relate to the first quarter of the reference year. For the Czech Republic, data relate to the fourth quarter of the reference year.
2. Individuals aged 16-74 years, except for Australia (18+), Canada (15+), the Czech Republic (15+), Japan (6+), Switzerland (14-74). Data generally refer to Internet use in the last 12 months.
3. Private data from *Arbeitsgruppe für Werbemedienforschung* (WEMF AG). Data refer to Internet users aged 14-74 who used the Internet at least once within the last six months.
4. Aged 6 years or over. The percentages may be relatively high compared to other countries as younger people tend to be greater users of the Internet than older age groups.
5. Individuals who use the Internet at least once a month. For 2000-03, data include Internet accessed only *via* computer. In the 2004 survey, Internet access through mobile phone was also included.
6. Percentage of all households with at least one member regularly using the Internet from any location.
7. Respondents are asked whether they use the Internet; no time period is specified.
8. Aged 18 years or over. For 2001, data for individuals aged over 64 have been estimated.
9. Used in the last 6 months.
10. Individuals in households in urban areas only.

StatLink: *http://dx.doi.org/10.1787/246801401553*

## D.8. Use of the Internet by individuals *(cont.)*

■ One of the most popular uses of the Internet, particularly in the Nordic countries, is to find information about goods or services. In 2004, Internet users in Iceland, Japan, Finland, Germany and Luxembourg used the Internet the most to find information about goods or services (at least 80% of users).

■ Adults in Japan, the United States, Korea, Germany, and Switzerland were most likely to use the Internet for online shopping. In Japan, the United States and Korea, more than a third of all individuals used the Internet for online shopping and represented at least half of these countries' Internet users.

■ Internet users in the Nordic countries (64% in Iceland and 70% in Finland and Norway) are most likely to use the Internet for online banking.

■ E-mail was the most popular of the Internet's communication services, and was used by more than half the adult population in many OECD countries. It was used by more than 60% of adults in each of the Nordic countries. Outside that region, the largest users were Switzerland, Luxembourg, Japan and the United States, with rates of between 56% and 60% of adults. Among Internet users, the rates were high for almost all OECD countries (over two-thirds of adult Internet users).

■ Use of Internet telephony was still relatively low in 2004 but growing, along with the uptake in broadband. The Nordic countries, Luxembourg, the Czech Republic and the United Kingdom used Internet telephony services the most. High rates in the Czech Republic and the UK probably reflect early adoption of Internet telephony by incumbent telecommunication carriers. The growing take-up of services, such as Skype, in the Nordic countries suggests that penetration is likely to increase rapidly in the future.

■ Playing or downloading games and music was most popular in Finland and Iceland. Other countries in which these activities are popular, with more than a quarter of the adult population participating, were Luxembourg and the United Kingdom. Among Internet users, Turkey, Finland and Greece had the highest participation, with over half of all adult Internet users playing/downloading games or music.

■ The Nordic countries, Luxembourg and Germany led the way in use of the Internet for interaction with public authorities (with over a third of adults). Internet users were also most likely to interact with public authorities in these countries, as well as in Hungary.

■ Using the Internet for job searches was most popular in Switzerland followed by the Nordic countries. Nearly a third of all Internet users in Switzerland and Finland searched for jobs online.

### Sources

- OECD, ICT database and Eurostat, Community Survey on ICT usage in households and by individuals, May 2005.

### For further reading

- OECD, *Information Technology Outlook*, 2004.
- OECD, *Communications Outlook*, 2005.
- OECD, "Digital Broadband Content: The Online Computer and Video Game Industry", DSTI/ICCP/IE(2004)13/FINAL.

### *The online games we play*

Online computer and video games are an increasingly popular use of the Internet, with games on mobile devices showing greatest growth. Online games include extensions of stand-alone games so that small groups of players can play together, to "Massively Multiplayer Online Role Playing Games" (MMORPGs), with more than 10 000 concurrent players. A major challenge for the online game industry is to produce new content appealing to the mass market or at least a market the size of Korea. The online market can be divided into three segments which are all growing in terms of absolute number of players: intensive, moderate and mass-market. On the one hand, Intensive PC game users are relatively few in number. They are usually male, aged 15-28, playing more than 20 hours per week. On the other hand, mass-market consumers tend to prefer playing games that are easy to learn and of short duration. With the moderate group being double the size of the intensive group and willing to spend approximately the same amount on games, it is becoming the key target of online game publishers. Two trends are: first, players are getting older and tend to have higher incomes. Second, more women are using computer games (MMORPGs increasingly attract women). These characteristics have important implications for games development as they suggest that market development will spread to broader population groups, specifically including women and older people.

## D.8. Use of the Internet by individuals *(cont.)*

**Internet use by type of activity,[1, 2] 2004**

As a percentage of adults

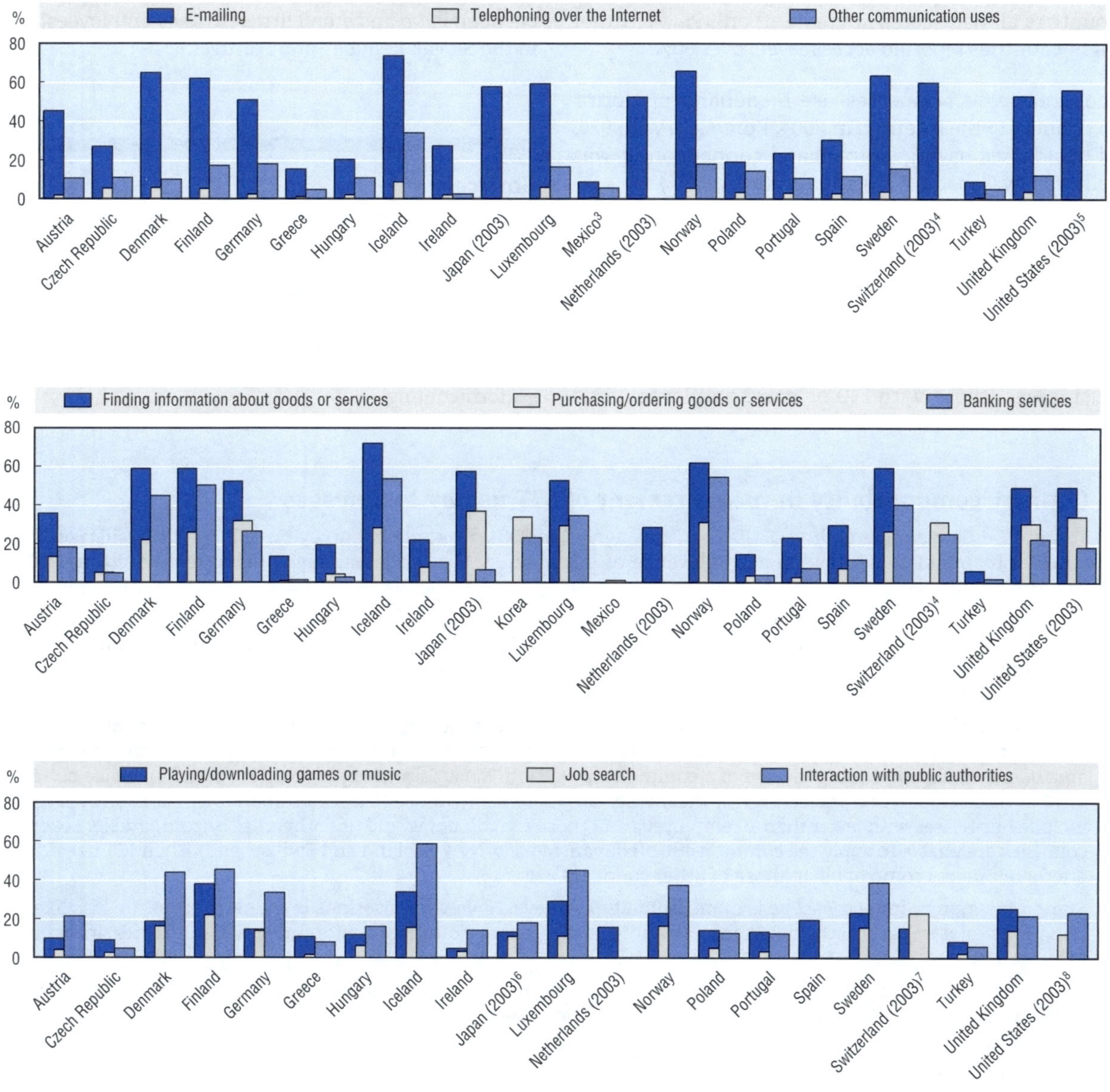


1. Data from the EU Community Survey on household use of ICT, which covers EU countries plus Iceland, Norway and Turkey, generally relate to the first quarter of the reference year. For the Czech Republic, data relate to the fourth quarter of the reference year.
2. Individuals aged 16-74 years, except for Australia (18+), Canada (15+), the Czech Republic (15+), Japan (15+), Switzerland (14-74). Data generally refer to Internet use in the last 12 months.
3. Telephoning over the Internet includes videoconferencing.
4. Private data from *Arbeitsgruppe für Werbemedienforschung* (WEMF AG). Data refer to Internet users aged 14-74 who used the Internet at least once within the last six months.
5. E-mailing includes instant-messaging.
6. Playing/downloading music only. Interaction with public authorities refers to obtaining government and local government information.
7. Playing/downloading games only. Private data from *Arbeitsgruppe für Werbemedienforschung* (WEMF AG). Data refer to Internet users aged 14-74 who used the Internet at least once within the last six months.
8. Interaction with public authorities refers to use of the Internet to search for information about government services or agencies.

StatLink: *http://dx.doi.org/10.1787/105112402428*

## D.9. Internet use by businesses

■ Use of the Internet by businesses (with 10 or more employees) has become fairly standard practice in most OECD countries. In 2004, Japan, Belgium and the Nordic countries all had access at greater than 95%. A further eight countries reported access levels over 90%.

■ Increasingly, businesses use broadband platforms to connect to the Internet. In 2004, Korea led, with 92% of businesses having a broadband connection. It was followed by Canada (82%) and Denmark (80%).

■ At more than 80%, Sweden and Denmark have the highest proportion of businesses with their own Web site. Japan, Finland, Germany and Austria recorded levels over 70%.

■ In most OECD countries, close to 100% of large businesses (those with 250 or more employees) had access to the Internet. Medium-sized firms (with 50 to 249 employees) also had very high rates of access. The most significant differences in Internet penetration rates between large and small firms (10 to 49 employees) were in the Slovak Republic and Portugal.

### Source

- OECD, ICT database and Eurostat, Community Survey on ICT usage in enterprises, May 2005.

### For further reading

- OECD, *Information Technology Outlook*, 2004.
- OECD, *Communications Outlook*, 2005.
- OECD, *Guide to Measuring the Information Society*, 2005 (forthcoming).

### *Country comparability in measurement of ICT use by businesses*

To improve data comparability, OECD countries agreed in 2001 on a model survey on ICT use by businesses. In order to maintain comparability and relevance of information, the model survey is being revised during 2005 (see D.9, p. 112).

The questionnaire part of the model is composed of self-contained modules which can be used either in their totality or as separate modules in specific national surveys. The model survey is intended to provide guidance for the measurement of ICT use (including e-commerce), and participating countries are encouraged to use it as a core part of their survey development work.

While the model survey has contributed to the use of common methodologies, concepts and data items across OECD countries, there is still some variation. The OECD has attempted to standardise data where possible, with the main area of standardisation being the use of a common size cut-off. Most countries provide data based on a size cut-off of 10 or more employees. Because larger businesses are more likely to use ICT, penetration rates for countries that include businesses with fewer than 10 employees and those that do not would not otherwise be comparable. Several countries are unable to apply the common cut-off (Japan, Mexico, New Zealand and Switzerland). Their ICT use rates are therefore less comparable to those of other countries.

Standardisation by industry scope is more difficult to achieve. However, variations in industry scope are less likely to have a major impact on the data than variations in size. Cross-country data for individual industries are found in D.9 p. 113.

While most countries provided data for 2004, some countries only had data available for earlier years. Given continuing growth in ICT use, this also affects data comparability.

Information on individual country variations regarding size, industry and survey year can be found in footnotes at the bottom of the next page.



OECD SCIENCE, TECHNOLOGY AND INDUSTRY SCOREBOARD 2005 – ISBN 92-64-01055-6 – © OECD 2005

## D.9. Internet use by businesses

### Business use of the Internet and Web sites, 2004

As a percentage of businesses with 10 or more employees[1]

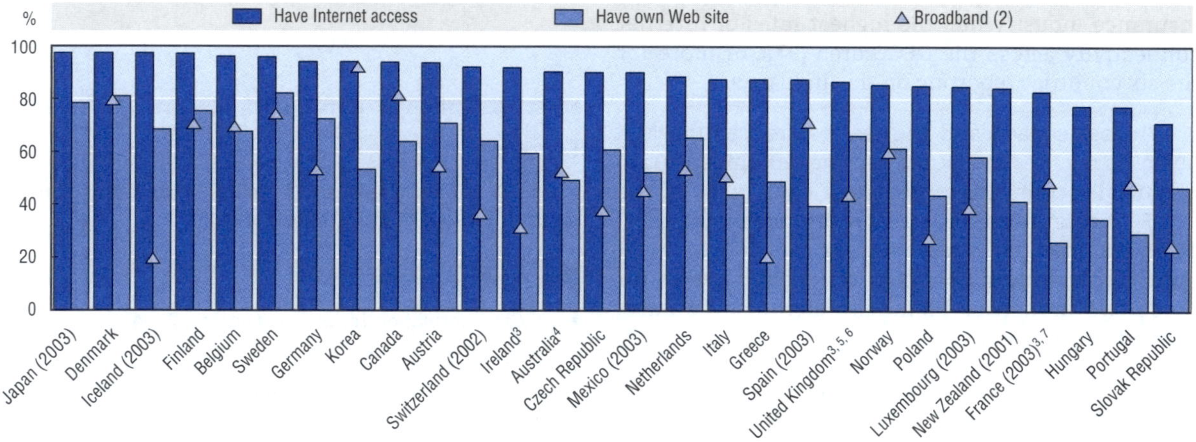


### Internet penetration by size class, 2004

As a percentage of businesses with 10 or more employees[1]

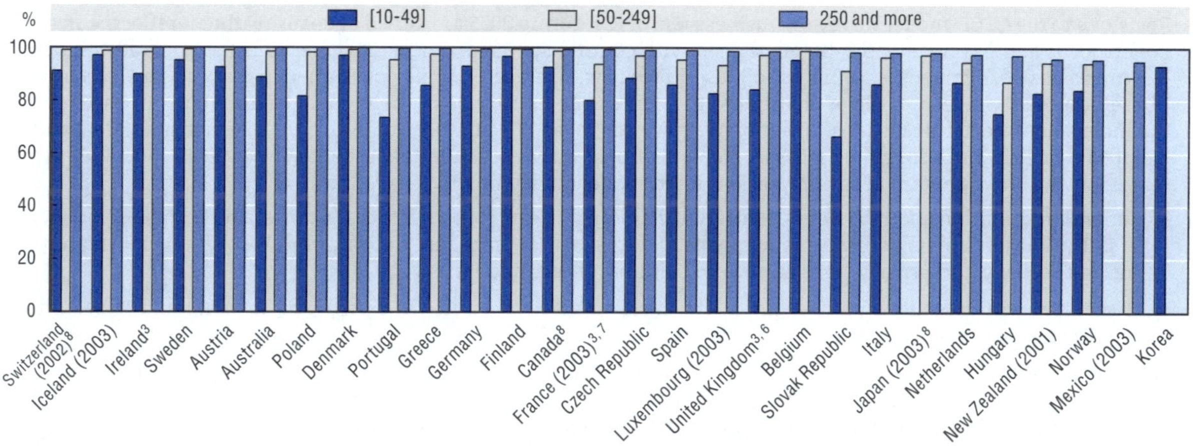


1. For most European countries, the following industries are included: Manufacturing, Construction, Wholesale and retail, Hotels and restaurants (part), Transport, storage and communication, Real estate, renting and business activities and Other community, social and personal service activities (part). For Australia, Agriculture, forestry and fishing, Education and Religious organisations are excluded. For Canada, Agriculture, fishing, hunting and trapping, and Construction – specialist contractors are excluded. For Japan, data refer to enterprises with 100 or more employees and exclude: Agriculture, forestry, fisheries and Mining. Korea includes: Agriculture and Fisheries, Light Industry, Heavy Industry, Petrochemicals, Construction, Distribution, Finance and Insurance, and Other services. For Mexico, data refer to enterprises with 50 or more employees and include: Manufacturing, Services and Construction. For New Zealand, data exclude Electricity, gas and water, Government administration and defence, and Personal and other services; the New Zealand survey also excludes businesses with five or fewer employees (FTEs) and those with turnover of less than NZD 30 000. For Switzerland, data refer to enterprises with 5 or more employees, and include the Manufacturing, Construction, Electricity, gas and water, and Services industries.
2. Most countries define broadband in terms of technology (*e.g.* ADSL, cable, etc.) rather than speed. However, Iceland only includes connections with bandwidth greater than or equal to 2 Mbps.
3. Includes all of NACE 92.
4. Web site includes a presence on another entity's Web site.
5. Broadband includes wireless connections.
6. Includes all of NACE 55.
7. Also includes Mining and quarrying, and Electricity, gas and water.
8. For Canada, 50-299 employees instead of 50-249 and 300 or more instead of 250 or more. For Japan, 100-299 instead of 50-249 and 300 or more instead of 250 or more. For Switzerland, 5-49 instead of 10-49 employees.

StatLink: *http://dx.doi.org/10.1787/378312630430*

## D.9. Internet use by businesses *(cont.)*

■ Internet penetration is relatively high in most sectors of the economy, at least among businesses with 10 or more employees. In 2004, the finance and insurance industry had the highest rates of Internet connectivity across the OECD area (97% or more for the six countries reporting on this industry).

■ Wholesale trade and the real estate, renting and business services industries had the next highest rate of Internet connectivity for most countries. Of the 21 OECD countries able to report on those industries, 14 had Internet penetration rates of over 90% for both. Countries reporting very high connectivity rates for these two industries included Belgium, Denmark, Finland and Sweden.

■ As in previous years, the retail industry had slightly lower penetration than other industries in most countries. Finland, Denmark, Sweden, Canada and Switzerland all had more than 90% of businesses in this category reporting an Internet connection.

### Source

- OECD, ICT database and Eurostat, Community Survey on ICT usage in enterprises, May 2005.

### For further reading

- OECD, *Information Technology Outlook*, 2004.
- OECD, *Communications Outlook*, 2005.
- OECD, *Guide to Measuring the Information Society*, 2005 (forthcoming).

### Measuring ICT use by businesses: revision of the OECD model survey

Revisions to the OECD model survey on business use of ICT during 2005 are aimed at ensuring that it reflects current policy needs and priorities and is better aligned with country survey practices. The revisions include questions on electronic business processes, selling of digitised products, use of electronic government services and IT security. These proposals will lead to major changes to the content and structure of the model questionnaire. In particular, the inclusion of electronic business questions requires changes to a number of the current questions that deal with electronic business (for instance, e-commerce questions, activities undertaken using the Internet and Web site features). The broad content of the proposed revised model questionnaire is as follows:

- General information about business use of ICT including: use of computers, the Internet and technologies such as LAN, WAN, intranets and extranets; means of accessing the Internet; Web site; and Web site "trust" features such as security and privacy statements and third party certification.
- IT security, with questions on IT security measures in place (*e.g.* anti-virus software, firewall) and IT security problems experienced.
- How business uses ICT in its operations including: incidence and value of e-commerce; the nature of products sold *via* the Internet and technologies used to sell those products; links between e-commerce and back-end systems, customer and supplier systems; benefits and barriers associated with e-commerce; use of the Internet for dealing with government and undertaking customer relationship functions; and use of computer networks in other areas of the business such as logistics, finance and human resources.
- Other information about business, for example, number of employees and annual turnover.

## D.9. Internet use by businesses *(cont.)*

### Internet penetration by industry, 2004

As a percentage of businesses with 10 or more employees in each industry group

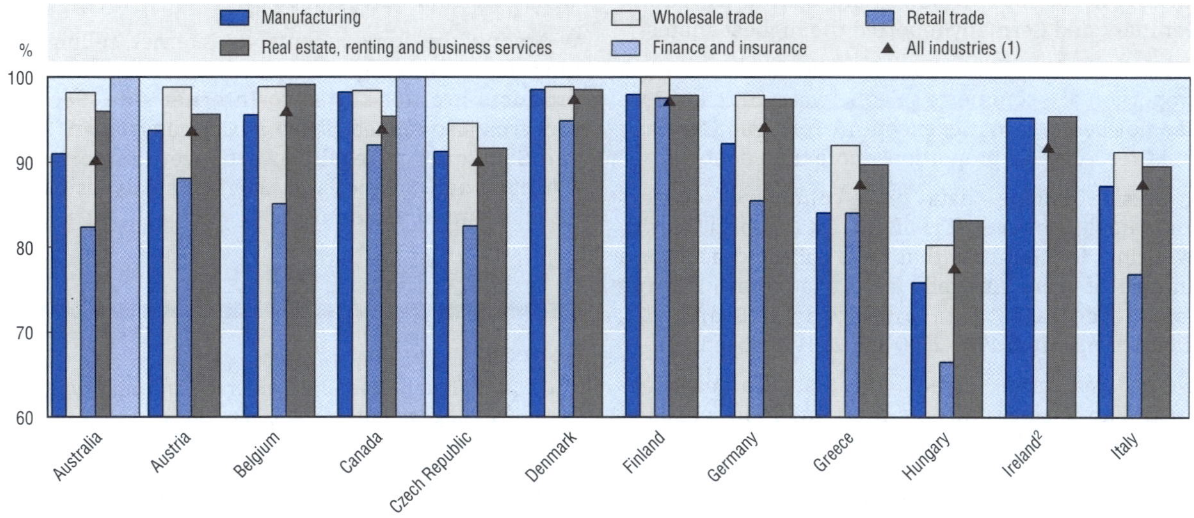


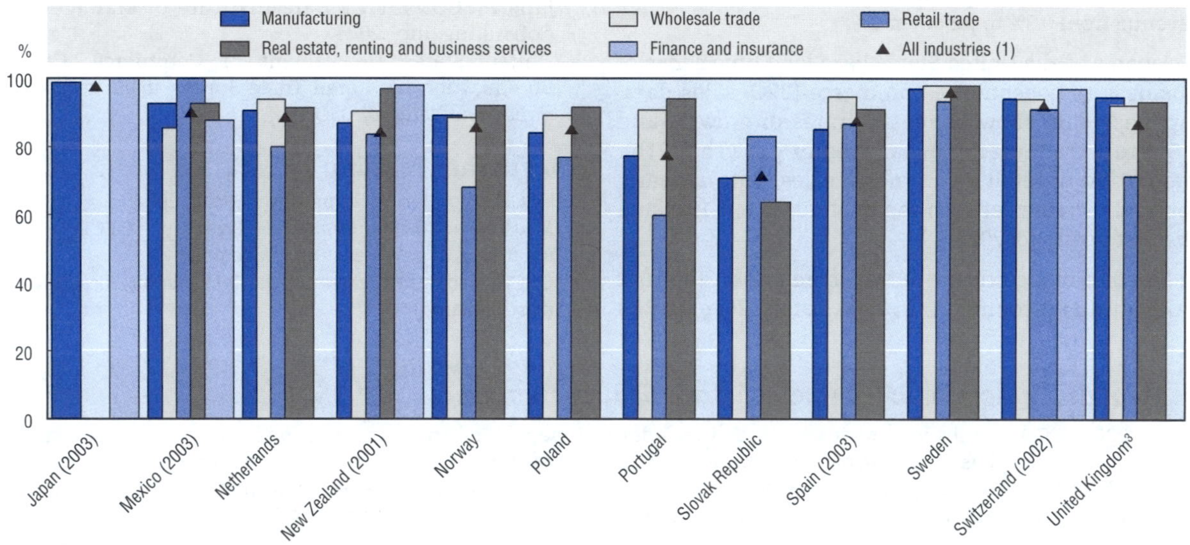


1. For most European countries, the following industries are included: Manufacturing, Construction, Wholesale and retail, Hotels and restaurants (part), Transport, storage and communication, Real estate, renting and business activities and Other community, social and personal service activities (part). For Australia, Agriculture, forestry and fishing, Education and Religious organisations are excluded. For Canada, Agriculture, fishing, hunting and trapping, and Construction – specialist contractors are excluded. For Japan, data refer to enterprises with 100 or more employees and exclude: Agriculture, forestry, fisheries and Mining. For Mexico, data refer to enterprises with 50 or more employees and include: Manufacturing, Services and Construction. For New Zealand, excludes Electricity, gas and water, Government administration and defence, and Personal and other services; the survey also excludes businesses with five or fewer employees (FTEs) and those with turnover of less than NZD 30 000. For Switzerland, data refer to enterprises with 5 or more employees, and include the Manufacturing, Construction, Electricity, gas and water, and Services industries.
2. "All industries" includes all of NACE 92.
3. "All industries" includes all of NACE 55 and NACE 92.

StatLink: *http://dx.doi.org/10.1787/171562525672*

## D.10. Electronic commerce volume

■ In most European countries, the volume of Internet and other e-commerce sales transactions (including proprietary EDI) is increasing as a percentage of total turnover. For 2004, Ireland, the United Kingdom, Denmark and Germany reported the highest shares.

■ For most European countries, the increase in the proportion of e-commerce sales between 2002 and 2004 has not been dramatic, except in Portugal, Germany and Greece, where proportions more than doubled.

■ Outside Europe, data on e-commerce are less comparable. However, it is of interest to look at growth over time for countries that have collected data for a number of years. Australia and Canada have Internet commerce sales data (including B2B and B2C transactions) from 1999-2000 and 2001, respectively.

■ The Australian Bureau of Statistics measures Australian business income from orders for goods or services received via the Internet or the Web. Survey results indicate that the value of Internet income increased significantly between 1999-2000 and 2003-04 (from less than 0.5% of total income to 2%). Statistics Canada's data for 2001 to 2004 show an increase in Internet sales as a proportion of total business operating revenue from 0.3% to just over 1%.

■ Japan and the United States have long time series of business-to-consumer e-commerce (B2C) sales data. Japanese data show increasing rates of growth, and US retail trade data reveal steady growth in the proportion of retail e-commerce sales, with a nearly fourfold increase between the final quarter of 1999 and the first quarter of 2005.

■ In spite of significant recent increases in Internet sales in many countries, in 2004, total B2C plus B2B Internet commerce still only represented 2% of turnover in Australia, 1% in Canada and ranged from 0.4 to 13% for European countries (see Annex Table D.10.1 for European data).

■ Among the impediments to Internet selling, the most commonly reported barrier, in 2004, was that products are not suited to Internet sale. Security concerns also ranked highly in Germany, Japan, Spain and Switzerland. Legal concerns were important in Germany and Switzerland. Barriers statistics can be found in Annex Table D.10.2.

### Sources

- OECD, ICT database and Eurostat, Community Survey on ICT usage in enterprises, May 2005.
- Australian Bureau of Statistics, Business Use of Information Technology, 1999-2000 to 2003-04, cat. No. 8129.0.
- Statistics Canada, CANSIM tables 187-0001 and 358-0010.
- Survey on Actual Condition and Market Size of Electronic Commerce, Ministry of Economy, Trade and Industry, Electronic Commerce Promotion Council of Japan (ECOM), NTT Data Institute of Management Consulting, Inc., 2004.
- United States Department of Commerce, Census Bureau, monthly Retail Trade Survey, *www.census.gov/mrts/www/data/pdf/05Q1.pdf*.

### For further reading

- OECD, *Information Technology Outlook*, 2004.
- *Measuring the Information Economy*, OECD, 2002, *www.oecd.org/sti/measuring-infoeconomy*.
- OECD, *Guide to Measuring the Information Society*, 2005 (forthcoming).

### Measuring electronic commerce: statistical challenges

In 2000, OECD member countries endorsed two definitions of electronic transactions (electronic sales and purchase orders) based on narrower and broader definitions of the communications infrastructure. According to the OECD definitions, it is the method by which the order is placed or received, not the payment or the channel of delivery, which determines whether the transaction is electronic commerce or not (see D.11).

While efforts have been made to harmonise definitions and concepts in this area, differences among countries remain. They include whether or not information on non-Internet e-commerce is collected; whether Internet commerce includes or excludes orders placed by conventional e-mail; and the conceptual basis of e-commerce value (for instance, the treatment of sales made by agents).

In addition, a number of conceptual and measurability issues remain unresolved. They include the challenge of converging technologies, which makes it increasingly difficult to split Internet and non-Internet e-commerce; the treatment of transactions in the finance sector; and statistical issues relating to the measurement of small values and rare events (these include high standard errors and the consequent reliability of disaggregated data). These and other issues are detailed in the forthcoming *Guide to Measuring the Information Society*, 2005.

Because of measurement differences, the approach taken here is, first, to make cross-country comparisons only on data sets that are reasonably comparable (*e.g.* Eurostat data on European countries) and, second, to look at longer time series from particular countries (Australia, Canada, Japan and the United States) and try to draw broad conclusions on e-commerce trends.

 OECD SCIENCE, TECHNOLOGY AND INDUSTRY SCOREBOARD 2005 – ISBN 92-64-01055-6 – 

## D.10. Electronic commerce volume

### Total e-commerce transaction value (including *via* the Internet), 2002 to 2004[1, 2]

As a percentage of total enterprise turnover

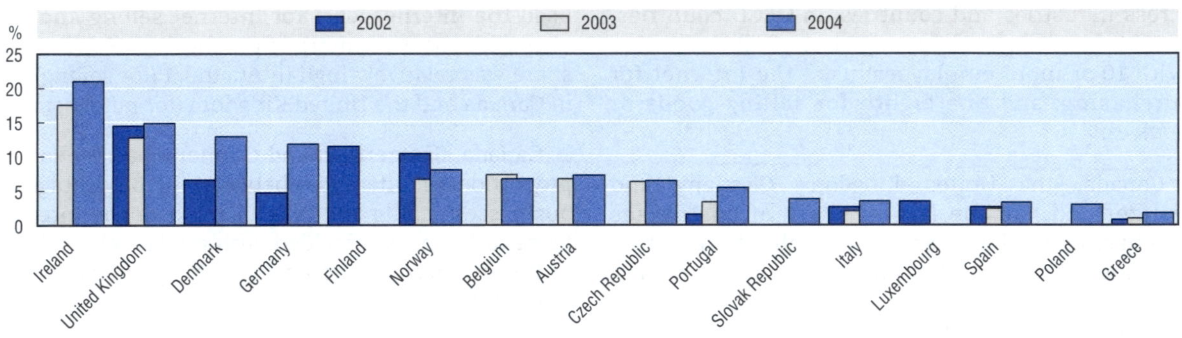


### Australian business[3] income from orders received *via* the Internet,[4] 1999-2000 to 2003-04

Percentage of total business income

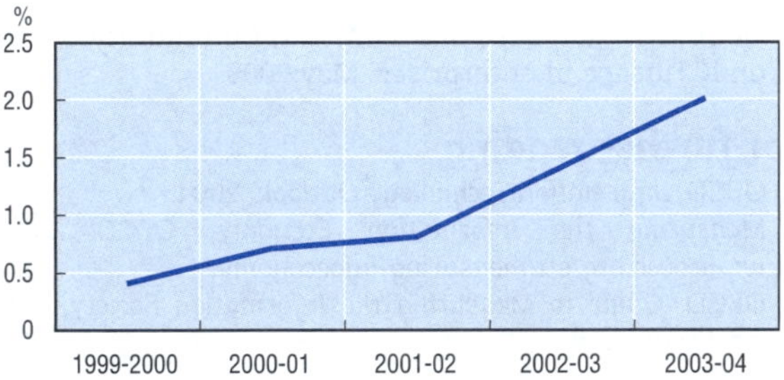


### Canadian business[5] sales conducted over the Internet,[6] 2001 to 2004

Percentage of total business operating revenue

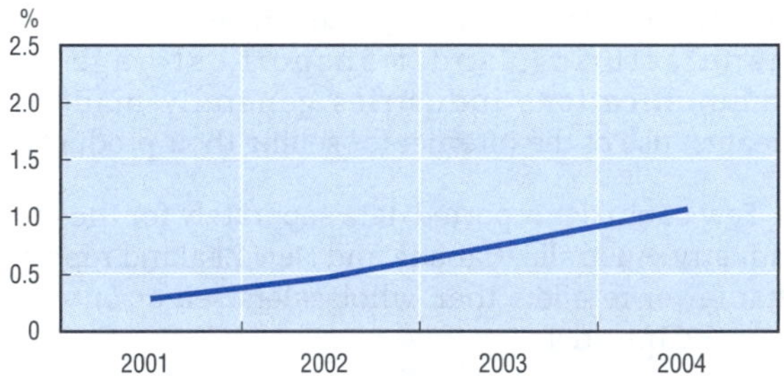


### Business-to-consumer electronic commerce in Japan,[7] 1998 to 2003

Percentage of total B2C sales

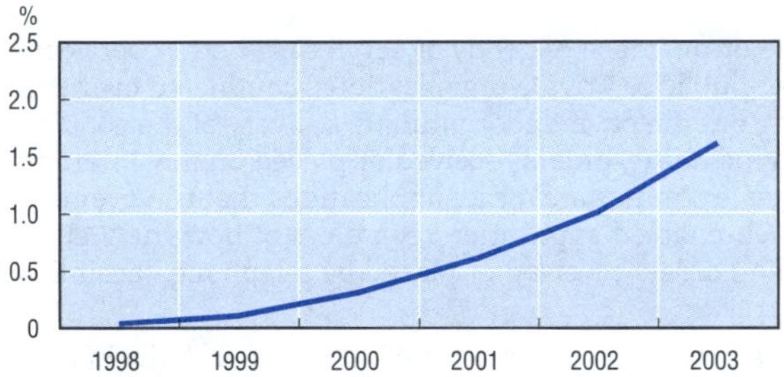


### Quarterly US e-commerce retail sales,[8, 9] 4th quarter 1999 to 1st quarter 2005

Percentage of total retail sales

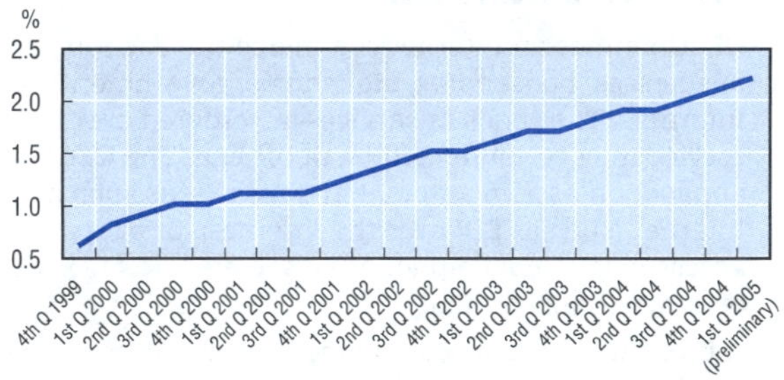


1. Enterprises in the following industries are included: Manufacturing, Wholesale and retail, Hotels and restaurants (part), Transport, storage and communication, and Real estate, renting and business activities.
2. Total sales *via* the Internet or other networks during reference year, excluding VAT.
3. Includes all employing businesses, except those in the following industries: Agriculture, forestry and fishing; Education; and Religious organisations.
4. Internet income is income resulting from orders received *via* the Internet or the Web for goods or services, whether or not payment and/or delivery were made over the Internet. E-mail orders over the Internet are explicitly included in the estimates. From 2003-04, an Internet order is defined as a commitment to purchase goods or services over the Internet.
5. Includes all but the smallest employing businesses (whose omission is considered to have a negligible impact on the value of e-commerce), except in the following industries: Agriculture, fishing, hunting and trapping, and Construction – specialist contractors.
6. Sales conducted over the Internet with or without online payment. Includes orders received by e-mail, on the business's Web site, by electronic data interchange (EDI) over the Internet and any other method of receiving orders *via* the Internet. Excludes Internet sales made on the business's behalf by other organisations and Internet sales made by the business on behalf of other organisations.
7. Includes mobile e-commerce.
8. E-commerce sales are sales of goods and services for which an order is placed by the buyer or price and terms of sale are negotiated over an Internet, extranet or EDI network, electronic mail, or other online system. Payment may or may not be made on line.
9. Estimates are adjusted for seasonal variation and holiday and trading-day differences, but not for price changes.

StatLink: *http://dx.doi.org/10.1787/815738050862*

## D.11. Internet commerce activity

■ Use of the Internet to sell goods or services varies across industries and countries. In OECD countries, in 2004, on average, about a quarter of all businesses (with 10 or more employees) used the Internet for purchasing, and one-eighth for selling goods or services.

■ Canada, the United Kingdom, Germany and Switzerland had the largest share of businesses purchasing *via* the Internet, with about half of all businesses doing so. The United Kingdom, Denmark, Sweden and Australia had the largest share selling goods or services *via* the Internet.

■ In most OECD countries for which data are available, the real estate, renting and business activities and the wholesale and retail industries made the most use of the Internet for purchasing. The wholesale and retail, manufacturing, and transport, storage and communications industries generally made the greatest use of the Internet for selling their products.

■ Few countries reported data separately for the retail industry. Australia, Canada and New Zealand reported that fewer retailers than wholesalers sell or purchase over the Internet.

■ As might be expected, the construction industry used the Internet least for Internet selling and was also a low user of Internet purchasing. However, its share was relatively high in Australia (for selling) and in Canada and the United Kingdom (for purchasing).

■ Canada, Switzerland and Germany had the largest proportionate differences between the percentages of businesses selling and purchasing over the Internet. Large differences coincided with a relatively high use of Internet purchasing and, generally, a low level of Internet selling.

### Source

- OECD, ICT database and Eurostat, Community Survey on ICT usage in enterprises, May 2005.

### For further reading

- OECD, *Information Technology Outlook*, 2004.
- *Measuring the Information Economy*, OECD, 2002, *www.oecd.org/sti/measuring-infoeconomy*.
- OECD, *Guide to Measuring the Information Society*, 2005 (forthcoming)

### *Measuring electronic commerce: OECD definitions of Internet and other electronic commerce transactions*

OECD defines an Internet commerce transaction as "the sale or purchase of goods or services, whether between businesses, households, individuals, governments, and other public or private organisations, conducted over the Internet". The goods or services are ordered over the Internet, but the payment or ultimate delivery of the good or service may be conducted on or off line. The OECD suggests including: orders received or placed on any Internet application used in automated transactions such as Web pages, extranets and other applications that run over the Internet (such as EDI over the Internet), or over any other Web-enabled application regardless of how the Web is accessed (*e.g.* mobile phone, TV set, etc.). It suggests excluding orders received or placed by telephone, facsimile or conventional e-mail.

A broader electronic commerce transaction may be conducted over any computer-mediated network (including the Internet). The OECD suggests including: orders received or placed on any online application used in automated transactions such as Internet applications, EDI over proprietary networks, Minitel or interactive telephone systems.

It should be noted that differences exist in the statistical treatment of e-commerce by countries. For more information, see box D.10 and the footnotes on the following page.

## D.11. Internet commerce activity

### Internet selling and purchasing[1] by industry,[2] 2004

Percentage of businesses with 10 or more employees in each industry group

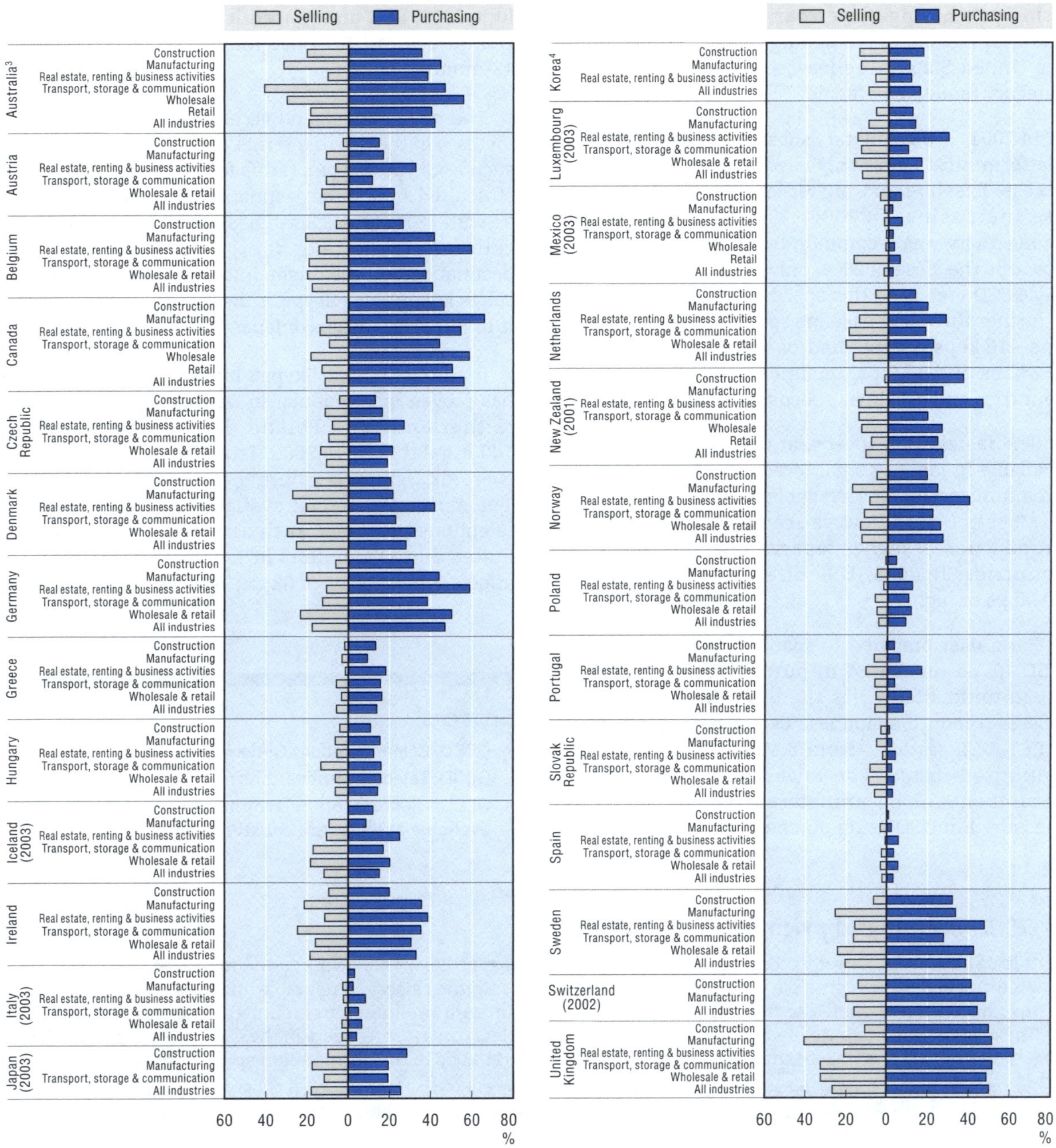

1. The definition of Internet selling and purchasing varies between countries, with some explicitly including orders placed by conventional e-mail (*e.g.* Australia and Canada) and others explicitly excluding such orders (*e.g.* Ireland, the United Kingdom and some other European countries). Most countries explicitly use the OECD concept of Internet commerce, that is, goods or services are ordered over the Internet but payment and/or delivery may be off line.
2. See Indicator D.9, note 1, on page 111.
3. Internet income results from orders received *via* the Internet or Web for goods or services, where an order is a commitment to purchase.
4. Data refer to enterprises with 1 or more employees.

StatLink: *http://dx.doi.org/10.1787/251333421086*

## D.12. Telecommunication pricing

■ The OECD compares mobile prices for users with low, medium and high volumes. For the low-user basket, the least expensive offers, measured in USD using purchasing power parity, were in Denmark, Finland, Iceland, Luxembourg, Sweden, Mexico and the United States. The least expensive offers in this category tend to be prepaid.

■ In 2004, DSL (digital subscriber line) was the platform most commonly used to provide broadband access. Baseline and higher-level broadband speeds are increasing. In 2002, 256 kbps downstream connectivity was a common baseline for DSL service. Towards the close of 2004, only six incumbents across the OECD area used this speed as their baseline offer. A further three had baseline speeds between 384 kbps and 416 kbps. Twelve had baseline speeds between 512 kbps and 1 Mbps. Incumbents in the remaining countries had baselines speeds at 1 Mbps or higher.

■ The fastest DSL speeds, at the close of 2004, were available in Japan, Korea, Sweden and France, where premium service was available to residential users at 10 Mbps or higher. However, competition is driving the introduction of higher capacity offers. In these four countries, in 2005, DSL offers were available at 20 Mbps or higher.

■ For a user prepared to spend between USD 30 and USD 40, as measured in purchasing power parity, Japan undoubtedly has the best offers. For around USD 34 a month a Japanese user can choose between NTT's DSL services from 8 Mbps to 24 Mbps with unlimited usage. The lowest-priced offer by an incumbent for an unmetered DSL service, when measured in USD using purchasing power parity, was Swisscom's 600 kbps service for USD 25.85, followed by SBC's baseline offer in the United States. Again, competition is forcing developments in pricing. In June 2005, SBC announced it would reduce baseline DSL prices to USD 14.95 for new customers with a 12-month contract.

■ The rise in broadband access has coincided with an increase in the use of Internet telephony from providers such as Skype. Skype's tariffs for Internet telephony are structured around the destination of the call rather than, as with PSTN (public switched telephone network) and cellular mobile telephony, a combination of the destination and the origin. In other words, the cost of a call to Japan, using Skype, is the same whether the caller is in Australia, Mexico or Japan.

■ In the OECD area, Skype's Internet telephony service has proven most popular in Denmark, followed by the Netherlands and Poland, in terms of users per 100 inhabitants. In 2005, Israel and Chinese Taipei overtook Denmark in terms of penetration of Skype. The early commercial availability of other Internet telephony providers, such as "Vonage" in the United States and "YahooBB!" in Japan, has undoubtedly affected the take-up of Skype in those countries.

### Sources


- OECD, *Communications Outlook* 2005, OECD, Paris.
- OECD, Telecommunications database 2005.
- OECD, Reports on telecommunications policy, 2005, available at *www.oecd.org/sti/telecom*.


### *OECD broadband pricing trends and VOIP*

It is not a simple matter to compare changes in prices and speeds for DSL owing to the modifications that have occurred in both. It is possible to compare offers from 2002 with the closest comparable offers for 2004, but speeds may have been upgraded or the closest offer has been changed from limited to unlimited data transfer or both. The overall trend for baseline offers, however, is relatively clear. On average, users in the OECD area paid USD 9.42 (USD 17 in PPP) less in 2004 than in 2002 for an increase of 514 kbps in the downstream speed of their connection.

By some estimates there were more than 1 100 Internet telephony providers in April 2005. At that time, Skype was the largest Internet telephony service in terms of users, with over 30 million. Skype makes available data on the total number of users in their largest 20 markets, and these data can be used to calculate the penetration rate for these countries.

## D.12. Telecommunication pricing

### OECD basket of low-user mobile telephone charges, August 2004

Annual charge, USD PPP, including tax

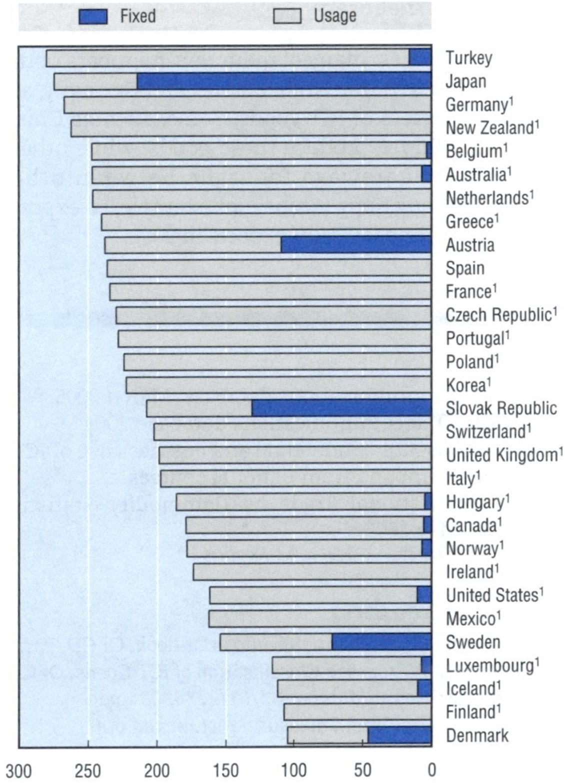


### Internet access by DSL in OECD member countries, November 2004

Monthly charge, USD PPP, including tax

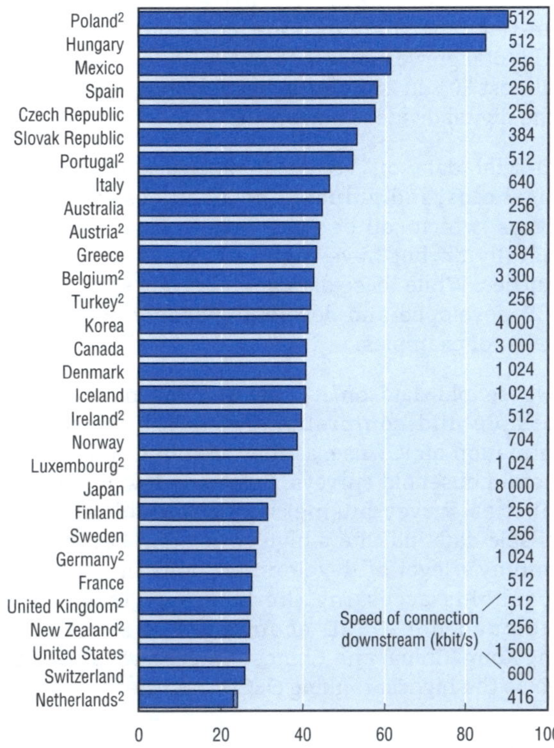


### Skype users per 100 inhabitants, April 2005

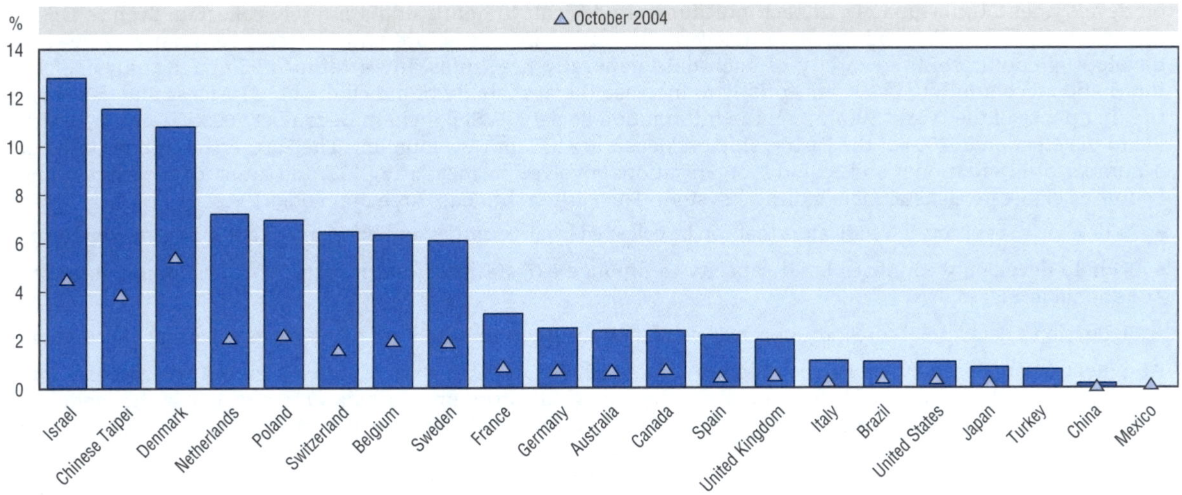


1. Package using prepaid card.
2. Offers that includes 1 Gbyte or more data transfer and capacity greater than 256 kbps. Other offers include unlimited data transfer.

StatLink: *http://dx.doi.org/10.1787/160652427415*

## D.13. ICT in non-OECD economies

■ Cellular wireless networks may offer the greatest potential for widespread access to and use of communication services in developing countries. The number of mobile subscribers has increased rapidly over the past decade and has recently grown more rapidly in developing countries than in OECD countries. The share of non-OECD countries in the world total grew from less than 10% in the early 1990s to almost 50% in 2003, an indication that at least part of the digital divide is narrowing.

■ Official data on access to and use of ICTs by households, individuals and businesses rely on surveys, which can be expensive to undertake and generally do not have high priority in developing countries. While these data are relatively scarce, non-OECD developed and developing economies offer a number of examples.

■ Household data on ICT use are the most widely available and comprehensive data in terms of information on ICT use, as they are often collected in general household surveys. Relatively few non-OECD countries survey businesses or individuals. The available data indicate a high correlation between an economy's level of development and the share of households accessing the Internet. The highly developed non-OECD economies of Singapore, Hong Kong (China) and Chinese Taipei have shares as high as the highest ranking OECD countries (see D.7).

■ In China, around 90 million persons aged 18 and over used the Internet in 2004, but they represent less than 8% of the corresponding population. China is expected soon to become the country with the largest number of Internet users.

■ Asian economies, many of them non-members of the OECD, together with the United States and Germany, are the main exporters of ICT goods. Some, such as China and Chinese Taipei, produce these goods, while others mainly act as gateways for trade between other countries. In Hong Kong (China), for example, re-exports accounted for almost 98% of exports in 2003.

### Sources

- OECD, Telecommunications database, March 2005.
- ITU, World Telecommunications database 2004.
- Data on household, individual and business use of ICTs have been compiled from national sources.
- OECD, International Trade by Commodity Statistics database, May 2005.
- UN COMTRADE database, May 2005.

### For further reading


- OECD (2005), *OECD Communications Outlook*, OECD, Paris.
- OECD (2003), *A Proposed Classification of ICT Goods*, OECD, Paris, *www.oecd.org/dataoecd/5/61/22343094.pdf*.
- Partnership site: *http://measuring-ict.unctad.org*.


### *Measuring ICT in non-OECD economies*

Because ICTs can be an effective tool for reducing poverty, policy makers wish to be informed about their impact on development. Unfortunately, impact indicators are difficult to define and are rarely collected. Even in OECD countries, such data, beyond supply of telecommunication infrastructure and services, are relatively new. In developing countries, the scarcity of such data generally precludes any attempt at impact analysis. The international community has been working to increase the availability of indicators of ICT access and use since the first phase of the World Summit on the Information Society (WSIS), held in December 2003 in Geneva, which led to the creation in 2004 of the Partnership on Measuring ICT for Development. The Partnership is composed of a number of international and regional organisations involved in measuring ICT and aims to help developing countries elaborate a sustainable indicator system. The Partnership has three main objectives:

- To develop a set of core ICT indicators that can be collected by all countries and harmonised at the international level.
- To help developing countries build capacity to produce ICT statistics and monitor ICT developments at the national level.
- To develop a database of core indicators and place it on the Internet, with links to relevant supporting information.

At a meeting organised by the Partnership in February 2005 in Geneva, a list of core indicators was agreed upon. The list currently consists of infrastructure indicators, indicators on access and use of ICT by households, individuals and businesses, and indicators on the ICT sector. It will be presented, along with a methodological annex, at the second phase of WSIS, to be held in November 2005 in Tunis. In time, other core indicators will be added, for example for ICT in relation to government, education and health.

## D.13. ICT in non-OECD economies

### Mobile cellular subscribers

OECD and non-OECD share in the world total, 1996-2003

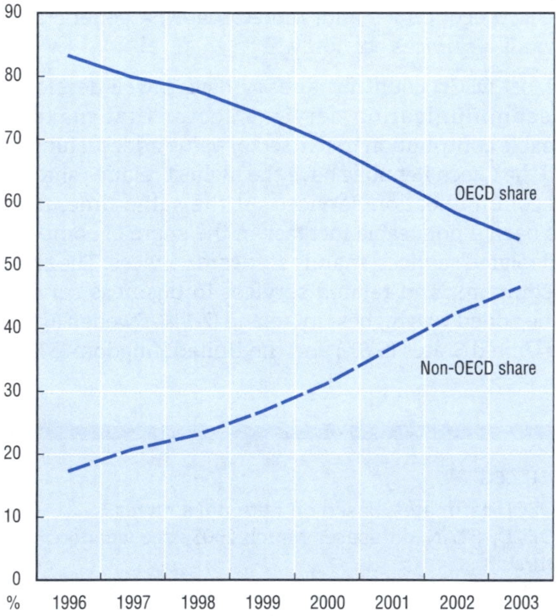


### Households and individuals[1] using the Internet

As a percentage of the total, 2004

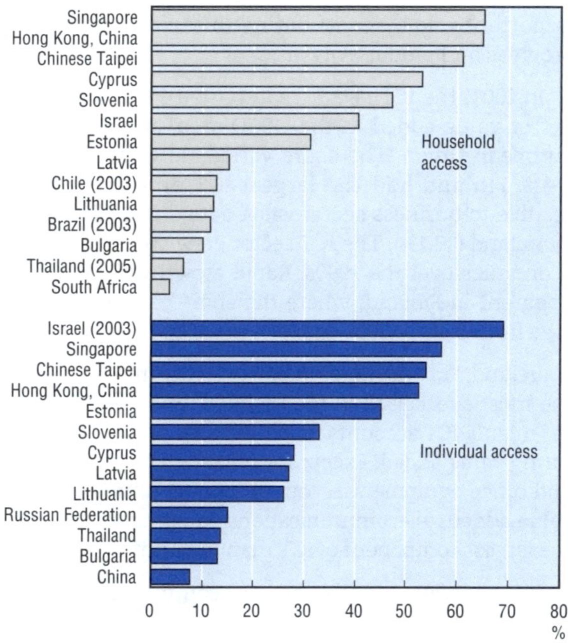


### Businesses using the Internet and with a Web site

As a percentage of the total, 2004

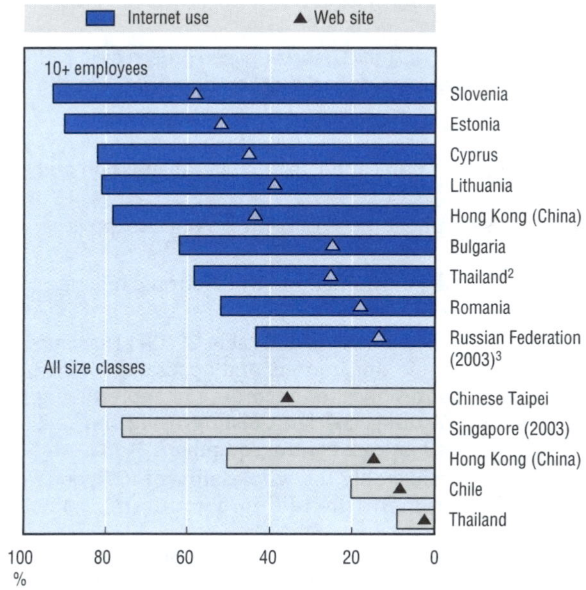


### Top exporting economies of ICT goods

Share of economy in the world total, 2003

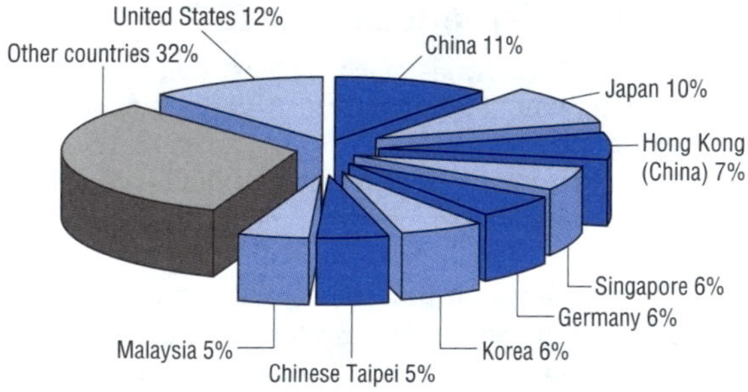


1. Age cut-off: Hong Kong (China) 10+; Singapore, Chinese Taipei and Thailand 15+; Bulgaria, Cyprus, Estonia, Latvia, Lithuania and Slovenia 16-74; China and the Russian Federation 18+; Israel 20+.
2. For Thailand 16+ employees.
3. For the Russian Federation, excluding enterprises with fewer than 100 employees in industry, construction and transport; 60 employees in agriculture and in R&D; 50 employees in wholesale trade; 30 employees in retail trade and consumer services; and 50 employees in other branches or fields of activity.

StatLink: *http://dx.doi.org/10.1787/524068603243*

## D.14. Size and growth of the ICT sector

■ Information and communication technologies (ICT) have been at the heart of economic change for more than a decade, and ICT-producing sectors play an important role by contributing to rapid technological progress and productivity growth.

■ In 2001, the ICT sector represented 9.6% of business sector value added in the OECD area, and 8.6% in the European Union. The share varied between 16.4% and 5.4%. Finland had the largest ICT-producing sector relative to business sector value added (16.4%) followed by Ireland (13.1%). The ICT sector grew strongly in OECD economies over the 1990s. Rapid growth was especially apparent in Finland, where the share of the ICT sector rose from 8.4% in 1995 to 16.4% in 2001.

■ Ireland, Finland, Korea, Japan and the United States are the most specialised in the manufacturing of ICT goods. In Finland, ICT accounts for almost 23% of total manufacturing value added. Except for Ireland, where computing and office equipment accounts for 6% of manufacturing value added, telecommunications equipment is typically the largest component of ICT manufacturing.

■ ICT services, such as telecommunication and computer services, often constitute between 70% and 90% of total ICT sector value added. In most OECD countries, ICT services have increased their relative share in the ICT sector, owing to the increasing importance of telecommunication services and software in OECD economies and, more broadly, a general shift towards a services economy.

■ Most OECD countries already have a well-developed telecommunication services sector that makes a sizeable contribution to ICT sector value added. Hungary and the Czech Republic have the highest relative share of telecommunication services. At the same time, there has been a noticeable increase in the share of computer and related services, mainly software services. The share of computer and related services in business services value added was highest in Ireland (7.1%), Sweden (6.2%), the United States (5.6%) and the United Kingdom (5%).

### Sources

- OECD estimates, based on national sources.
- OECD, STAN database, March 2005, see *www.oecd.org/sti/stan*.
- OECD, National Accounts databases, March 2005, see *www.oecd.org/std/national-accounts*.
- OECD, Education database, May 2005.

### *The OECD definition of the ICT sector*

In 1998, OECD countries reached agreement on an industry-based definition of the ICT sector based on Revision 3 of the International Standard Industrial Classification (ISIC Rev. 3). The principles underlying the definition are the following:

For manufacturing industries, the products of a candidate industry:

- Must be intended to fulfil the function of information processing and communication, including transmission and display.
- Must use electronic processing to detect, measure and/or record physical phenomena or control a physical process.

For services industries, the products of a candidate industry:

- Must be intended to enable the function of information processing and communication by electronic means.

The classes included in the 1998 definition are as follows:

**Manufacturing**: 3000 – Office, accounting and computing machinery; 3130 – Insulated wire and cable; 3210 – Electronic valves and tubes and other electronic components; 3220 – Television and radio transmitters and apparatus for line telephony and line telegraphy; 3230 – Television and radio receivers, sound or video recording or reproducing apparatus, and associated goods; 3312 – Instruments and appliances for measuring, checking, testing, navigating and other purposes, except industrial process control equipment; 3313 – Industrial process control equipment.

**Services**: 5150 – Wholesale of machinery, equipment and supplies (if possible only the wholesaling of ICT goods should be included); 7123 – Renting of office machinery and equipment (including computers); 6420 – Telecommunications; 72 – Computer and related activities.

In 2002, the definition of the ICT sector was amended to split 5150 into two classes (based on ISIC Rev. 3.1): 5151 – Wholesale of computers, computer peripheral equipment and software; 5152 – Wholesale of electronic and telecommunications parts and equipment.

The existence of a widely accepted definition of the ICT sector is the first step towards making comparisons across time and countries. However, the definition is not as yet consistently applied and data provided by member countries have been combined with different data sources to estimate ICT aggregates compatible with national accounts totals. For this reason, statistics presented here may differ from figures contained in national reports and in previous OECD publications.

## D.14. Size and growth of the ICT sector

### Share of ICT value added in business sector value added, 2001

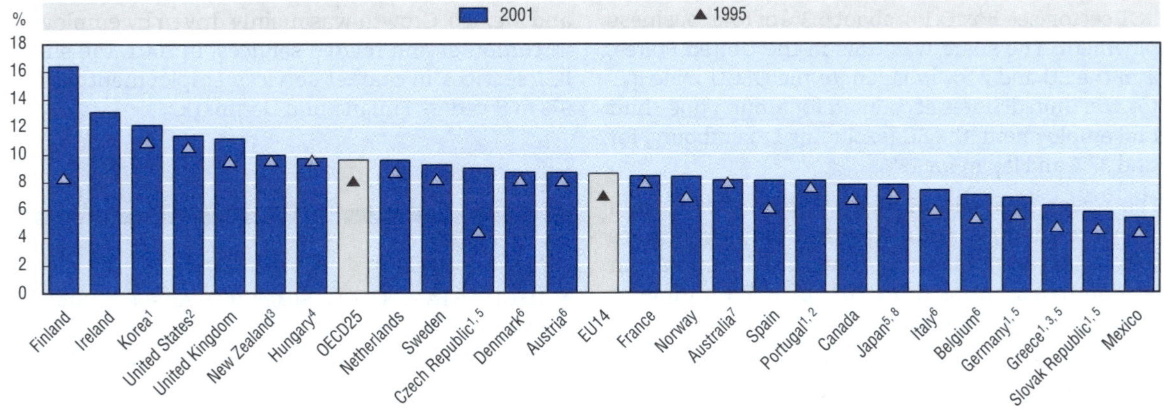

### Share of ICT manufacturing in total manufacturing value added, 2001

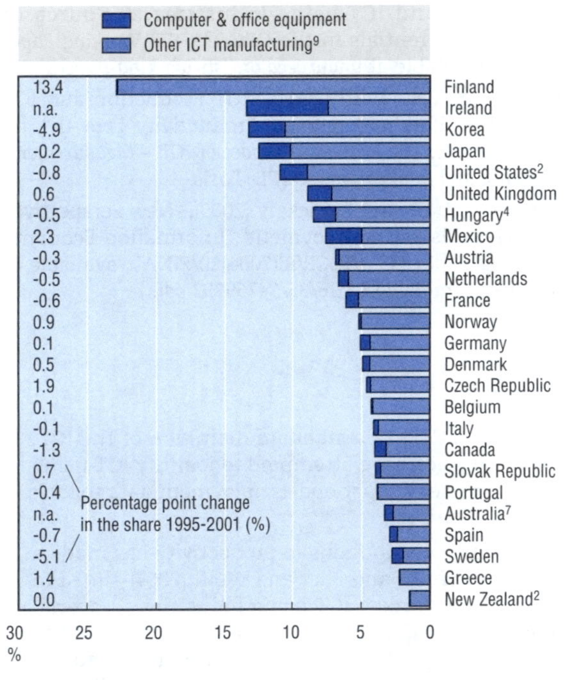

### Share of ICT services in total business services value added, 2001

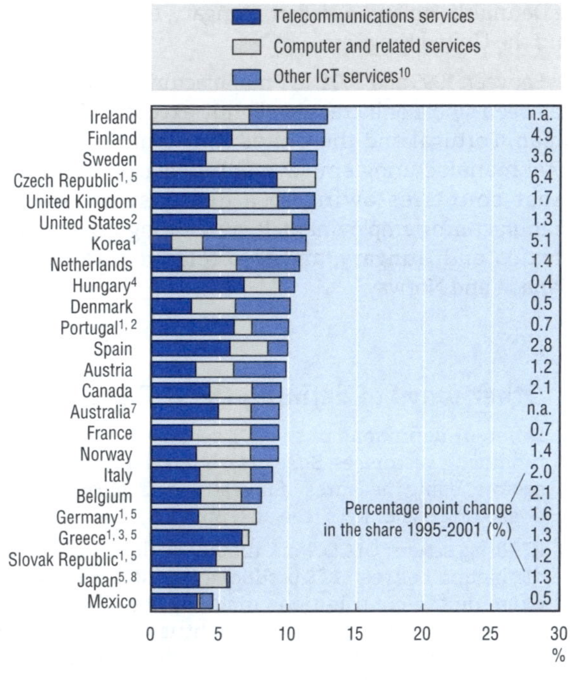

1. Rental of ICT goods (7123) is not available.
2. 1996 instead of 1995.
3. Postal services included with telecommunication services.
4. 1998 instead of 1995.
5. ICT wholesale is not available.
6. 2002.
7. 1998/99 and 2000/01 instead of 1995 and 2001 respectively.
8. Includes only part of computer-related activities (72).
9. "Other ICT manufacturing" includes communication equipment, insulated wire and cable and precision instruments, except for Greece, with communication equipment only.
10. "Other ICT services" includes wholesale and rental of ICT goods, except for Ireland where telecommunications services are also included.

StatLink: *http://dx.doi.org/10.1787/381515003783*

## D.15. Contribution of the ICT sector to employment

■ In 2001, the 23 OECD countries for which estimates are available employed more than 17 million persons in the ICT sector (see Box D.14), about 6.3% of total business employment. The share was 6.5% in the United States, 6.3% in the EU and 7.5% in Japan. In the OECD-wide ICT sector, the United States accounted for around one-third of total employment, the EU (excluding Luxembourg) for around 37% and Japan for 15%.

■ The Czech Republic, Hungary, Japan, Mexico and Korea were the only countries that employed more people in ICT manufacturing than in ICT services. In most countries, more than 70% of ICT employees worked in services activities.

■ The ICT sector has been a major source of employment growth. Over the period 1995-2001, OECD-area employment in the sector grew by more than 3.5 million, for average annual growth of over 4% a year. In all OECD countries except Portugal, employment in the ICT sector increased in relative terms, most notably in Denmark, Finland, Sweden, Hungary, the Netherlands and the United Kingdom.

■ Between 1995 and 2001, ICT manufacturing employment has been stable or increased slightly except in Germany, Japan, Portugal and the United Kingdom. Its share in total manufacturing employment increased slightly in most countries owing to a decrease in overall manufacturing employment. It grew strongly in Finland, Mexico and Hungary, and also relatively rapidly in Canada and Norway.

■ The share of ICT services in employment has increased since 1995 in all countries except Portugal and Mexico. Growth was mainly driven by employment in computer and related services. In 2001, the share of ICT services in market services employment was over 9% in Sweden, Finland and Denmark.

### Sources

- OECD, STAN: OECD Structural Analysis Statistics, March 2005.
- OECD, National Accounts database, March 2005.

### *For further reading*


- OECD, *OECD Information Technology Outlook 2004*, available at *www.oecd.org/sti/ito/*.
- Pilat, D. and F. Lee (2001), "Productivity Growth in ICT-producing and ICT-using Industries: A Source of Growth Differentials in the OECD?", *STI Working Paper* 2001/4, available at *www.oecd.org/sti/working-papers/*.
- Pilat, D. and A. Wölfl (2004), "ICT Production and ICT Use: What Role in Aggregate Productivity Growth", in: OECD (2004), *The Economic Impact of ICT – Measurement, Evidence and Implications,* OECD, Paris.
- Van Welsum, D. and G. Vickery (2005), "New Perspectives on ICT Skills and Employment", Information Economy working paper DSTI/ICCP/IE(2004)10/FINAL, available at *www.oecd.org/dataoecd/26/35/34769393.pdf*.


### *Other ways of defining the ICT sector*

Different definitions of the ICT sector serve different purposes. The OECD has a standard definition of the ICT-producing sector (see Box D.14), but other definitions exist. Various studies have attempted to identify ICT-using sectors, using measures of investment in ICTs. Another approach is to use occupational employment data to look at sectors' use of ICTs (see also Box D.2).

*ICT-using sectors*: OECD work mainly dealing with the analysis of sectoral contributions to productivity has made a distinction between ICT-producing and ICT-using sectors. Pilat and Lee (2001) and Pilat and Wölfl (2004) aimed to examine the contributions made by the ICT-producing sector and certain key ICT-using industries to overall productivity growth in OECD countries. The standard OECD definition of the ICT-producing sector was used to describe the behaviour of the ICT-producing industries. However, to identify key ICT-using industries, these studies examined empirical evidence on ICT use by industry based on capital flow matrices and capital stock estimates. They found that, while industrial classifications are not entirely compatible, some patterns emerge. In particular, certain manufacturing industries and certain services industries were the largest relative investors in ICT equipment. The use of ICT was mainly concentrated in the services sector and in some manufacturing industries.

*The ICT-skilled employment approach*: The term "ICT employment" can be interpreted in two ways: *i)* employment in industries traditionally identified as belonging to the ICT sector, including all types of occupations, even those bearing no relation to the use of ICTs; and *ii)* employment in occupations that use ICTs to variable degrees across all industries. Following the latter approach, ICT-using sectors are identified by their employment of ICT-skilled personnel, *i.e.* by the level of actual ICT usage, rather than by their investment in ICT capital. Industries are then ranked according to the degree of ICT-skills specialisation of their workforce, or the share of the industry's ICT-skilled employment. Many business services sectors have a very high share of such ICT-skilled employment (*e.g.* computer and related services, insurance, financial services, R&D), as do certain manufacturing sectors (*e.g.* electrical machinery and apparatus).


OECD SCIENCE, TECHNOLOGY AND INDUSTRY SCOREBOARD 2005 – ISBN 92-64-01055-6 – © OECD 2005

## D.15. Contribution of the ICT sector to employment

### Share of the ICT sector in business sector employment, 1995 and 2001

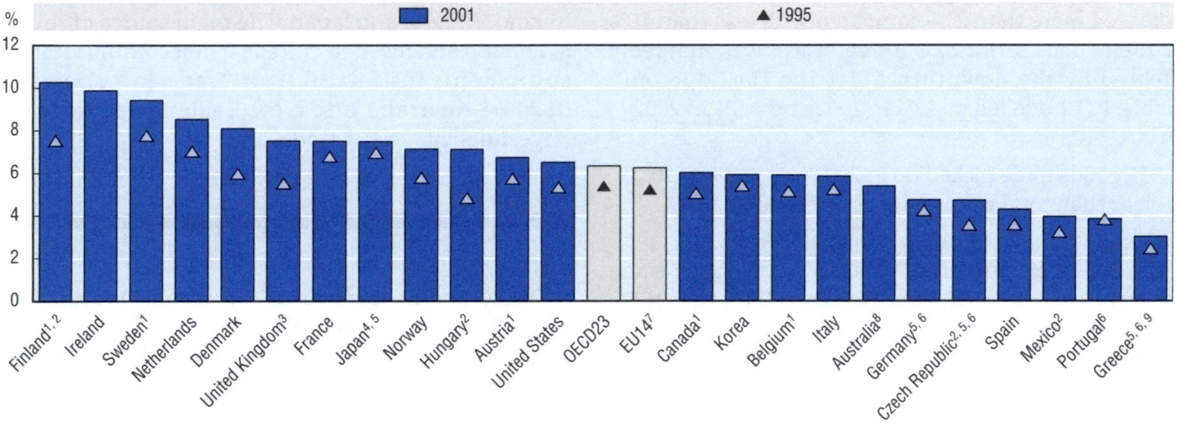


### Share of ICT manufacturing in total manufacturing employment, 2001

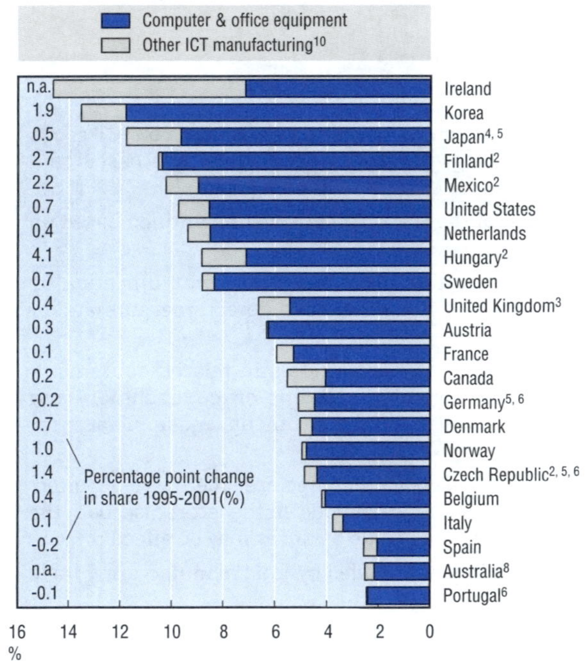


### Share of ICT services in market services employment, 2001

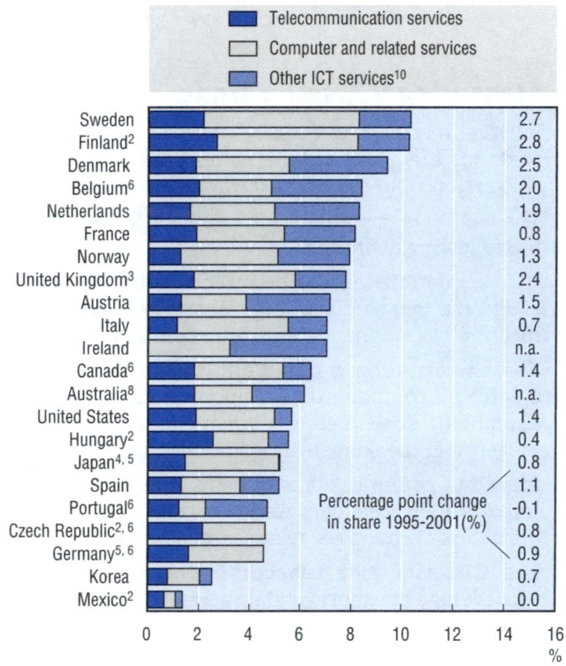


1. 2002.
2. Based on employees figures only.
3. Excludes self-employment.
4. ICT services include market research and public opinion polling.
5. ICT wholesale (5150) is not available.
6. Rental of ICT goods (7123) is not available.
7. Luxembourg not included.
8. 2000-01.
9. ICT manufacturing includes ISIC 30 and 32 only; postal services are included with telecommunication services.
10. "Other ICT manufacturing" includes communication equipment, insulated wire and cable and precision instruments. "Other ICT services" include wholesale and rental of ICT goods, except for Ireland, where telecommunication services are also included.

StatLink: *http://dx.doi.org/10.1787/003250155157*

## D.16. International trade in ICT goods

■ ICT goods trade grew much more rapidly than total trade in goods during the 1990s. In 2000, ICT trade increased more than 20% compared with less than 10% for total goods. After 2000, trade in ICT was markedly affected by the downturn following the "dotcom" bubble; ICT trade fell by 13% in 2001 and 4.5% in 2002.

■ ICT goods trade picked up in 2003 and grew by 10.2%, but less than total goods which increased at 16.4%.

■ In 2003, the share of ICT trade in total goods trade was very close to 1996 levels for the EU15, the OECD area and Japan, while that of the United States decreased by 2.6 percentage points.

■ ICT goods trade plays a particularly important role in Korea (28% of manufacturing trade in 2003), Ireland (25%), Hungary (25%), Mexico (21%), the Netherlands (21%) and Japan (20%). In the OECD, the share is 13% and 11% in the EU15.

■ Only eight countries showed a positive ICT trade balance in 2003. The surplus was highest in Korea, Ireland, Finland and Japan. The main source of surplus in Finland and Sweden is trade in telecommunications equipment; in Ireland, it is trade in computers. In 2003, Australia and New Zealand recorded the largest deficits in ICT trade.

### Sources

- OECD, International Trade by Commodity Statistics (ITCS) database, May 2005.
- OECD, STAN: OECD Structural Analysis Statistics, May 2005, see *www.oecg.org/sti/stan*.

### For further reading

- OECD, "A Proposed Classification of ICT Goods", available at *www.oecd.org/dataoecd/5/61/22343094.pdf*.
- OECD, *Communications Outlook* 2005, OECD, Paris.
- OECD, *Information Technology Outlook*, 2004.

### *Measuring ICT sector trade*

In December 2003, the OECD finalised a classification of ICT goods which was used to prepare data on ICT goods trade for this publication. The approach differs from the methodology previously used which was based on a conversion from the ICT sector to the Harmonized System (HS) used for classifying traded goods.

The OECD classification of ICT goods is based on the 2002 version of the HS. ICT goods were identified based on the following definition:

"ICT goods must either be intended to fulfil the function of information processing and communication by electronic means, including transmission and display, or use electronic processing to detect, measure and/or record physical phenomena, or to control a physical process".

The classification is broad and covers: telecommunications equipment, computers and related equipment, electronic components, audio and video equipment, and other ICT goods (including office machinery and equipment, some medical equipment, industrial process control equipment, and instruments and appliances for measuring, checking, testing and navigating).

Individual countries' data for both imports and exports include imported goods that are subsequently re-exported. Imports and subsequent re-exports may be in the same or in different reference periods. In the latter case, both the indicators of countries' relative trade performance and the indicators of their trade balances may be affected.

The ICT sector trade balance is calculated as ICT exports minus ICT imports divided by total manufacturing trade (the average of exports and imports).

## D.16. International trade in ICT goods

### ICT goods trade[1] by area, 1996-2003

As a percentage of total goods trade

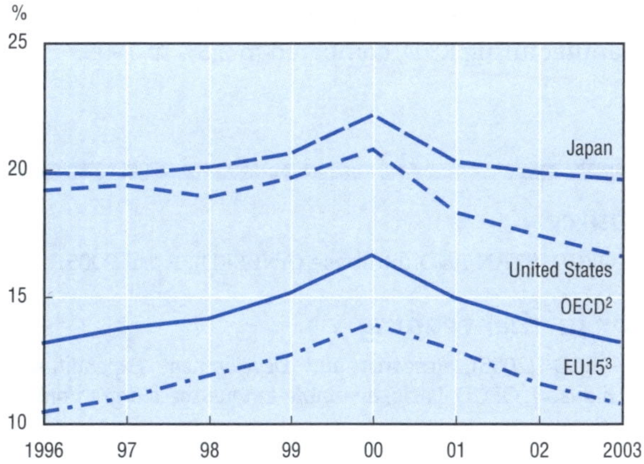


### ICT and total goods trade for the OECD,[2] 1996-2003

Index 1996 = 100

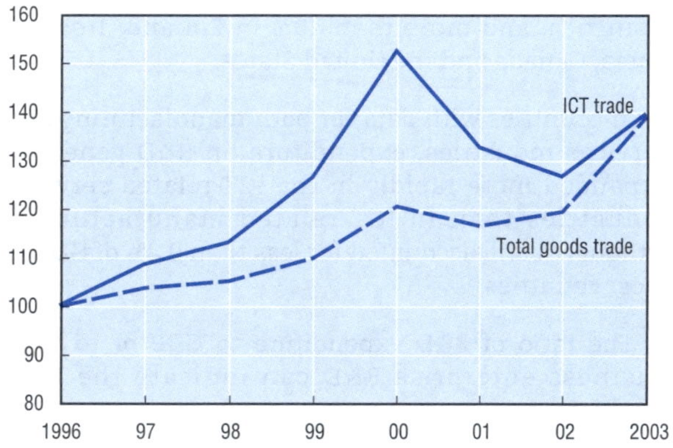


### ICT goods trade,[1] 2003

As a percentage of total goods trade

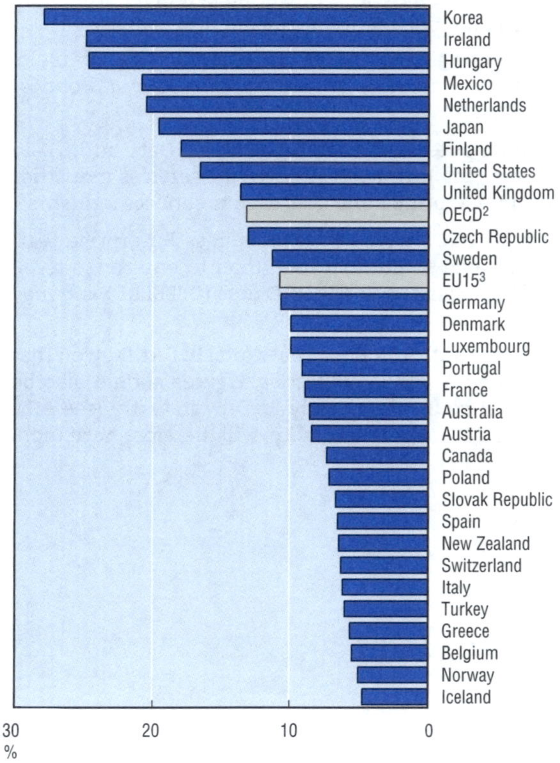


### ICT goods trade balance, 2003

As a percentage of total goods trade

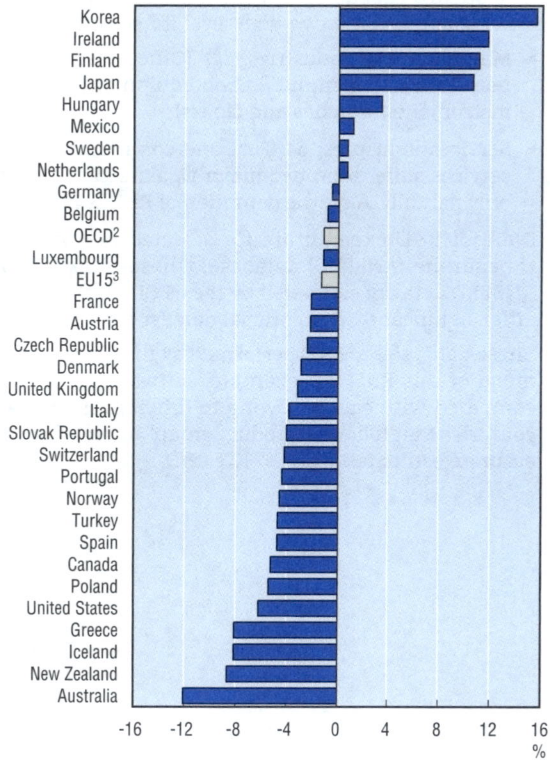


1. Average of imports and exports.
2. The OECD includes all member countries except the Slovak Republic in 1996 and Luxembourg from 1996 to 1998.
3. From 1996 to 1998, the EU15 includes all European Union member states except Luxembourg.

StatLink: *http://dx.doi.org/10.1787/538145685102*

## D.17. R&D in selected ICT industries

■ The ICT sector invests heavily in R&D and is highly innovative. In 2002, ICT manufacturing industries accounted for more than a quarter of total business R&D expenditure in manufacturing in most OECD countries, and more than 40% in Finland, Ireland, Korea, Canada and the United States.

■ In countries with data for both manufacturing and services industries, expenditure on R&D generally expanded more rapidly in the ICT-related services industries than in ICT-related manufacturing, although it still accounted for less than 0.2% of GDP in most countries.

■ The ratio of R&D expenditure to GDP or to total business enterprise R&D can indicate the R&D specialisation of ICT industries. Finland, Korea and Sweden are relatively more specialised than large countries in both ICT manufacturing and services. In 2003, Finland allocated 1.4% of GDP to ICT-related manufacturing R&D, compared to 0.5% in 1995.

### Source

- OECD, STAN R&D database (ANBERD), April 2005.

### For further reading

- OECD (2005), *Research and Development Expenditure in Industry*, OECD, Paris, available at *www.oecd.org/sti/anberd*.

### *Measuring ICT R&D expenditure*

The OECD definition of the ICT sector is largely based on the four-digit level of ISIC Rev. 3.1 (see D.14); however, data on R&D expenditure at the four-digit level are often lacking. Therefore, the ICT R&D indicators reported here are calculated at the two-digit level for selected ICT industries and include the following ISIC Rev. 3 divisions:

- Manufacturing industries: 30 (Office, accounting and computing machinery); 32 (Manufacture of radio, television and communication equipment apparatus); and 33 (Manufacture of medical, precision and optical instruments, watches and clocks).
- Services industries: 64 (Post and communications); and 72 (Computer and related activities). Data on R&D in services suffer from two major weaknesses. In certain countries, the R&D surveys cover the services industries only partially. Also, the definition of R&D is better suited to manufacturing industries than to services industries.

Data for R&D expenditure for selected ICT industries are from OECD's Analytical Business Enterprise R&D Expenditure (ANBERD) database, whose basis is more closely related to product field than to enterprise level. ANBERD data are estimated by the OECD on the basis of official business enterprise R&D data (OFFBERD) and may differ significantly from official data (see A.7).

These data refer to R&D performed by the ICT sector and may significantly underestimate total ICT R&D given that much of this R&D (for example, software R&D) may be performed in other industries. Figures should also be compared with caution owing to differences in the way in which countries classify R&D by industry (see A.7): countries that follow a "product group" approach (instead of principal economic activity) will therefore have more accurate estimates of "true" ICT R&D.

## D.17. R&D in selected ICT industries

### Business R&D expenditure by selected ICT manufacturing industries, 1995 and 2002

As a percentage of GDP

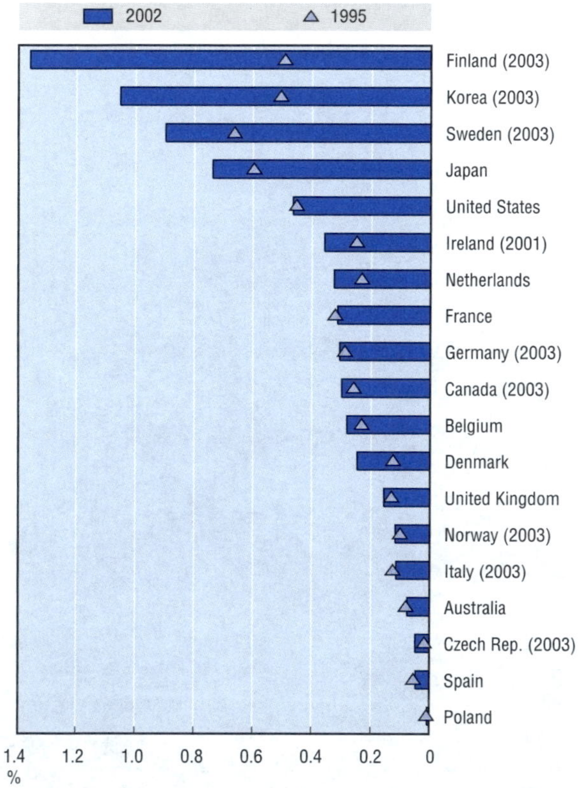


### Business R&D expenditure by selected ICT services industries, 1992 and 2002[1]

As a percentage of GDP

1. Owing to unavailability of R&D for class 642 (Telecommunications), division 64 (Post and telecommunications) is used as a proxy. Available information shows that in the United States, class 642 accounts for 97-98% of the R&D in division 64.

StatLink: *http://dx.doi.org/10.1787/610050068883*

# E. KNOWLEDGE FLOWS AND THE GLOBAL ENTERPRISE

## E.1. Trends in international trade and investment flows

■ In the dynamic, multidimensional process of globalisation, national economies can integrate their activities and internationalise through various channels: trade in goods and services, capital and labour flows, transfer of production facilities and/or technology.

■ Such economic linkages are not new, but the intensity and multiplicity of transactions have accelerated over the past decade, making the economic implications of globalisation harder to quantify.

■ More advanced information and communication technology, lower transport costs, firms' strategies regarding location and the need to exploit technological and organisational advantages worldwide, liberalisation of trade and financial flows, etc., have all contributed to the speed-up of the globalisation process.

■ Financial transactions (portfolio investment, direct investment, other investment) have been the fastest-growing segment of international transactions. The upsurge in direct investment and portfolio investment was especially significant in the second half of the 1990s.

■ Such investment flows have also proved highly volatile. Portfolio investment, for instance, declined in the early 1990s, tripled between 1995 and 1999, declined again from 1999 and only showed a significant increase in 2003. For its part, foreign direct investment rose sharply from 1997, but has steadily declined since 2000.

■ The lowering of tariff and non-tariff barriers has contributed to a steady rise in international trade. The share of trade in international transactions has remained high, averaging 15% of OECD GDP over the 1990s.

■ In terms of the composition of international trade, the share of trade in goods is more than four times the share of trade in services.

### Sources

- OECD, National Accounts database, April 2005.
- IMF, Balance of Payments Statistics, April 2005.

### For further reading

- OECD (2005), *Measuring Globalisation – OECD Handbook on Economic Globalisation Indicators*, OECD, Paris, available at: *www.oecd.org/sti/measuring-globalisation.*
- OECD (2005), *Measuring Globalisation – Economic Globalisation Indicators*, OECD, Paris, forthcoming.

### *Main components of international trade and investment*

**Balance of payments current account**

*Trade in goods and services.* Data relating to trade in goods and services correspond to each country's exports to, and imports from, the rest of the world. These data are collected to determine the balance of payments. Data relating to international trade in goods are also collected in customs surveys, but are generally not systematically comparable to balance of payment data. Since trade data need to be compared with data on international investment, the balance of payments has been chosen as source data to ensure comparability of trade and investment data.

*Investment income.* This covers receipts and payments on external financial assets and liabilities, including receipts and payments on portfolio investment, direct investment and other investments, and receipts on reserve assets.

**Balance of payments financial account**

*Foreign direct investment.* Foreign investment is defined as being "direct" if the foreign investor holds at least 10% of the ordinary shares or voting rights in the firm in which the investment is made. This 10% threshold means that the direct investor is able to influence and participate in the management of a firm but does not necessarily have complete control.

*Portfolio investments.* In cases where the foreign investor holds less than 10% of the capital (ordinary shares or voting rights) of a firm, the investment is considered to be a "portfolio investment". This type of investment usually corresponds to "short-term" investments for which the investor does not intend to influence the management of the firm.

*Other investment.* This is a residual category that covers all financial transactions not covered by direct investment, portfolio investment or reserve assets. It includes trade credits, loans, currency and deposits, and other assets and liabilities.

 OECD SCIENCE, TECHNOLOGY AND INDUSTRY SCOREBOARD 2005 – ISBN 92-64-01055-6 – © OECD 2005

## E.1. Trends in international trade and investment flows

### Trends in international trade and investment components,[1] OECD[2]

1990 = 100, current prices

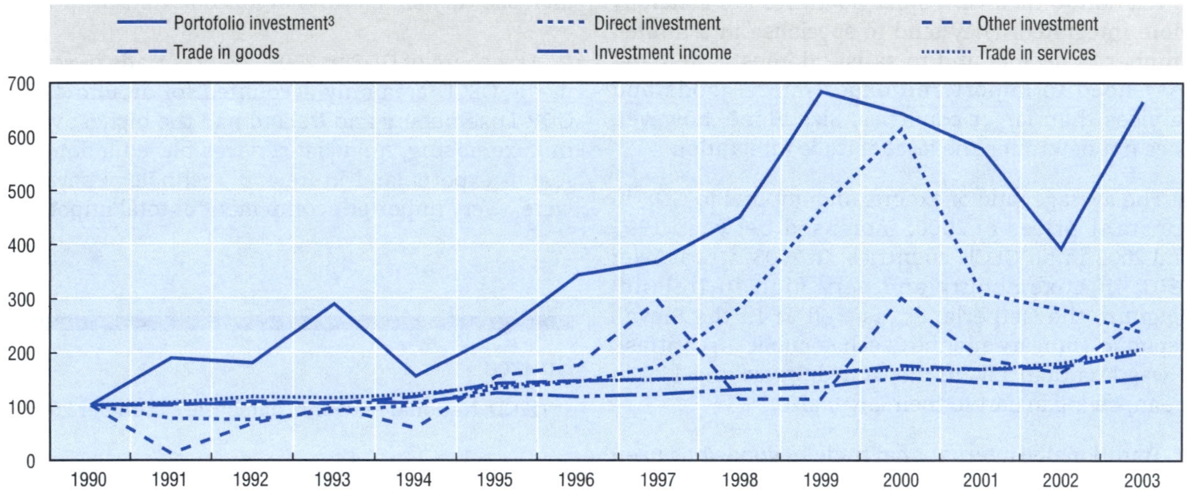


### Main components of the current account, OECD,[4] average 1999-2003

As a percentage of GDP,[5] gross basis

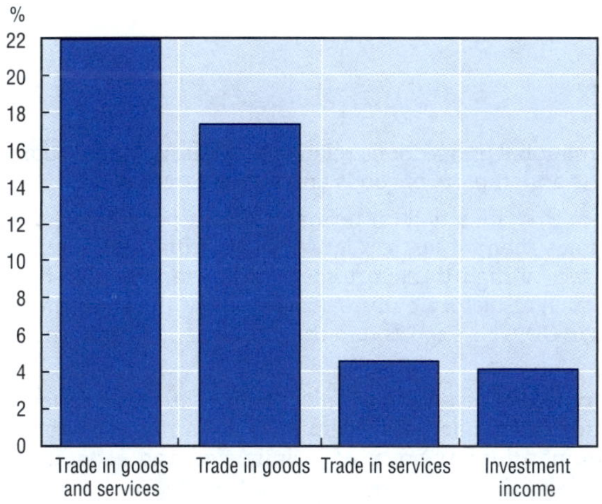


### Main components of the financial account, OECD,[4] average 1999-2003

As a percentage of GDP,[6] net basis

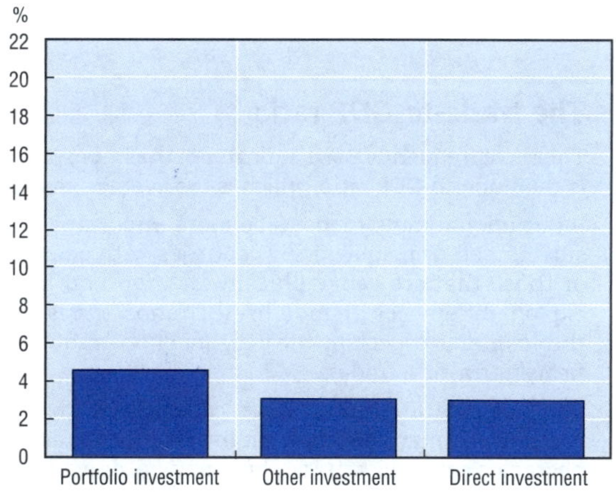


1. Average imports + exports or average assets + liabilities.
2. OECD excludes the Czech Republic 1990-92, Greece 1998, the Slovak Republic 1990-92 and 2001.
3. Excluding financial derivatives.
4. Excluding the Slovak Republic in 2001.
5. Imports + exports divided by 2 and by GDP.
6. Assets + liabilities (in absolute terms) divided by 2 and by GDP.

StatLink: *http://dx.doi.org/10.1787/674320182036*

## E.2. International trade

■ Their international trade in goods and services reflects countries' integration into the world economy. In relation to their GDP, small countries are generally more integrated. They tend to specialise in a limited number of sectors and to satisfy domestic demand they need to import and export more goods and services than larger countries. Size alone, however, does not determine the level of trade integration.

■ The average ratio of exports and imports to GDP, in constant prices of 2000, increased between 1995 and 2003 in all OECD countries. In 2003, it was over 130% in Luxembourg and very high in Ireland, Belgium, the Netherlands, as well as in the Slovak Republic, Hungary and the Czech Republic. In contrast, it was less than 13% in the United States and 11% in Japan, owing in part to their larger size.

■ Traditionally, international trade in goods has been the principal channel for economic integration. Over the past 20 years, however, other forms of transactions have become increasing prevalent (*e.g.* foreign direct investment, portfolio investment) as firms increasingly implement global strategies and capital movements are liberalised.

■ In 2003, the average trade-to-GDP ratio of goods in the OECD area was 35.8%, up from 26.4% in 1995, an increase very similar to that for total trade.

■ As a share of GDP in 2003, average trade in services in the OECD area only accounted for around 4.4% of GDP. Luxembourg and Ireland had the highest values. In Luxembourg, financial services played a dominant role in exports, and in Ireland, technology payments were a very important component of total imports.

### Source

- OECD, National Accounts database, December 2004.

### For further reading


- OECD (2005), *Measuring Globalisation – OECD Handbook on Economic Globalisation Indicators*, OECD, Paris, available at: *www.oecd.org/sti/measuring-globalisation.*
- OECD (2005), *Measuring Globalisation – Economic Globalisation Indicators*, OECD, Paris, forthcoming.


### *The trade-to-GDP ratio*

The most frequently used indicator of the importance of international transactions relative to domestic transactions is the trade-to-GDP ratio, which is the average share of exports and imports of goods and services in GDP.

International trade tends to be more important for countries that are small (in terms of size or population) and surrounded by neighbouring countries with open trade regimes than for large, relatively self-sufficient countries or those that are geographically isolated and thus penalised by high transport costs. Other factors also help explain differences in trade-to-GDP ratios across countries, such as history, culture, (trade) policy, the structure of the economy (especially the weight of non-tradable services in GDP), re-exports and the presence of multinational firms (intra-firm trade).

The trade-to-GDP ratio is often called the trade openness ratio. However, the term "openness" to international competition may be somewhat misleading. In fact, a low ratio does not necessarily imply high (tariff or non-tariff) obstacles to foreign trade, but may be due to the factors mentioned above, especially size and geographic remoteness from potential trading partners.

## E.2. International trade

### Total exports and imports, 2003

Average, as a percentage of GDP

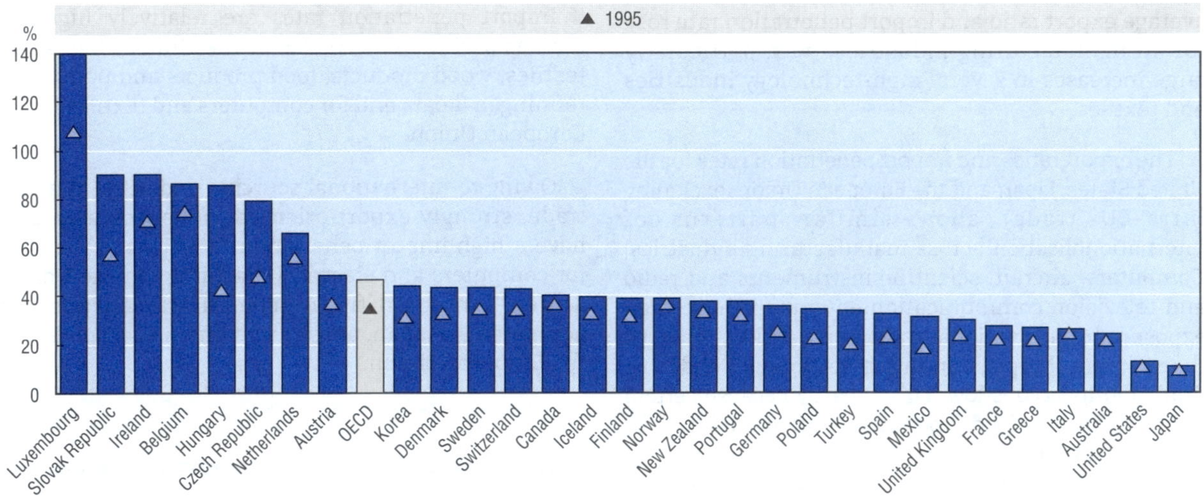


### Exports and imports of goods, 2003

Average, as a percentage of GDP

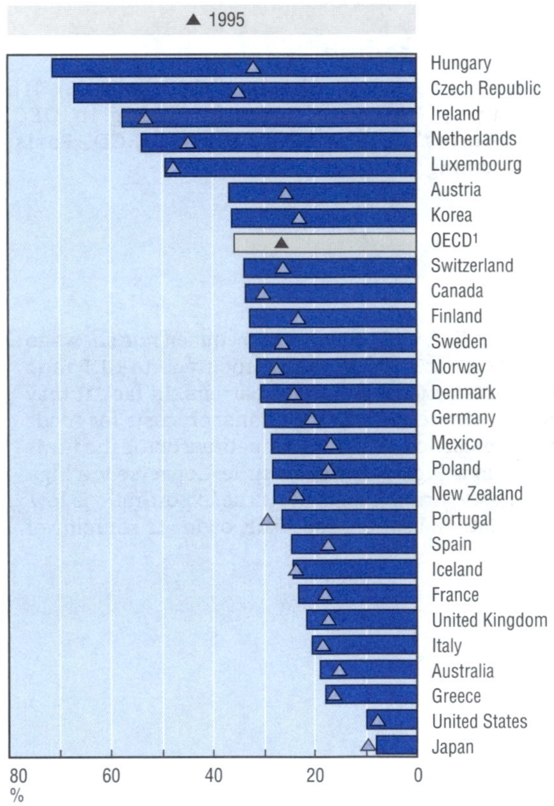


### Exports and imports of services, 2003

Average, as a percentage of GDP

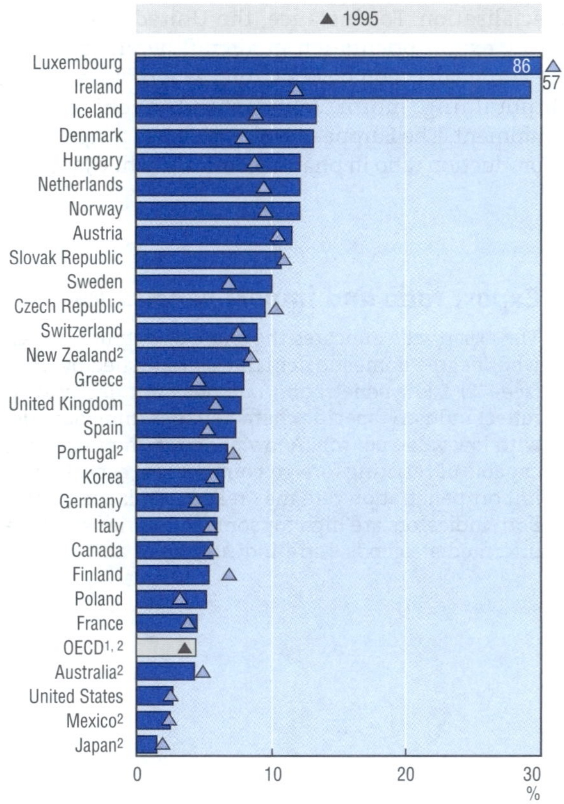


1. Belgium and Turkey are not included in the OECD total.
2. Data for Australia, Japan, Mexico, New Zealand and Portugal refer to 2002, which also affects the OECD average.

StatLink: *http://dx.doi.org/10.1787/766280153661*

## E.3. Exposure to international trade competition by industry

The exposure of manufacturing industries to international trade increased in OECD countries over the past decade. For the 1992-2001 period, the average export ratio and import penetration rate rose for all manufacturing industries, with particularly large increases in several high-technology industries and textiles.

The export ratios and import penetration rates for the United States, Japan and the European Union (excluding intra-EU trade) show similar patterns of internationalisation across manufacturing industries. Computers, aircraft, scientific instruments and radio and television communication equipment have high exposure to international trade competition, whereas the exposure of paper, printing, metal products and food, drink and tobacco is low. This is partly because certain products, such as food products, are often produced for local or regional markets, while others, such as television equipment, may serve global markets and be involved in considerable intra-industry trade.

A marked difference between the export ratio and import penetration rate for specific manufacturing industries may indicate patterns of national specialisation. For instance, the United States has a strong export orientation in aircraft, while Japan and the European Union have a strong export orientation in shipbuilding, motor vehicles and machinery and equipment. The European Union also has a high export to production ratio in pharmaceuticals, while Japan has a strong export orientation in scientific instruments, electrical machinery and rubber and plastics.

Import penetration rates are relatively high for textiles and motor vehicles in the United States, for textiles, wood products, food products and petroleum refining in Japan, and for computers and textiles in the European Union.

Owing to international sourcing and intra-industry trade, strongly export-oriented industries may also have a high import penetration rate. This is the case for computers and electrical machinery in the United States, for scientific instruments and transport equipment in Japan, and for aircraft and computers in the European Union.

### Sources

- OECD, STAN Indicators Database, March 2005, see: *www.oecd.org/sti/stan/indicators*.
- OECD, STAN BTD – Bilateral Trade Database, March 2005, see: *www.oecd.org/sti/btd*.

### For further reading


- D. Pilat, A. Cimper, K. Olsen and C. Webb (2005), "The Changing Nature of Manufacturing in OECD Economies", *STI Working Paper*, OECD, Paris, forthcoming.


### Export ratio and import penetration

The *export ratio* indicates the share of output Y which is exported, *i.e.* X/Y, and the *import penetration rate* shows to what degree domestic demand D is satisfied by imports M, *i.e.* $M/D = M/(Y - X + M)$. As for the trade-to-GDP ratio (see E.2) a low penetration rate does not necessarily imply the existence of high import barriers. In fact, it may reflect industry-specific characteristics unfavourable to international trade, such as high transport costs for goods with low value per ton. A low penetration rate may also reflect the presence of highly competitive domestic firms capable of resisting foreign competition, especially if the export ratio is high at the same time. Conversely, a high import penetration rate may reflect weak competitiveness of domestic firms, especially if the export ratio is low. Both indicators are high for some industries and reflect their internationalisation, especially owing to sourcing of intermediate goods, intra-industry trade and intra-firm trade.

## E.3. Exposure to international trade competition by industry

### Exposure to international trade competition for manufacturing industries in OECD countries,[1] 2001

Average of export to production ratio and import penetration

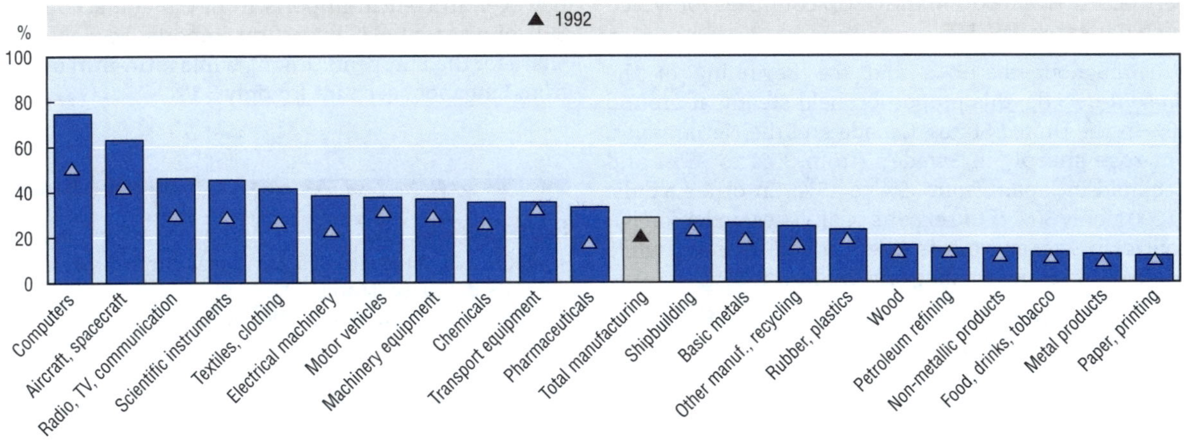


### Exposure of manufacturing industries, 2001

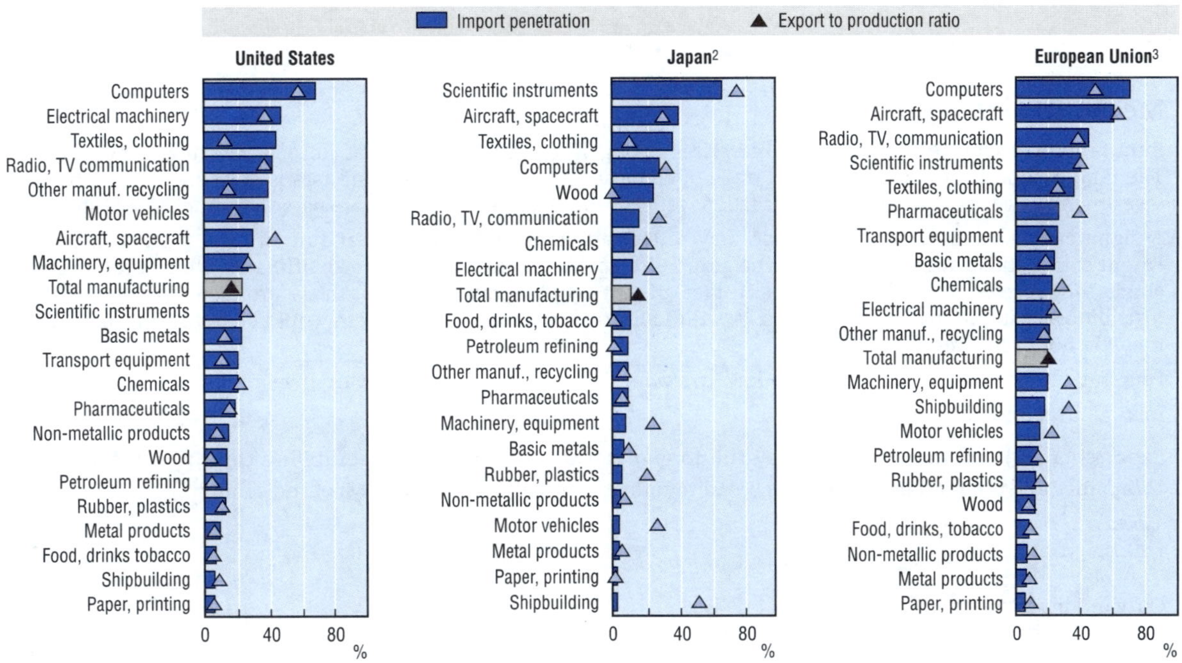


1. Including Austria, Canada, Denmark, Finland, France, Germany, Italy, Japan, Korea, the Netherlands, Norway, Portugal, Spain, Sweden, the United Kingdom and the United States. Data include intra-OECD trade.
2. Motor vehicles (ISIC 34) include Railroad and other transport equipment (ISIC 352 + 359).
3. Including Austria, Denmark, Finland, France, Germany, Italy, the Netherlands, Portugal, Spain, Sweden and the United Kingdom. Intra-EU trade is excluded.

StatLink: *http://dx.doi.org/10.1787/740268554017*

## E.4. Intra-firm trade

■ The share of intra-firm exports in total exports of manufacturing affiliates under foreign control ranges between 15% and 60% in the OECD countries for which such data are available.

■ Throughout the 1990s and the beginning of the present decade, this proportion held steady at around 50% in the United States, Canada and the Netherlands, but rose sharply in Sweden (from 35% to 75%) and declined in Japan (from 35% to 15%). In other words, in 2001, only 30% of the exports of affiliates under foreign control in Sweden were destined for non-affiliates, while in Japan the corresponding proportion was 85%.

■ In 2002, the ratio of intra-firm trade by US parent companies was highest in Switzerland, Argentina, Panama and Singapore for exports, and in Singapore, Ireland and Hong Kong (China), for imports.

■ Intra-firm trade with partner countries, even if it represents substantial value, may account for only a small percentage of overall intra-firm trade. For example, intra-firm imports from Canada account for less than 30% of aggregate US imports from Canada, but almost 60% of those from Singapore. In absolute value, however, intra-firm imports from Canada account for 36% of aggregate US intra-firm imports (*i.e.* double the share for the European Union), while intra-firm imports from Singapore account for only 5.1%.

### Sources

- OECD, OECD Statistics on Measuring Globalisation – AFA database, March 2005.
- OECD, International Trade by Commodity Statistics database, May 2005.

### For further reading

- OECD (2005), *Measuring Globalisation – OECD Handbook on Economic Globalisation Indicators*, OECD, Paris, available at: *www.oecd.org/sti/measuring-globalisation*.
- OECD (2005), *Measuring Globalisation – Economic Globalisation Indicators*, OECD, Paris, forthcoming.

### Measuring intra-firm trade

Intra-firm trade refers to trade between enterprises belonging to the same group that are located in different countries. The ratio of intra-firm trade to the total trade of countries publishing the relevant data is quite high. Once foreign investments have been made, these transactions reflect centralised decisions that are part of a group's global strategy.

A significant portion of intra-firm trade may reflect affiliates' better understanding of local market demand. Parent corporations and other firms in the group often prefer to export to their own affiliates, which then sell the goods they receive to local consumers. In fact, parent corporations could sell these products directly to local distributors, without involving affiliates. It is difficult to determine whether there would be fewer transactions if they did not pass through affiliates.

Four basic indicators are proposed: two for inward investment and two for outward investment.

Inward investment:

Exports ($X_F^{intra}$) and imports ($M_F^{intra}$) by the foreign-controlled affiliates in compiling countries with parent companies and other affiliates located abroad to total exports (*X*) and imports (*M*) of the compiling countries:

$$\frac{X_F^{intra}}{X}, \frac{M_F^{intra}}{M}$$

Outward investment:

Exports ($X_{out}^{intra}$) and imports ($M_{out}^{intra}$) by parent companies in the compiling country with their affiliates abroad to total exports and imports:

$$\frac{X_{out}^{intra}}{X}, \frac{M_{out}^{intra}}{M}$$

These indicators might also be calculated in terms of total exports and imports by these firms, and by industrial sector and by country of origin and destination.

In the case of imports by affiliates under foreign control in host countries and by parent companies controlled by compiling countries, it would also be very useful to distinguish between imports destined for use in their own production, those resold as same-state goods on the domestic market, and those re-exported, either in the same state or after further processing.

 OECD SCIENCE, TECHNOLOGY AND INDUSTRY SCOREBOARD 2005 – ISBN 92-64-01055-6 – © OECD 2005

## E.4. Intra-firm trade

### Share of intra-firm exports in total exports of affiliates under foreign control (inward investment),[1] 1990-2001

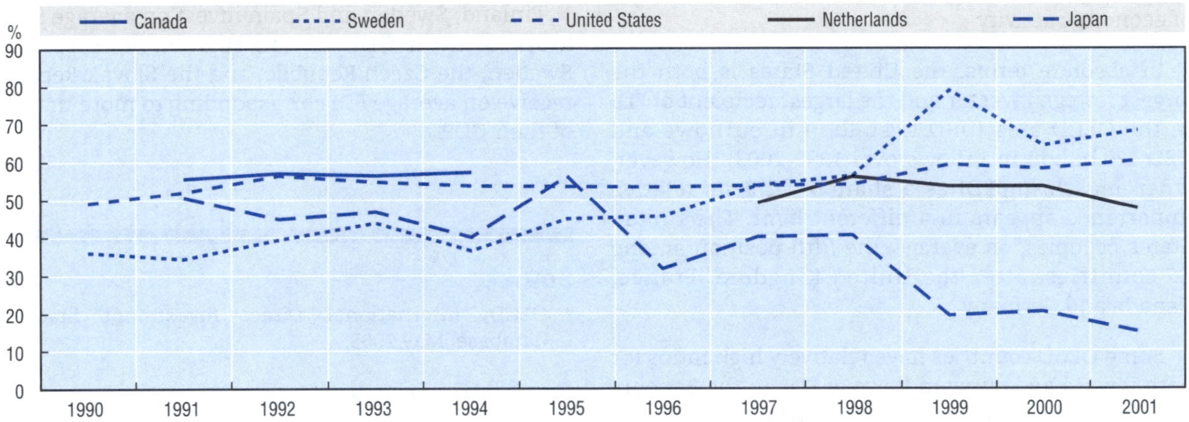


### US intra-firm trade in goods from outward investment, 2002

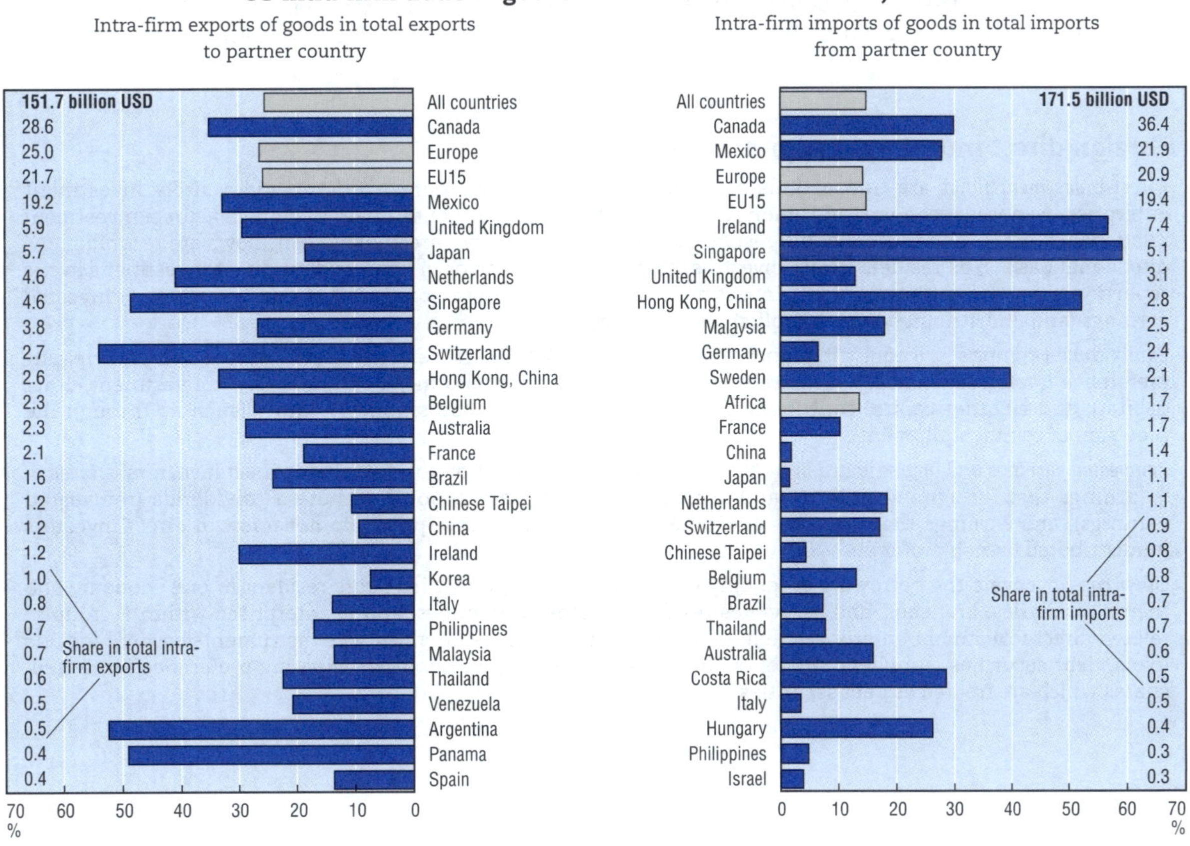


1. The US data also include minority-controlled affiliates. For the United States, Japan and the Netherlands, trade in goods only.

StatLink: http://dx.doi.org/10.1787/081403516407

## E.5. Foreign direct investment flows

■ Flows of direct investment as a percentage of GDP help measure the relative importance of globalisation by relating an economy's direct investment to its level of economic activity.

■ In absolute terms, the United States is both the largest foreign investor and the largest recipient of FDI in the OECD area (USD 124 billion in outflows and USD 120 billion in inflows over 1992-2003). However, when measuring FDI as a share of GDP, its relative importance appears in a different light. The United States occupies, on average, the fifth position among G7 countries, after the United Kingdom, France, Canada and Germany.

■ Some OECD countries have relatively high ratios for both inward and outward flows of FDI. In the Benelux countries, for example, some of these flows are largely due to the activities of special purpose entities and holding companies established by multinationals to finance and manage their cross-border investment. Owing to the methodology currently used for FDI statistics, a significant share of the transactions of such entities is included in FDI statistics.

■ Finland, Sweden and Spain invest on average 5% or more of their GDP in non-resident enterprises. Sweden, the Czech Republic, and the Slovak Republic receive on average FDI corresponding to more than 5% of their GDP.

### Source

- OECD, International Direct Investment Statistics database, May 2005.

### For further reading

- OECD (2005), *Measuring Globalisation – OECD Handbook on Economic Globalisation Indicators*, OECD, Paris, available at: *www.oecd.org/sti/measuring-globalisation*.
- OECD (2005), *Measuring Globalisation – Economic Globalisation Indicators*, OECD, Paris, forthcoming.

### Foreign direct investment capital transactions

*Direct investment flows* are transactions between a direct investor in one economy and a direct investment enterprise in another economy, and among affiliated direct investment enterprises that are in a direct investment relationship, other than those that are resident in the same economy. Direct investment flows are recorded on a directional basis: *i)* as resident direct investment abroad (outflows); or *ii)* non-resident direct investment in the reporting economy (inflows). Direct investment financial flows are composed of equity capital, reinvested earnings (and undistributed branch profits) and other capital.

*Equity capital* comprises: *i)* equity in branches; *ii)* all shares in subsidiaries and associates (except non-participating preference [preferred] shares, which are treated as debt securities and included under direct investment, other capital); and *iii)* other capital contributions, including non-cash acquisitions of equity (such as through the provision of capital equipment).

*Reinvested earnings and undistributed branch profits* comprise in proportion to equity held, direct investors' shares of *i)* earnings that foreign subsidiaries and associated enterprises do not distribute as dividends (reinvested earnings), and earnings that branches and other unincorporated enterprises do not remit to direct investors (undistributed branch profits).

*Other capital*: covers the borrowing or lending of funds between *i)* direct investors resident in one economy and their subsidiaries, branches, and associates resident in other economies, and *ii)* enterprises within a group of related direct investment enterprises that are resident in different economies. The instruments covered include loans, debt securities, suppliers' (trade) credits, financial leases, and non-participating preference [preferred] shares which are treated as debt securities.



OECD SCIENCE, TECHNOLOGY AND INDUSTRY SCOREBOARD 2005 – ISBN 92-64-01055-6 – © OECD 2005

## E.5. Foreign direct investment flows

### FDI outflows from G7 countries, 1992-2003

As a percentage of GDP

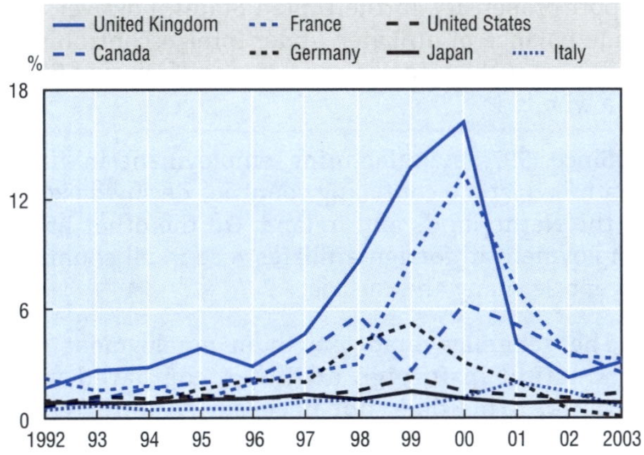


### FDI inflows to G7 countries, 1992-2003

As a percentage of GDP

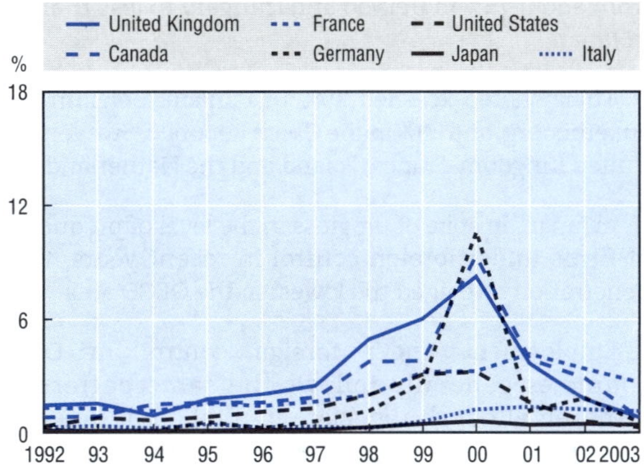


### FDI outflows from OECD countries, average 2000-03

As a percentage of GDP

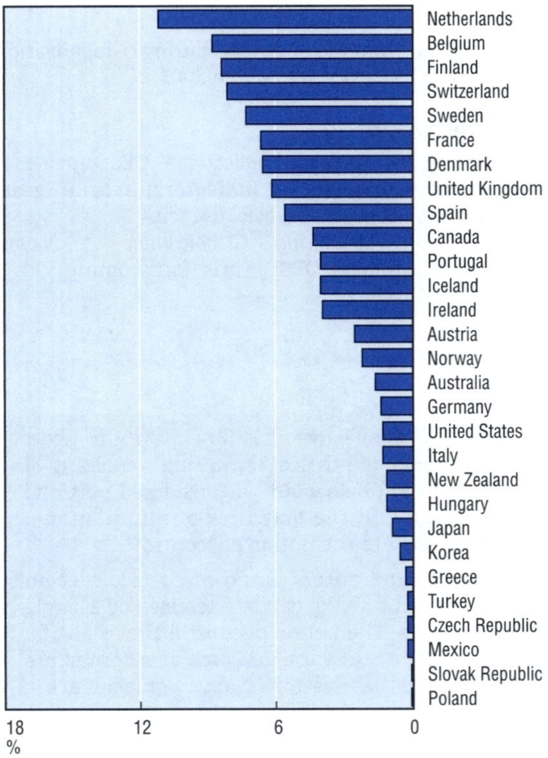


### FDI inflows to OECD countries, average 2000-03

As a percentage of GDP

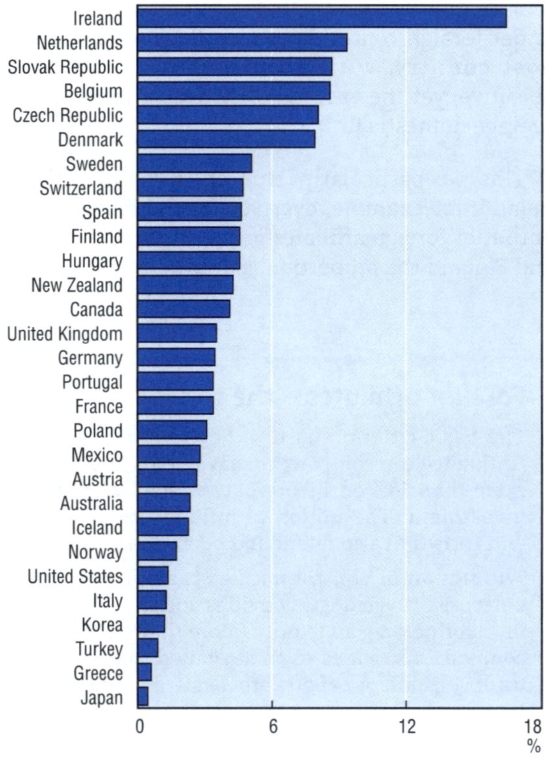


StatLink: http://dx.doi.org/10.1787/121572871043

## E.6. Activity of affiliates under foreign control in manufacturing

■ The share of firms under foreign control in total manufacturing sector turnover in 2001 or 2002 varied from about 75% in Ireland and Hungary to less than 3% in Japan.

■ Their share exceeded 40% in Canada, Belgium and Luxembourg, and 30% in the Czech Republic, Sweden, the United Kingdom, France, Poland and the Netherlands.

■ In Japan, in spite of progress in the level of production of firms under foreign control in recent years, their penetration remained the lowest in the OECD area.

■ Employment under foreign control in OECD countries generally follows the same pattern as turnover, although the share in total employment is smaller, since foreign direct investment is more capital- than labour-intensive. However, while turnover under foreign control is about the same in France and in the United Kingdom, the share of employment under foreign control is greater in France.

■ It might be supposed that the main task of affiliates under foreign control is to meet local demand in the host country, with exports being a secondary objective, yet the vast majority export more than the average domestic firm.

■ This is particularly true in manufacturing. In Ireland, for example, over 90% of the manufacturing output of foreign affiliates is exported, and in Austria and Finland the proportion is over half.

■ In a majority of countries, the import propensity of affiliates under foreign control is lower than their export propensity. In the United States, however, the trade balance of affiliates under foreign control is in deficit, as is the trade balance of manufacturing firms as a whole.

■ Since 1997, manufacturing employment in firms controlled by the compiling countries declined except in the Netherlands and Ireland. On the other hand, employment in foreign affiliates rose in all countries except Germany and Austria.

■ The generally rapid growth in employment and production in foreign affiliates compared with national firms does not necessarily point to the creation of new foreign affiliates. In most cases, it reflects changes of ownership owing to acquisitions.

### Source

- OECD, OECD Statistics on Measuring Globalisation – AFA and FATS databases, March 2005.

### For further reading

- OECD (2005), Measuring *Globalisation – OECD Handbook on Economic Globalisation Indicators*, available at: *www.oecd.org/sti/measuring-globalisation*.
- OECD (2005), *Measuring Globalisation – Economic Globalisation Indicators*, OECD, Paris, forthcoming.

### *Foreign affiliates – the concepts of influence and control*

The basic criterion used to determine whether an investment is a direct investment is its capacity to exert "influence" on company management. The notion of influence is reflected, in statistical terms, in the holding of more than 10% of the ordinary shares or voting rights, while any investment below 10% is considered portfolio investment. The notion of influence is not sufficient for collecting data on the activities of multinational enterprises in a coherent and operational manner, whence the need to resort to the notion of "control".

The notion of control implies the ability to appoint a majority of administrators empowered to direct an enterprise, to guide its activities and determine its strategy. In most cases, this ability can be exercised by a single investor holding a majority (more than 50%) of the shares with voting rights. The notion of control allows all of a company's activities to be attributed to the controlling investor. This means that variables such as a company's turnover, staff or exports are all attributed to the controlling investor and to the investor's country of residence.

The term "foreign affiliate" is restricted to majority-owned affiliates under foreign control. Accordingly, the geographical origin of a foreign affiliate is the country of residence of the ultimate controller. An investor (company or individual) is considered to be the investor of ultimate control if it is at the head of a chain of companies and controls directly or indirectly all the enterprises in the chain without itself being controlled by any other company or individual.

 OECD SCIENCE, TECHNOLOGY AND INDUSTRY SCOREBOARD 2005 – ISBN 92-64-01055-6 – © OECD 2005

# E.6. Activity of affiliates under foreign control in manufacturing

### Foreign-controlled affiliates' share of manufacturing turnover[1] and employment, 2002

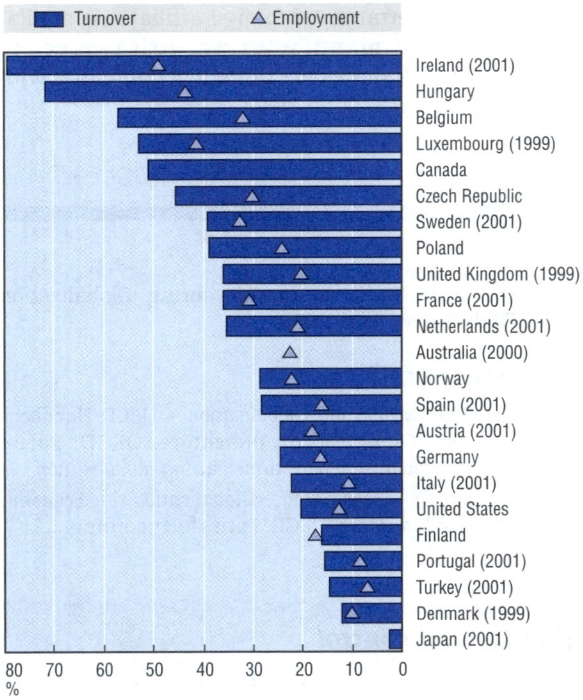


### Export and import propensity[2] of affiliates under foreign control in the manufacturing sector, 2002

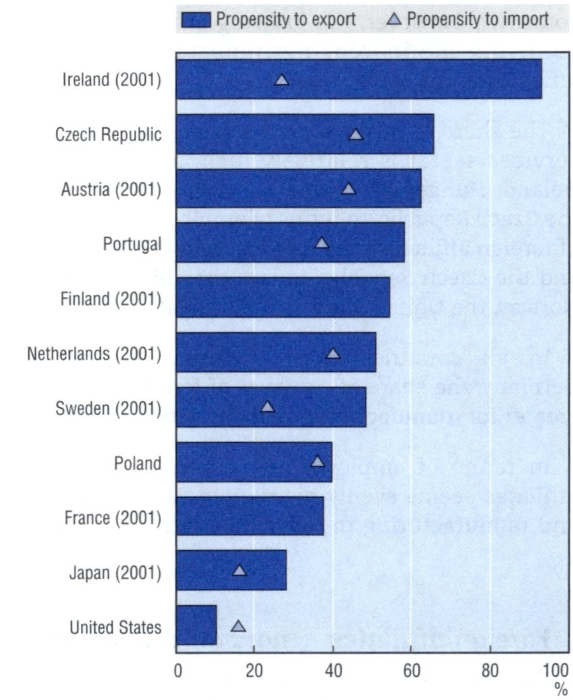


### Turnover[1] and employment of manufacturing foreign affiliates and firms controlled by compiling countries, 1997-2002

Average annual growth rate (%)

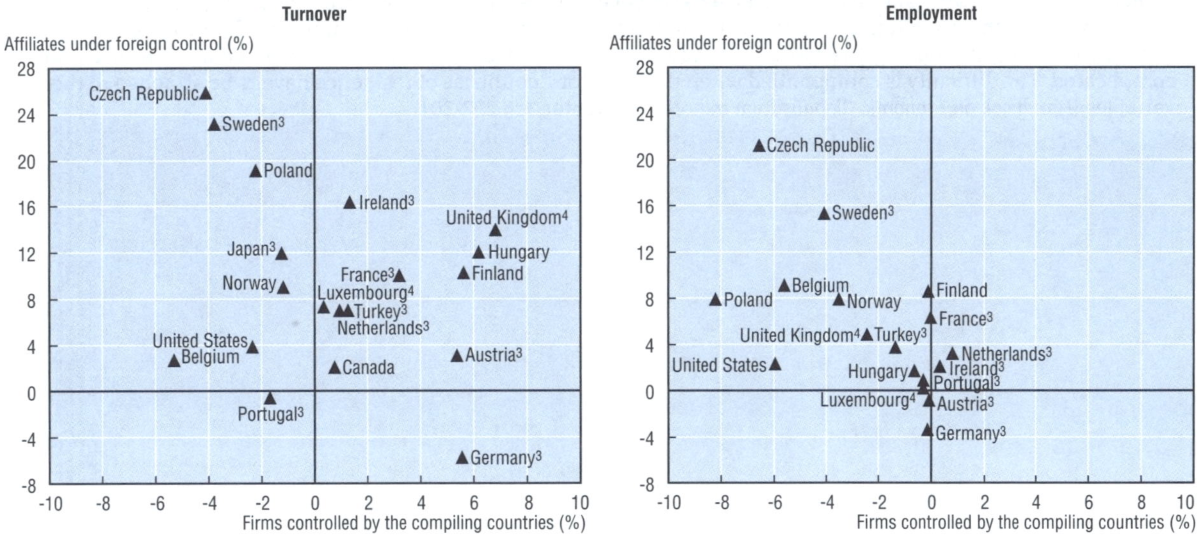


1. Production rather than turnover for Canada and Ireland.
2. Exports and imports as a percentage of turnover (or production for Ireland).
3. 1997-2001.
4. 1995-99.

StatLink: *http://dx.doi.org/10.1787/310134226534*

## E.7. Activity of affiliates under foreign control in services

■ Collection of data on the activity of foreign affiliates in services did not start until the second half of the 1990s, and data are not yet available for all OECD countries. However, the growing availability of data confirms the increasing importance of foreign affiliates in the services sector.

■ The share of turnover under foreign control in the services sector is relatively high, at over 25%, for Ireland, Hungary, Belgium, Luxembourg, Poland and the Czech Republic. In terms of employment, the share of foreign affiliates ranges from around 20% in Ireland and the Czech Republic, to less than 5% in Germany, Norway, the United States and Portugal.

■ In all countries except Norway, Finland and Germany, the share of turnover of foreign affiliates is greater for manufacturing than for services (see E.6).

■ In terms of employment, penetration of foreign affiliates seems evenly distributed between services and manufacturing in Germany, Denmark, Portugal and Norway. The largest differences are in Luxembourg, Hungary, Belgium and Sweden.

■ In Japan, penetration of foreign affiliates is similar in services and manufacturing with respect to turnover, but the shares are quite low compared with those of other OECD countries.

### Source

- OECD, OECD Statistics on Measuring Globalisation – FATS database, April 2005.

### For further reading

- OECD (2005), *Measuring Globalisation – OECD Handbook on Economic Globalisation Indicators*, OECD, Paris, available at: *www.oecd.org/sti/measuring-globalisation*.
- OECD (2005), *Measuring Globalisation – Economic Globalisation Indicators*, OECD, Paris, forthcoming.

### *Foreign affiliates – more on the concepts of influence and control*

Data on the activity of multinationals use the notion of "control" to a greater degree than the notion of "influence". Influence implies attributing production, value added, the number of employees and other variables according to shareholders' percentage stake in the enterprise, and it is the "financial" aspect that predominates. In the case of control, it is the "power to take decisions" and "decide corporate strategy" that comes first.

When control of all of an enterprise's economic variables is attributed to a single majority shareholder, this does not mean that the latter appropriates all of the enterprise's output or profits, but that it makes all of the strategic choices. Where a firm's activity is concerned, however, there are other reasons for taking a control-based approach. When there are numerous minority shareholders and when the chain of indirectly owned companies is also included, attributing the variables according to the principles of ownership becomes much more complicated. The difficulty is compounded when the investors' countries of residence have to be attached to these variables (*Handbook on Economic Globalisation Indicators*, Chapter 3, § 297-301).

# E.7. Activity of affiliates under foreign control in services

### Share of foreign affiliates in services, 2002[1]

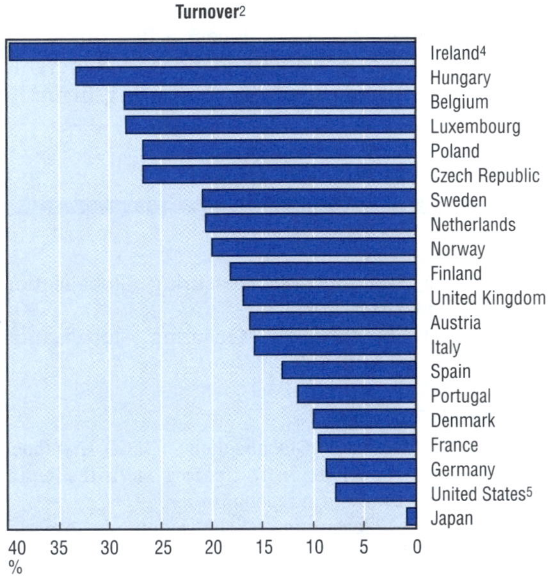


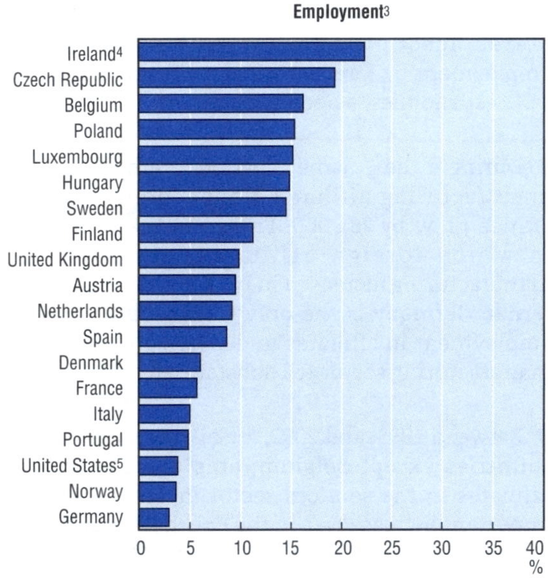


### Share of foreign affiliates in the services and manufacturing sectors, 2002[1]

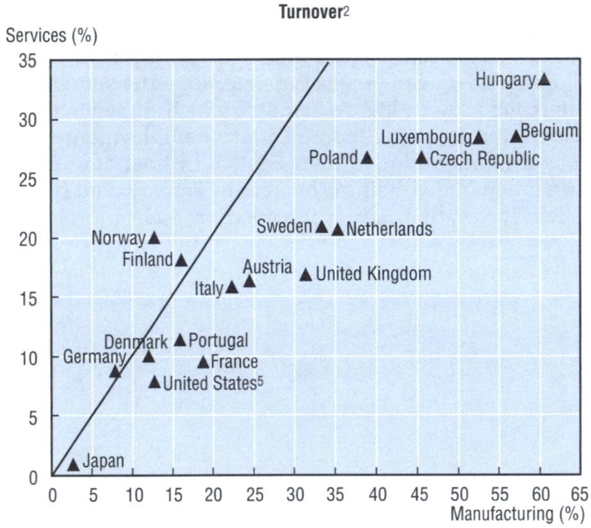


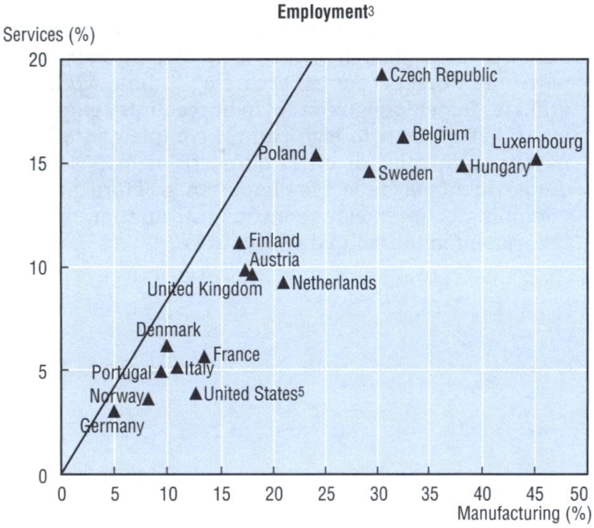


1. 2001 for Austria, Finland, France, Italy, Japan, the Netherlands and Portugal; 2000 for Sweden; 1999 for Denmark; 1998 for Luxembourg; 1997 for Norway and the United Kingdom.
2. Turnover: Financial intermediation (ISIC 65 to 67) excluded completely or in part for all countries except the Czech Republic and France; Community, social and personal services (ISIC 80 to 93) excluded for Austria, Denmark, Germany, Ireland, Portugal and the United Kingdom.
3. Employment: Financial intermediation (ISIC 65 to 67) excluded completely or in part for all countries except Austria, the Czech Republic, Finland, France, Italy, Luxembourg and Norway. Community, social and personal services (ISIC 80 to 93) excluded for Austria, Denmark, Germany, Ireland, Portugal and the United Kingdom.
4. Enterprises with 20 employees or more.
5. The data used here for foreign affiliates are broken down by industry of sales to be compatible with total national data.

StatLink: *http://dx.doi.org/10.1787/030222401615*

## E.8. Trends in the employment of foreign affiliates

■ Between 1995 and 2001, employment by affiliates under foreign control in the manufacturing sector of OECD countries increased by 24%. In 2001, the United States accounted for more than 34% of total employment by foreign affiliates in manufacturing in OECD economies, a decrease from its share in 1995.

■ During the same period, employment in manufacturing affiliates under foreign control in France grew by 281 000. France is the only country in which foreign affiliates' employment in manufacturing increased in both absolute and relative terms. Germany is the only OECD country in which employment in affiliates under foreign control in the manufacturing sector fell substantially (by 120 000).

■ Between 1995 and 2002, in all the selected OECD countries except Belgium, employment in foreign affiliates in the services sector increased. The most important increase was in the Czech Republic, with an increase of approximately 200 000. This may partly reflect the importance of temporary recruitment firms in the services sector.

■ These changes do not necessarily imply job creation. They are often due to changes in ownership resulting from the acquisition of existing firms by foreign investors.

### Sources

- OECD, OECD Statistics on Measuring Globalisation – AFA database, April 2005.
- OECD, OECD Statistics on Measuring Globalisation – FATS database, April 2005.

### *For further reading*


- OECD (2005), *Measuring Globalisation – OECD Handbook on Economic Globalisation Indicators*, available at: *www.oecd.org/sti/measuring-globalisation.*
- OECD (2005), *Measuring Globalisation – Economic Globalisation Indicators*, OECD, Paris, forthcoming.


### *Share of foreign affiliates in employment*

Employment in foreign affiliates should normally be measured as the number of persons on the payrolls of affiliates under foreign control. Employment data are sometimes converted to a full-time equivalent (FTE), with part-time workers counted according to time worked. Employment data can be used to determine the share of affiliates under foreign control in host country employment or to help determine the extent to which employment by affiliates under foreign control complements or substitutes for domestic (home country) employment by parent companies or other domestic firms. The share of affiliates under foreign control in host country employment may reflect the importance of foreign direct investment in maintaining or creating employment in a compiling country. However, this information does not allow for evaluating net job creation due to foreign investment in the compiling countries.

## E.8. Trends in the employment of foreign affiliates

### Trends in manufacturing employment of foreign affiliates in selected OECD countries, 1995 and 2001

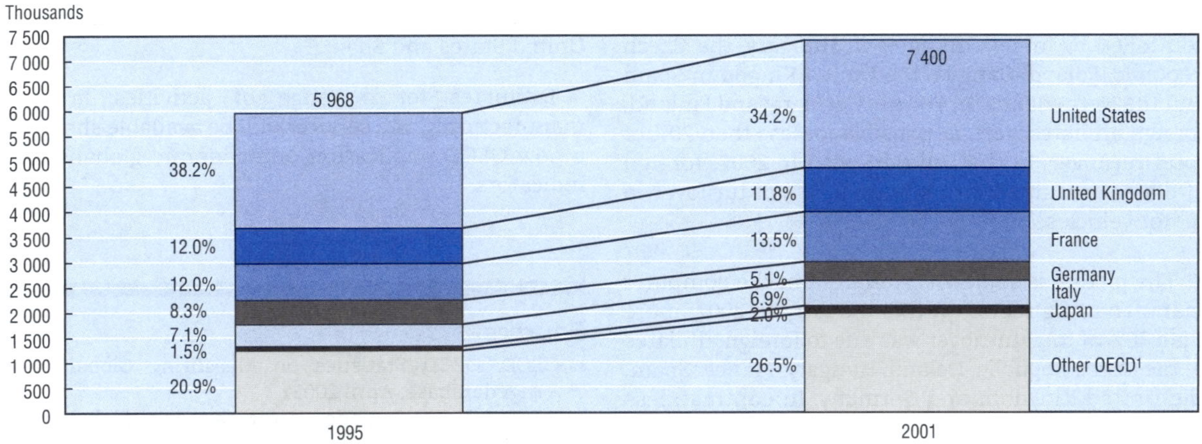


### Share of foreign affiliates in services employment in selected OECD countries, 2002

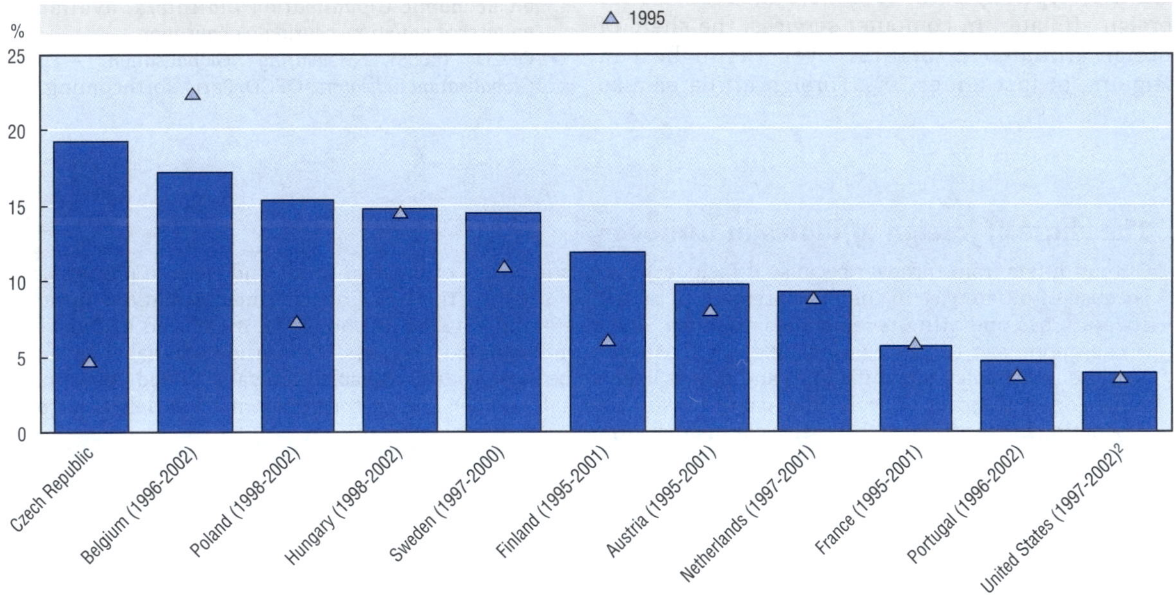


1. Consists of the Czech Republic, Hungary, Finland, Ireland, Luxembourg, the Netherlands, Norway, Poland, Portugal, Sweden and Turkey.
2. The data used here for foreign affiliates are broken down by industry of sales to be compatible with national total data.

StatLink: *http://dx.doi.org/10.1787/570251827111*

## E.9. Share of turnover under foreign control in selected manufacturing and services sectors

The contribution of foreign affiliates to turnover differs considerably across countries and activities. In 2001, more than 70% of motor vehicle turnover was controlled by foreign affiliates in Hungary, the Czech Republic, Poland, Canada, the United Kingdom, Spain and the Netherlands. In France, Germany and Finland, foreign affiliates were responsible for less than 20% of total turnover. In the United States in 2002, foreign affiliates accounted for more than 30% of turnover in motor vehicles.

The picture is somewhat different in the computer manufacturing sector. In this industry in 2002, more than 70% of total turnover was due to foreign affiliates in the Czech Republic, Ireland, Hungary, France, Spain, the United Kingdom and Germany. In contrast, less than 20% was due to foreign affiliates in the Netherlands and the United States.

Similar data can be derived for the services sector, and they typically point to a more modest role for foreign affiliates. In computer services, the share of foreign affiliates in total turnover was highest in Belgium, at just under 50%. Foreign affiliates also played a relatively important role in the United Kingdom, the Czech Republic and Norway. They played a relatively minor role in Austria, Germany, the United States and Spain.

Estimates for a range of activities in both manufacturing and services will be available shortly in a new OECD publication on economic globalisation indicators.

### Sources

- OECD, OECD Statistics on Measuring Globalisation – AFA database, April 2005.
- OECD, OECD Statistics on Measuring Globalisation – FATS database, April 2005.

### For further reading

- OECD (2005), *Measuring Globalisation – OECD Handbook on Economic Globalisation Indicators*, available at: *www.oecd.org/sti/measuring-globalisation*.
- OECD (2005), *Measuring Globalisation – Economic Globalisation Indicators*, OECD, Paris, forthcoming.

### *The share of foreign affiliates in turnover*

Output differs from turnover because it includes changes in stocks of finished goods and work in progress and because of differences in the measurement of activities involving trade or financial intermediation. Turnover covers gross operating revenues less rebates, discounts and returns. It should be measured exclusive of consumption and turnover (sales) taxes on consumers and value-added taxes. The turnover variable generally presents fewer collection difficulties and thus is likely to be more widely available than value added. Also, unlike value added, turnover indicates the extent to which affiliates under foreign control are used to deliver outputs originating in the affiliates themselves or in other firms.

## E.9. Share of turnover under foreign control in selected manufacturing and services sectors

### Motor vehicles (ISIC 34), 2002

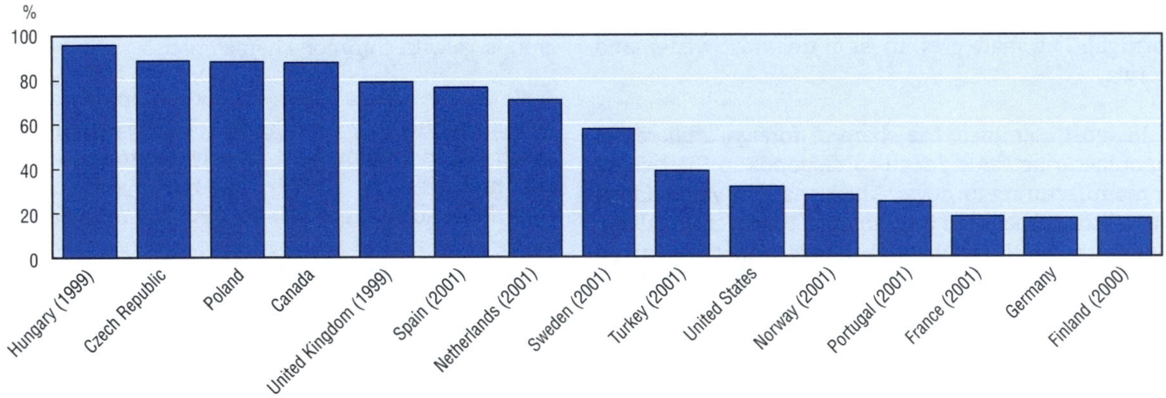


### Computer manufacturing (ISIC 30), 2002

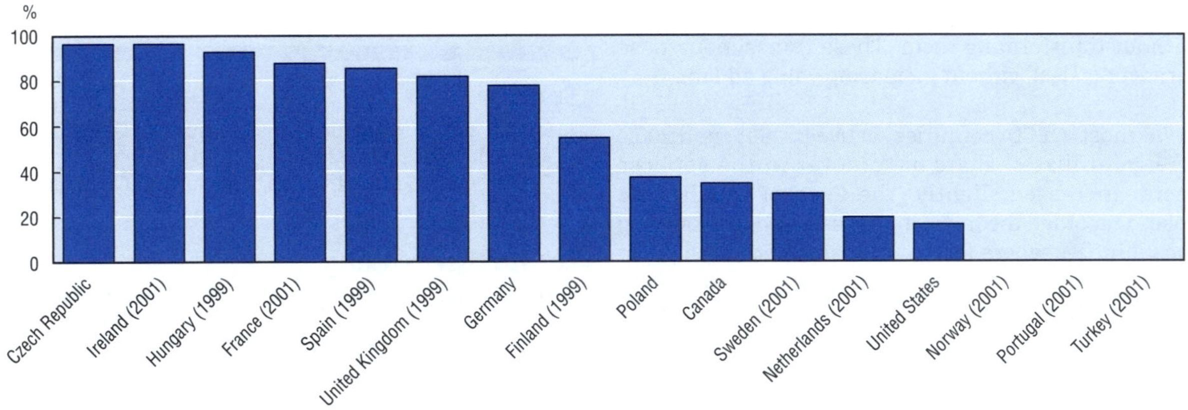


### Computer and related services (ISIC 72), 2002

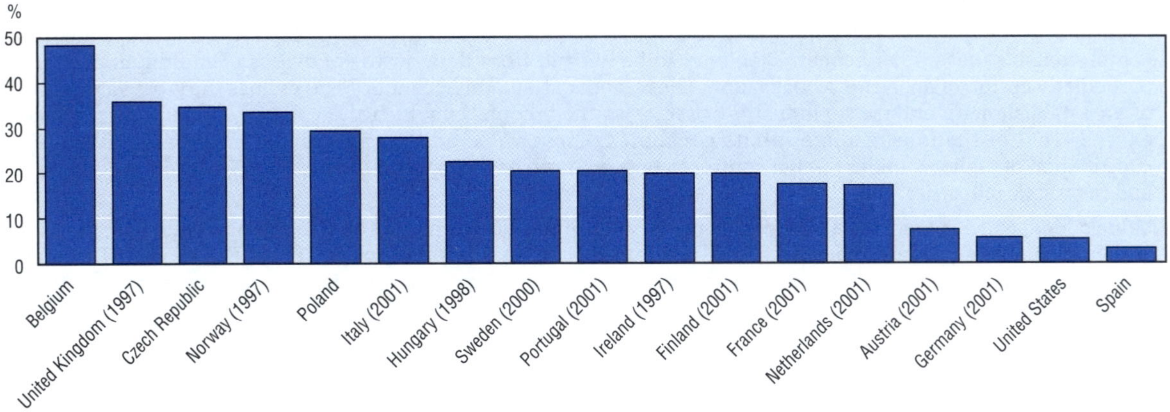


StatLink: *http://dx.doi.org/10.1787/544520841363*

## E.10. The contribution of multinationals to value added and labour productivity

■ Between 1995 and 2001, foreign-controlled affiliates increased their share in manufacturing value added in all countries for which data are available except Portugal. The share grew most in Ireland, Sweden and Norway.

■ In most countries, the share of foreign affiliates in manufacturing value added corresponds to their share in manufacturing turnover. Their share in value added was a little higher than their share in turnover in Ireland, Sweden and Norway. In Hungary and the United Kingdom, their share in manufacturing value added was lower than their share in manufacturing turnover.

■ Leaving aside the role of intermediate consumption in the production process, the difference between the shares of foreign affiliates in manufacturing turnover and in value added reflects the fact that some foreign affiliates import goods from their parent company or parent group and sell them on the domestic market without transforming them. These transactions raise turnover (sales) without increasing value added.

■ In most OECD countries between 1995 and 2002, foreign affiliates' share of turnover in the services sector increased slightly. The Czech Republic and Poland recorded the highest increase, and were among the countries where foreign affiliates had the highest shares in total national services sector turnover. In Japan and the United States, foreign affiliates had the smallest share in services turnover among OECD countries and did not show any significant change over the period.

■ A comparison of employment and labour productivity trends in foreign-controlled affiliates between 1997 and 2002 reveals some striking differences and some groupings with common characteristics.

■ Germany saw a drop in both employment and labour productivity. The Czech Republic experienced a sharp rise in employment, largely due to acquisitions, accompanied by a slight upturn in productivity. Ireland's modest growth in employment occurred along with a sharp rise in labour productivity, the strongest recorded in OECD countries.

■ Countries in which productivity improved more than employment include Hungary, Poland, the United Kingdom and the Netherlands. In Belgium, Finland, France, Japan, Norway and Turkey, employment grew but productivity growth was low or negative. Sweden had both high productivity and employment growth.

### Sources

- OECD, OECD Statistics on Measuring Globalisation – AFA database, May 2005.
- OECD, OECD Statistics on Measuring Globalisation – FATS database, May 2005.

### For further reading

- OECD (2005), *Measuring Globalisation – OECD Handbook on Economic Globalisation Indicators*, OECD, Paris, available at: *www.oecd.org/sti/measuring-globalisation*.
- OECD (2005), *Measuring Globalisation – Economic Globalisation Indicators*, OECD, Paris, forthcoming.

### Measuring value added

Value added – the portion of an enterprise's output that originates within the enterprise itself – is perhaps the most comprehensive measure of economic activity to be derived from data on the activities of multinationals. It is particularly useful for analysing globalisation. The System of National Accounts (SNA) defines the gross value added of an establishment, enterprise, industry or sector as the amount by which the value of the outputs produced exceeds that of the intermediate inputs consumed. Gross value added can provide information about the contribution of affiliates under foreign control to host country gross domestic product (GDP), both in the aggregate and in specific industries.

Value added, when it concerns all the components of a country's economy, is equal to the sum of its GDP, the most widely available aggregate measure of the size of an economy and its growth. Thus, the shares of foreign-controlled affiliates in total GDP and in the relevant industrial sector are a useful measure of the extent to which an economy has become globalised.

 OECD SCIENCE, TECHNOLOGY AND INDUSTRY SCOREBOARD 2005 – ISBN 92-64-01055-6 – © OECD 2005

## E.10. The contribution of multinationals to value added and labour productivity

### Share of affiliates under foreign control in manufacturing value added, 2002

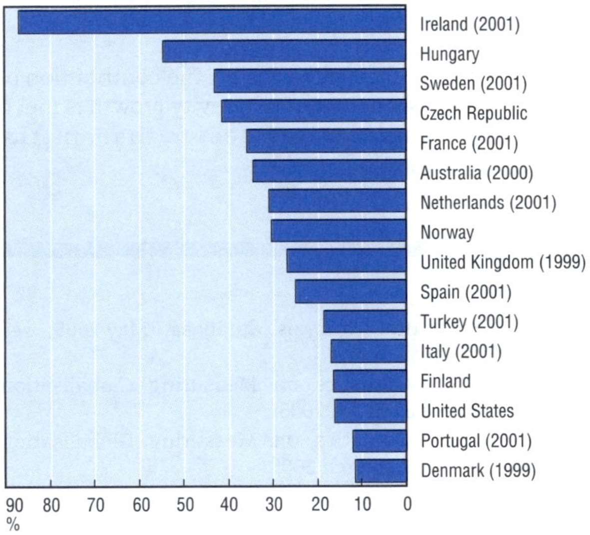


### Share of affiliates under foreign control in services value added, 2002

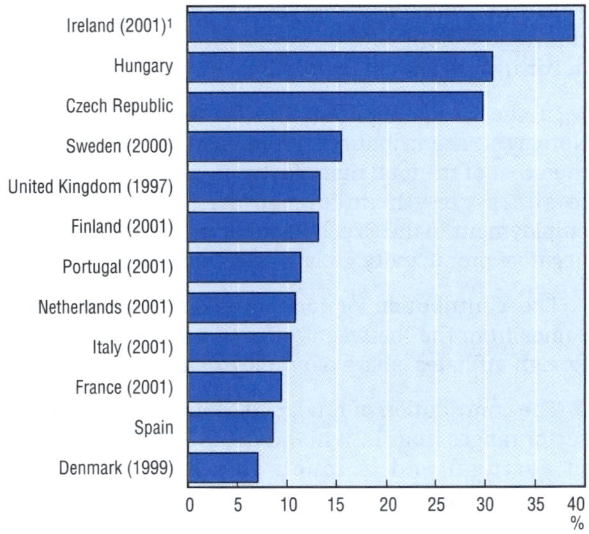


### Employment and labour productivity[2] of affiliates under foreign control in the manufacturing sector, 1997-2002

Average annual growth rate (%)

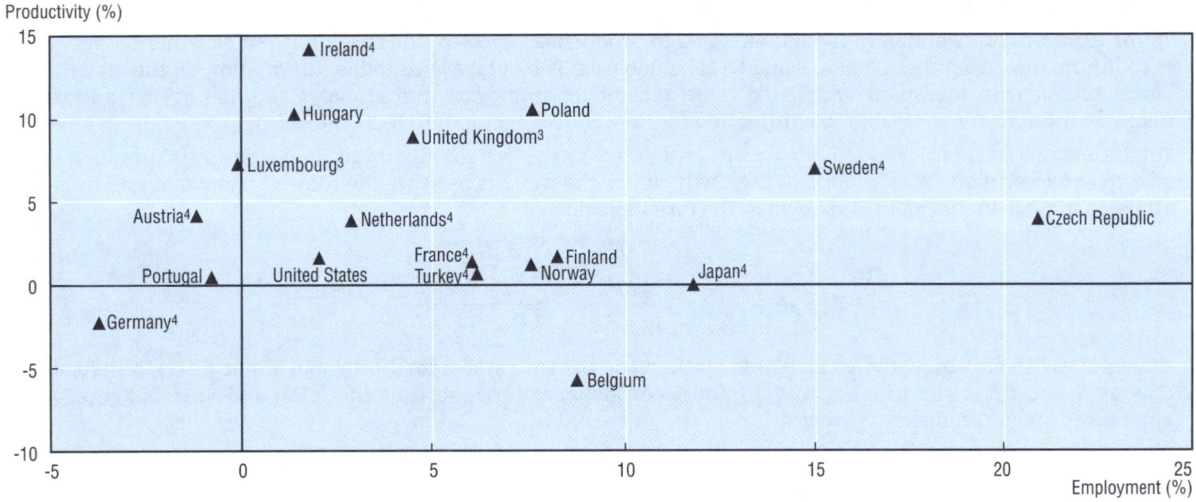


1. Enterprises with at least 20 employees.
2. Turnover to employment.
3. 1995-99.
4. 1997-2001.

StatLink: *http://dx.doi.org/10.1787/421816067734*

## E.11. The contribution of multinationals to productivity growth

■ Multinationals often make an important contribution to productivity growth.

■ In the manufacturing sector, foreign affiliates contributed from 6.7% in the Czech Republic to –0.4% in Portugal to annual productivity growth.

■ In the Czech Republic, the United Kingdom and Norway, the contribution of foreign affiliates is greater than that of the total manufacturing sector. This is due to sharp growth in foreign affiliates' share of employment in the Czech Republic and Norway and to negative productivity growth in UK domestic firms.

■ The contribution of foreign affiliates most often comes from the "between" effect, *i.e.* the sharp rise in foreign affiliates' share of employment.

■ The contribution of foreign affiliates in the services sector ranges from 1.2% in the Czech Republic to –0.2% in Portugal and is much smaller than in the manufacturing sector.

■ As in the manufacturing sector, the between effect in the services sector accounts for most of the contribution of foreign affiliates to productivity growth. Hungary is an exception.

■ In both the manufacturing and services sector, the contribution of foreign affiliates is largest in the Czech Republic and Sweden and smallest in Japan and Portugal.

■ In France and the United States, the contribution of foreign affiliates to labour productivity growth is much smaller in the services sector than in the manufacturing sector.

### Sources

- OECD, Structural Analysis database, May 2005, see *www.oecd.org/sti/stan*.
- OECD, OECD Statistics on Measuring Globalisation – AFA database, March 2005.
- OECD, OECD Statistics on Measuring Globalisation – FATS database, March 2005.

### For further reading

- C. Criscuolo (2005), "The Contribution of Foreign Affiliates to Productivity Growth: Evidence from OECD Countries", *STI Working Papers* 2005/08, OECD, available at *www.oecd.org/sti/working-papers*.

### Calculating foreign affiliates' contribution to productivity growth

To measure the contribution of foreign affiliates to productivity growth, the OECD has put together a database with information from the AFA, FATS and STAN databases. The database contains information on the growth of labour productivity, measured as deflated value added over employment of affiliates and non-affiliates for the manufacturing sector of 12 OECD countries and for the services sector of 9 OECD countries.

Total annualised labour productivity growth is defined as the weighted sum of domestic firms' productivity growth and foreign affiliates' productivity growth, where the weights used are the shares of domestic and foreign affiliates in total employment, as shown in the formula below:

$$\frac{1}{k}*\frac{\Delta LP_t}{LP_{t-k}} = \sum_{i=DOM,FOR} \frac{\frac{EMP_{it}}{EMP_t}LP_{it} - \frac{EMP_{it-k}}{EMP_{t-k}}LP_{it-k}}{LP_{t-k}} * \frac{1}{k}$$

Where *LP* is labour productivity calculated as the ratio of real value added to labour input (EMP), $\Delta$ indicates change; *k* indicates the number of years between observations, so that the left-hand side is aggregate annualised labour productivity growth.

For each sector therefore the contribution to labour productivity growth of foreign affiliates can be calculated as:

$$1/k*\left(\left(\frac{EMP_{FOR,t}}{EMP_t}*LP_{FOR,t} - \frac{EMP_{FOR,t-k}}{EMP_{t-k}}*LP_{FOR,t-k}\right)\Big/LP_{t-k}\right) = \underbrace{\frac{1}{k}*\frac{\Delta LP_{FOR,t}}{LP_{t-k}}*\overline{w}_{FOR}}_{within} + \underbrace{\Delta w_{FOR,t}*\frac{1}{k}*\frac{\overline{LP}_{FOR}}{LP_{t-k}}}_{between}$$

Foreign affiliates' contribution to productivity growth derives from switches in labour resources between domestic and more productive foreign affiliates, the "between effect", and from labour productivity growth within the group of foreign affiliates, the "within effect". The first term of the right-hand side is the "within" effect and the second is the "between" effect. Thus, foreign affiliates' contribution to labour productivity growth might increase if there is an increase in its rate of productivity growth or if their average employment share is higher (from the first term); and if their employment share increases or their labour productivity level is higher relative to the domestic average (from the second term).



OECD SCIENCE, TECHNOLOGY AND INDUSTRY SCOREBOARD 2005 – ISBN 92-64-01055-6 – © OECD 2005

# E.11. The contribution of multinationals to productivity growth

### Labour productivity growth and average contribution of foreign affiliates, 1995-2001

Percentage points

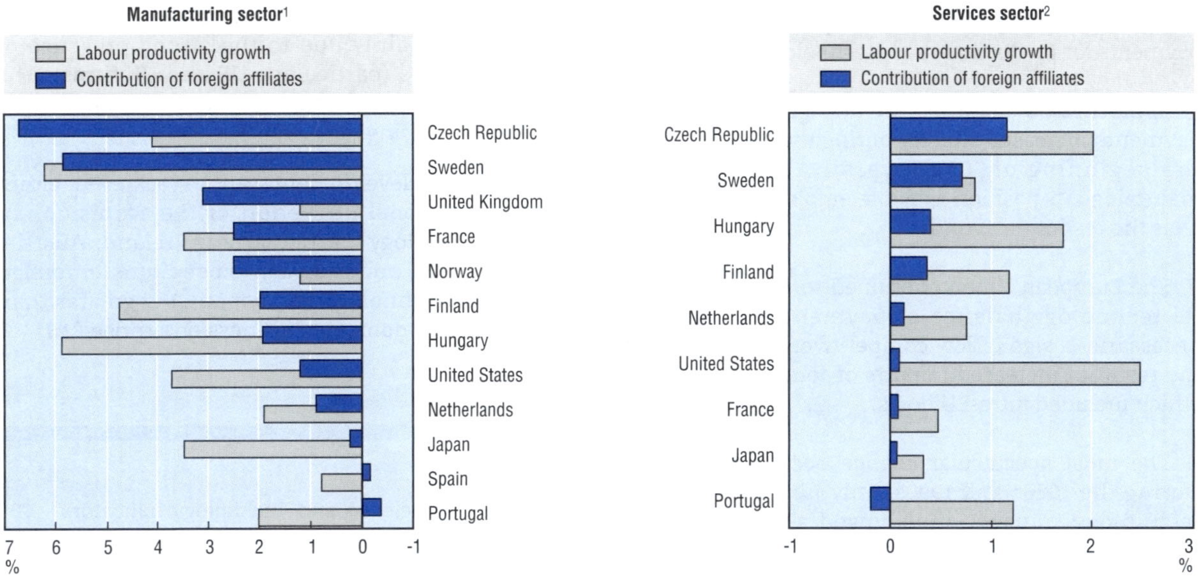


### Breakdown of foreign affiliates' contribution, 1995-2001

Percentage points

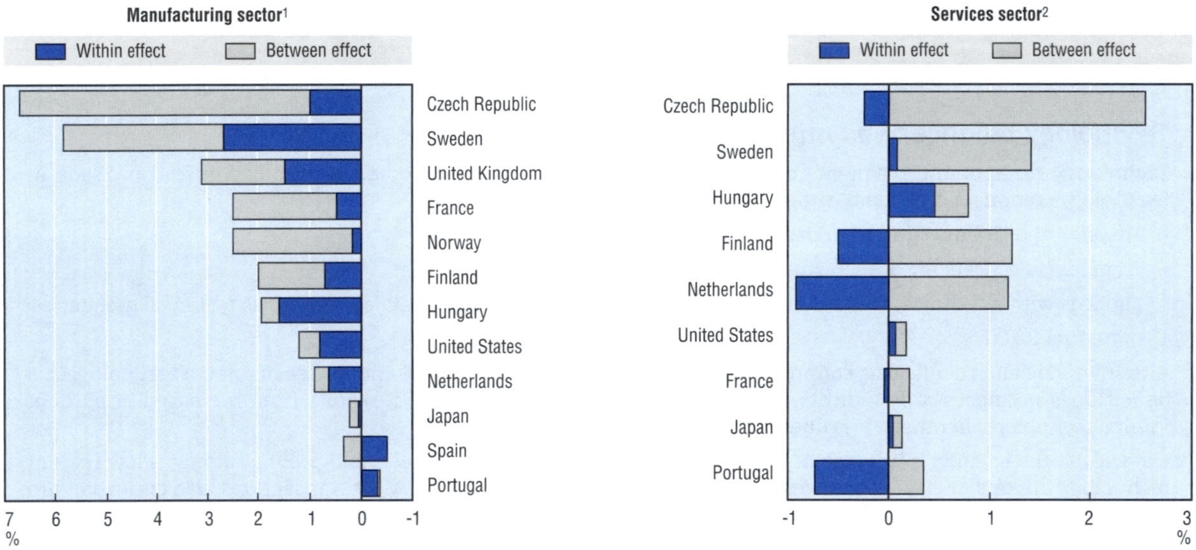


1. Labour productivity is measured as value added in constant prices over employment.
2. Or nearest available year: Czech Republic 1997-2002; United Kingdom 1995-1999; Finland 1995-2002; Hungary 1996-2002; Spain 1999-2001; and Portugal 1996-2002.
3. Or nearest available year: Czech Republic 1995-2002; Sweden 1997-2000; Hungary 1998-2002; Netherlands 1997-2001; Japan 1997-2000; and Portugal 1996-2002.

StatLink: *http://dx.doi.org/10.1787/280675232405*

## E.12. Technological balance of payments

■ The technology balance of payments measures international technology transfers: licence fees, patents, purchases and royalties paid, know-how, research and technical assistance. Unlike R&D expenditure, these are payments for production-ready technologies.

■ In most OECD countries, technological receipts and payments increased sharply during the 1990s through the beginning of 2001. Overall, the OECD area maintained its position as net technology exporter *vis-à-vis* the rest of the world.

■ The European Union continued to run a deficit on its technology balance of payments. This is not necessarily a sign of low competitiveness but may be the result of increased imports of foreign technology, which included intra-EU flows.

■ The most spectacular change occurred in Japan. During the 1980s and 1990s, only new contracts for technology transactions showed a positive trade balance, while total technology transactions were in deficit. In 2003, these transactions showed a very large surplus (receipts-payments).

■ In 2003, the main technology exporters as a percentage of GDP were the United Kingdom, Belgium, Denmark, the United States, Japan, Canada, Finland, France and Norway. Ireland, Hungary, the Czech Republic, Poland and Korea imported the most technology.

■ The magnitude of the deficit in Ireland's technology payments is mainly due to the strong presence of foreign affiliates (particularly US and UK firms). The figures may also be affected by intra-firm transactions and transfer pricing.

■ Technology development can be achieved either through a national R&D effort or the acquisition of foreign technology. Particularly in Ireland, Austria, Poland, Portugal and Hungary, expenditure for foreign technology (technological payments) is greater than expenditure for domestic business enterprise R&D.

### Source

- OECD, Main Science and Technology Indicators – TBP database, April 2005.

### For further reading

- OECD (2005), *Measuring Globalisation – OECD Handbook on Economic Globalisation Indicators*, OECD, Paris, available at: *www.oecd.org/sti/measuring-globalisation*.
- OECD (2005), *Measuring Globalisation – Economic Globalisation Indicators*, OECD, Paris, forthcoming.

### Technology balance of payments

Technology receipts and payments constitute the main form of disembodied technology diffusion. Trade in technology comprises four main categories:

- Transfer of techniques (through patents and licences, disclosure of know-how).
- Transfer (sale, licensing, franchising) of designs, trademarks and patterns.
- Services with a technical content, including technical and engineering studies, as well as technical assistance.
- Industrial R&D.

Although the balance reflects a country's ability to sell its technology abroad and its use of foreign technologies, a deficit does not necessarily indicate low competitiveness. In some cases, it results from increased imports of foreign technology; in others, it is due to declining receipts.

Likewise, if the balance is in surplus, this may be due to a high degree of technological autonomy, a low level of technology imports or a lack of capacity to assimilate foreign technologies. Most transactions also correspond to operations between parent companies and affiliates. Thus, it is important to have additional qualitative and quantitative information to analyse correctly a country's deficit or surplus position in a given year.

There is also the difficulty of dissociating the technological from the non-technological content of trade in services, which falls under the heading of pure industrial property. Thus, trade in services may be underestimated when a significant portion does not give rise to financial payments or when payments are not in the form of technology payments.

## E.12. Technological balance of payments

### Trends in technology flows[1] by main areas, 1991-2003

As a percentage of GDP

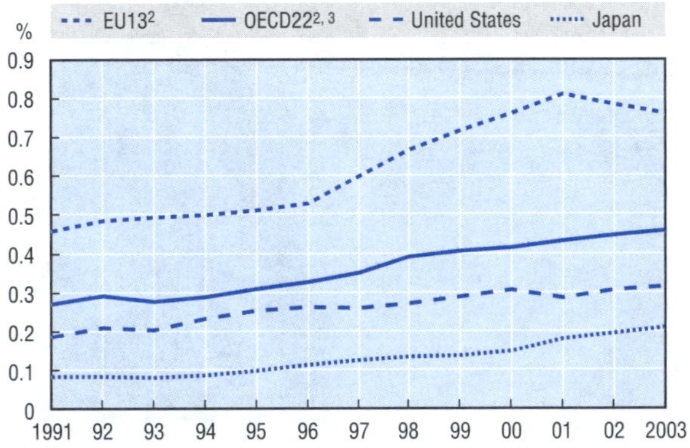


### Change in the technology balance of payments by main areas, 1993-2003

As a percentage of GDP

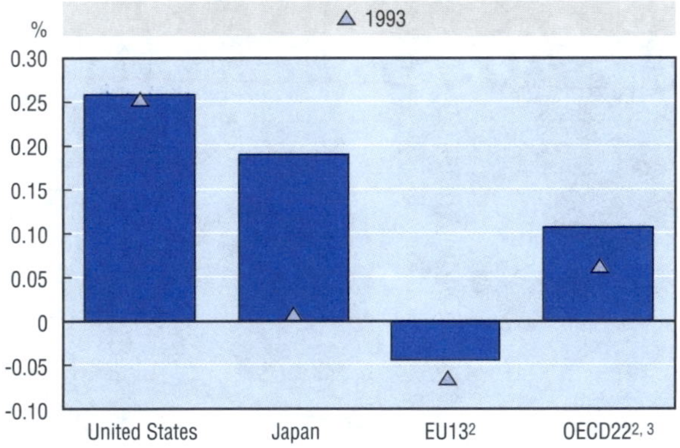


### Technology flows, 2003

As a percentage of GDP

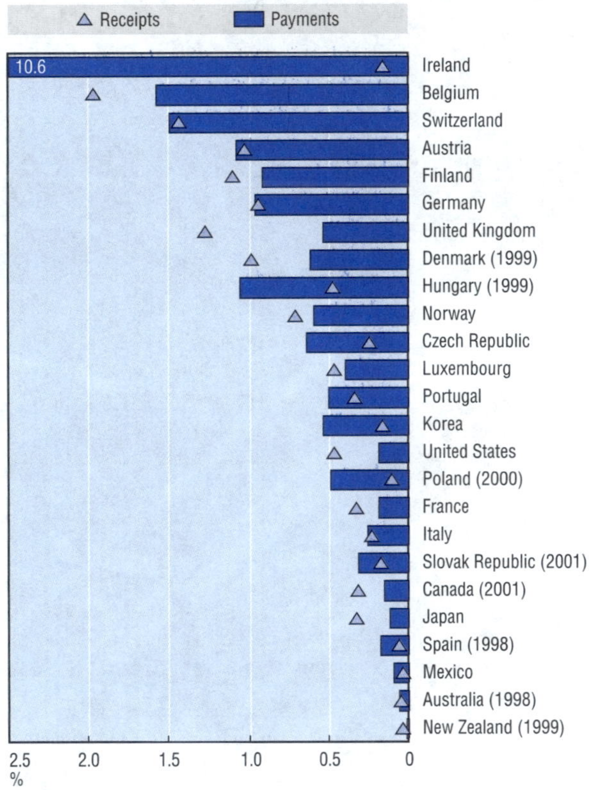


### Technology balance of payments, 2003

As a percentage of GDP

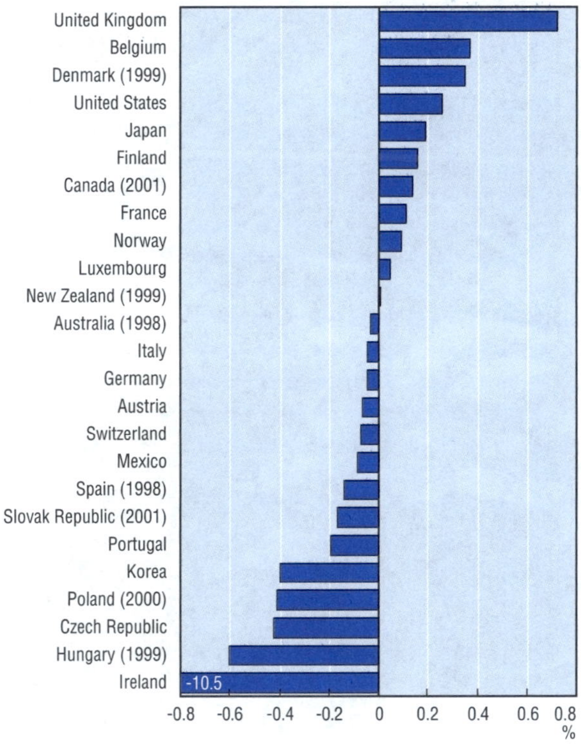


1. Average of technological payments and receipts.
2. Including intra-area flows. Excluding Denmark and Greece. Data partially estimated.
3. Excluding Iceland and Turkey.

StatLink: *http://dx.doi.org/10.1787/848421764553*

YYYY CAD CAM
PRESS ENTER

# F. THE IMPACT OF KNOWLEDGE ON PRODUCTIVE ACTIVITIES

## F.1. Income and productivity levels

■ In 2004, GDP per capita in the OECD area ranged from over USD 35 000 in Ireland, Luxembourg, Norway and the United States to less than USD 15 000 in Mexico, Poland, the Slovak Republic and Turkey. For most OECD countries, income levels are 70-85% of US income levels.

■ The differences in income reflect a combination of labour productivity, measured as GDP per hour worked, and labour utilisation, measured as hours worked per capita. A country's labour productivity level is typically the most significant factor in determining differences in income, particularly in countries with low levels of GDP per capita.

■ Most OECD countries have higher levels of GDP per hour worked than GDP per capita because they have lower levels of labour utilisation. The difference between income and productivity levels is largest in European countries; GDP per hour worked surpasses the US productivity level in Belgium, France, Ireland and Norway, whereas income levels in most of these countries are substantially lower than in the United States.

■ In many OECD countries, labour use, as measured by hours worked per capita, is substantially lower than in the United States. This is because of disparities in working hours but also in several countries because of high unemployment and low participation of the working-age population in the labour market. In Iceland and Korea, however, labour input per capita is considerably higher than in the United States, owing to relatively long working hours and high rates of labour force participation. Labour input per capita is also relatively high in Australia, Canada, the Czech Republic, Japan, New Zealand and Switzerland.

### Sources

- OECD, Productivity database, July 2005, available at *www.oecd.org/statistics/productivity.*
- OECD, National Accounts database, July 2005.

### For further reading


- OECD (2001), *Measuring Productivity – OECD Manual*, OECD, Paris.
- Pilat, D. and P. Schreyer (2004), "The OECD Productivity Database – An Overview", *International Productivity Monitor*, No. 8, Spring, pp. 59-65.
- OECD (2004), "Clocking In (and Out): Several Facets of Working Time", *OECD Employment Outlook 2004*, Chapter 1, OECD, Paris.


### Comparisons of income and productivity levels

Comparisons of income and productivity levels face several measurement problems. First, they require comparable data on output. In the 1993 System of National Accounts (SNA), the measurement and definition of GDP are treated systematically across countries. Most countries have implemented this system; in the OECD area, Turkey is the only exception, and its output is likely to be understated relative to other OECD countries. Other differences, such as the measurement of software investment, also affect the comparability of GDP across countries, although the differences are typically quite small.

The second problem is the measurement of labour input. Some countries integrate the measurement of labour input in the national accounts; this may ensure that estimates of labour input are consistent with those of output. In most countries, however, employment data are derived from labour force surveys which are not entirely consistent with the national accounts. Labour input also requires measures of hours worked, which are typically derived either from labour force surveys or from business surveys. Several OECD countries estimate hours worked from a combination of these sources or integrate these sources in a system of labour accounts, which are comparable to the national accounts. The OECD Productivity Database includes estimates of total hours worked which aim at consistency between estimates of employment and hours worked. The cross-country comparability of hours worked remains somewhat limited, however, with a margin of uncertainty in estimates of productivity levels.

Third, international comparisons require price ratios to convert output expressed in a national currency into a common unit. Exchange rates are of limited use for this purpose because they are volatile and reflect many influences, including capital movements and trade flows. The alternative is to use purchasing power parities (PPP), which measure the relative prices of the same basket of consumption goods in different countries. The estimates shown here use official OECD PPPs for 2004.

## F.1. Income and productivity levels

### Income and productivity levels, 2004

Percentage point differences with respect to the United States

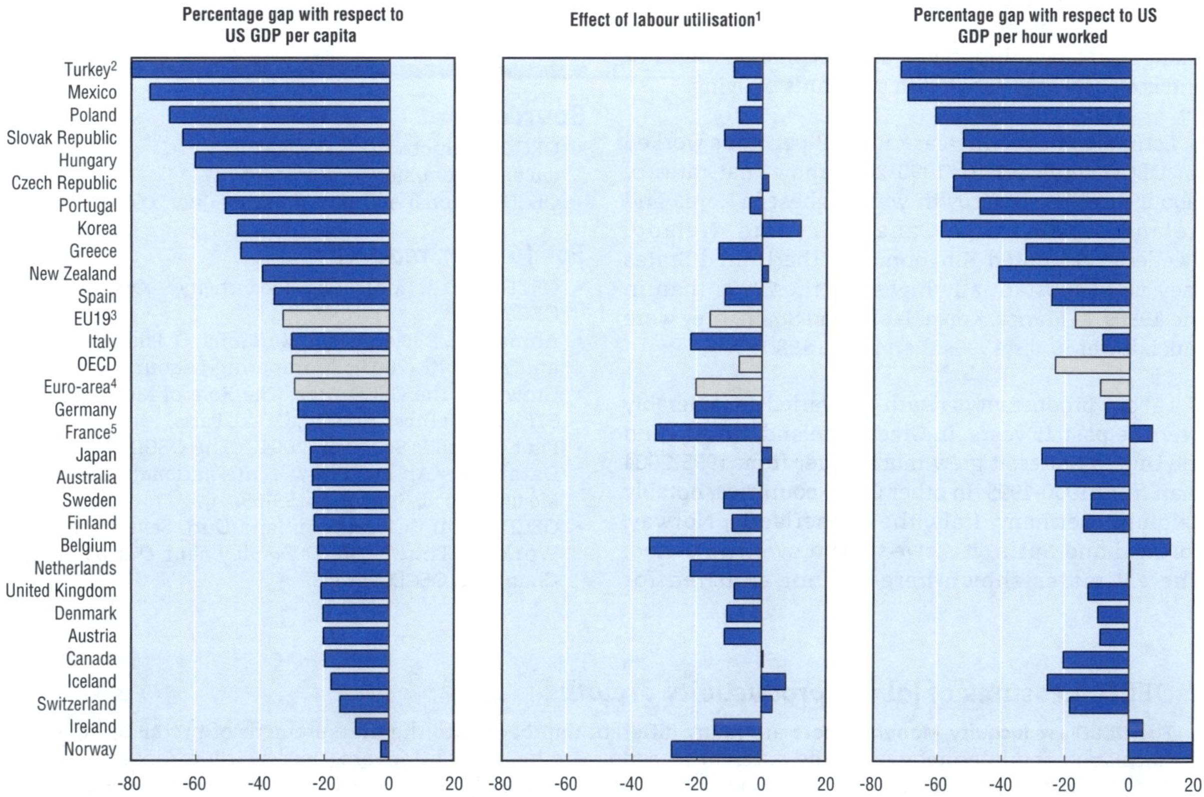


### GDP per capita and GDP per hour worked, 2004

United States = 100

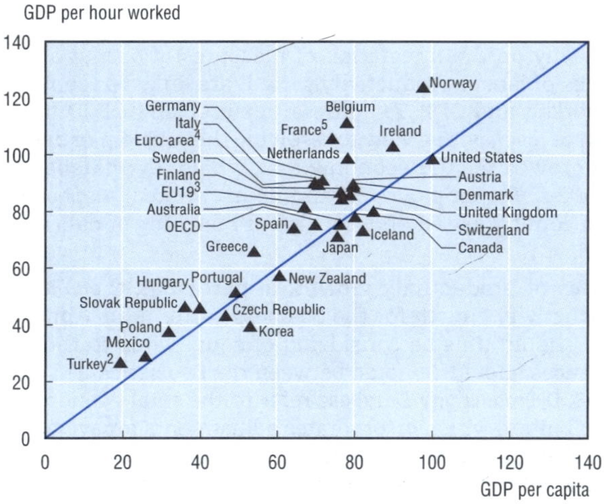


### GDP per hour worked and hours per capita, 2004

United States = 100

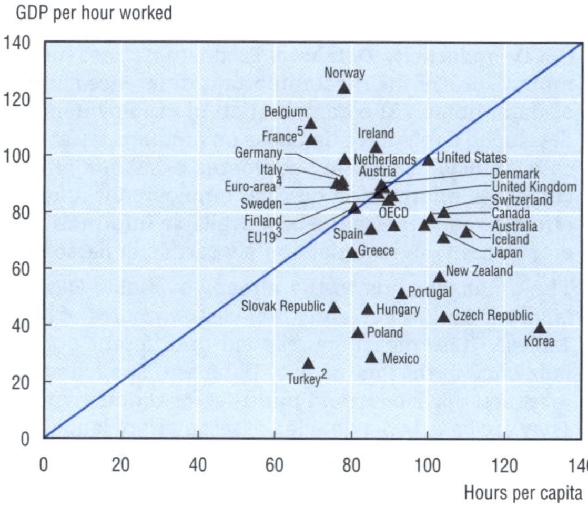


1. Based on total hours worked per capita.
2. GDP for Turkey is based on the 1968 System of National Accounts.
3. EU member countries that are also member countries of the OECD.
4. Austria, Belgium, Finland, France, Germany, Greece, Ireland, Italy, Luxembourg, Netherlands, Portugal, Spain.
5. Includes overseas departments.

StatLink: *http://dx.doi.org/10.1787/237173503560*

## F.2. Labour productivity growth

■ Productivity growth can be measured by relating changes in output to changes in one or more inputs to production. The most common productivity measure is labour productivity, which links changes in output to changes in labour input. It is a key economic indicator and is closely associated with standards of living.

■ Estimates of the increase in GDP per hour worked for OECD countries for 1990-2004 show that rates of labour productivity growth were highest in Korea and Ireland. In Australia, Canada, Iceland, Ireland, Sweden, the United Kingdom and the United States they were substantially higher in the 1990s than in the 1980s. In France, Korea, Japan and Spain, they were much lower in the 1990s than in the 1980s.

■ Labour productivity growth has varied considerably over the past 15 years. In Greece, Iceland, Ireland and the United States, it grew much faster from 1995-2004 than from 1990-1995. In other OECD countries, notably Belgium, Germany, Italy, the Netherlands, Norway, Portugal and Spain, it slowed down over the period. The estimates shown here are not adjusted for differences in the business cycle; cyclically adjusted estimates might show a somewhat different pattern.

### Sources

- OECD Productivity database: *www.oecd.org/statistics/productivity.*
- OECD, National Accounts database, July 2005.

### For further reading


- OECD (2001), *Measuring Productivity – OECD Manual*, OECD, Paris.
- Ahmad, N., F. Lequiller, P. Marianna, D. Pilat, P. Schreyer and A. Wölfl (2003), "Comparing Labour Productivity Growth in the OECD Area: The Role of Measurement", *STI Working Paper 2003/14*, OECD, Paris.
- Pilat, D. and P. Schreyer (2004), "The OECD Productivity Database – An Overview", *International Productivity Monitor*, No. 8, Spring, pp. 59-65.
- OECD (2004), "Clocking In (and Out): Several Facets of Working Time", *OECD Employment Outlook 2004*, Chapter 1, OECD, Paris.


### OECD measures of labour productivity growth

**The OECD Productivity Manual.** There are many different approaches to the measurement of productivity. The calculation and interpretation of the different measures are not straightforward, particularly for international comparisons. To give guidance to statisticians, researchers and analysts who work with productivity measures, the OECD released the *OECD Productivity Manual* in 2001. It is the first comprehensive guide to various productivity measures and focuses on the industry level. It presents the theoretical foundations of productivity measurement, discusses implementation and measurement issues and is accompanied by examples from OECD member countries to enhance its usefulness and readability. It also offers a brief discussion of the interpretation and use of indicators of productivity. See *www.oecd.org/sti/measuring-ind-performance.*

**OECD Productivity Database.** Productivity measures rely heavily on the integration of measures of output and input. Some of the most important differences among studies of labour productivity growth are linked to choice of data, notably the combination of employment, hours worked and GDP. To address this problem, OECD has developed a reference database on productivity at the aggregate level, with a view to resolving the problem of data consistency. In deriving estimates of labour productivity growth for the economy as a whole, the database combines information on GDP, employment and hours worked. For employment and hours worked, a special effort is made to use the best available information for each country, based on a consistent matching of data on employment and annual hours worked per person employed.

The database adds to the already available OECD estimates of productivity growth. In particular, the *OECD Economic Outlook* currently includes estimates of labour productivity growth for the business sector in its Annex Tables. These measures respond to different purposes and should thus be considered of equal value to those published in the Productivity Database. The following differences should be noted between the two series: 1) The measures for labour and multi-factor productivity in the *OECD Productivity Database* refer to the total economy. They are based on a detailed assessment of labour and capital input, which incorporates adjustments for average hours worked per person employed and for capital services. These economy-wide productivity measures provide a close link to changes in GDP per capita. 2) The measures of labour productivity in the *OECD Economic Outlook* cover the business sector only and do not adjust for average hours worked and for capital services. The main advantage of these measures is that it excludes a large part of the economy, *i.e.* the public sector, in which productivity is typically poorly measured. More sophisticated measures of productivity growth in the business sector are currently under development.

More information is available on the special website for the database: *www.oecd.org/statistics/productivity.*

## F.2. Labour productivity growth

**Growth in GDP per hour worked, 1980-1990 compared with 1990-2004**

Total economy, percentage change at annual rate

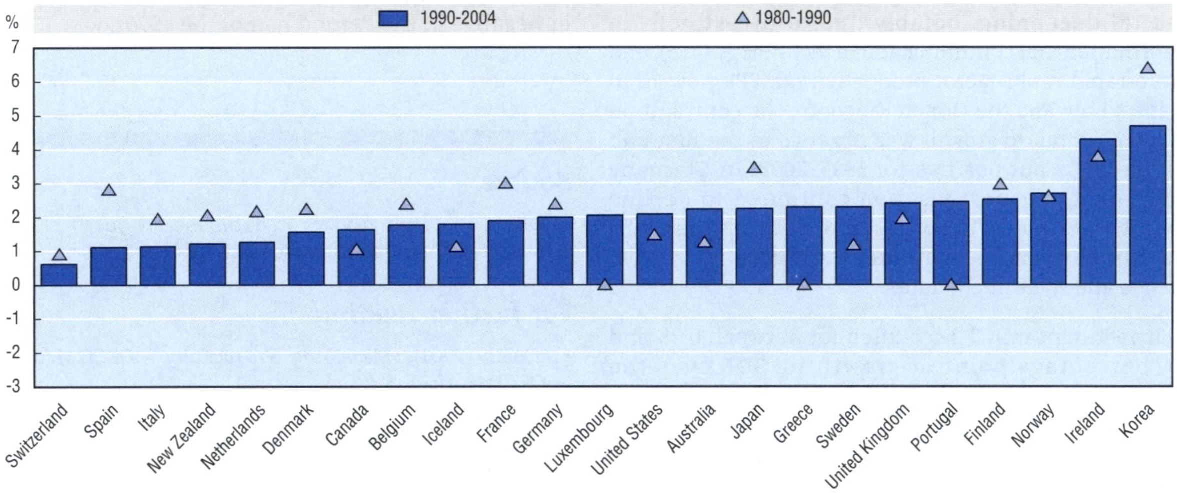


**Growth in GDP per hour worked, 1990-1995 compared with 1995-2004**

Total economy, percentage change at annual rate

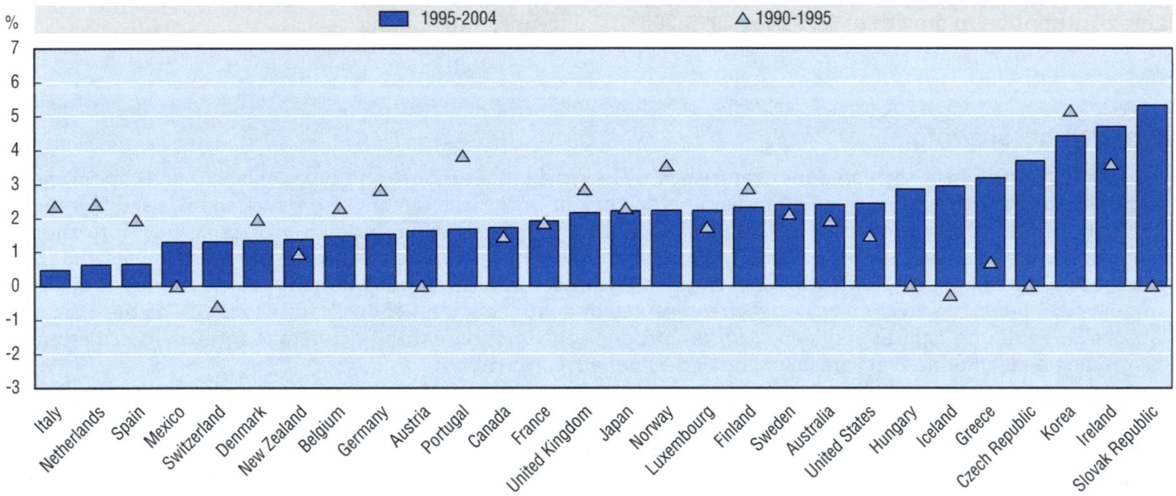


StatLink: *http://dx.doi.org/10.1787/381177605583*

## F.3. Growth accounts for OECD countries

■ Stronger growth in Canada, France, the United Kingdom and the United States over the 1990s was due to several factors, including higher labour utilisation, capital deepening, notably due to investment in information and communications technology (ICT), and more rapid multi-factor productivity (MFP) growth. In France, Italy and the United Kingdom, the contribution of labour input to growth was negative in the first half of the 1990s but positive for 1995-2003. In Germany and Japan, labour utilisation continued to decline from 1995 onwards. In several European countries, MFP growth fell from 1995 onwards, but it rose in Canada, France and the United States.

■ Investment in ICT accounted for between 0.35 and 0.9 percentage point of growth in GDP over the period 1995-2003. Australia, Sweden and the United States received the largest boost from ICT capital; Japan and Canada a more modest one; and Austria, France and Germany a much smaller one. In several countries, ICT accounts for the bulk of capital's contribution to GDP growth.

■ In Canada, Finland, Ireland, the Netherlands, New Zealand and Spain, increased labour utilisation made a large contribution to growth of GDP over 1995-2003.

■ In Ireland, Finland and Greece, MFP growth was also an important source of GDP growth. In Denmark, Italy, the Netherlands and Spain, MFP growth was very low or negative in the second half of the 1990s.

### Source

- OECD Productivity database, July 2005, *www.oecd.org/statistics/productivity.*

### For further reading


- OECD (2001), *Measuring Productivity – OECD Manual*, OECD, Paris.
- Schreyer, P., P.E. Bignon and J. Dupont (2003), "OECD Capital Services Estimates: Methodology and a First Set of Results", *OECD Statistics Working Paper 2003/6*, OECD, Paris.
- Schreyer, P. (2004), "Capital Stocks, Capital Services and Multi-factor Productivity Measures", *OECD Economic Studies No. 37, 2003/2*, OECD, Paris, pp. 163-184.
- Wölfl, A., and D. Hajkova (2005), "Measuring Multi-factor Productivity Growth", *STI Working Papers*, OECD, Paris, forthcoming.


### Growth accounting

Economic growth can be increased in several ways; by increasing the amount and types of labour and capital used in production, and by attaining greater overall efficiency in how these factors of production are used together, *i.e.* higher multi-factor productivity. Growth accounting involves breaking down growth of GDP into these contributions; *i.e.* labour input, capital input and MFP. The growth accounting model is based on the microeconomic theory of production and rests on a number of assumptions, among which the following are important: *i)* production technology can be represented by a production function relating total GDP to the primary inputs labour *L* and capital services *K*; *ii)* this production function exhibits constant returns to scale; and *iii)* product and factor markets are characterised by perfect competition.

For any desired level of output, the firm minimises costs of inputs, subject to the production technology discussed above. Factor input markets are competitive, so that the firm takes factor prices as given and adjusts quantities of factor inputs to minimise costs. The rate of growth of output is a weighted average of the rates of growth of the various inputs and of the multi-factor productivity term. The weights attached to each input are the output elasticities for each factor of production. Output elasticities cannot be directly observed, however, and the factor shares of labour and capital are often used as weights.


OECD SCIENCE, TECHNOLOGY AND INDUSTRY SCOREBOARD 2005 – ISBN 92-64-01055-6 – © OECD 2005

## F.3. Growth accounts for OECD countries

### Contributions to growth of GDP, G7 countries, 1990-95 and 1995-2003[1]

In percentage points

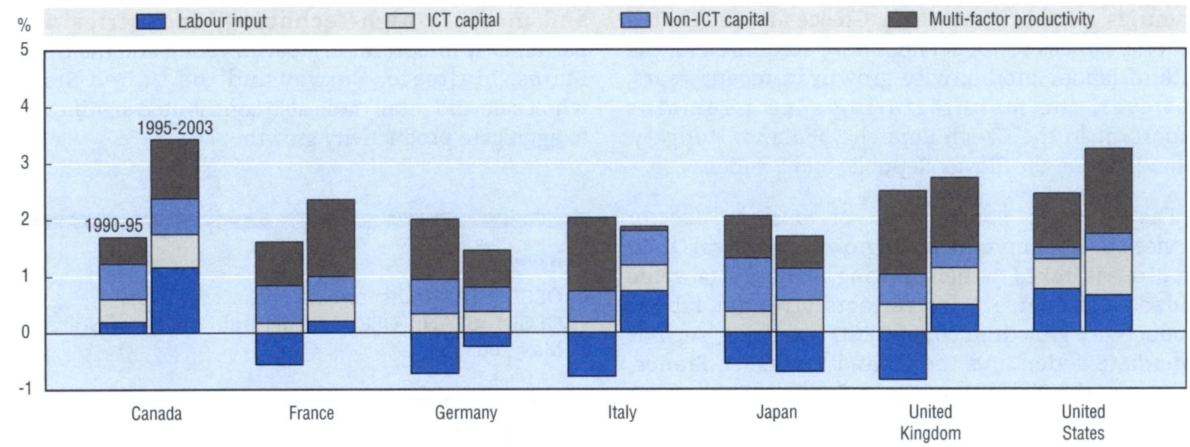


### Contributions to GDP growth, all OECD countries, 1995-2003[2]

In percentage points

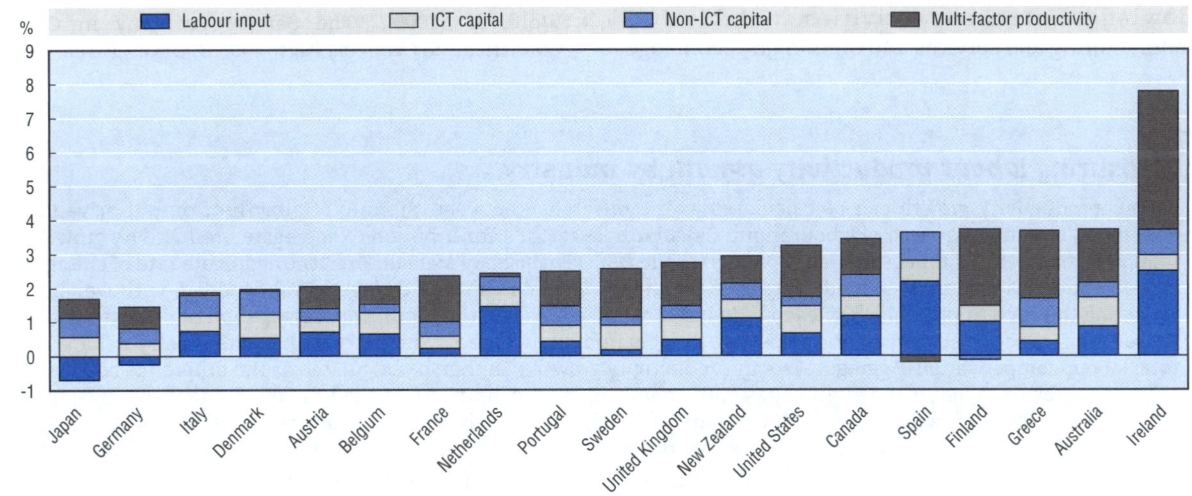


1. 1991-1995 for Germany; 1995-2001 for Italy, 1995-2002 for France and Japan.
2. 1995-2001 for Italy; 1995-2002 for Australia, France, Japan, New Zealand and Spain.

StatLink: *http://dx.doi.org/10.1787/483730666483*

## F.4. Labour productivity growth by industry

■ A breakdown of productivity growth by activity can show which industries are particularly important for overall productivity performance. In many OECD countries, notably in Australia, Greece and the United States, business sector services have accounted for the bulk of labour productivity growth in recent years. However, the manufacturing sector remains important in the Czech Republic, Finland, Hungary, Poland, Korea, the Slovak Republic and Sweden.

■ The growing contribution of business sector services to labour productivity growth in several OECD countries is linked to their growing share in total value added. However, it also reflects stronger labour productivity growth in some OECD countries, such as Canada, Sweden and the United States. In France, Germany, the Netherlands and Spain, on the other hand, labour productivity growth in business services slowed over the past decade, a trend that can also be observed at the aggregate level (see F.2).

■ A large share of labour productivity growth in the non-agricultural business sector is attributable to knowledge-intensive activities, notably ICT manufacturing and services and other high-technology and medium-high-technology manufacturing. ICT manufacturing and services were particularly important in Finland and Sweden, whereas other high- and medium-high-technology industries were particularly important in Japan, Sweden and the United States. In Greece, Norway and the United States, wholesale and retail trade also contributed significantly to aggregate productivity growth.

### Sources

- OECD, STAN Indicators database, May 2005.
- OECD, STAN: OECD Structural Analysis Statistics, May 2005.

### For further reading


- OECD (2001), *Measuring Productivity – OECD Manual*, OECD, Paris.
- Wölfl, A. (2003), "Productivity Growth in Service Industries: An Assessment of Recent Patterns and the Role of Measurement", *STI Working Paper 2003/7*, OECD, Paris.
- Wölfl, A. (2005), "The Service Economy in OECD Countries", *STI Working Paper 2005/3*, OECD, Paris.


### *Measuring labour productivity growth by industry*

Labour productivity growth can be calculated as the difference between the rate of growth of output or value added and the rate of growth of labour input. Calculating a sector's contribution to aggregate productivity growth requires a number of simple steps, as explained in the *OECD Productivity Manual*. First, the aggregate rate of change in value added is a share-weighted average of the industry-specific rate of change in value added, with weights reflecting the current price share of each industry in value added. On the input side, aggregation of industry-level labour input is achieved by weighting the growth rates in hours worked by industry with each industry's share in total labour compensation. Aggregate labour productivity growth can then be calculated as the difference between aggregate growth in value added and aggregate growth in labour input. An industry's contribution to aggregate labour productivity growth is therefore the difference between its contribution to total value added and total labour input. If value added and labour shares are the same, total labour productivity growth is a simple weighted average of industry-specific labour productivity growth. Similar approaches can be followed when production, instead of value added, is used as the output measure. However, OECD work on the basis of the STAN database has typically focused on value added, since constant price series of value added are more widely available across OECD countries than constant price series of production. Difficulties in measuring output and productivity in services sectors should also be taken into consideration when interpreting the results (see Wölfl, 2003).

# F.4. Labour productivity growth by industry

### Labour productivity growth by industry

Contributions to average annual growth rate, 1995-2003[1]

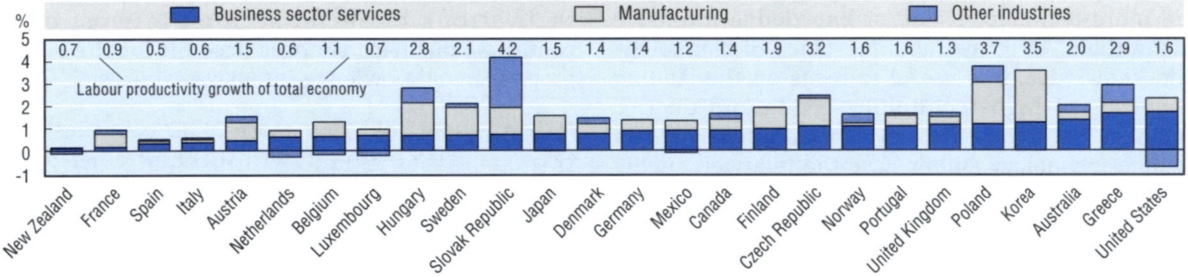


### Share of business sector services in total value added

1980 and 2003[1]

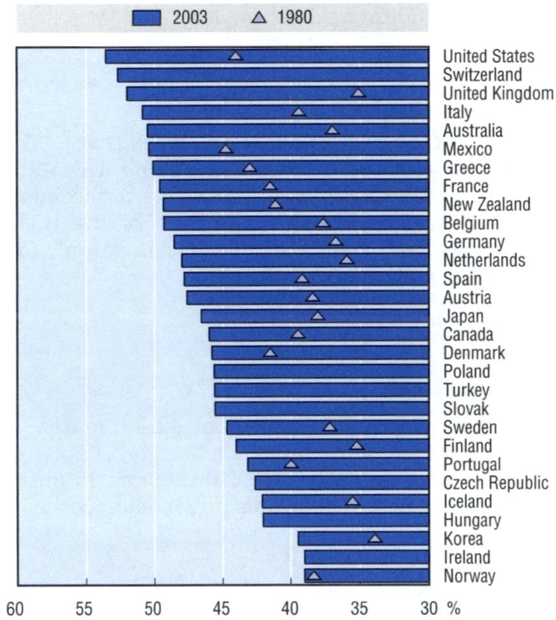


### Growth in business sector services labour productivity

Annual average growth rates

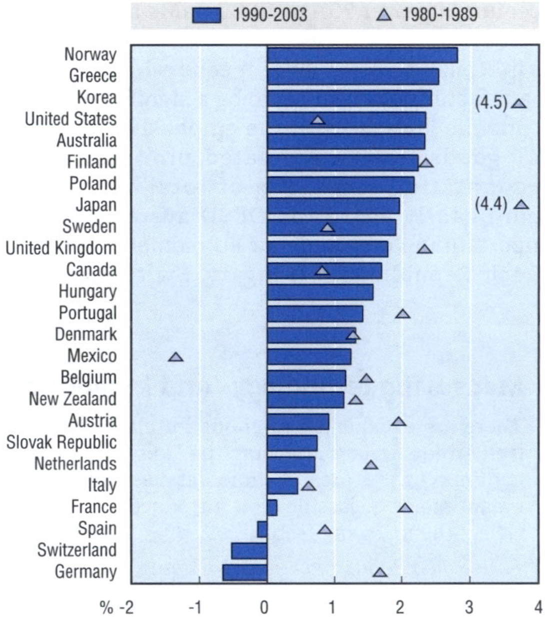


### Contributions of key sectors to labour productivity growth in the non-agricultural business sector

Contributions to average annual growth rate, 1990-2003[1]

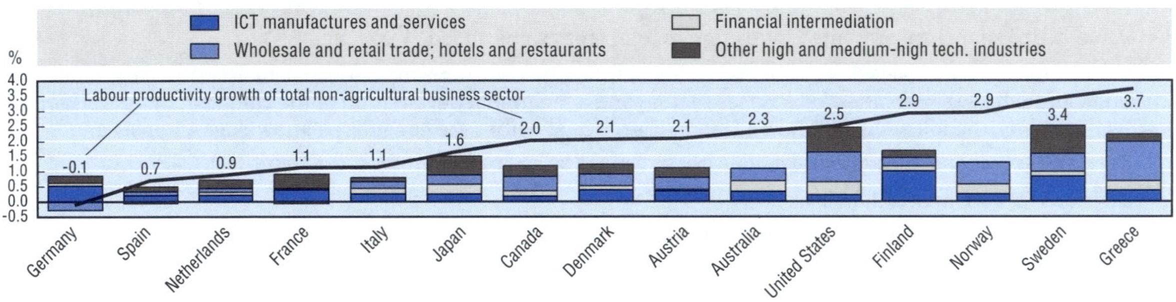


*Note:* Business sector services cover "Wholesale and retail trade, hotels and restaurants" (ISIC 50-55), "Transport, storage and communication" (ISIC 60-64), "Finance, insurance, real estate and business services" (ISIC 65-74).

1. Or nearest year available.

StatLink: *http://dx.doi.org/10.1787/522633271125*

## F.5. Technology- and knowledge-intensive industries

■ All industries generate and/or exploit new technology and knowledge to some extent, but some are more technology- and/or knowledge-intensive than others. To gauge the importance of technology and knowledge, it is useful to focus on the leading *producers* of high-technology goods and on the activities (including services) that are intensive *users* of high technology and/or have the relatively highly skilled workforce necessary to benefit fully from technological innovations.

■ In 2002, high- and medium-high-technology manufacturing accounted for about 7.5% of total OECD value added, compared to about 8.5% in 2000. Meanwhile, the share of knowledge-based "market" services (see box) continues to rise and now accounts for over 20% of OECD value added.

■ In Ireland, high- and medium-high-technology manufacturing continues to be a significant driver of economic growth (with the emphasis moving from ICT goods to health-related products). It now accounts for about 21% of total value added, significantly above the OECD average. It is also important in Korea and new EU members such as the Czech Republic and Hungary. Switzerland's and Luxembourg's high shares of knowledge-intensive services (over 25% of total value added) are due to their strong financial sectors. In most other countries, business services account for the largest proportion of knowledge-intensive services.

■ Throughout the 1990s most OECD countries have experienced steady growth in knowledge-based services. Among the largest OECD countries, the United States has had particularly strong growth, while Japan's development of knowledge-based services continues to lag behind.

### Sources

- OECD, STAN Indicators database, May 2005.
- OECD, STAN: OECD Structural Analysis Statistics, May 2005.

### For further reading


- Pilat, D., A. Cimper, K. Olsen and C. Webb (2005), "The Changing Nature of Manufacturing in OECD Economies", *STI Working Paper*, OECD, Paris, forthcoming.
- Hatzichronologou, T. (1997), "Revision of the High-Technology Sector and Product Classification", *STI Working Paper 1997/2*, OECD, Paris.


### *Measuring technology- and knowledge-intensive industries*

There are established methods for classifying manufacturing industries according to technological intensity (see Annex A), but capturing the "knowledge-intensive" services sectors has proved more challenging. Efforts continue in this area as more detailed data on the services sector become available in OECD countries. In the meantime, the classification introduced in the 2003 *STI Scoreboard* is used here. The figures presented opposite reflect the following features:

- Use of an industry breakdown based on ISIC Rev. 3.
- A technology classification of manufacturing industries based on ISIC Rev. 3 R&D intensities in the 1990s (see Annex A).
- A relatively narrow definition of knowledge-based services, which reflects improved data availability. "Real estate activities" (over 10% of total OECD area value added) are excluded, as a significant proportion consists of "Imputed rent of owner-occupied dwellings".
- Value-added shares are presented in relation to total gross value added.

Based on previous analysis of users of embodied technology (based on input-output tables), recently available (though limited) R&D intensities for services sectors and a preliminary evaluation of the composition of workforce skills by activity, the following ISIC Rev. 3 "market" service activities are considered knowledge-intensive:

- Division 64: Post and telecommunications (these cannot be separated out for most countries).
- Divisions 65-67: Finance and insurance.
- Divisions 71-74: Business activities (not including real estate).

In addition, although not shown in the figures, the value-added shares of the education and health sectors (about 11% of the total for the OECD area) are presented for most countries in Annex Table F.5.

## F.5. Technology- and knowledge-intensive industries

### Share of total gross value added, 2002

High- and medium-high-technology manufactures

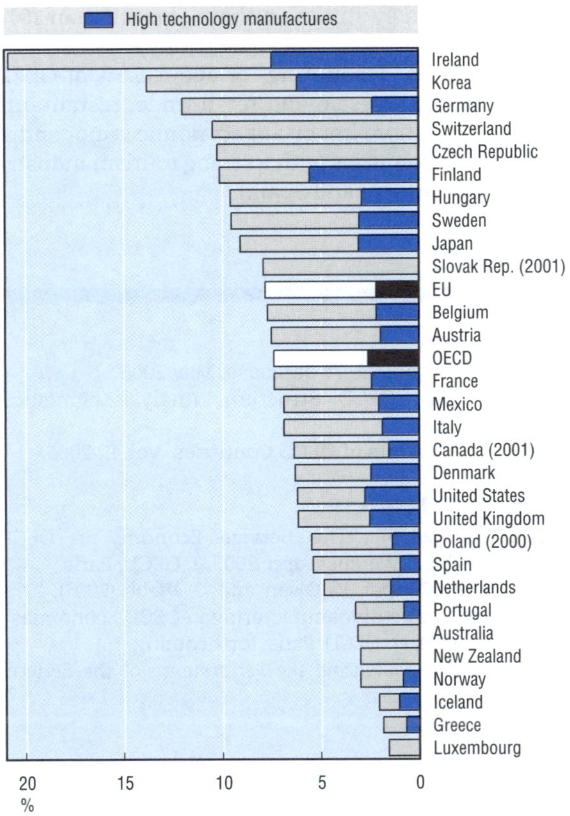


Knowledge-intensive "market" services

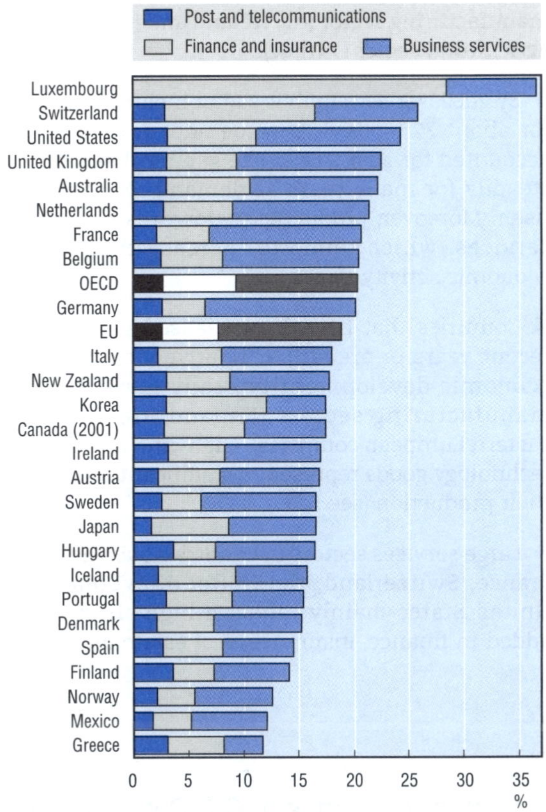


### Shares of gross value added 1990-2002

High- and medium-high-technology manufactures

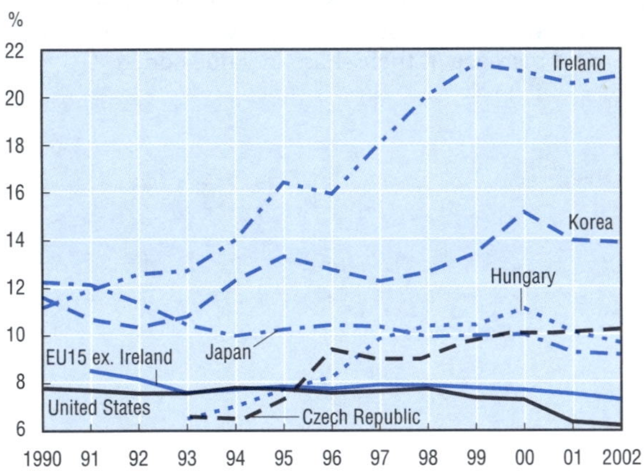


Knowledge-intensive "market" services

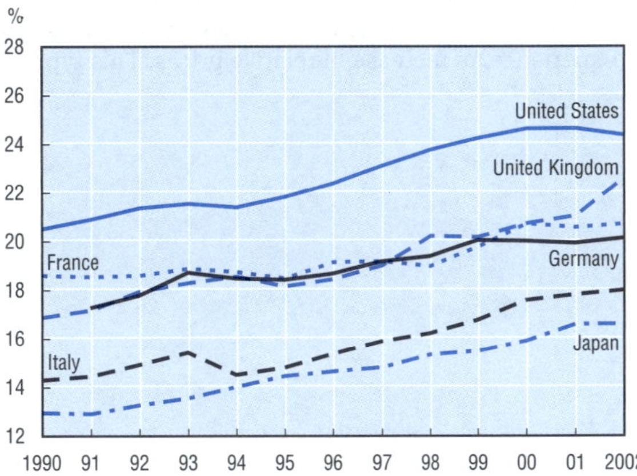


StatLink: http://dx.doi.org/10.1787/381402335886

## F.6. The structure of OECD economies

■ Sectoral shares of value added provide a good perspective on the structure of OECD economies. Some economies are heavily oriented towards services (*e.g.* the United States), while others have a significant manufacturing sector (*e.g.* Ireland and Korea) or a large agricultural sector (Turkey).

■ By 2002, services (public sector included) accounted for about 72% of OECD value added; manufactures accounted for about 17%. The gap has been widening steadily for many years as demand for services has risen. Moreover, productivity growth is slow in some services, which tends to increase their share in economic activity.

■ Countries that have industrialised very rapidly in recent years or are still at relatively early stages of economic development typically have the largest manufacturing sectors (Finland, Ireland, Korea, eastern European countries). High- and medium-high-technology goods represent a significant proportion of their production (see F.5).

■ Large services sectors in countries such as Belgium, France, Switzerland, the United Kingdom and the United States mainly reflect a high share of value added in finance, insurance, real estate and business services, and a large community, social and personal services sector.

■ Agriculture accounts for just 2% of OECD value added. Only Turkey still has a share of more than 10%. The construction sector is also relatively small in most OECD countries, accounting for about 5.5% of OECD value added. Wholesale and retail trade, restaurants and hotels is a more important economic sector and is often large in countries with a strong tourism industry (*e.g.* Greece, Portugal and Spain).

### Sources


- OECD, STAN Indicators database, May 2005.
- OECD, STAN: OECD Structural Analysis Statistics, May 2005.
- National Accounts of OECD Countries, Vol. II, 2005.


### *For further reading*


- Wölfl, A. (2005), "The Service Economy in OECD Countries", *STI Working Paper 2005/3*, OECD, Paris.
- Pilat, D., A. Cimper, K. Olsen and C. Webb (2005), "The Changing Nature of Manufacturing in OECD Economies", *STI Working Paper*, OECD, Paris, forthcoming.
- OECD (2005), *Enhancing the Performance of the Services Sector*, OECD, Paris.


### *Structural change in OECD economies*

Economic development in OECD economies has long been characterised by a gradual process of structural change. In the initial stages, the share of agriculture in total value added and employment declines and the manufacturing sector grows as economies industrialise. In recent years, many OECD economies have seen a decline in the share of manufacturing in overall economic activity. This is partly due to saturated demand for many manufactured goods but also to the difference in productivity growth between the manufacturing and the services sectors. Since productivity typically grows faster in manufacturing, relative prices decline and the sector's share in value added may decline. In contrast, some services sectors may have little scope for productivity growth and therefore experience an increase in relative prices. This typically leads to an increase in their share in value added.



OECD SCIENCE, TECHNOLOGY AND INDUSTRY SCOREBOARD 2005 – ISBN 92-64-01055-6 – © OECD 2005

## F.6. The structure of OECD economies

### Shares of total gross value added, 2002 – Major activities

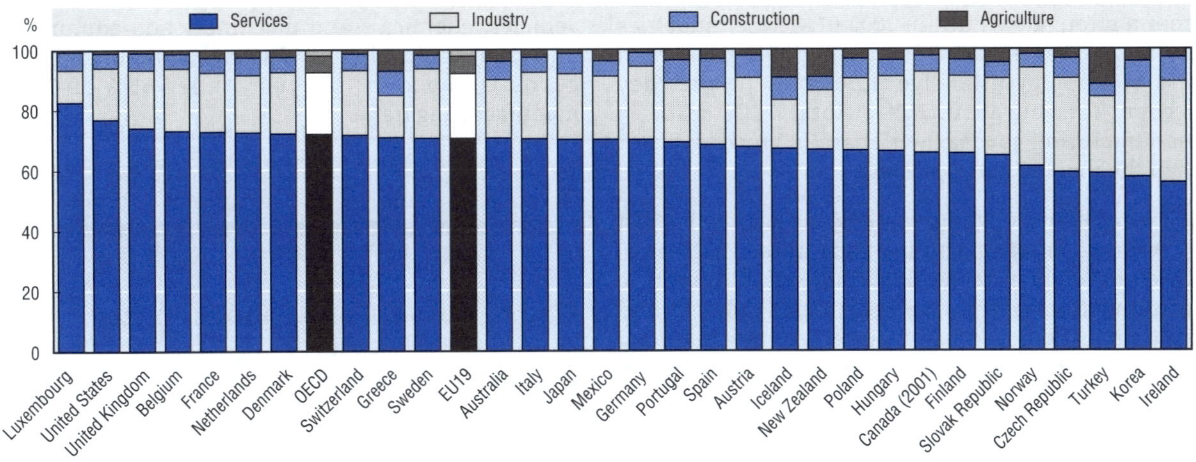


### Distribution of gross value added of the services sector, 2002

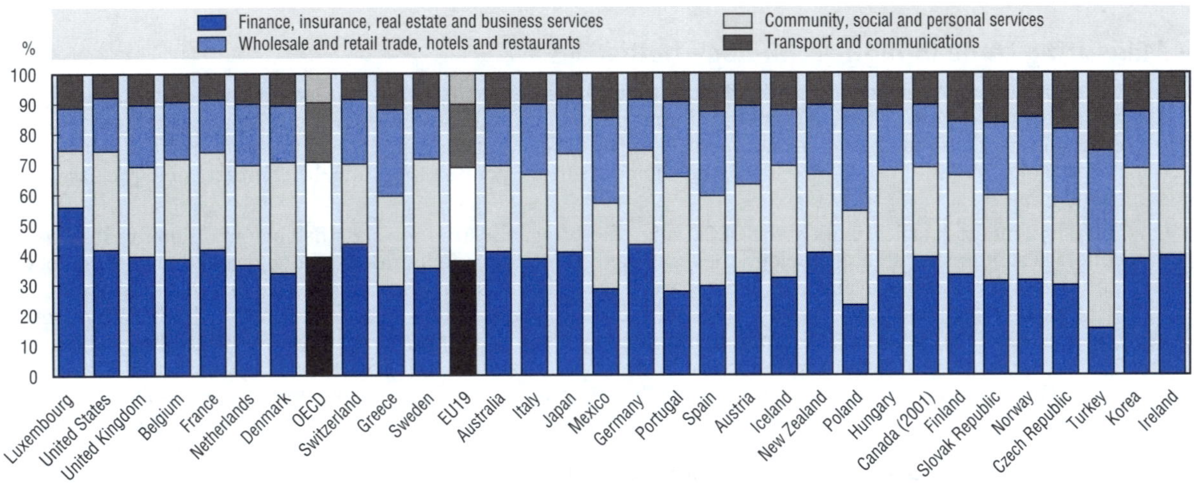


### Shares of total gross value added, 2002 – Mining, manufacturing and utilities

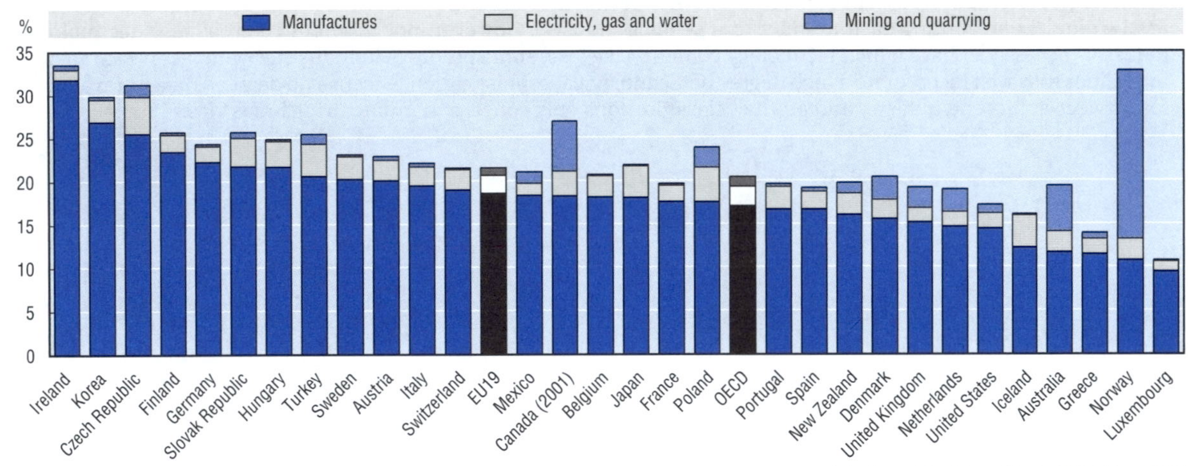


StatLink: *http://dx.doi.org/10.1787/620680374058*

## F.7. International trade by technology intensity

■ Trade in high-technology industries has recovered from a strong downturn in 2000-01. These industries are more oriented towards international trade than less technology-intensive industries. While they account for only about 25% of total OECD trade in manufacturing goods, their share is growing faster than the manufacturing average.

■ From 1994 to 2003, pharmaceuticals had the highest growth rate in manufacturing trade in the OECD area. Three other high-technology industries, scientific instruments, aircraft and spacecraft, and radio, TV and communication, also had high growth rates. Among high-technology industries, only office machinery and computers had relatively slow growth.

■ The share of high-technology industries in total OECD trade has declined marginally in recent years. Medium-high-technology industries (notably motor vehicles, chemicals and machinery and equipment) and high-technology industries, taken together, currently account for just under 65% of OECD manufacturing trade.

### Source

- OECD, STAN Indicators database, March 2005.

### For further reading

- Hatzichronoglou, T. (1997), "Revision of the High-technology Sector and Product Classification", *STI Working Paper 1997/2*.

### *Measuring trade in high-technology industries*

The very concept of a "high-technology" industry is subject to debate. Is it one that largely *produces* technology or one that largely *uses* technology? A certain number of potential indicators range from input-related measures (*e.g.* expenditures on research and development, number of scientists and engineers) to output-related measures (*e.g.* number of patents). For such indicators, the choice of cut-off points separating different technology classes is somewhat arbitrary.

On the basis of methodological work at the OECD, manufacturing industries are classified in four different categories of technological intensity: high technology, medium-high technology, medium-low technology and low technology (see Annex A). For reasons of availability of comparable statistics, this classification is based on indicators of (direct as well as indirect) technological intensity which reflect to some degree "technology-producer" or "technology-user" aspects. These indicators are R&D expenditures divided by value added, R&D expenditures divided by production and R&D expenditures plus technology embodied in intermediate and capital goods divided by production. The level of detail in the industrial breakdown is limited only by the availability of comparable input-output tables and R&D surveys. The indicators were calculated in the aggregate for 1990 for ten OECD countries for which the embodied technology variable is available using purchasing power parities in 1990 USD. Embodied technology intensities appear to be highly correlated with direct R&D intensities; this reinforces the view that the latter largely reflect an industry's technological sophistication.

This classification is particularly useful for analysing industry information on employment or value added by technological intensity, for example. To do likewise for international trade flows – which are defined at product level – requires attributing each product to a specific industry. However, not all products in a "high-technology industry" necessarily have a high technology content. Likewise, some products in industries with lesser technology intensities may well incorporate a high degree of technological sophistication. Because no detailed data are available for services at present, industry and product classifications only concern manufacturing industries.

 OECD SCIENCE, TECHNOLOGY AND INDUSTRY SCOREBOARD 2005 – ISBN 92-64-01055-6 – © OECD 2005

## F.7. International trade by technology intensity

### OECD[1] manufacturing trade[2] by technology intensity

Index 1994 = 100

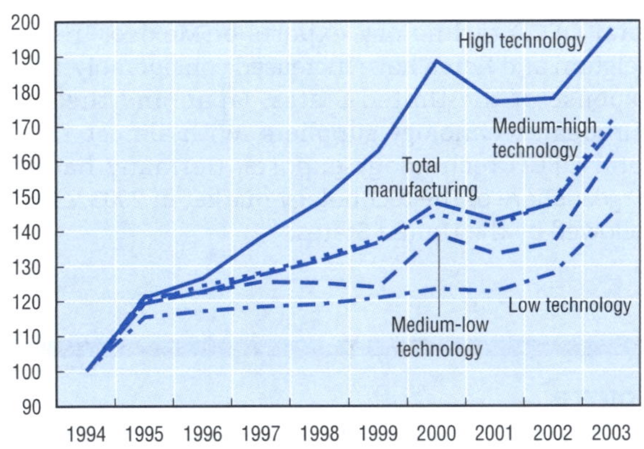


### Structure of OECD[1] manufacturing trade[2] by technology intensity

Share in total manufacturing trade

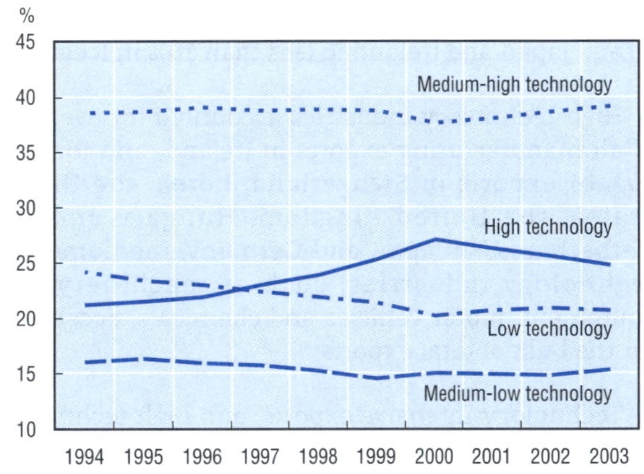


### Growth of OECD[1] manufacturing trade[2] by industry and technological intensity

Average annual growth rate, 1994-2003

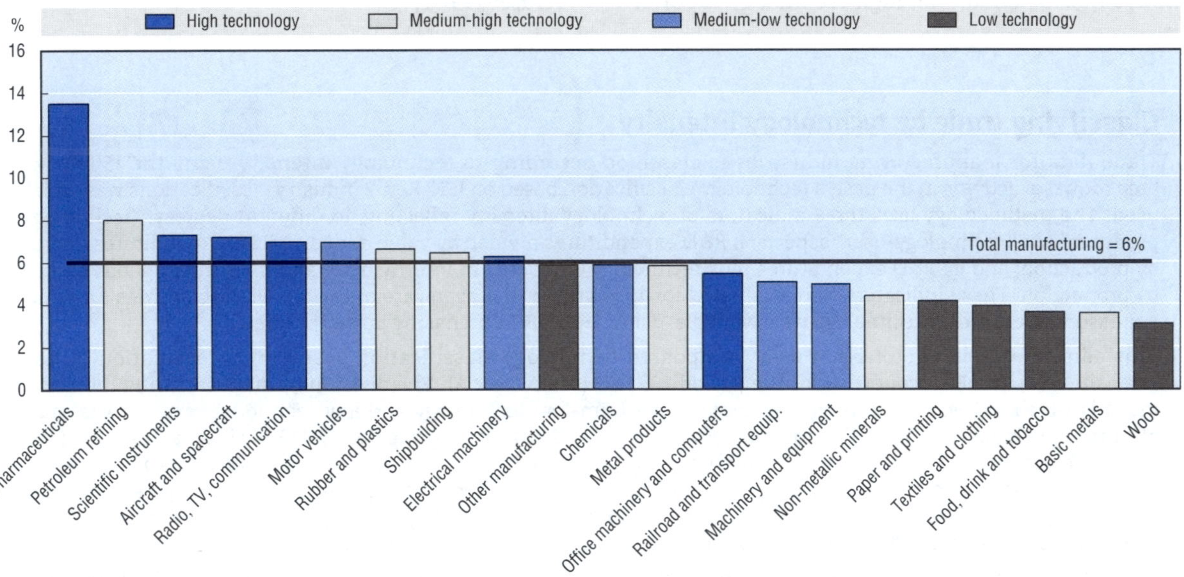


1. Excluding Luxembourg and the Slovak Republic.
2. Average value of total OECD exports and imports of goods.

StatLink: *http://dx.doi.org/10.1787/545400655443*

## F.8. Exports from high- and medium-high-technology industries

Industries of high- and medium-high-technology intensity accounted for over two-thirds of total OECD manufacturing exports in 2003. Differences among countries are substantial; the share of high- and medium-high-technology industries ranges from over 80% in Japan and Ireland to less than 10% in Iceland.

High-technology industries accounted for over 50% of all manufacturing exports in Ireland, and for over 30% of exports in Switzerland, Korea, the United States, the United Kingdom, Hungary and the Netherlands. In Japan and Germany, medium-high technology industries, such as machinery and equipment, motor vehicles and chemicals, accounted for the bulk of total exports.

Technology-intensive exports, and high technology exports in particular, accounted for much of the growth in trade over the past decade. In all OECD countries, they grew more rapidly than total manufacturing exports. Japan is the only country in which total manufacturing exports grew faster over the 1994-2003 period than high-technology exports.

Technology exports grew very rapidly in Iceland, Turkey and the eastern European countries, although most of these countries, with Hungary and the Czech Republic as exceptions, still focus primarily on low- and medium-low-technology exports. The shares in total OECD technology exports of Mexico, Ireland, Belgium and Korea have increased considerably, at the expense of the United States, Japan and the large European technology suppliers. With almost 17% of total OECD technology exports, Germany had the largest share of the technology market in 2003, closely followed by the United States.

### Source

- OECD, STAN Indicators database, March 2005.

### For further reading

- Hatzichronoglou, T. "Revision of the High-technology Sector and Product Classification", *STI Working Paper* 1997/2.

### Classifying trade by technology intensity

Trade data for manufacturing industries is classified according to technology intensity using the ISIC Rev. 3 breakdown of activity. In the past, a technology classification based on ISIC Rev. 2 industry classifications was widely used. The methodology uses three indicators of technology intensity reflecting, to different degrees, "technology-producer" and "technology-user" aspects: *i)* R&D expenditures divided by value added; *ii)* R&D expenditures divided by production; and *iii)* R&D expenditures plus technology embodied in intermediate and investment goods divided by production. These indicators were evaluated for 1990 and for the aggregate of the ten OECD countries for which a measure of embodied technology was available, using 1990 USD purchasing power parities.

This edition of the *STI Scoreboard* uses an updated technology classification based on an evaluation of R&D intensities for 12 OECD countries for the period 1991-99 (see Annex A). The division of manufacturing industries into high-technology, medium-high-technology, medium-low-technology and low-technology groups was made after ranking industries according to their average for 1991-99 against aggregate OECD R&D intensities. Industries classified to higher categories have a higher average intensity for both indicators than industries in lower categories. Also considered were: *i)* temporal stability: for adjacent years, industries classified to higher categories have a higher average intensity than those in lower categories; and *ii)* country median stability: industries classified to the higher categories have a higher median intensity than those in lower categories.

The cut-off points between these groups are clear except possibly the distinction between the medium-low- and low-technology groups. The low-technology group consists of relatively aggregate sectors, owing to limited detailed R&D expenditure data across countries. The few cases in which R&D intensities are available for more detailed (2-digit) breakdowns confirm the allocation of these industries to low technology.

The classification concerns the OECD area as a whole. For individual countries, allocation to technology groups may differ. Also, at national level, finer technology classifications may be generated from more detailed underlying data.

## F.8. Exports from high- and medium-high-technology industries

### Share of technology industries in manufacturing exports, 2003

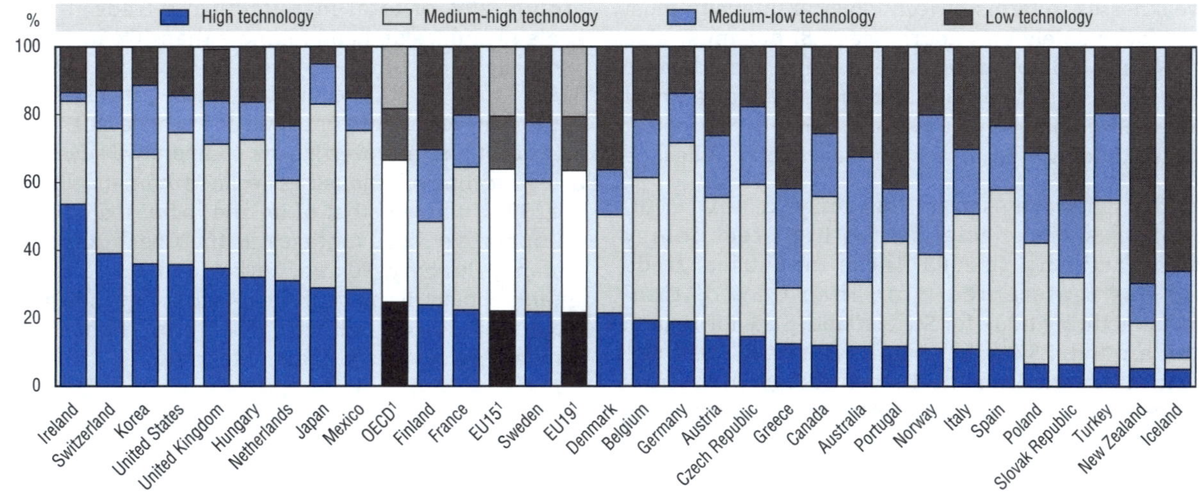


### Growth of high- and medium-high-technology exports, 1994-2003

Annual average growth rate

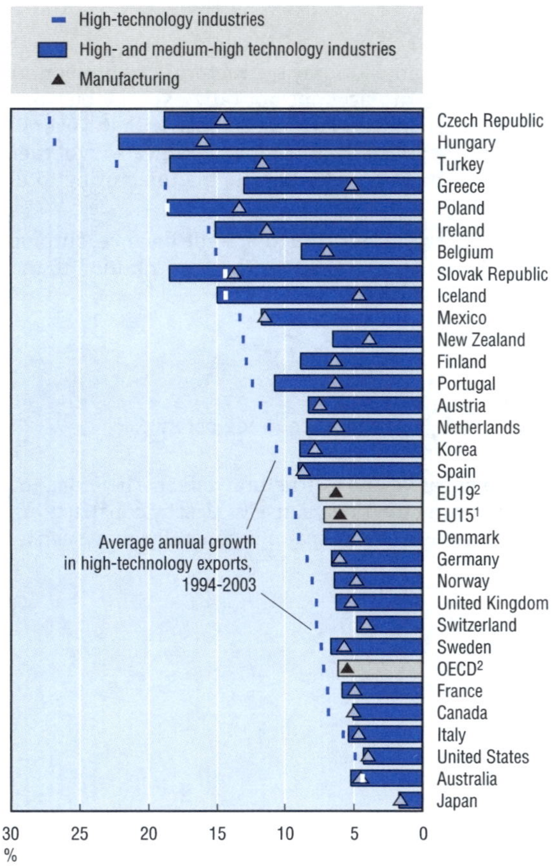


### Share in total OECD[2] high- and medium-high-technology exports, 1994-2003

Percentage change in exports' growth shares

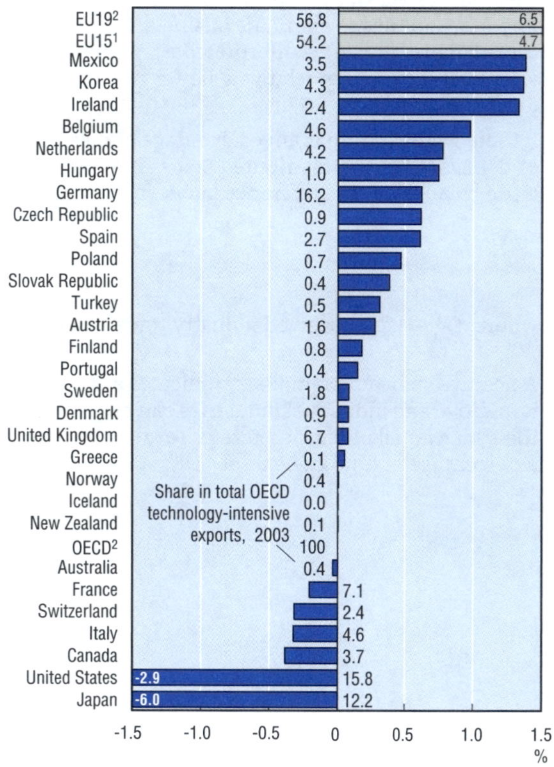


1. Excluding Luxembourg.
2. Excluding Luxembourg and the Slovak Republic.

StatLink: *http://dx.doi.org/10.1787/520574817683*

## F.9. Contributions to the manufacturing trade balance

■ An assessment of countries' strengths and weaknesses in terms of technological intensity must not focus solely on exports (see F.8) but must also gauge the role of imports, as exports may depend heavily on imports in the same industry. Indicators of revealed comparative advantage allow for a better understanding of countries' specialisation profiles.

■ This indicator shows that only a few OECD countries are specialised in high-technology manufacturing. In 2003, these industries' trade surplus represented more than 6.5% of total manufacturing trade for Switzerland, 5.5% for Ireland and around 4.5% for the United States. The trade surplus in medium-high-technology industries represented more than 15% of total manufacturing trade in Japan and over 7% in Germany.

■ A considerable number of OECD countries still have a strong comparative advantage in medium-low-technology and low-technology industries. The structural surplus in these industries accounted for around 20% of total manufacturing trade in New Zealand and Iceland and for more than 10% in Turkey.

■ For most OECD countries, these specialisation patterns have changed little over the past decade. There are exceptions, however. Japan's comparative advantage in high-technology industries declined dramatically over the 1990s, whereas that of Ireland increased strongly. Comparative disadvantages in the Czech Republic, Finland, Hungary, Poland, Turkey and New Zealand shrank notably. In medium-high-technology industries, larger shifts occurred, with an improvement in the comparative advantage in many countries.

### Source

- OECD STAN Indicators database, March 2005.

### *Measuring contributions to the trade balance*

The "contribution to the trade balance" makes it possible to identify an economy's structural strengths and weaknesses via the composition of international trade flows. It takes into account not only exports, but also imports, and tries to eliminate business cycle variations by comparing an industry's trade balance with the overall trade balance. It can be interpreted as an indicator of "revealed comparative advantage", as it indicates whether an industry performs relatively better or worse than the manufacturing total, whether the manufacturing total itself is in deficit or surplus.

If there were no comparative advantage or disadvantage for any industry i, a country's total trade balance (surplus or deficit) should be distributed across industries according to their share in total trade. The "contribution to the trade balance" is the difference between the actual and this theoretical balance:

$$(X_i - M_i) - (X - M)\frac{(X_i + M_i)}{(X + M)}$$

where $(X_i - M_i)$ = observed industry trade balance, and $(X - M)\frac{(X_i + M_i)}{(X + M)}$ = theoretical trade balance.

A positive value for an industry indicates a structural surplus and a negative one a structural deficit. The indicator is additive and individual industries can be grouped together by summing their respective values: by construction, the sum over all industries is zero. To allow comparisons across industries, the indicator is generally expressed as a percentage of total trade or of GDP.


OECD SCIENCE, TECHNOLOGY AND INDUSTRY SCOREBOARD 2005 – ISBN 92-64-01055-6 – © OECD 2005

## F.9. Contributions to the manufacturing trade balance

### Contribution to the manufacturing trade balance, 2003

As a percentage of manufacturing trade

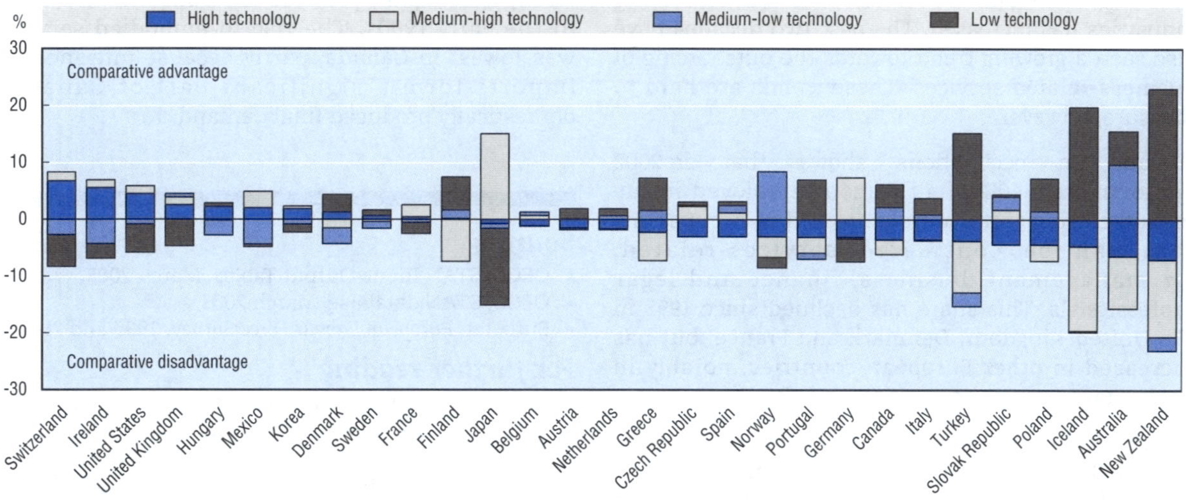


### Change in contribution to the manufacturing trade balance, 2003

As a percentage of total manufacturing trade

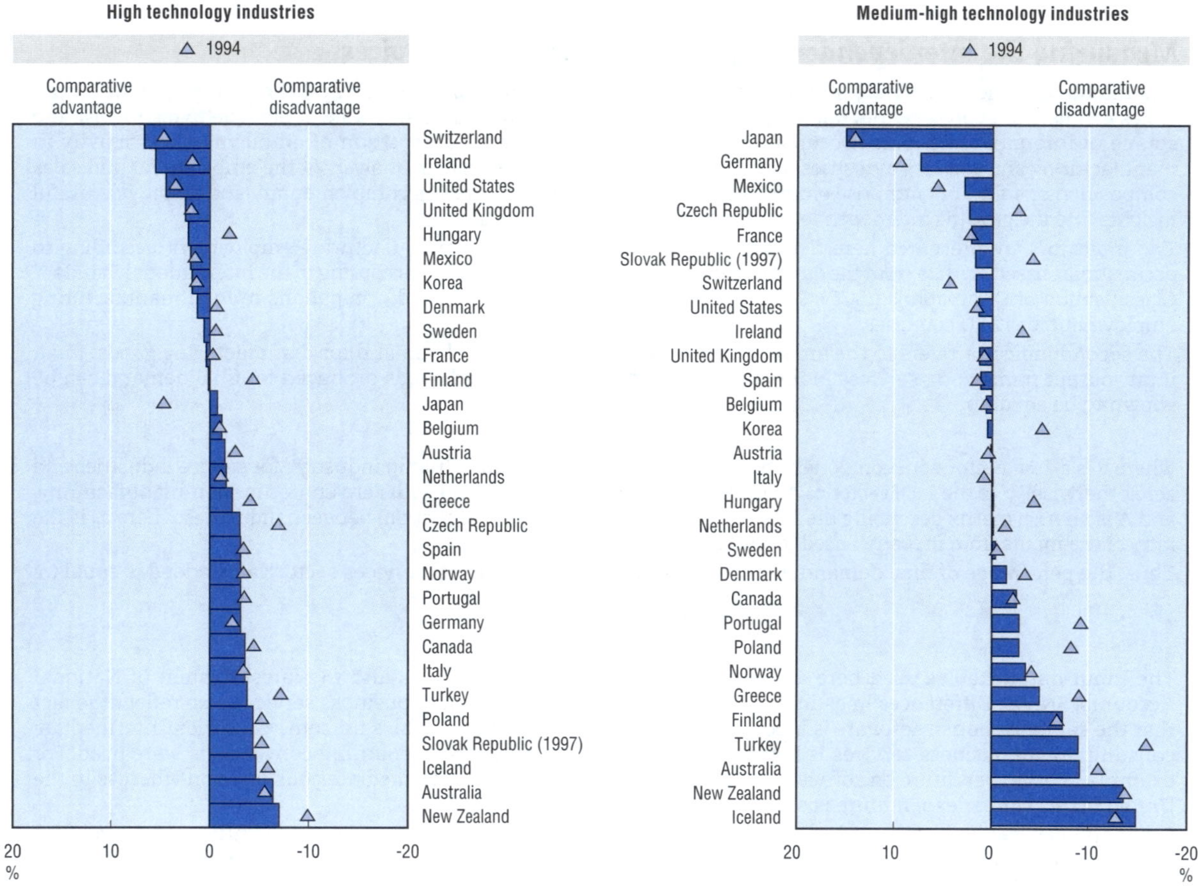


StatLink: *http://dx.doi.org/10.1787/348820837440*

## F.10. The interdependence of services and manufacturing

As the amount of services activities that enters manufacturing production has risen in recent years, the interdependence of services and manufacturing industries has increased. The past two decades have also seen a growing trend towards the outsourcing of business-related services. These trends are hard to measure, however.

Data on occupations shows that in 2002 approximately 40% of all persons employed in the manufacturing sector were employed in occupations that can be considered services-related, *e.g.* management, business, finance and legal professionals. This share has declined since 1995 in the United Kingdom, Denmark and France, but has increased in other European countries, notably in Spain, Italy and Germany.

Data from input-output tables show that by the mid-1990s the amount of services embodied in one unit of final demand for manufactured goods was significantly higher than in the early 1970s for all ten countries covered. In the Netherlands, the contribution nearly doubled, albeit from a relatively low starting point (to 15.7% from 8.2%). The amount of services embodied in manufacturing also grew strongly in Japan, particularly from the mid-1980s to the early 1990s. The rise in embodied services was lowest in Canada, partly because intermediate imports form a significant part of Canada's domestically produced final demand.

### Sources

- OECD, STAN Input-Output Tables, March 2005.
- OECD, STAN database, March 2005.
- Eurostat, *European Labour Force Survey*, 1995 and 2002.

### *For further reading*


- Wölfl, A. (2005), "The Service Economy in OECD Countries", *STI Working Paper 2005/3*, OECD, Paris.
- Pilat, D. and A. Wölfl, (2005), "Measuring the Interaction between Manufacturing and Services", *STI Working Paper 2005/5*, OECD, Paris.
- Pilat, D., A. Cimper, K. Olsen and C. Webb (2005), "The Changing Nature of Manufacturing in OECD Economies", *STI Working Paper*, OECD, Paris, forthcoming.


### *Measuring the interdependence of manufacturing and services*

The interdependence of services and manufacturing can be measured in several ways. For example, input-output tables can help to analyse output and employment flows between industries and make it possible to distinguish the source of intermediate inputs. Occupation data can help to see the composition of employment or activity in manufacturing and services industries. Firm (micro) level data may enable an analysis of the employment and sales composition of a firm or enterprise group. These – and other – approaches are complementary and all provide useful insights into the growing interdependence of services and manufacturing.

Two indicators are presented here. The first shows the composition of manufacturing employment according to occupations, based on data from the *European Labour Force Survey* and classified according to the International Standard Classification of Occupations (ISCO). This shows the share of services-related occupations in total manufacturing employment for 12 EU countries.

The second indicator refers to the amount of services embodied in final demand for manufacturing goods. In an input-output framework, services indirectly embodied in manufactured goods produced for final demand can be shown to be equal to:

$$v \times (I - A)^{-1} \times y'$$

where $v$ is a $1 \times n$ vector with components $v_j$ (the ratio of value added to output in industry $j$ for service industries and zero otherwise), y' is the $1 \times n$ vector of domestically produced final demand with zero entries for non-manufacturing, and A is an $n \times n$ matrix describing the inter-relationships (or production function) between industries where $a_{ij}$ is the ratio of the inputs from industry i used to make the output of industry $j$.

Thus, the percentage of final demand in manufactured goods that reflects services sector value added is equal to:

$$v \times (I - a)^{-1} \times \frac{y'}{\sum y'}$$

The input-output tables used here are based on ISIC Rev. 3 classifications and the latest System of National Accounts, SNA93. Differences in estimates of intermediate consumption of business services also reflect the fact that the capitalisation of software is inconsistent across countries. In the tables for some countries, intermediate consumption of business services is higher than it would be if different accounting conventions were used. For example, most expenditure on software in the UK tables is recorded as intermediate consumption whereas in the United States similar expenditure is often capitalised.

Other approaches can be followed to examine the interdependence of services and manufacturing. Firm-level data can be particularly revealing as they suggest that manufacturing firms increasingly engage in services activities (see Pilat and Wölfl, 2005).



OECD SCIENCE, TECHNOLOGY AND INDUSTRY SCOREBOARD 2005 – ISBN 92-64-01055-6 – © OECD 2005

## F.10. The interdependence of services and manufacturing

### Share of employment in services-related occupations in the manufacturing sector[1]

As a percentage of total manufacturing employment, 1995 and 2002[2]

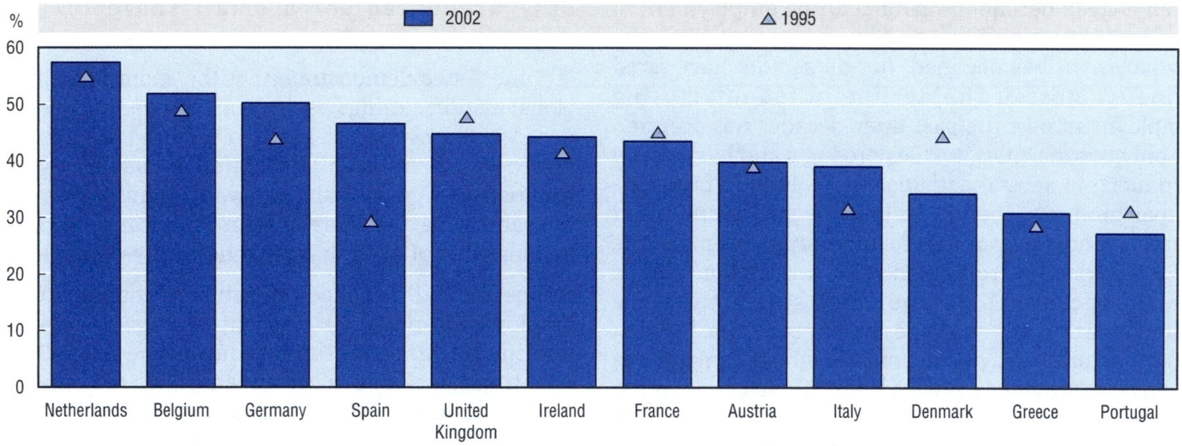


### Services sector value added embodied in manufactured goods

Percentage of total value added of manufactured goods in final demand

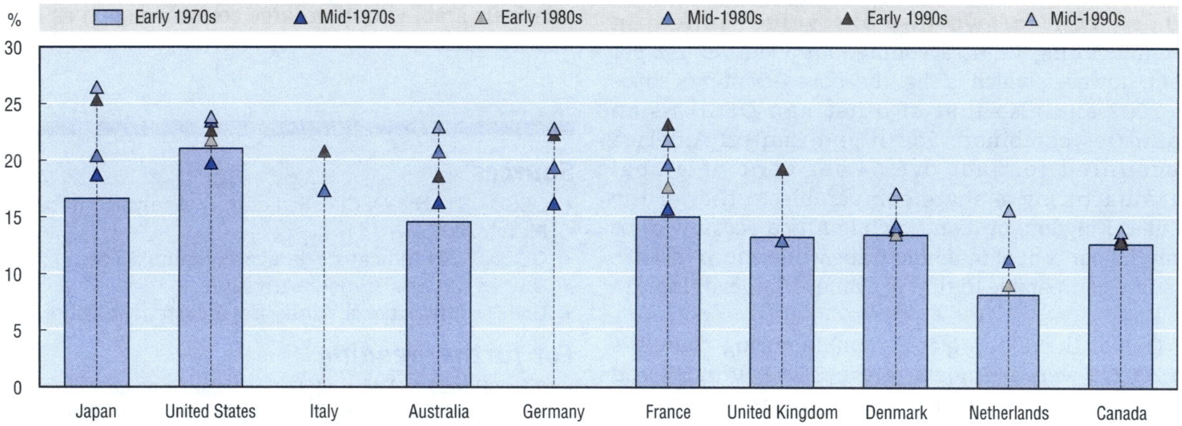


1. Services-related occupations include ISCO classes 100-500, 830, 910 and 933, *i.e.* legislators, senior officials and managers, professionals and associate professionals, clerks, service workers, shop and market sales workers, as well as drivers, sales and services elementary occupations and transport workers.
2. Data for Germany refer to 2001.

StatLink: *http://dx.doi.org/10.1787/053332582475*

## F.11. The changing nature of manufacturing

■ Concerns about deindustrialisation are back on the agenda in many OECD countries. Recent years have seen a steep decline in manufacturing employment in many OECD countries. While overall manufacturing employment has declined, not all sectors have fared equally. Most of the decline in manufacturing employment over the past three decades has occurred in only two activities, textiles products and basic metal products. In several activities, notably food products, paper products, chemicals, motor vehicles and other manufacturing, manufacturing employment in the G7 countries has remained relatively stable. This is partly because OECD countries still maintain a comparative advantage in certain sectors of manufacturing activity, in some of which demand has been quite strong, *e.g.* pharmaceuticals. In certain other industries, such as food products, manufacturing production is often located close to the market.

■ In terms of the importance of different countries in global manufacturing, OECD countries still dominated global manufacturing in 2002, accounting for just below 80 per cent of world-wide value added in manufacturing. China accounted for about 7.5 to 8 per cent, however, which is slightly above Germany's share in 2002 and also that of other non-OECD Asian countries combined. South and Central America accounted for just over 4 per cent of global manufacturing, a share comparable to that of the United Kingdom or France, while Africa accounted for only 1.3 per cent of manufacturing value added in 2002, a share comparable to that of Chinese Taipei or India.

■ Out of the 10 top global manufacturing countries in 2002, 9 were members of the OECD, with US and Japanese manufacturing being substantially larger than any other country. In 2002, China's manufacturing value added was slightly above that of Germany. However, given recent trends, China has now clearly become the third-largest manufacturing country in the world. Other non-OECD countries, including Brazil, India and the Russian Federation, only accounted for a small share of total manufacturing in 2002.

■ Time series demonstrate that the share of China in global manufacturing has risen rapidly over the past few decades. Strong growth has also occurred in East Asia, while South Asia and the Middle East have also experienced a growing share in world manufacturing. At the same time, the share of Latin America has declined whereas that of Africa has remained at a very low level.

■ The limited evidence on trends in manufacturing employment in non-OECD countries suggests that the decline in manufacturing employment in OECD countries has not been accompanied by an increase in non-OECD countries. ILO and UNIDO employment estimates for key non-OECD countries such as Brazil, China and the Russian Federation shows that manufacturing employment has also declined in these countries, and very substantially in some of them. Manufacturing employment has also remained relatively stable in other large countries such as India and Indonesia.

### Sources

- OECD STAN: OECD Structural Analysis database, March 2005.
- OECD STAN Indicators database, March 2005.
- United Nations Statistics Division.
- UNIDO, *International Yearbook of Industrial Statistics.*

### For further reading


- Pilat, D and A. Wölfl (2005), "Measuring the Interaction between Manufacturing and Services", *STI Working Paper 2005/5*, OECD, Paris.
- Pilat, D., A. Cimper, K. Olsen and C. Webb (2005), "The Changing Nature of Manufacturing in OECD Economies", *STI Working Paper*, OECD, Paris, forthcoming.


### *Measuring the share of countries in global manufacturing value added*

Comparing manufacturing production or value added across countries is no simple task. Estimates of purchasing power parities are available for total GDP, but these do not reflect the relative prices of manufacturing production or value added. Conversion factors for manufacturing production and value added have been estimated on the basis of information on manufacturing prices and unit value ratios for some countries, but these are not available for all countries. In the calculations presented here, value added is converted at exchange rates, as manufacturing is typically highly exposed to international trade. The estimates are therefore subject to some uncertainty and should be interpreted with caution.

 OECD SCIENCE, TECHNOLOGY AND INDUSTRY SCOREBOARD 2005 – ISBN 92-64-01055-6 – © OECD 2005

## F.11. The changing nature of manufacturing

### Manufacturing employment by key activity, G7 countries, 1970-2001

Million workers

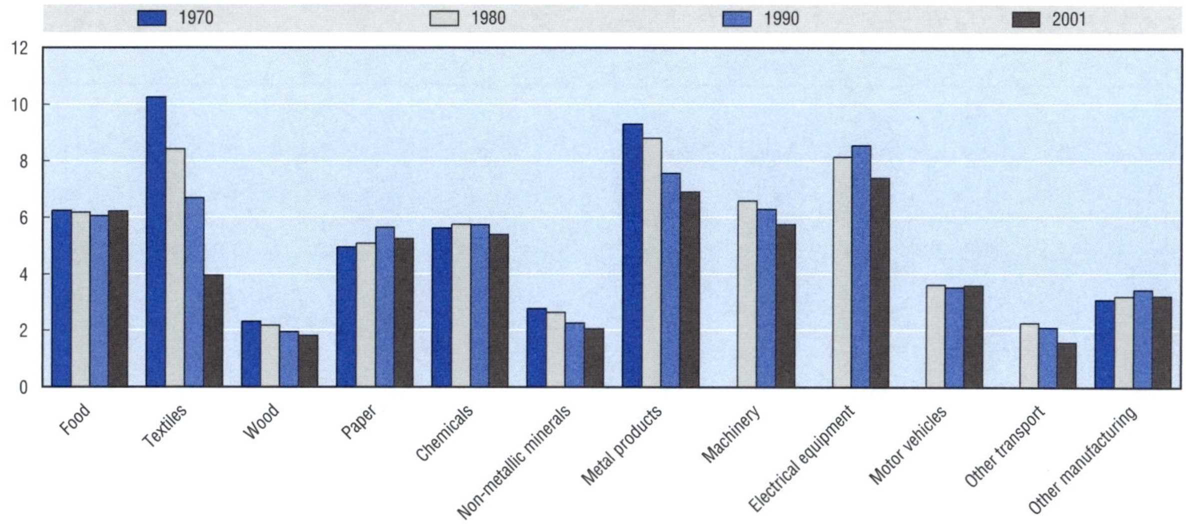


### Share of major regions in global manufacturing value added, 2002 (%)

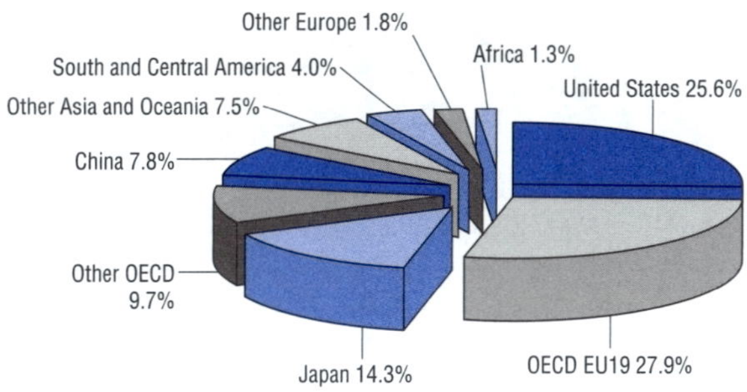


### Top 20 manufacturing economies, 2002

Manufacturing value added, USD billions

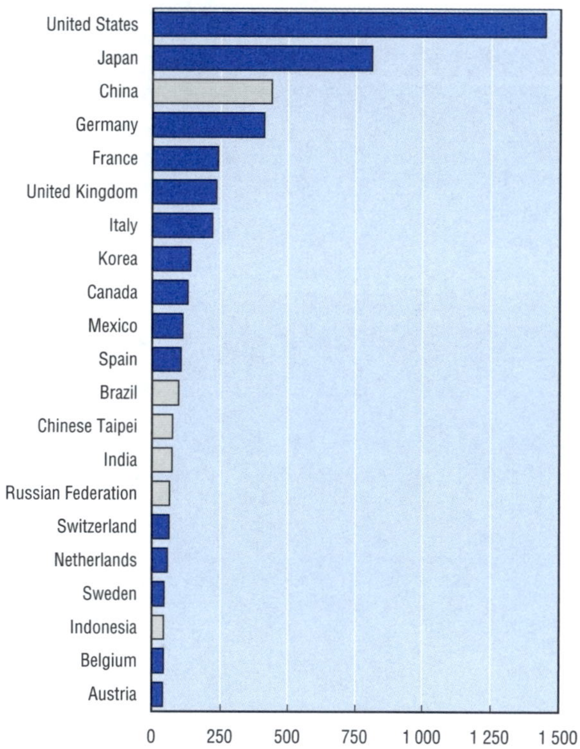


StatLink: *http://dx.doi.org/10.1787/337356816574*

# ANNEX A

# *Classification of manufacturing industries based on technology*

Annex Table 1.1 presents manufacturing industries classified according to technology intensity using the ISIC Rev. 3 breakdown of activity.

Technological effort is a critical determinant of productivity growth and international competitiveness. However, since it is not spread evenly across the economy, analyses of industry performance and structural change attach much importance to technological criteria. Methodological work carried out at the OECD is used to determine these criteria.

In the past, a technology classification based on ISIC Rev. 2 industry classifications was widely used. The methodology uses three indicators of technology intensity reflecting, to different degrees, "technology-producer" and "technology-user" aspects: *i)* R&D expenditures divided by value added; *ii)* R&D expenditures divided by production; and *iii)* R&D expenditures plus technology embodied in intermediate and investment goods divided by production. These indicators were evaluated for 1990 and for the aggregate of the ten OECD countries for which a measure of embodied technology was available, using 1990 USD purchasing power parities (see T. Hatzichronoglou, "Revision of the High-Technology Sector and Product Classification", STI Working Paper 1997/2).

The current classification is based on analysis of R&D expenditure and output of 12 OECD countries according to ISIC Rev. 3 (NACE Rev. 1 in Europe) and covering the period 1991-99. In the absence of updated ISIC Rev. 3 input-output tables (required for estimating embodied technology), only the first two indicators could be calculated.

The division of manufacturing industries into high-technology, medium-high-technology, medium-low-technology and low-technology groups was made after ranking the industries according to their average over 1991-99 against aggregate OECD R&D intensities. Industries classified to higher categories have a higher average intensity for both indicators than industries in lower categories. Also considered were: *i)* temporal stability: for adjacent years, industries classified to higher categories have a higher average intensity than those in lower categories (see Annex Table 1.2); and *ii)* country median stability: industries classified to the higher categories have a higher median intensity than those in lower categories.

Points to note:

- The cut-off points are clear except possibly the distinction between the medium-low- and low-technology groups.

Annex 1.1. **Classification of manufacturing industries based on technology**[1]

| | ISIC Rev. 3 | 1999 | | | | 1991 | | | |
|---|---|---|---|---|---|---|---|---|---|
| | | R&D divided by production | | R&D divided by value added | | R&D divided by production | | R&D divided by value added | |
| | | Aggregate intensity[2] | Median intensity | Aggregate intensity[2] | Median intensity | Aggregate intensity[2] | Median intensity | Aggregate intensity[2] | Median intensity |
| **High-technology industries** | | | | | | | | | |
| Aircraft and spacecraft | 353 | 10.3 | 10.4 | 29.1 | 27.5 | 13.9 | 12.9 | 34.7 | 32.1 |
| Pharmaceuticals | 2423 | 10.5 | 10.1 | 22.3 | 25.8 | 9.4 | 8.7 | 20.6 | 19.7 |
| Office, accounting and computing machinery | 30 | 7.2 | 4.6 | 25.8 | 15.1 | 10.9 | 6.4 | 29.4 | 15.2 |
| Radio, TV and communciations equipment | 32 | 7.4 | 7.6 | 17.9 | 22.4 | 7.9 | 8.2 | 17.0 | 21.5 |
| Medical, precision and optical instruments | 33 | 9.7 | 5.6 | 24.6 | 11.9 | 6.6 | 6.1 | 15.6 | 12.5 |
| **Medium-high-technology industries** | | | | | | | | | |
| Electrical machinery and apparatus, n.e.c. | 31 | 3.6 | 2.3 | 9.1 | 6.7 | 4.2 | 2.6 | 9.3 | 5.9 |
| Motor vehicles, trailers and semi-trailers | 34 | 3.5 | 2.8 | 13.3 | 11.7 | 3.7 | 3.0 | 14.3 | 11.9 |
| Chemicals excluding pharmaceuticals | 24 excl. 2423 | 2.9 | 2.2 | 8.3 | 7.1 | 3.4 | 2.8 | 9.8 | 8.0 |
| Railroad equipment and transport equipment, n.e.c. | 352 + 359 | 3.1 | 2.8 | 8.7 | 7.9 | 2.9 | 2.1 | 7.6 | 5.4 |
| Machinery and equipment, n.e.c. | 29 | 2.2 | 2.1 | 5.8 | 5.3 | 1.9 | 2.0 | 4.6 | 4.7 |
| **Medium-low-technology industries** | | | | | | | | | |
| Building and repairing of ships and boats | 351 | 1.0 | 1.0 | 3.1 | 2.9 | 0.9 | 0.9 | 2.8 | 2.6 |
| Rubber and plastics products | 25 | 1.0 | 1.1 | 2.7 | 3.0 | 1.0 | 0.6 | 2.6 | 1.5 |
| Coke, refined petroleum products and nuclear fuel | 23 | 0.4 | 0.3 | 1.9 | 2.7 | 1.2 | 0.7 | 5.4 | 3.8 |
| Other non-metallic mineral products | 26 | 0.8 | 0.6 | 1.9 | 1.3 | 1.0 | 0.6 | 2.4 | 1.5 |
| Basic metals and fabricated metal products | 27-28 | 0.6 | 0.5 | 1.6 | 1.4 | 0.7 | 0.6 | 2.0 | 1.6 |
| **Low-technology industries** | | | | | | | | | |
| Manufacturing, n.e.c.; Recycling | 36-37 | 0.5 | 0.5 | 1.3 | 1.2 | 0.5 | 0.4 | 1.2 | 0.9 |
| Wood, pulp, paper, paper products, printing and publishing | 20-22 | 0.4 | 0.1 | 1.0 | 0.3 | 0.3 | 0.1 | 0.8 | 0.3 |
| Food products, beverages and tobacco | 15-16 | 0.3 | 0.3 | 1.1 | 1.0 | 0.3 | 0.3 | 1.1 | 1.1 |
| Textiles, textile products, leather and footwear | 17-19 | 0.3 | 0.4 | 0.8 | 1.0 | 0.2 | 0.3 | 0.7 | 0.7 |
| **Total manufacturing** | 15-37 | 2.6 | 2.2 | 7.2 | 6.5 | 2.5 | 2.0 | 7.0 | 5.7 |

1. Based on data for 12 OECD countries: United States, Canada, Japan, Denmark, Finland, France, Germany, Ireland, Italy, Spain, Sweden, United Kingdom
2. Aggregate R&D intensities calculated after converting countries' R&D expenditures, value added and production using GDP PPPs

*Source:* OECD: ANBERD and STAN databases, May 2003

StatLink: *http://dx.doi.org/10.1787/585330067651*

Annex 1.2. **R&D intensity[1] for aggregate of 12 OECD countries, 1991-1999**

| | *ISIC Rev.3* | **1991** | **1992** | **1993** | **1994** | **1995** | **1996** | **1997** | **1998** | **1999** | mean intensity 1991-1999 |
|---|---|---|---|---|---|---|---|---|---|---|---|
| Aircraft and spacecraft | 353 | 13.9 | 13.9 | 13.5 | 13.9 | 16.2 | 14.8 | 12.8 | 10.7 | 10.3 | 13.3 |
| Pharmaceuticals | 2423 | 9.4 | 10.1 | 10.8 | 10.9 | 10.6 | 10.3 | 11.0 | 11.1 | 10.5 | 10.5 |
| Office, accounting and computing machinery | 30 | 10.9 | 10.4 | 9.3 | 8.8 | 7.5 | 9.1 | 10.4 | 8.9 | 7.2 | 9.2 |
| Radio, TV and communciations equipment | 32 | 7.9 | 8.3 | 7.9 | 7.8 | 7.7 | 8.2 | 8.0 | 8.6 | 7.4 | 8.0 |
| Medical, precision and optical instruments | 33 | 6.6 | 6.8 | 7.1 | 7.7 | 7.7 | 7.4 | 8.0 | 8.0 | 9.7 | 7.7 |
| Electrical machinery and apparatus, n.e.c. | 31 | 4.2 | 4.0 | 4.0 | 3.8 | 4.0 | 3.9 | 3.9 | 4.0 | 3.6 | 3.9 |
| Motor vehicles, trailers and semi-trailers | 34 | 3.7 | 3.4 | 3.5 | 3.4 | 3.5 | 3.7 | 3.5 | 3.3 | 3.5 | 3.5 |
| Chemicals excluding pharmaceuticals | 24 excl. 24 | 3.4 | 3.3 | 3.4 | 3.1 | 2.8 | 3.1 | 2.7 | 3.1 | 2.9 | 3.1 |
| Railroad equipment and transport equipment, n.e.c. | 352 + 359 | 2.9 | 2.4 | 2.4 | 2.7 | 2.6 | 3.2 | 3.5 | 3.0 | 3.1 | 2.9 |
| Machinery and equipment, n.e.c. | 29 | 1.9 | 2.0 | 2.0 | 2.1 | 2.0 | 2.1 | 2.1 | 2.1 | 2.2 | 2.1 |
| Building and repairing of ships and boats | 351 | 0.9 | 1.0 | 1.0 | 0.9 | 0.9 | 1.0 | 0.8 | 1.0 | 1.0 | 1.0 |
| Rubber and plastics products | 25 | 1.0 | 1.0 | 0.9 | 1.0 | 0.8 | 0.9 | 0.9 | 0.9 | 1.0 | 0.9 |
| Coke, refined petroleum products and nuclear fuel | 23 | 1.2 | 1.2 | 1.1 | 1.0 | 0.9 | 0.8 | 0.7 | 0.9 | 0.4 | 0.9 |
| Other non-metallic mineral products | 26 | 1.0 | 0.9 | 0.9 | 0.9 | 0.8 | 0.9 | 0.9 | 0.9 | 0.8 | 0.9 |
| Basic metals and fabricated metal products | 27-28 | 0.7 | 0.7 | 0.7 | 0.6 | 0.6 | 0.7 | 0.7 | 0.6 | 0.6 | 0.6 |
| Manufacturing, n.e.c.; Recycling | 36-37 | 0.5 | 0.5 | 0.5 | 0.4 | 0.4 | 0.4 | 0.4 | 0.6 | 0.5 | 0.5 |
| Wood, pulp, paper, paper products, printing and publishing | 20-22 | 0.3 | 0.3 | 0.3 | 0.3 | 0.3 | 0.4 | 0.3 | 0.4 | 0.4 | 0.3 |
| Food products, beverages and tobacco | 15-16 | 0.3 | 0.3 | 0.3 | 0.3 | 0.3 | 0.3 | 0.4 | 0.4 | 0.3 | 0.3 |
| Textiles, textile products, leather and footwear | 17-19 | 0.2 | 0.3 | 0.3 | 0.3 | 0.3 | 0.3 | 0.3 | 0.3 | 0.3 | 0.3 |
| **Total manufacturing** | **15-37** | **2.5** | **2.5** | **2.5** | **2.4** | **2.4** | **2.6** | **2.6** | **2.6** | **2.6** | **2.5** |
| **High-technology industries** | | **9.4** | **9.5** | **9.3** | **9.3** | **9.2** | **9.3** | **9.5** | **9.3** | **8.7** | **9.3** |
| **Medium-high-technology industries** | | **3.1** | **3.0** | **3.1** | **3.0** | **2.9** | **3.1** | **2.9** | **3.0** | **3.0** | **3.0** |
| **Medium-low-technology industries** | | **0.9** | **0.9** | **0.9** | **0.8** | **0.8** | **0.8** | **0.8** | **0.8** | **0.7** | **0.8** |
| **Low-technology industries** | | **0.3** | **0.3** | **0.3** | **0.3** | **0.3** | **0.4** | **0.4** | **0.4** | **0.4** | **0.3** |

1. R&D intensity defined as direct R&D expenditures as a percentage of production (gross output), calculated after converting countries' R&D expenditures and production using GDP PPPs

*Source:* OECD: ANBERD and STAN databases, May 2003

StatLink: *http://dx.doi.org/10.1787/303453114276*

- The low-technology group consists of relatively aggregate sectors, owing to limited detailed R&D expenditure data across countries. The few cases in which R&D intensities are available for more detailed (2-digit) breakdowns confirm the allocation of these industries to low technology.
- The classification concerns the OECD area as a whole. For individual countries, allocation to the technology groups may differ. Also, at national level, finer technology classifications may be generated from more detailed underlying data.



OECD SCIENCE, TECHNOLOGY AND INDUSTRY SCOREBOARD 2005 – ISBN 92-64-01055-6 – © OECD 2005

# ANNEX B

# *Main OECD Databases Used*

**STAN – Industry:** The STAN database for **Industrial Analysis** includes annual measures of output, labour input, investment and international trade by economic activity which allow users to construct a wide range of indicators focused on areas such as productivity growth, competitiveness and general structural change. The industry list based on the International Standard Industrial Classification (ISIC) Rev. 3, provides sufficient details to enable users to highlight high-technology sectors and is compatible with those lists used in related OECD databases in the "STAN" family (see below). STAN-Industry is primarily based on member countries' annual National Accounts by activity tables and uses data from other sources, such as national industrial surveys/censuses, to estimate any missing detail. Since many of the data points in STAN are estimated, they do not represent the official member country submissions. See *www.oecd.org/sti/stan.*

*Publication*: STAN-industry is available on line via SourceOECD (*www.sourceoecd.org*) where it is regularly updated (new tables are posted as soon as they are ready). A "snapshot" of STAN-industry is also available on CD-ROM together with the latest versions of STAN – R&D (ANBERD), STAN – Bilateral Trade and a set of derived STAN Indicators. See *www.oecd.org/sti/stan/indicators.*

**STAN – R&D (ANBERD)**: The **Analytical Business Enterprise Research and Development** database is an estimated database constructed with a view to creating a consistent data set that overcomes the problems of international comparability and time discontinuity associated with the official business enterprise R&D data provided to the OECD by its member countries. ANBERD contains R&D expenditures for the period 1987-2003, by industry (ISIC Rev. 3), for 19 OECD countries. See *www.oecd.org/sti/anberd.*

*Publication*: OECD (2004), *Research and Development Expenditure in Industry 2004*. Annual. ANBERD is also available online *via* SourceOECD (under the STAN heading) as well as on the STAN family CD-ROM.

**STAN – Bilateral Trade (BTD):** This database presents detailed **trade flows** by manufacturing industry between a set of OECD *declaring* countries and a selection of *partner* countries and geographical regions. Data are presented in thousands of USD at current prices, and cover the period 1988-2003. The data have been derived from the OECD database *International Trade by Commodities Statistics* (ITCS – formerly *Foreign Trade Statistics* or FTS). Imports and exports are grouped according to the country of origin and the country of destination of the goods. The data have been converted from product classification schemes to an activity classification scheme based on ISIC Rev. 3, compatible with those the OECD's STAN-Industry, Input-Output tables and ANBERD databases. See *www.oecd.org/sti/btd.*

*Publication:* OECD (2005), *Bilateral Trade Database, 2004.* BTD is available online *via* SourceOECD (under the STAN heading) as well as on the STAN family CD-ROM.

**STAN – I-O**: The latest set of OECD **Input-Output** tables consists of matrices of inter-industrial transaction flows of goods and services (domestically produced and imported) in current prices for 18 OECD countries and two non-member OECD economies (Brazil and China) covering one or more years around the mid-1990s. The tables are based on ISIC Rev. 3 and are available for free in zipped Excel format. See *www.oecd.org/std/io-tables/data.*

**R&D:** The **R&D** database contains the full results of the OECD surveys on **R&D expenditure and personnel.** This database serves, *inter alia*, as raw material for both the ANBERD and MSTI databases.

*Publication:* OECD (2005), *Research and Development Statistics: 2004 Edition* (formerly *Basic Science and Technology Statistics*) Updated annually on CD-ROM as *OECD Science and Technology Statistics* (a printed edition is also available every two years).

**MSTI:** The **Main Science and Technology Indicators** database provides a selection of the most frequently used annual data on the scientific and technological performance of OECD member countries and nine non-member economies (Argentina, China, Israel, Romania, Russian Federation, Singapore, Slovenia, South Africa, Chinese Taipei). The indicators, expressed in the form of ratios, percentages, growth rates, cover resources devoted to R&D, patent families, technology balance of payments and international trade in highly R&D-intensive industries.

*Publication:* OECD (2005), *Main Science and Technology Indicators 2005/1.* Biannual. Also available on CD-ROM as *OECD Science and Technology Statistics.*

**TBP:** The **TBP** database presents information on the **technology balance of payments**. The database serves, *inter alia*, as raw material for the MSTI database and publications.

**Patent database:** This database contains patents filed at the largest national patent offices – European Patent Office (EPO); US Patent and Trademark Office (USPTO); Japanese Patent Office (JPO) – and other national or regional offices. Each patent is referenced by: patent numbers and dates (publication, application and priority); names and countries of residence of the applicants and of the inventors; and technological categories, using the national patent classification as well as the International Patent Classification (IPC). The compiled indicators mainly refer to single patent counts in a selected patent office, as well as counts of triadic patent families (patents filed at the EPO, the USPTO and the JPO to protect a single invention). See *www.oecd.org/sti/ipr-statistics.*

The series are published on a regular basis in OECD, *Main Science and Technology Indicators.*

**AFA:** The **Activities of Foreign Affiliates** database presents detailed data on the performance of foreign affiliates in the **manufacturing** industry of OECD countries (inward and outward investment). The data indicate the increasing importance of foreign affiliates in the economies of host countries, particularly in production, employment, value added, research and development, exports, wages and salaries. AFA contains 18 variables broken down by country of origin and by industrial sector (based on ISIC Rev. 3) for 23 OECD countries.

## Current country coverage of main DSTI databases used in this publication

| | Industry | Science and technology | | | | | Globalisation | | | ICT |
|---|---|---|---|---|---|---|---|---|---|---|
| | STAN | R&D | TBP | MSTI | ANBERD | Patents | AFA | FATS | BTD | Telecom. |
| **Australia** | X | X | X | X | X | X | X | | X | X |
| Austria | X | X | X | X | | X | | X | X | X |
| **Belgium** | X | X | X | X | X | X | | X | X | X |
| Canada | X | X | X | X | X | X | X | X | X | X |
| **Czech Republic** | X | X | X | X | X | X | X | X | X | X |
| Denmark | X | X | X | X | X | X | | | X | X |
| **Finland** | X | X | X | X | X | X | X | X | X | X |
| France | X | X | X | X | X | X | X | X | X | X |
| **Germany** | X | X | X | X | X | X | X | X | X | X |
| Greece | X | X | | X | | X | X | X | X | X |
| **Hungary** | X | X | X | X | | X | X | X | X | X |
| Iceland | X | X | | X | | X | | | X | X |
| **Ireland** | X | X | X | X | X | X | X | X | X | X |
| Italy | X | X | X | X | X | X | X | X | X | X |
| **Japan** | X | X | X | X | X | X | X | X | X | X |
| Korea | X | X | X | X | X | X | | | X | X |
| **Luxembourg** | X | X | | X | | X | X | X | X | X |
| Mexico | X | X | X | X | | X | X | | X | X |
| **Netherlands** | X | X | X | X | X | X | X | X | X | X |
| New Zealand | X | X | X | X | | X | | | X | X |
| **Norway** | X | X | X | X | X | X | X | X | X | X |
| Poland | X | X | X | X | X | X | X | X | X | X |
| **Portugal** | X | X | X | X | | X | X | X | X | X |
| Slovak Republic | X | X | X | X | | X | X | | X | X |
| **Spain** | X | X | X | X | X | X | X | X | X | X |
| Sweden | X | X | X | X | X | X | X | X | X | X |
| **Switzerland** | X | X | X | X | | X | | | X | X |
| Turkey | | X | | X | | X | X | | X | X |
| **United Kingdom** | X | X | X | X | X | X | X | X | X | X |
| United States | X | X | X | X | X | X | X | X | X | X |

StatLink: *http://dx.doi.org/10.1787/455742184222*

*Publication:* OECD, *Measuring Globalisation: The Role of Multinationals in OECD Economies*, 2001 Edition. Vol. I: Manufacturing. Biennial. Also available annually online on SourceOECD (*www.sourceoecd.org*).

**FATS:** This database gives detailed data on the **activities of foreign affiliates** in the **services** sector of OECD countries (inward and outward investment). The data indicate the increasing importance of foreign affiliates in the economies of host countries and of affiliates of national firms implanted abroad. FATS contains five variables (production, employment, value added, imports and exports) broken down by country of origin (inward investments) or implantation (outward investments) and by industrial sector (based on ISIC Rev. 3) for 21 OECD countries.

*Publication:* OECD, *Measuring Globalisation: The Role of Multinationals in OECD Economies*, 2001 Edition. Vol. II: Services. Biennial.

**Telecommunications:** This database is produced in association with the biennial *Communications Outlook*. It provides time-series data covering all OECD countries, where available, for the period 1980-2004. It contains both telecommunication and economic indicators.

*Publication*: OECD (2005), *Telecommunications Database* 2005. Only available on diskette and CD-ROM.

**ICT:** Work is under way to develop a database on ICT supply and ICT usage statistics. Statistics on employment, value added, production, wages and salaries, number of enterprises, R&D, imports and exports for the ICT sector are been collected following the OECD ICT sector definition.

## Other OECD databases

**ANA:** SNA93 – Annual National Accounts (Statistics Directorate).

**Database on Immigrants and Expatriates** (Directorate for Employment, Labour and Social Affairs).

**Education** (Directorate for Education).

**Educational Attainment** (Directorate for Education).

**ITCS:** International Trade by Commodity Statistics (Statistics Directorate).

**International Direct Investment** (Directorate for Financial and Enterprise Affairs).

**LFS:** Labour Force Statistics (Statistics Directorate).

**Productivity** (Statistics Directorate, Directorate for Employment, Labour and Social Affairs, Directorate for Science, Technology and Industry).

Further details on OECD statistics are available at: *www.oecd.org/statistics/*.

# ANNEX C

## *Statistical Tables*

Table A.2.1 **R&D intensity**
Gross domestic expenditure on R&D as a percentage of GDP

| | 1991 | 1995 | 1996 | 1997 | 1998 | 1999 | 2000 | 2001 | 2002 | 2003 | 2004 |
|---|---|---|---|---|---|---|---|---|---|---|---|
| Canada | 1.60 | 1.72 | 1.68 | 1.68 | 1.79 | 1.82 | 1.93 | 2.08 | 1.96 | 1.94 | 1.91 |
| Mexico[1] | 0.22 | 0.31 | 0.31 | 0.34 | 0.38 | 0.43 | 0.37 | 0.39 | .. | .. | .. |
| United States | 2.71 | 2.51 | 2.55 | 2.58 | 2.61 [8] | 2.65 | 2.72 | 2.73 | 2.66 | 2.60 | .. |
| Australia[2] | 1.52 | .. | 1.67 | .. | 1.51 | .. | 1.56 | .. | 1.62 | .. | .. |
| Japan[3] | 2.76 | 2.69 | 2.78 [8] | 2.84 | 2.95 | 2.96 | 2.99 | 3.07 | 3.12 | 3.15 | .. |
| Korea | 1.82 | 2.37 | 2.42 | 2.48 | 2.34 | 2.25 | 2.39 | 2.59 | 2.53 | 2.64 | .. |
| New Zealand | 0.98 | 0.96 [8] | .. | 1.10 | .. | 1.01 | .. | 1.14 [8] | .. | 1.16 | .. |
| Austria | 1.44 | 1.54 | 1.59 | 1.69 | 1.77 | 1.88 | 1.91 | 2.04 | 2.12 | 2.20 | 2.27 |
| Belgium | 1.62 | 1.72 [8] | 1.80 | 1.87 | 1.90 | 1.96 | 2.04 | 2.17 | 2.23 | 2.31 | 2.38 |
| Czech Republic | 1.90 | 0.95 [8] | 0.98 | 1.09 | 1.17 | 1.16 | 1.23 | 1.22 | 1.22 | 1.26 | .. |
| Denmark | 1.64 | 1.84 | 1.85 | 1.94 | 2.06 | 2.19 | .. | 2.41 | 2.53 | .. | .. |
| Finland | 2.04 | 2.28 | 2.54 | 2.71 | 2.88 | 3.23 | 3.40 | 3.41 | 3.44 | 3.49 | .. |
| France | 2.37 | 2.31 | 2.30 | 2.22 [8] | 2.17 | 2.18 | 2.18 [8] | 2.23 | 2.26 | 2.19 | .. |
| Germany[4] | 2.52 | 2.25 | 2.25 | 2.29 | 2.31 | 2.44 | 2.49 | 2.51 | 2.53 | 2.55 | .. |
| Greece | 0.36 | 0.49 [8] | .. | 0.51 | .. | 0.67 | .. | 0.65 | .. | .. | .. |
| Hungary | 1.06 | 0.73 [8] | 0.65 | 0.72 | 0.68 | 0.69 | 0.80 | 0.95 | 1.02 | 0.95 | .. |
| Iceland | 1.17 | 1.57 | .. | 1.88 | 2.07 | 2.38 | 2.75 | 3.06 | 3.09 | 3.04 | .. |
| Ireland | 0.93 | 1.28 | 1.32 | 1.29 | 1.25 | 1.19 | 1.14 | 1.11 | 1.12 | .. | .. |
| Italy | 1.23 | 1.00 | 1.01 | 1.05 [8] | 1.07 | 1.04 | 1.07 | 1.11 | 1.16 | .. | .. |
| Luxembourg | .. | .. | .. | .. | .. | .. | 1.71 | .. | .. | .. | .. |
| Netherlands | 1.97 | 1.99 [8] | 2.01 [8] | 2.04 | 1.94 | 2.02 | 1.90 | 1.88 | 1.80 | .. | .. |
| Norway | 1.64 | 1.70 [8] | .. | 1.64 | .. | 1.65 | .. | 1.60 | 1.67 | 1.75 | .. |
| Poland | 0.76 | 0.65 [8] | 0.67 | 0.67 | 0.68 | 0.70 | 0.66 | 0.64 | 0.58 | 0.56 | .. |
| Portugal | 0.57 | 0.57 | 0.60 | 0.62 | 0.69 | 0.75 | 0.80 | 0.85 | 0.94 | .. | .. |
| Slovak Republic | 2.13 | 0.93 [8] | 0.92 | 1.09 [8] | 0.79 | 0.66 | 0.65 | 0.64 | 0.58 | 0.58 | .. |
| Spain | 0.84 | 0.81 [8] | 0.83 | 0.82 | 0.89 | 0.88 | 0.94 | 0.95 | 1.03 | 1.10 | .. |
| Sweden | 2.72 | 3.35 [8] | .. | 3.54 | .. | 3.65 | .. | 4.27 | .. | 3.98 | .. |
| Switzerland[2] | 2.59 | .. | 2.67 | .. | .. | .. | 2.57 | .. | .. | .. | .. |
| Turkey | 0.53 | 0.38 | 0.45 | 0.49 | 0.50 | 0.63 | 0.64 | 0.72 | 0.66 | .. | .. |
| United Kingdom | 2.07 | 1.95 [8] | 1.88 | 1.81 | 1.80 | 1.87 | 1.86 | 1.87 | 1.90 | 1.89 | .. |
| EU15[5] | 1.90 | 1.80 [8] | 1.80 | 1.80 | 1.81 | 1.86 | 1.89 | 1.92 | 1.95 | 1.95 | .. |
| EU25[6] | .. | 1.72 | 1.71 | 1.72 | 1.72 | 1.77 | 1.80 | 1.83 | 1.85 | 1.85 | .. |
| Total OECD[7] | 2.21 | 2.09 [8] | 2.11 | 2.13 | 2.15 | 2.19 | 2.23 | 2.27 | 2.25 | 2.24 | .. |

1. 1993 instead of 1991.
2. 1992 instead of 1991.
3. Adjusted by OECD up to 1995.
4. Figures for Germany refer to unified Germany.
5. Includes Luxembourg from 2000.
6. Malta is excluded; includes Luxembourg from 2000.
7. Includes Czech Republic, Hungary, Poland and Slovak Republic from 1995, and Luxembourg from 2000.
8. Break in series from previous year for which data are available.

*Source:* OECD, MSTI database, May 2005.

StatLink: *http://dx.doi.org/10.1787/025470526535*

Table A.2.2 **Gross domestic expenditure on R&D (GERD)**
Millions of 2000 PPP dollars

| | 1991 | 1995 | 1996 | 1997 | 1998 | 1999 | 2000 | 2001 | 2002 | 2003 | 2004 | Average annual growth rate (1995-2003) | |
|---|---|---|---|---|---|---|---|---|---|---|---|---|---|
| Canada | 10 075.5 | 12 093.7 | 11958.2 | 12522.75 | 13828.52 | 14898.98 | 16 643.7 | 18 223.5 | 17 762.0 | 17 926.9 | 18 211.9 | | 5.0 |
| Mexico[1] | 1 547.8 | 2 133.2 | 2245.98 | 2667.33 | 3068.3 | 3619.25 | 3 348.5 | 3 538.5 | .. | .. | .. | 1995-2001 | 8.8 |
| United States | 191 111.3 | 199 886.4 | 210716.37 | 222916.36 | 235058.35 [8] | 249343.13 | 265 194.1 | 268 294.9 | 266 177.7 | 268 439.0 | .. | 1998-2003 | 2.7 |
| Australia[2] | 5 674.5 | .. | 7274.55 | | | | 7 930.7 | .. | 8 815.5 | .. | .. | 1996-2002 | 3.3 |
| Japan[3] | 81 219.0 | 82 580.0 | 88618.06 [8] | 92352.06 | 94779.48 | 95345.69 | 99 003.7 | 102 102.9 | 103 382.0 | 106 921.1 | .. | 1996-2003 | 2.7 |
| Korea | 8 597.3 | 14 686.3 | 16098.39 | 17237.88 | 15154.38 | 15952.42 | 18 395.1 | 20 668.6 | 21 616.9 | 23 261.9 | .. | | 5.9 |
| New Zealand | 580.7 | 671.1 [8] | .. | 807.41 | .. | 780.51 | .. | 939.3 [8] | .. | 1 035.6 | .. | 2001-2003 | 5.0 |
| Austria | 2 661.4 | 3 065.6 | 3242.74 | 3511.27 | 3809.33 | 4188.53 | 4 407.8 | 4 724.2 | 4 971.2 | 5 198.6 | 5 483.4 | | 6.8 |
| Belgium | 3 590.6 | 4 032.1 [8] | 4292.23 | 4595.35 | 4766.24 | 5075.41 | 5 476.4 | 5 880.7 | 6 088.7 | 6 407.0 | 6 741.9 | | 6.0 |
| Czech Republic | 2 455.0 | 1 327.9 [8] | 1420.9 | 1571.44 | 1658.78 | 1669.12 | 1 844.2 | 1 880.5 | 1 908.4 | 2 044.6 | .. | | 5.5 |
| Denmark | 2 009.2 | 2 447.0 | 2531.12 | 2728.24 | 2968.11 | 3235.45 | .. | 3 714.0 | 3 948.0 | .. | .. | 1995-2002 | 7.1 |
| Finland | 2 103.7 | 2 407.2 | 2783.75 | 3162.65 | 3528.77 | 4088.71 | 4 518.0 | 4 581.6 | 4 728.4 | 4 910.0 | .. | | 9.3 |
| France | 30 866.0 | 31 417.5 | 31573.73 | 31083.37 [8] | 31419.39 | 32584.96 | 33 829.7 [8] | 35 317.5 | 36 258.9 | 35 297.5 | .. | 2000-2003 | 1.4 |
| Germany[4] | 45 278.2 | 42 501.8 | 42807.16 | 44271.05 | 45613.96 | 48990.14 | 51 588.5 | 52 308.3 | 52 872.4 | 53 217.1 | .. | | 2.9 |
| Greece | 525.8 | 729.6 [8] | .. | 805.95 | .. | 1148.18 | .. | 1 202.0 | .. | .. | .. | 1995-2001 | 8.7 |
| Hungary | 1 061.2 | 739.8 [8] | 665.09 | 772.21 | 761.86 | 800.5 | 981.8 | 1 206.7 | 1 351.1 | 1 286.7 | .. | | 7.2 |
| Iceland | 71.9 | 97.6 | .. | 128.68 | 149.56 | 179.45 | 219.3 | 249.1 | 250.3 | 256.5 | .. | | 12.8 |
| Ireland | 513.5 | 866.7 | 969.05 | 1047.07 | 1108.72 | 1174.68 | 1 233.4 | 1 276.0 | 1 364.5 | .. | .. | 1995-2002 | 6.7 |
| Italy | 15 320.0 | 13 125.4 | 13367.99 | 14238.93 [8] | 14704.59 | 14578.67 | 15 425.0 | 16 368.4 | 17 085.1 | .. | .. | 1997-2002 | 3.7 |
| Luxembourg | .. | .. | .. | .. | .. | .. | 368.3 | .. | .. | .. | .. | | |
| Netherlands | 6 577.4 | 7 198.5 [8] | 7515.24 [8] | 7905.77 | 7842.31 | 8503.37 | 8 248.7 | 8 300.0 | 7 994.5 | .. | .. | 1996-2002 | 1.0 |
| Norway | 1 727.8 | 2 016.7 [8] | .. | 2214.05 | .. | 2347.51 | .. | 2 623.7 | 2 687.6 | 2 813.9 | .. | | 4.3 |
| Poland | 1 956.3 | 2 005.2 [8] | 2188.46 | 2338.56 | 2498.15 | 2692.19 | 2 635.6 | 2 566.7 | 2 358.3 | 2 366.2 | .. | | 2.1 |
| Portugal | 797.9 | 837.1 | 915.6 | 981.87 | 1141.02 | 1296.13 | 1 424.7 | 1 531.3 | 1 699.2 | .. | .. | 1995-2002 | 10.6 |
| Slovak Republic | 899.5 | 452.4 [8] | 476.45 | 585.56 [8] | 442.26 | 374.81 | 378.8 | 386.5 | 363.9 | 385.2 | .. | 1997-2003 | -6.7 |
| Spain | 5 441.3 | 5 514.0 [8] | 5780.32 | 5922.47 | 6752.01 | 6961.88 | 7 706.5 | 8 053.5 | 8 902.8 | 9 772.7 | .. | | 7.4 |
| Sweden | 5 284.2 | 6 818.3 [8] | .. | 7485.33 | .. | 8358.09 | .. | 10 294.5 | .. | 9 943.6 | .. | | 7.1 |
| Switzerland[2] | 5 072.9 | .. | 5320.74 | .. | .. | .. | 5 627.0 | .. | .. | .. | .. | 1996-2000 | 1.4 |
| Turkey | 1 725.6 | 1 440.4 | 1830.97 | 2143.63 | 2241.23 | 2706.24 | 2 946.9 | 3 080.0 | 3 048.9 | .. | .. | 1995-2002 | 11.3 |
| United Kingdom | 24 162.0 | 25 106.8 [8] | 24841.16 | 24690.25 | 25324.24 | 27125.08 | 28 015.5 | 28 799.2 | 29 698.2 | 30 233.9 | .. | | 2.4 |
| EU15[5] | 145 086.5 | 146 068.4 [8] | 148497.94 | 152429.28 | 157820.42 | 167287.11 | 176 103.1 | 182 730.9 | 187 294.1 | 188 941.8 | .. | | 3.3 |
| EU25[6] | .. | 151 280.4 | 153902.41 | 158384.75 | 163923.61 | 173594.67 | 182 792.6 | 189 729.3 | 194 279.9 | 196 106.9 | .. | | 3.3 |
| Total OECD[7] | 451 983.1 | 479 030.2 [8] | 500272.06 | 523320.97 | 543156.75 | 570842.75 | 604 566.3 | 622 799.9 | 627 444.3 | 638 020.5 | .. | | 3.7 |

1. 1993 instead of 1991.
2. 1992 instead of 1991
3. Adjusted by OECD up to 1995.
4. Figures for Germany refer to unified Germany.
5. Includes Luxembourg from 2000.
6. Malta is excluded; includes Luxembourg from 2000.
7. Includes Czech Republic, Hungary, Poland and Slovak Republic from 1995, and Luxembourg from 2000.
8. Break in series from previous year for which data are available.

*Source:* OECD, MSTI database, May 2005.

StatLink: *http://dx.doi.org/10.1787/471706711372*

Table A.3.1 **R&D expenditure by source of financing**

Percentages

| | Business enterprise | | | | | Government | | | | | Other national sources | | | | | Abroad | | | | |
|---|---|---|---|---|---|---|---|---|---|---|---|---|---|---|---|---|---|---|---|---|
| | 1995 | 1997 | 1999 | 2001 | 2003 | 1995 | 1997 | 1999 | 2001 | 2003 | 1995 | 1997 | 1999 | 2001 | 2003 | 1995 | 1997 | 1999 | 2001 | 2003 |
| Canada | 45.7 | 48.0 | 44.9 | 49.4 | 47.5 | 35.9 | 32.0 | 31.2 | 29.8 | 34.5 | 6.9 | 7.7 | 8.5 | 8.0 | 9.9 | 11.6 | 12.3 | 15.3 | 12.8 | 8.1 |
| Mexico | 17.6 | 16.9 | 23.6 | 29.8 | .. | 66.2 | 71.1 | 61.3 | 59.1 | .. | .. | 9.5 | 9.8 | 9.8 | .. | 6.7 | 2.5 | 5.3 | 1.3 | .. |
| United States | 60.2 [6] | 64.0 [6] | 66.9 [6] | 67.3 [6] | 63.1 [6] | 35.4 [6] | 31.5 [6] | 28.5 [6,7] | 27.8 [6] | 31.2 [6] | 4.4 [6] | 4.4 [6] | 4.6 [6] | 4.9 [6] | 5.7 [6] | .. | .. | .. | .. | .. |
| Australia[1] | 47.8 | 45.9 | 46.3 | 46.4 | .. | 45.8 | 46.9 | 45.5 | 44.4 | .. | .. | .. | .. | .. | .. | .. | .. | .. | .. | .. |
| Japan[2] | 72.3 [8] | 74.0 [7] | 72.2 | 73.0 | 74.5 | 20.9 [6] | 18.2 [7] | 19.6 | 18.6 | 17.7 | 9.9 | 7.5 | 7.8 | 8.0 | 7.5 | 0.1 | 0.3 | 0.4 | 0.4 | 0.3 |
| Korea | 76.3 [6] | 72.5 [6] | 70.0 [6] | 72.5 [6] | 74.0 [6] | 19.0 [6] | 22.9 [6] | 24.9 [6] | 25.0 [6] | 23.9 [6] | 4.7 [6] | 4.5 [6] | 5.1 [6] | 2.1 [6] | 1.7 [6] | 0.0 [6] | 0.1 [6] | 0.1 [6] | 0.5 [6] | 0.4 [6] |
| New Zealand | 33.7 | 30.5 | 34.1 | 37.1 [7] | .. | 52.3 | 52.3 | 50.6 | 46.3 [7] | 42.8 | 10.1 | 12.0 | 11.0 | 10.0 [7] | .. | 3.9 | 5.2 | 4.3 | 6.6 [7] | .. |
| Austria | 45.7 | 43.3 | 41.1 | 41.8 | 43.9 | 46.9 | 41.0 | 38.9 | 38.3 | 34.7 | 0.4 | 0.4 | 0.3 | 0.3 | 0.4 | 7.0 | 15.3 | 19.6 | 19.7 | 21.0 |
| Belgium | 67.1 | 67.6 | 66.2 | 64.3 | .. | 23.1 | 22.2 | 23.5 | 21.4 | .. | 2.3 | 3.4 | 3.0 | 2.5 | .. | 7.5 | 6.8 | 7.3 | 11.8 | .. |
| Czech Republic | 63.1 | 59.8 | 52.6 | 52.5 | 51.4 | 32.3 [6] | 30.8 [6] | 42.6 [7] | 43.6 | 41.8 | 1.3 [8] | 7.5 [8] | 0.8 [7] | 1.7 | 2.2 | 3.3 | 1.9 | 4.0 | 2.2 | 4.6 |
| Denmark | 45.2 | 53.4 | 59.0 | 61.4 | .. | 39.6 | 36.1 | 31.2 | 28.2 | .. | 4.2 | 4.1 | 3.3 | 2.6 | .. | 11.0 | 6.4 | 5.4 | 7.8 | .. |
| Finland | 59.5 | 62.9 | 66.9 [7] | 70.8 | 70.0 | 35.1 | 30.9 | 29.2 | 25.5 | 25.7 | .. | 0.9 | 0.9 | 1.2 | 1.1 | 4.5 | 5.3 | 3.0 | 2.5 | 3.1 |
| France | 48.3 | 51.6 [7] | 54.1 | 54.2 [7] | .. | 41.9 | 38.8 [7] | 36.9 | 36.9 [7] | .. | 1.7 | 1.6 | 1.9 | 1.7 | .. | 8.0 | 7.9 | 7.0 | 7.2 | .. |
| Germany[3] | 60.0 | 61.3 | 65.4 | 65.7 | 66.1 | 37.9 | 35.9 | 32.1 | 31.4 | 31.1 | 0.3 | 0.3 | 0.4 | 0.4 | 0.4 | 1.8 | 2.4 | 2.1 | 2.5 | 2.3 |
| Greece | 25.5 | 21.6 | 24.2 | 33.0 | .. | 54.0 | 54.5 | 48.9 | 46.6 | .. | 2.5 | 1.6 | 2.5 | 2.0 | .. | 18.0 | 22.3 | 24.5 | 18.4 | .. |
| Hungary | 38.4 | 36.6 | 38.5 | 34.8 | 30.7 | 53.1 | 54.8 | 53.2 | 53.6 | 58.0 | 0.5 | 0.5 | 0.3 | 0.4 | 0.4 | 4.8 | 4.3 | 5.6 | 9.2 | 10.7 |
| Iceland | 34.6 | 41.9 | 43.4 | 46.2 | .. | 57.3 | 50.9 | 41.2 | 34.0 | .. | 3.7 | 0.9 | 1.5 | 1.6 | .. | 4.4 | 6.2 | 13.9 | 18.3 | .. |
| Ireland | 72.3 | 67.3 | 64.4 | 66.8 | .. | 22.5 | 24.3 | 21.9 | 25.5 | .. | 1.9 | 1.7 | 1.8 | 1.7 | .. | 8.5 | 6.7 | 12.0 | 6.0 | .. |
| Italy | 41.7 | .. | .. | .. | .. | 53.0 | .. | .. | .. | .. | .. | .. | .. | .. | .. | 5.3 | .. | .. | .. | .. |
| Luxembourg[1] | .. | .. | 90.7 | .. | .. | .. | .. | 7.7 | .. | .. | .. | .. | .. | .. | .. | | | 1.7 | | |
| Netherlands | 46.0 | 45.6 [7] | 49.7 | 51.9 | .. | 42.2 | 39.1 [7] | 35.7 | 35.8 | .. | 2.6 | 2.6 [7] | 3.4 | 1.3 [7] | .. | 9.3 | 12.8 [7] | 11.2 | 11.0 | .. |
| Norway | 49.9 | 49.4 | 49.5 | 51.6 | 49.2 | 44.0 | 42.9 | 42.5 | 39.8 | 41.9 | 1.2 | 1.2 | 1.6 | 1.4 | 1.5 | 4.9 | 6.5 | 6.3 | 7.1 | 7.4 |
| Poland | 36.0 | 35.1 | 38.1 | 30.8 | 30.3 | 60.2 | 61.7 | 58.5 | 64.8 | 62.7 | 2.1 | 1.6 | 1.7 | 2.0 | 2.4 | 1.7 | 1.6 | 1.7 | 2.4 | 4.6 |
| Portugal | 19.5 | 21.2 | 21.3 | 31.5 | .. | 65.3 | 68.2 [7] | 69.7 | 61.0 | .. | .. | 4.4 | 3.7 | 2.4 | .. | 11.9 | 6.1 [7] | 5.3 | 5.1 | .. |
| Slovak Republic | 60.4 [6] | 63.5 [7,8] | 49.9 [8] | 56.1 [8] | 45.1 [8] | 37.8 [6] | 34.5 [6,7] | 47.9 | 41.3 | 50.8 | 0.1 | 0.1 | 0.0 | 0.8 | 0.7 | 1.6 | 1.9 | 2.3 | 1.9 | 3.3 |
| Spain | 44.5 | 44.7 | 48.9 | 47.2 | 48.4 | 43.6 | 43.6 | 40.8 | 39.9 | 40.1 | 5.2 | 4.9 | 4.7 | 5.3 | 5.8 | 6.7 | 6.7 | 5.6 | 7.7 | 5.7 |
| Sweden | 65.5 | 67.8 | 67.8 | 71.9 | 65.0 | 28.8 | 25.8 [7] | 24.5 | 21.0 | 23.5 | 2.2 | 2.8 [7] | 4.2 | 3.8 | 4.3 | 3.4 | 3.5 [7] | 3.5 | 3.4 | 7.3 |
| Switzerland[1] | 67.5 | .. | 69.1 | .. | .. | 26.9 | .. | 23.2 | .. | .. | 2.5 | .. | 3.4 | .. | .. | 3.1 | .. | 4.3 | .. | .. |
| Turkey | 30.8 | 41.8 | 43.3 | 44.9 | .. | 62.4 | 53.7 | 47.7 | 48.0 | .. | 2.7 | 2.6 | 4.2 | 6.3 | .. | 2.0 | 1.8 | 4.8 | 0.8 | .. |
| United Kingdom | 48.2 | 49.9 | 48.5 | 46.9 | 43.9 | 32.8 | 30.7 | 29.2 | 29.1 | 31.3 | 4.5 | 4.8 | 5.0 | 5.7 | 5.4 | 14.5 | 14.6 | 17.3 | 18.2 | 19.4 |
| EU15[4] | 52.2 | 53.7 | 55.6 | 56.0 | .. | 39.1 | 37.1 | 34.8 | 34.0 | .. | 1.8 | 2.0 | 2.2 | 2.2 | 1.5 | 6.9 | 7.3 | 7.4 | 7.8 | .. |
| EU25[5] | 51.9 | 53.3 | 55.2 | 55.5 | .. | 39.5 | 37.5 | 35.5 | 34.7 | .. | 1.9 | 2.0 | 2.1 | 2.2 | 1.4 | 6.7 | 7.1 | 7.2 | 7.6 | .. |
| Total OECD[4] | 59.4 | 61.9 | 63.0 | 63.6 | 61.6 | 34.0 | 31.2 | 29.7 | 28.9 | 30.5 | 4.0 | 4.3 | 4.5 | 4.6 | 4.9 | .. | .. | .. | .. | .. |

1. For relevant years, 1996 instead of 1995; 1998 instead of 1997; 2000 instead of 1999; 2002 instead of 2001.
2. Adjusted by OECD up to 1995.
3. Figures for Germany refer to unified Germany.
4. Includes Luxembourg from 2000.
5. Malta is excluded; includes Luxembourg from 2000.
6. Underestimated.
7. Break in series from previous year for which data are available.
8. Overestimated.

*Source:* OECD, MSTI database, May 2005.

StatLink: *http://dx.doi.org/10.1787/140583080361*

Table A.3.2 **R&D expenditure by performing sector**

Percentages

| | Business enterprise | | | | | Higher education | | | | | Government | | | | | Private non-profit | | | | |
|---|---|---|---|---|---|---|---|---|---|---|---|---|---|---|---|---|---|---|---|---|
| | 1995 | 1997 | 1999 | 2001 | 2003 | 1995 | 1997 | 1999 | 2001 | 2003 | 1995 | 1997 | 1999 | 2001 | 2003 | 1995 | 1997 | 1999 | 2001 | 2003 |
| Canada | 58.1 | 59.7 | 59.0 | 60.9 | 53.0 | 26.8 | 26.5 | 28.8 | 28.3 | 35.7 | 14.4 | 13.2 | 11.9 | 10.6 | 11.0 | 0.7 | 0.6 | 0.4 | 0.2 | 0.3 |
| Mexico | 20.8 | 19.7 | 25.5 | 30.3 | .. | 45.8 | 39.9 | 26.3 | 30.4 | .. | 33.0 | 38.8 | 45.0 | 39.1 | .. | 0.4 | 1.6 | 3.1 | 0.2 | .. |
| United States | 71.8 [6] | 74.1 [6] | 74.9 [6] | 73.0 [6] | 68.9 [6] | 15.2 [6] | 14.3 [6] | 13.9 [6] | 14.5 [6] | 16.8 [6] | 9.4 [6] | 8.2 [6] | 7.5 [6] | 7.9 [6] | 9.1 [6] | 3.6 [6] | 3.5 [6] | 3.8 [6] | 4.7 [6] | 5.3 [6] |
| Australia[1] | 48.2 | 45.9 | 47.8 | 48.8 | .. | 26.3 | 28.7 | 26.8 | 28.0 | .. | 23.5 | 22.9 | 22.6 | 20.3 | | 2.1 | 2.5 | 2.8 | 2.9 | .. |
| Japan[2] | 70.3 | 72.0 [7] | 70.7 | 73.7 | 75.0 | 14.5 [6] | 14.3 [7] | 14.8 | 14.5 | 13.7 | 10.4 [6] | 8.8 [7] | 9.9 | 9.5 | 9.3 | 4.8 [6] | 4.9 | 4.6 | 2.3 [7] | 2.1 |
| Korea | 73.7 [6] | 72.6 [6] | 71.4 [6] | 76.2 [6] | 76.1 [6] | 8.2 [6] | 10.4 [6] | 12.0 [6] | 10.4 [6] | 10.1 [6] | 17.0 [6] | 15.8 [6] | 14.5 [6] | 12.4 [6] | 12.6 [6] | 1.2 [6] | 1.2 [6] | 2.2 [6] | 1.1 [6] | 1.2 [6] |
| New Zealand | 27.0 | 28.2 | 29.7 | 36.8 [7] | 40.5 | 30.7 | 36.4 | 34.3 | 30.8 [7] | 28.4 | 42.2 | 35.3 | 36.0 | 32.5 [7] | 31.1 | .. | .. | .. | .. | .. |
| Austria[1] | .. | 63.6 | .. | 66.8 | .. | .. | 29.7 | .. | 27.0 | | .. | 6.4 | .. | 5.7 | | .. | 0.3 | .. | 0.5 | .. |
| Belgium | 71.3 | 71.6 | 71.6 | 73.7 | 74.1 | 22.5 | 21.6 | 21.0 | 19.2 | 18.4 | 4.8 | 5.5 | 6.2 | 6.0 | 6.4 | 1.4 | 1.3 | 1.2 | 1.1 | 1.1 |
| Czech Republic | 65.1 | 62.8 | 62.9 | 60.2 | 61.0 | 8.5 | 9.1 | 12.3 | 15.7 | 15.3 | 26.5 | 26.6 | 24.3 | 23.7 | 23.3 | .. | 1.4 | 0.6 | 0.5 | 0.4 |
| Denmark | 57.4 | 61.5 | 64.9 | 68.6 | .. | 24.5 | 22.2 | 19.4 | 18.8 | .. | 17.0 | 15.4 | 14.5 | 11.9 | .. | 1.1 | 1.0 | 1.1 | 0.7 | .. |
| Finland | 63.2 | 66.0 | 68.2 | 71.1 | 70.5 | 19.5 | 20.0 [7] | 19.7 | 18.1 | 19.2 | 16.7 | 13.6 | 11.4 | 10.2 | 9.7 | 0.6 | 0.5 | 0.7 | 0.6 | 0.6 |
| France | 61.0 | 62.5 [7] | 63.2 | 63.2 [7] | 62.3 | 16.7 | 17.4 [7] | 17.2 | 18.9 | 19.3 | 21.0 | 18.7 [7] | 18.1 | 16.5 | 17.1 | 1.3 | 1.4 [7] | 1.5 | 1.4 | 1.4 |
| Germany[3] | 66.3 | 67.5 | 69.8 | 69.9 | 69.8 | 18.2 | 17.9 | 16.5 | 16.4 | 16.8 | 15.5 | 14.6 | 13.8 | 13.7 | 13.4 | .. | .. | .. | .. | .. |
| Greece | 29.5 | 25.6 | 28.5 | 32.7 | .. | 44.3 | 50.6 | 49.5 | 44.9 | .. | 25.5 | 23.4 | 21.7 | 22.1 | .. | 0.7 | 0.4 | 0.3 | 0.4 | .. |
| Hungary | 43.4 | 41.5 | 40.2 | 40.1 | 36.7 | 24.8 | 23.0 | 22.4 | 25.7 | 26.7 | 25.6 | 25.1 | 32.3 | 25.9 | 31.3 | .. | .. | .. | .. | .. |
| Iceland | 31.9 | 40.6 | 46.7 | 58.9 | 54.9 | 27.5 | 28.3 | 20.9 | 18.8 | 20.1 | 37.5 | 29.8 | 30.2 | 20.1 | 21.9 | 3.2 | 1.3 | 2.2 | 2.3 | 3.1 |
| Ireland | 70.0 | 71.0 | 73.3 | 70.1 | .. | 20.4 | 20.7 | 20.7 | 21.8 | .. | 9.0 | 7.6 | 6.0 | 8.1 | .. | 0.8 | 0.7 | .. | .. | .. |
| Italy | 53.4 | 49.8 [7] | 49.3 | 49.1 | .. | 25.5 | 30.8 [7] | 31.5 | 32.6 | .. | 21.1 | 19.4 [7] | 19.2 | 18.4 | .. | .. | .. | .. | .. | .. |
| Luxembourg[1] | .. | .. | 92.6 | .. | .. | .. | .. | 0.3 | .. | .. | .. | .. | 7.1 | .. | .. | .. | .. | .. | .. | .. |
| Netherlands | 52.1 | 54.6 | 56.4 | 58.4 | .. | 28.8 | 27.3 | 26.2 | 27.0 | .. | 18.1 | 17.1 | 16.5 | 13.8 | .. | 1.0 | 1.0 | 0.9 | 0.8 | .. |
| Norway | 56.7 | 56.9 | 56.0 | 59.7 | 57.5 | 26.0 | 26.6 | 28.6 | 25.7 | 27.5 | 17.3 | 16.4 | 15.4 | 14.6 | 15.1 | .. | .. | .. | .. | .. |
| Poland | 38.7 | 39.4 | 41.3 | 35.8 | 27.4 | 26.3 | 28.6 | 27.8 | 32.7 | 31.7 | 35.0 | 32.0 | 30.8 | 31.3 | 40.7 | .. | .. | 0.1 | 0.2 | 0.2 |
| Portugal | 20.9 | 22.5 | 22.7 | 31.8 | .. | 37.1 | 40.0 | 38.6 | 36.7 | .. | 27.0 | 24.2 | 27.9 | 20.8 | .. | 15.0 | 13.3 | 10.8 | 10.8 | .. |
| Slovak Republic | 53.9 | 75.6 [7,8] | 62.6 [8] | 67.3 [8] | 55.2 [8] | 5.9 [6] | 6.7 [7,8] | 9.9 [8] | 9.0 [8] | 13.2 [8] | 40.2 | 17.7 [6,7] | 27.5 [6] | 23.7 [6] | 31.6 [6] | 0.0 | 0.0 | 0.0 | 0.0 | 0.0 |
| Spain | 48.2 | 48.8 | 52.0 | 52.4 | 54.1 | 32.0 | 32.7 | 30.1 | 30.9 | 30.3 | 18.6 | 17.4 | 16.9 | 15.9 | 15.4 | 1.1 | 1.1 | 1.0 | 0.8 | 0.2 |
| Sweden | 74.3 | 74.9 | 75.1 | 77.6 | 74.1 | 21.9 [8] | 21.4 [7,8] | 21.4 [8] | 19.4 [8] | 22.0 [8] | 3.7 [6] | 3.5 [6] | 3.4 [6] | 2.8 [6] | 3.5 [6] | 0.2 | 0.1 | 0.1 | 0.1 | 0.4 |
| Switzerland[1] | 70.7 | .. | 73.9 | .. | .. | 24.3 | .. | 22.9 | | .. | 2.5 [6] | .. | 1.3 [6,7] | .. | .. | 2.5 | .. | 1.9 | .. | .. |
| Turkey | 23.6 | 32.3 | 38.1 | 33.7 | .. | 69.0 | 57.2 | 55.3 | 58.9 | .. | 7.4 | 10.5 | 6.7 | 7.4 | .. | .. | .. | .. | .. | .. |
| United Kingdom | 65.0 | 65.2 | 66.8 | 66.2 [7] | 65.7 | 19.2 | 19.7 | 19.6 | 21.7 | 21.4 | 14.6 | 13.8 | 12.2 | 9.8 [7] | 9.6 | 1.3 | 1.3 | 1.4 | 2.3 | 3.2 |
| EU15[4] | 62.1 | 62.8 | 64.2 | 64.7 | 64.2 | 20.8 | 21.4 | 20.7 | 21.3 | .. | 16.3 | 15.0 | 14.2 | 13.0 | 12.8 | 0.9 | 0.9 | 0.9 | 1.0 | 1.3 |
| EU25[5] | 61.6 | 62.3 | 63.6 | 64.1 | 63.4 | 20.8 | 21.3 | 20.8 | 21.4 | 21.9 | 16.8 | 15.5 | 14.7 | 13.5 | 13.5 | 0.9 | 0.9 | 0.9 | 1.0 | 1.2 |
| Total OECD[4] | 67.3 | 68.8 | 69.3 | 69.3 | 67.3 | 17.5 | 17.2 | 17.1 | 17.5 | 18.7 | 12.6 | 11.2 | 10.8 | 10.4 | 10.9 | 2.7 | 2.7 | 2.8 | 2.8 | 3.1 |

1. For relevant years, 1996 instead of 1995; 1998 instead of 1997; 2000 instead of 1999; 2002 instead of 2001.
2. Adjusted by OECD up to 1995.
3. Figures for Germany refer to unified Germany.
4. Includes Luxembourg from 2000.
5. Malta is excluded; includes Luxembourg from 2000.
6. Underestimated.
7. Break in series from previous year for which data are available.
8. Overestimated.

*Source:* OECD, MSTI database, May 2005.

StatLink: *http://dx.doi.org/10.1787/074117410852*

Table B.7 **Researchers per thousand employment**
by sector of employment

| | Business enterprise | | | | | Government | | | | | Higher education | | | | |
|---|---|---|---|---|---|---|---|---|---|---|---|---|---|---|---|
| | 1995 | 1997 | 1999 | 2001 | 2003 | 1995 | 1997 | 1999 | 2001 | 2003 | 1995 | 1997 | 1999 | 2001 | 2003 |
| Canada | 3.6 | 3.7 | 3.9 | 4.8 | .. | 0.6 | 0.5 | 0.5 | 0.5 | .. | 2.2 | 2.4 | 2.2 | 2.2 | .. |
| Mexico | 0.1 | 0.1 | 0.1 | .. | .. | 0.2 | 0.2 | 0.2 | .. | .. | 0.3 | 0.3 | 0.3 | .. | .. |
| United States | 6.2 | 7.0 | 7.5 | .. | .. | 0.4[7] | 0.4[7] | 0.4[7] | .. | .. | 1.4 | 1.4 | 1.4 | .. | .. |
| Australia[1] | 1.9 | 1.7 | 1.8 | 1.9 | .. | 1.1 | 1.0 | 1.0 | 0.9 | .. | 4.2 | 4.4 | 4.4 | 4.6 | .. |
| Japan[2] | 5.8 | 6.0[8] | 6.5 | 6.5 | 7.0 | 0.5 | 0.4 | 0.5 | 0.5 | 0.5 | 3.6[9] | 2.6 | 2.7 | 3.0 | 2.6 |
| Korea | 3.3 | 3.3 | 3.2 | 4.6 | 5.0 | 0.6[7] | 0.6[7] | 0.6[7] | 0.6[7] | 0.5[7] | 1.0[7] | 0.9[7] | 1.1[7] | 1.1[7] | 1.2[7] |
| New Zealand | 1.2 | 1.3 | 1.5 | 1.7[8] | 2.6 | 1.2 | 1.3 | 1.2 | 1.4 | 1.4 | 2.4 | 3.6 | 3.5 | 6.0[8] | .. |
| Austria[1] | .. | 2.9 | .. | 3.9 | .. | .. | 0.2 | .. | 0.2 | .. | .. | 1.5 | .. | 1.7 | .. |
| Belgium | 3.1 | 3.7 | 4.0 | 4.3 | 4.7 | 0.3 | 0.4 | 0.4 | 0.5 | 0.6 | 2.6 | 2.5 | 2.9 | 2.9 | 3.0 |
| Czech Republic | 1.0 | 1.0 | 1.2 | 1.2 | 1.3 | 0.8[8] | 0.9 | 0.9 | 1.0 | 1.0 | 0.5[8] | 0.6 | 0.7 | 0.9 | 0.9 |
| Denmark | 2.5 | 2.8 | 3.3 | 3.5 | .. | 1.4 | 1.4 | 1.4 | 1.3 | 0.9 | 2.1 | 2.3 | 2.1 | 2.2 | 2.8 |
| Finland | 3.3 | 6.4[8] | 7.7 | 9.0 | 10.0 | 1.7 | 1.8[8] | 2.0 | 1.9 | 2.0 | 3.2 | 4.0[8] | 4.7 | 4.7 | 5.5 |
| France | 2.9 | 3.1[8] | 3.2 | 3.6[8] | .. | 1.2 | 1.1[7,8] | 1.1[7] | 0.9[7] | .. | 2.4 | 2.4[8] | 2.4 | 2.5 | .. |
| Germany[3] | 3.5 | 3.6 | 3.9 | 4.1 | 4.0 | 1.0 | 1.0 | 1.0 | 1.0 | 1.0 | 1.7 | 1.8 | 1.8 | 1.7 | 1.9 |
| Greece | 0.4 | 0.5 | 0.6 | 1.0 | 1.1 | 0.5 | 0.5 | 0.5 | 0.5 | .. | 1.6[8] | 1.9 | 2.7 | 2.2 | .. |
| Hungary | 0.8 | 0.8 | 0.9 | 1.1 | 1.1 | 1.0 | 1.1 | 1.2 | 1.2 | 1.2 | 1.1 | 1.2 | 1.3 | 1.5 | 1.5 |
| Ireland | 2.6 | 3.1 | 3.3 | 3.4 | 3.3 | 0.2 | 0.2 | 0.2 | 0.3[8] | 0.3 | 1.5 | 1.6 | 1.4 | 1.4[8] | .. |
| Italy | 1.2 | 1.2 | 1.2 | 1.1 | .. | 0.6 | 0.6 | 0.6 | 0.6 | .. | 1.6 | 1.1[8] | 1.1 | 1.2 | .. |
| Luxembourg[4] | .. | .. | 5.3 | .. | .. | .. | .. | 0.8 | 1.0 | 1.1 | .. | .. | 0.1 | 0.1 | .. |
| Netherlands | 1.9 | 2.3 | 2.4 | 2.7 | .. | 1.1 | 1.0 | 1.0 | 0.8 | 0.9[8] | 1.8 | 1.6 | 1.6 | 1.9 | .. |
| Norway | 3.7 | 4.2 | 4.2 | 4.9 | 5.0 | 1.4 | 1.4 | 1.3 | 1.3 | 1.4 | 2.4 | 2.3 | 2.4 | 2.5 | 2.7 |
| Poland | 0.7 | 0.7 | 0.7 | 0.6 | 0.5 | 0.7 | 0.7 | 0.7 | 0.7 | 1.0 | 1.8 | 2.0 | 2.2 | 2.4 | 2.9 |
| Portugal | 0.2 | 0.3 | 0.4 | 0.5 | .. | 0.6 | 0.6 | 0.7 | 0.7 | .. | 1.3[8] | 1.6 | 1.7 | 1.8 | .. |
| Slovak Republic | 1.0 | 1.6[8] | 1.2 | 1.1 | 0.9 | 1.7 | 1.2[8] | 1.2 | 1.2 | 1.2 | 1.9 | 1.9 | 2.1 | 2.4 | 2.6 |
| Spain | 0.8 | 0.8 | 1.0 | 1.2 | 1.7 | 0.6 | 0.7 | 0.8 | 0.8 | 0.9 | 2.0 | 2.2 | 2.2 | 2.9 | 3.0 |
| Sweden | 4.6 | 5.2 | 5.5 | 6.4 | 6.5 | 0.7 | 0.6 | 0.6 | 0.5 | .. | 2.9 | 3.4 | 3.5 | 3.6 | .. |
| Switzerland[1] | 3.2 | .. | 4.0 | .. | .. | 0.1 | .. | 0.1 | .. | .. | 2.3 | .. | 2.2 | .. | .. |
| Turkey | 0.1 | 0.2 | 0.1 | 0.2 | .. | 0.1 | 0.1 | 0.1 | 0.1 | .. | 0.6 | 0.6 | 0.7 | 0.8 | .. |
| United Kingdom | 3.0 | 2.9 | 3.2 | 3.1[8] | 3.4 | 0.5 | 0.4 | 0.5 | 0.3[8] | 0.3 | 1.7 | 1.7 | .. | .. | .. |
| EU15[5] | 2.5 | 2.6 | 2.8 | 3.0 | .. | 0.8 | 0.8[8] | 0.8 | 0.7 | .. | 1.9 | 1.9[8] | 1.9 | 2.1 | .. |
| EU25[6] | 2.2 | 2.3[8] | 2.5 | 2.7 | .. | 0.8 | 0.8[8] | 0.8 | 0.8 | .. | 1.8 | 1.8[8] | 1.9 | 2.1 | .. |
| Total OECD[5] | 3.6 | 3.9 | 4.2 | .. | .. | 0.6[8] | 0.5 | 0.5 | 0.5 | .. | 1.6[8] | 1.7 | 1.7 | .. | .. |

1. For relevant years, 1996 instead of 1995; 1998 instead of 1997; 2000 instead of 1999; 2002 instead of 2001.
2. Adjusted by OECD up to 1995.
3. Figures for Germany refer to unified Germany.
4. 2000 instead of 1999.
5. Includes Luxembourg from 2000.
6. Malta is excluded; includes Luxembourg from 2000.
7. Underestimated.
8. Break in series from previous year for which data are available.
9. Overestimated.

*Source:* OECD, MSTI database, May 2005.

StatLink: *http://dx.doi.org/10.1787/704453421600*

Table D.9 **Business use of the Internet, 2000-04. Percentage of businesses with 10 or more employees**[1]

| | 2000 | 2001 | 2002 [2] | 2003 | 2004 |
|---|---|---|---|---|---|
| Japan | .. | 91.5 | 96.1 | 97.5 | .. |
| Denmark | .. | .. | 94.8 | 96.7 | 97.4 |
| Hungary | .. | .. | .. | 97.4 | 77.5 |
| Finland [3] | .. | .. | 96.0 | 97.3 | 97.1 |
| Belgium | .. | .. | .. | 91.4 | 96.0 |
| Sweden | .. | .. | 95.2 | 80.2 | 95.9 |
| Spain | .. | 82.5 | 95.2 | 87.4 | |
| Germany | .. | .. | 83.9 | 94.9 | 94.1 |
| Korea | .. | 81.2 | 86.5 | 91.6 | 94.0 |
| Canada | .. | 84.8 | 89.1 | 91.4 | 93.9 |
| Austria | .. | .. | 84.9 | 89.1 | 93.7 |
| Switzerland | 78.0 | 83.0 | 92.0 | .. | .. |
| Ireland [4] | .. | .. | .. | 83.0 | 91.8 |
| Australia | 77.0 | 86.0 | 88.6 | 88.9 | 90.2 |
| Czech Republic[5] | .. | .. | .. | 87.7 | 90.1 |
| Mexico | .. | .. | .. | 90.0 | .. |
| Netherlands[6] | .. | .. | 85.5 | 88.3 | 88.5 |
| Greece | .. | .. | 64.4 | 87.5 | 87.4 |
| Italy | .. | .. | 74.3 | 85.0 | 87.4 |
| United Kingdom [7] | .. | .. | 74.0 | .. | 86.6 |
| Iceland | .. | .. | .. | 86.3 | .. |
| Luxembourg | .. | .. | 78.2 | 85.7 | .. |
| Norway | .. | .. | 82.4 | 69.6 | 85.5 |
| Poland | .. | .. | .. | .. | 85.0 |
| New Zealand | .. | 84.3 | .. | .. | .. |
| France [8] | .. | .. | .. | 82.9 | .. |
| Portugal | .. | .. | 68.7 | 81.6 | 77.3 |
| Slovak Republic | .. | .. | .. | .. | 71.3 |

1. For most European countries, the following industries are included: Manufacturing, Construction, Wholesale and retail, Hotels and restaurants (part), Transport, storage & communication, Real estate, renting and business activities and Other community, social and personal service activities (part).

For Australia, Agriculture, forestry and fishing, Education and Religious organisations are excluded. For Canada, Agriculture, fishing, hunting and trapping, and Construction – specialist contractors are excluded. For Japan, data refer to enterprises with 100 or more employees and exclude: Agriculture, forestry, fisheries and Mining. Korea includes: Agriculture & Fisheries, Light Industry, Heavy Industry, Petrochemicals, Construction, Distribution, Finance and Insurance, and Other services. For Mexico, data refer to enterprises with 50 or more employees and include: Manufacturing, Services and Construction. For New Zealand, data exclude Electricity, gas and water, Government administration and defence, and Personal and other services; the NZ survey also excludes businesses with five or fewer employees (FTEs) and those with turnover of less than NZD 30 000. For Switzerland, data refer to enterprises with five or more employees, and include the Manufacturing, Construction, Electricity, Gas, Water and Services industries.

2. For European countries, 2002 data include only the following industries: Manufacturing, Wholesale and retail, (part) Hotels and restaurants, Transport, storage & communication, and Real estate, renting and business activities.
3. Data for 2002 include NACE J (Financial intermediation). Data for 2003, include NACE 92.4 and 92.71.
4. Data include all of NACE 92.
5. Data for 2003 include all of NACE O (Other community, social and personal service activities).
6. Data for 2003 include all of NACE 55 and all of NACE 92.
7. Data for 2004 include all of NACE 55 and all of NACE 92.
8. Data also include Mining and quarrying, and Electricity, gas and water and all of NACE 92.

*Source:* OECD, ICT database and Eurostat, Community Survey on ICT usage in enterprises, May 2005.

StatLink: *http://dx.doi.org/10.1787/776314817627*

Table D.10.1 **Internet commerce transaction value, 2002 to 2004** [1,2]

As a percentage of total enterprise turnover

| | 2002 | 2003 | 2004 |
|---|---|---|---|
| Ireland | | 10.0 | 12.8 |
| Denmark [2] | 1.0 | 1.6 | 4.4 |
| Czech Republic | | 2.8 | 1.9 |
| Sweden | | 2.8 | |
| Norway | 2.2 | 2.4 | 2.7 |
| Germany [3] | 1.0 | 0.7 | 2.7 |
| United Kingdom | 1.2 | 1.5 | 2.3 |
| Belgium | | 1.8 | 1.5 |
| Portugal | 0.6 | 0.6 | 1.3 |
| Poland | | | 1.3 |
| Italy | 0.3 | 0.3 | 1.2 |
| Finland [4] | 1.1 | | |
| Austria | | 0.9 | 1.0 |
| Greece [5] | 0.5 | 0.2 | 1.0 |
| Slovak Republic | | | 0.8 |
| Iceland | | 0.5 | |
| Luxembourg | 0.4 | | |
| Spain | 0.3 | 0.3 | 0.4 |

1. Enterprises in the following industries are included: Manufacturing, Wholesale and retail, Hotels and restaurants (part), Transport, storage and communication, and Real estate, renting and business activities.
2. Refers to sales via the Internet during reference year, excluding VAT.
3. For Germany, 2003 data are more precise and as a result not comparable with 2002.
4. For Finland, 2002 does not include NACE 67. Data for 2004 are not comparable to previous years due to better coverage.
5. For Greece, 2003 data are estimated.

*Source:* Eurostat, Community Survey on ICT usage in enterprises, May 2005.

StatLink: *http://dx.doi.org/10.1787/544173163388*

Table D.10.2 **Businesses recognising specific barriers to use of the Internet for selling, 2004.**

Percentage of businesses with 10 or more employees [1,2] which did not sell their products over the Internet

| | Australia | Belgium | Canada | Germany | Hungary | Ireland | Japan (2003) | Korea (2003) | Poland | Slovak Republic | Spain | Switzerland (2002) |
|---|---|---|---|---|---|---|---|---|---|---|---|---|
| Products of the business are not suited to Internet sale | 61.8 | 28.7 | 47.8 | 39.0 | 31.8 | 27.6 | .. | 79.8 | 37.5 | 26.2 | 60.2 | 58.0 |
| Prefer to maintain current business model *e.g.* face to face interaction | 34.2 | .. | 33.9 | .. | .. | .. | 23.2 | .. | .. | .. | .. | .. |
| Customers not ready/lack of customer demand | 16.0 | 8.8 | 14.9 | 16.6 | 12.6 | 10.2 | .. | 12.1 | 21.7 | 12.2 | 33.7 | 33.0 |
| Security concerns | 6.2 | 21.1 | 19.3 | 33.5 | 5.0 | 13.7 | 33.0 | 5.9 | 21.6 | 21.3 | 28.1 | 25.0 |
| Costs too high | 9.9 | .. | 14.1 | .. | .. | .. | .. | .. | .. | .. | .. | 16.0 |
| Legal concerns | .. | 11.3 | .. | 22.4 | 2.0 | 8.8 | .. | .. | 17.8 | 15.7 | 33.3 | 22.0 |

1. For most European countries, the following industries are included: Manufacturing, Construction, Wholesale and retail, Hotels and restaurants (part), Transport, storage & communication, Real estate, renting and business activities and Other community, social and personal service activities (part). For Australia, Agriculture, forestry and fishing, Education and Religious organisations are excluded. For Canada, Agriculture, fishing, hunting and trapping, and Construction – specialist contractors are excluded. For Japan, data refer to enterprises with 100 or more employees and exclude: Agriculture, forestry, fisheries and Mining. Korea includes: Agriculture & Fisheries, Light Industry, Heavy Industry, Petrochemicals, Construction, Distribution, Finance and Insurance, and Other services. For Switzerland, data refer to enterprises with 5 or more employees, and include the Manufacturing, Construction, Electricity, gas, water and Services industries.

2. OECD countries vary in how they ask barriers questions and what alternatives they provide. Some countries (e.g. Korea) have a very small number of barriers. Others (e.g. Japan) offer a large number. Other differences between countries occur in how the question is asked, for instance, whether countries are asked to rate each barrier, tick the most important one, or tick all which apply. Because of these differences in approach, it is suggested that users focus on the relative importance of barriers within each country rather than making comparisons between countries.

*Source:* OECD, ICT database and Eurostat, Community Survey on ICT usage in enterprises, May 2005.

StatLink: *http://dx.doi.org/10.1787/454614844138*

Table E.3.1 **Export ratio by industry**[1]

| | Total manufacturing | | High-technology industries: Total | | Aircraft and spacecraft | | Pharmaceuticals | | Office, accounting and computing machinery | | Radio, television and communication equipment | | Medical, precision and optical instruments | | Medium-high-technology industries: Total | | Electrical machinery and apparatus, n.e.c. | | Motor vehicles, trailers and semi-trailers | | Chemicals excluding pharmaceuticals | | Railroad equipment and transport equipment, n.e.c. | | Machinery and equipment, n.e.c. | |
|---|---|---|---|---|---|---|---|---|---|---|---|---|---|---|---|---|---|---|---|---|---|---|---|---|---|---|
| | 1992 | 2001 | 1992 | 2001 | 1992 | 2001 | 1992 | 2001 | 1992 | 2001 | 1992 | 2001 | 1992 | 2001 | 1992 | 2001 | 1992 | 2001 | 1992 | 2001 | 1992 | 2001 | 1992 | 2001 | 1992 | 2001 |
| Canada[2] | 42 | 52 | 57 | 83 | 74 | 105 | 10 | 26 | 117 | 131 | 40 | 58 | .. | .. | 62 | 72 | 41 | 68 | 81 | 82 | 38 | 54 | 32 | 38 | 47 | 66 |
| United States | 13 | 17 | 26 | 35 | 35 | 44 | 10 | 15 | 47 | 58 | 24 | 37 | 16 | 26 | 20 | 24 | 24 | 38 | 18 | 19 | 17 | 22 | 11 | 11 | 24 | 27 |
| Japan[3] | 13 | 16 | 27 | 30 | 13 | 31 | 4 | 6 | 34 | 33 | 27 | 28 | 43 | 77 | 20 | 25 | 16 | 24 | 23 | 26 | 14 | 21 | .. | .. | 19 | 25 |
| Austria | 45 | 63 | 55 | 102 | .. | .. | 56 | 111 | 1045 | 175 | 32 | 73 | 71 | 109 | 73 | 87 | 81 | 91 | 96 | 101 | 55 | 78 | 32 | 69 | 71 | 80 |
| Denmark[4] | 57 | 67 | 101 | 117 | .. | .. | 85 | 98 | 206 | 347 | 95 | 139 | 102 | 100 | 75 | 82 | 58 | 80 | 113 | 130 | 63 | 87 | 118 | 142 | 76 | 74 |
| Finland | 38 | 48 | 59 | 61 | 9 | 70 | 36 | 55 | 69 | 384 | 62 | 59 | 71 | 64 | 50 | 58 | 49 | 73 | 137 | 195 | 38 | 48 | 9 | 21 | 46 | 47 |
| France | 29 | 39 | 42 | 62 | 68 | 66 | 24 | 53 | 62 | 102 | 39 | 66 | 29 | 45 | 41 | 51 | 37 | 53 | 40 | 44 | 47 | 61 | 39 | 36 | 39 | 55 |
| Germany | 32 | 47 | 54 | 101 | 100 | 142 | 46 | 90 | 46 | 117 | 51 | 108 | 47 | 74 | 42 | 54 | 24 | 38 | 48 | 55 | 46 | 60 | 42 | 39 | 43 | 57 |
| Italy | 23 | 35 | 31 | 56 | 48 | 72 | 15 | 50 | 76 | 79 | 26 | 53 | 32 | 55 | 33 | 50 | 19 | 32 | 39 | 50 | 22 | 37 | 35 | 52 | 42 | 61 |
| Netherlands | 64 | 85 | 93 | 222 | .. | 75 | 61 | 101 | 392 | 1624 | 46 | 84 | 108 | 237 | 82 | 94 | 102 | 160 | 99 | 120 | 76 | 90 | .. | 128 | 82 | 73 |
| Norway | 37 | 43 | 67 | 78 | 55 | 237 | 64 | 62 | 179 | 259 | 57 | 64 | 55 | 54 | 40 | 49 | 26 | 52 | 96 | 82 | 41 | 46 | 11 | 23 | 40 | 47 |
| Portugal | 29 | 39 | 42 | 71 | .. | .. | 11 | 36 | 52 | 97 | 59 | 72 | 46 | 59 | 38 | 64 | 57 | 56 | 56 | 97 | 20 | 36 | 30 | 23 | 36 | 51 |
| Spain | 19 | 31 | 28 | 50 | 121 | 85 | 10 | 33 | 52 | 51 | 33 | 66 | 24 | 47 | 36 | 52 | 25 | 37 | 49 | 67 | 22 | 39 | 15 | 44 | 34 | 45 |
| Sweden | 41 | 51 | 66 | 67 | 46 | 103 | 67 | 79 | 97 | 136 | 65 | 55 | 65 | 72 | 50 | 58 | 49 | 66 | 54 | 50 | 43 | 66 | 18 | 23 | 52 | 64 |
| United Kingdom | 31 | 43 | 57 | 101 | 70 | 124 | 40 | 74 | 69 | 102 | 52 | 128 | 51 | 64 | 45 | 53 | 36 | 54 | 45 | 48 | 46 | 58 | 17 | 19 | 51 | 55 |
| EU[5] (intra-EU trade is excluded) | 13 | 21 | 24 | 44 | 49 | 63 | 17 | 40 | 21 | 49 | 20 | 38 | 23 | 40 | 19 | 27 | 13 | 24 | 16 | 22 | 20 | 29 | 15 | 18 | 23 | 33 |
| EU[5] (intra-EU trade is included) | 31 | 44 | 50 | 87 | 78 | 100 | 32 | 68 | 72 | 151 | 45 | 83 | 45 | 70 | 43 | 55 | 30 | 47 | 47 | 55 | 43 | 58 | 36 | 43 | 46 | 58 |
| OECD[6] | 21 | 28 | 34 | 50 | 48 | 66 | 18 | 33 | 49 | 71 | 31 | 46 | 31 | 46 | 31 | 39 | 24 | 39 | 33 | 38 | 28 | 37 | 34 | 35 | 33 | 41 |

.. Not available.

1. Exports as a percentage of production. Values greater than 100 can occur when exports exceed production because of the inclusion of re-exports - products that are imported and then re-exported without any further transformation.
2. Medical, precision and optical instruments is included in Manufacturing, n.e.c. and recycling.
3. Railroad equipment and transport equipment, n.e.c. is included in Motor vehicles.
4. Aircraft and spacecraft is included in Railroad equipment and transport equipment, n.e.c.
5. European Union includes Austria, Denmark, Finland, France, Germany, Italy, Netherlands, Portugal, Spain, Sweden and United Kingdom.
6. Calculated with the above fifteen countries.

*Sources:* OECD, STAN Indicators and Bilateral Trade Database (BTD), March 2005.

StatLink: *http://dx.doi.org/10.1787/584517447771*

Table E.3.1 **Export ratio by industry**[1] *(cont)*

| | Medium-low-technology industries | | | | | | | | | | | | | | Low-technology industries | | | | | | | | | | | |
|---|---|---|---|---|---|---|---|---|---|---|---|---|---|---|---|---|---|---|---|---|---|---|---|---|---|---|
| | Total | | Coke, refined petroleum products and nuclear fuel | | Rubber and plastic products | | Other non-metallic mineral products | | Building and repairing of ships and boats | | Basic metals | | Fabricated metal products, except machinery and equipment | | Total | | Manufacturing, n.e.c. and recycling | | Wood and products of wood and cork | | Pulp, paper, paper products, printing and publishing | | Food products, beverages and tobacco | | Textiles, textile products, leather and footwear | |
| | 1992 | 2001 | 1992 | 2001 | 1992 | 2001 | 1992 | 2001 | 1992 | 2001 | 1992 | 2001 | 1992 | 2001 | 1992 | 2001 | 1992 | 2001 | 1992 | 2001 | 1992 | 2001 | 1992 | 2001 | 1992 | 2001 |
| Canada[2] | 33 | 36 | 21 | 28 | 27 | 42 | 18 | 27 | 15 | 66 | 60 | 53 | 15 | 24 | 29 | 37 | 25 | 43 | 60 | 59 | 45 | 41 | 14 | 22 | 13 | 36 |
| United States | 7 | 8 | 5 | 5 | 8 | 11 | 6 | 7 | 10 | 9 | 10 | 13 | 5 | 6 | 6 | 7 | 12 | 15 | 6 | 4 | 5 | 6 | 6 | 6 | 7 | 13 |
| Japan[3] | 6 | 8 | 2 | 1 | 15 | 21 | 5 | 7 | 54 | 53 | 6 | 10 | 4 | 5 | 3 | 3 | 5 | 7 | - | - | 2 | 2 | 1 | 1 | 6 | 10 |
| Austria | 40 | 44 | 6 | 15 | 67 | 65 | 26 | 26 | 38 | 402 | 56 | 65 | 37 | 36 | 30 | 47 | 32 | 48 | 35 | 43 | 41 | 48 | 8 | 31 | 64 | 87 |
| Denmark[4] | 43 | 40 | 42 | 33 | 54 | 59 | 32 | 27 | 54 | 37 | 54 | 67 | 35 | 32 | 48 | 59 | 61 | 57 | 42 | 39 | 18 | 20 | 51 | 63 | 82 | 162 |
| Finland | 34 | 40 | 30 | 40 | 34 | 35 | 18 | 24 | 44 | 77 | 47 | 51 | 22 | 21 | 32 | 40 | 23 | 23 | 48 | 45 | 51 | 54 | 5 | 10 | 38 | 50 |
| France | 21 | 24 | 14 | 16 | 26 | 31 | 16 | 20 | 24 | 49 | 42 | 45 | 12 | 14 | 20 | 26 | 19 | 26 | 12 | 18 | 13 | 17 | 20 | 24 | 31 | 51 |
| Germany | 22 | 31 | 15 | 21 | 26 | 39 | 15 | 23 | 46 | 66 | 36 | 47 | 15 | 22 | 20 | 27 | 25 | 37 | 9 | 18 | 16 | 23 | 13 | 18 | 49 | 77 |
| Italy | 17 | 24 | 14 | 18 | 23 | 34 | 17 | 23 | 11 | 58 | 22 | 31 | 12 | 17 | 19 | 29 | 33 | 48 | 5 | 8 | 9 | 14 | 9 | 15 | 30 | 44 |
| Netherlands | 56 | 60 | 76 | 86 | 76 | 76 | 31 | 22 | .. | 33 | 94 | 104 | 32 | 28 | 50 | 54 | 33 | 44 | 33 | 21 | 31 | 33 | 52 | 57 | 121 | 151 |
| Norway | 63 | 61 | .. | .. | 30 | 34 | 13 | 13 | 51 | 33 | 75 | 77 | 26 | 21 | 18 | 23 | 23 | 28 | 19 | 14 | 21 | 26 | 16 | 22 | 32 | 40 |
| Portugal | 19 | 25 | 24 | 13 | 15 | 34 | 18 | 20 | 30 | 19 | 12 | 42 | 21 | 33 | 29 | 32 | 19 | 22 | 38 | 42 | 20 | 25 | 9 | 13 | 49 | 56 |
| Spain | 17 | 21 | 25 | 18 | 18 | 30 | 11 | 17 | 47 | 26 | 27 | 30 | 10 | 13 | 9 | 19 | 10 | 21 | 7 | 11 | 9 | 16 | 7 | 16 | 15 | 36 |
| Sweden | 39 | 44 | 48 | 49 | 45 | 56 | 17 | 26 | 71 | 57 | 52 | 61 | 25 | 27 | 28 | 39 | 34 | 41 | 36 | 42 | 40 | 50 | 6 | 15 | 58 | 107 |
| United Kingdom | 21 | 24 | 24 | 30 | 21 | 21 | 16 | 16 | 15 | 16 | 33 | 44 | 13 | 16 | 16 | 17 | 26 | 24 | 3 | 5 | 11 | 12 | 14 | 15 | 30 | 44 |
| EU[5] (intra-EU trade is excluded) | 9 | 13 | 12 | 14 | 9 | 15 | 7 | 11 | 24 | 33 | 14 | 19 | 6 | 9 | 8 | 13 | 12 | 18 | 4 | 8 | 6 | 9 | 6 | 9 | 14 | 26 |
| EU[5] (intra-EU trade is included) | 23 | 29 | 23 | 27 | 28 | 35 | 17 | 21 | 34 | 46 | 36 | 45 | 15 | 19 | 21 | 28 | 26 | 35 | 15 | 20 | 18 | 22 | 16 | 22 | 36 | 53 |
| OECD[6] | 15 | 18 | 11 | 13 | 19 | 24 | 12 | 14 | 34 | 36 | 19 | 25 | 10 | 12 | 13 | 16 | 15 | 20 | 11 | 14 | 11 | 13 | 10 | 12 | 22 | 33 |

.. Not available. - Nil or negligible.

1. Exports as a percentage of production. Values greater than 100 can occur when exports exceed production because of the inclusion of re-exports - products that are imported and then re-exported without any further transformation.
2. Medical, precision and optical instruments is included in Manufacturing, n.e.c. and recycling.
3. Railroad equipment and transport equipment, n.e.c. is included in Motor vehicles.
4. Aircraft and spacecraft is included in Railroad equipment and transport equipment, n.e.c.
5. European Union includes Austria, Denmark, Finland, France, Germany, Italy, Netherlands, Portugal, Spain, Sweden and United Kingdom.
6. Calculated with the above fifteen countries.

*Sources:* OECD, STAN Indicators and Bilateral Trade Database (BTD), March 2005.

Table E.3.2 **Import penetration by industry**[1]

| | Total manufacturing | | High-technology industries: Total | | Aircraft and spacecraft | | Pharmaceuticals | | Office, accounting and computing machinery | | Radio, television and communication equipment | | Medical, precision and optical instruments | | Medium-high-technology industries: Total | | Electrical machinery and apparatus, n.e.c. | | Motor vehicles, trailers and semi-trailers | | Chemicals excluding pharmaceuticals | | Railroad equipment and transport equipment, n.e.c. | | Machinery and equipment, n.e.c. | |
|---|---|---|---|---|---|---|---|---|---|---|---|---|---|---|---|---|---|---|---|---|---|---|---|---|---|---|
| | 1992 | 2001 | 1992 | 2001 | 1992 | 2001 | 1992 | 2001 | 1992 | 2001 | 1992 | 2001 | 1992 | 2001 | 1992 | 2001 | 1992 | 2001 | 1992 | 2001 | 1992 | 2001 | 1992 | 2001 | 1992 | 2001 |
| Canada[2] | 43 | 51 | 72 | 88 | 73 | 107 | 32 | 52 | 107 | 111 | 56 | 68 | 147 | 171 | 66 | 74 | 65 | 81 | 79 | 77 | 42 | 60 | 31 | 50 | 69 | 77 |
| United States | 16 | 23 | 23 | 37 | 14 | 30 | 8 | 19 | 52 | 69 | 32 | 42 | 13 | 23 | 22 | 31 | 27 | 47 | 30 | 37 | 11 | 21 | 17 | 21 | 20 | 27 |
| Japan[3] | 6 | 12 | 9 | 22 | 44 | 41 | 8 | 9 | 9 | 29 | 5 | 17 | 23 | 67 | 4 | 8 | 4 | 13 | 2 | 4 | 8 | 13 | .. | .. | 4 | 8 |
| Austria | 49 | 64 | 68 | 102 | 136 | 661 | 63 | 109 | 152 | 126 | 42 | 72 | 79 | 107 | 76 | 87 | 76 | 90 | 97 | 101 | 67 | 83 | 38 | 62 | 71 | 77 |
| Denmark[4] | 53 | 65 | 101 | 120 | .. | .. | 73 | 95 | 126 | 145 | 95 | 129 | 103 | 100 | 77 | 83 | 62 | 74 | 106 | 111 | 76 | 90 | 111 | 112 | 68 | 67 |
| Finland | 31 | 37 | 67 | 52 | 50 | 84 | 58 | 74 | 78 | 123 | 63 | 39 | 75 | 58 | 54 | 56 | 49 | 70 | 128 | 152 | 50 | 54 | 25 | 50 | 45 | 37 |
| France | 29 | 38 | 42 | 59 | 55 | 49 | 19 | 47 | 72 | 101 | 45 | 64 | 33 | 48 | 38 | 48 | 30 | 48 | 35 | 38 | 44 | 57 | 40 | 43 | 41 | 56 |
| Germany | 29 | 40 | 56 | 101 | 100 | 156 | 36 | 84 | 62 | 109 | 57 | 107 | 38 | 65 | 29 | 39 | 17 | 32 | 34 | 35 | 36 | 53 | 39 | 43 | 26 | 37 |
| Italy | 21 | 31 | 40 | 64 | 46 | 76 | 20 | 49 | 83 | 91 | 41 | 62 | 43 | 61 | 32 | 45 | 16 | 28 | 52 | 59 | 36 | 48 | 25 | 43 | 23 | 38 |
| Netherlands | 63 | 84 | 93 | 211 | -7335 | 80 | 62 | 101 | 296 | -2437 | 52 | 90 | 107 | 291 | 83 | 94 | 102 | 148 | 99 | 113 | 70 | 85 | 173 | 122 | 85 | 72 |
| Norway | 44 | 49 | 84 | 89 | 80 | 128 | 70 | 71 | 114 | 115 | 77 | 77 | 75 | 64 | 55 | 61 | 50 | 67 | 99 | 95 | 35 | 38 | 37 | 67 | 64 | 62 |
| Portugal | 38 | 48 | 69 | 85 | 176 | 180 | 36 | 67 | 92 | 99 | 72 | 79 | 81 | 85 | 66 | 75 | 60 | 57 | 82 | 98 | 47 | 63 | 67 | 36 | 70 | 73 |
| Spain | 25 | 35 | 50 | 68 | 114 | 89 | 19 | 47 | 76 | 75 | 58 | 80 | 58 | 71 | 43 | 56 | 33 | 41 | 45 | 66 | 37 | 48 | 36 | 41 | 52 | 59 |
| Sweden | 37 | 45 | 65 | 62 | 50 | 103 | 48 | 57 | 98 | 109 | 58 | 45 | 64 | 70 | 46 | 52 | 54 | 66 | 41 | 40 | 55 | 73 | 23 | 27 | 45 | 54 |
| United Kingdom | 34 | 48 | 57 | 101 | 60 | 125 | 29 | 71 | 75 | 102 | 59 | 131 | 50 | 64 | 46 | 57 | 39 | 55 | 52 | 62 | 43 | 55 | 31 | 39 | 49 | 55 |
| EU[5] (intra-EU trade is excluded) | 12 | 20 | 28 | 48 | 42 | 61 | 11 | 27 | 44 | 70 | 30 | 45 | 24 | 40 | 13 | 19 | 10 | 22 | 11 | 15 | 16 | 22 | 20 | 26 | 11 | 20 |
| EU[5] (intra-EU trade is included) | 31 | 42 | 54 | 87 | 74 | 100 | 28 | 63 | 81 | 130 | 52 | 84 | 46 | 68 | 39 | 50 | 27 | 44 | 45 | 51 | 43 | 56 | 40 | 48 | 37 | 49 |
| OECD[6] | 21 | 29 | 32 | 50 | 37 | 59 | 17 | 32 | 52 | 78 | 29 | 46 | 28 | 44 | 26 | 36 | 21 | 38 | 29 | 37 | 25 | 34 | 30 | 35 | 25 | 33 |

.. Not available.

1. Imports as a percentage of domestic demand (estimated as production minus exports plus imports). Values greater than 100 can occur when exports exceed production because of the inclusion of re-exports - products that are imported and then re-exported without any further transformation.
2. Medical, precision and optical instruments is included in Manufacturing, n.e.c. and recycling.
3. Railroad equipment and transport equipment, n.e.c. is included in Motor vehicles.
4. Aircraft and spacecraft is included in Railroad equipment and transport equipment, n.e.c.
5. European Union includes Austria, Denmark, Finland, France, Germany, Italy, Netherlands, Portugal, Spain, Sweden and United Kingdom.
6. Calculated with the above fifteen countries.

*Sources:* OECD, STAN Indicators and Bilateral Trade Database (BTD), March 2005.

StatLink: *http://dx.doi.org/10.1787/000512480504*

Table E.3.2 **Import penetration by industry**[1] *(cont.)*

| | Medium-low-technology industries | | | | | | | | | | | | | | Low-technology industries | | | | | | | | | | | |
|---|---|---|---|---|---|---|---|---|---|---|---|---|---|---|---|---|---|---|---|---|---|---|---|---|---|---|
| | **Total** | | Coke, refined petroleum products and nuclear fuel | | Rubber and plastic products | | Other non-metallic mineral products | | Building and repairing of ships and boats | | Basic metals | | Fabricated metal products, except machinery and equipment | | **Total** | | Manufacturing, n.e.c. and recycling | | Wood and products of wood and cork | | Pulp, paper, paper products, printing and publishing | | Food products, beverages and tobacco | | Textiles, textile products, leather and footwear | |
| | 1992 | 2001 | 1992 | 2001 | 1992 | 2001 | 1992 | 2001 | 1992 | 2001 | 1992 | 2001 | 1992 | 2001 | 1992 | 2001 | 1992 | 2001 | 1992 | 2001 | 1992 | 2001 | 1992 | 2001 | 1992 | 2001 |
| Canada[2] | 28 | 32 | 11 | 12 | 36 | 43 | 30 | 35 | 16 | 71 | 39 | 42 | 27 | 30 | 22 | 27 | 39 | 44 | 17 | 16 | 23 | 22 | 13 | 18 | 41 | 56 |
| United States | 10 | 14 | 10 | 13 | 9 | 13 | 10 | 15 | 2 | 6 | 15 | 23 | 6 | 9 | 11 | 17 | 28 | 40 | 9 | 14 | 4 | 6 | 5 | 7 | 28 | 45 |
| Japan[3] | 5 | 7 | 11 | 10 | 4 | 6 | 2 | 5 | 4 | 3 | 5 | 7 | 2 | 4 | 8 | 13 | 6 | 10 | 16 | 25 | 2 | 3 | 9 | 11 | 15 | 37 |
| Austria | 38 | 45 | 23 | 40 | 64 | 66 | 21 | 27 | 52 | 241 | 53 | 59 | 35 | 38 | 31 | 45 | 38 | 50 | 20 | 23 | 33 | 36 | 12 | 31 | 71 | 90 |
| Denmark[4] | 45 | 46 | 47 | 42 | 52 | 58 | 26 | 31 | 25 | 42 | 78 | 82 | 31 | 32 | 38 | 51 | 38 | 44 | 50 | 50 | 28 | 30 | 29 | 43 | 85 | 143 |
| Finland | 28 | 28 | 31 | 32 | 40 | 36 | 19 | 20 | 25 | 28 | 31 | 38 | 21 | 17 | 14 | 19 | 30 | 33 | 8 | 9 | 9 | 10 | 7 | 16 | 59 | 70 |
| France | 22 | 25 | 22 | 19 | 27 | 32 | 15 | 20 | 14 | 29 | 42 | 47 | 12 | 15 | 22 | 28 | 27 | 35 | 16 | 23 | 17 | 21 | 16 | 19 | 39 | 61 |
| Germany | 22 | 27 | 28 | 27 | 22 | 29 | 16 | 20 | 16 | 50 | 37 | 45 | 12 | 15 | 27 | 31 | 30 | 40 | 20 | 19 | 16 | 21 | 17 | 20 | 64 | 85 |
| Italy | 16 | 20 | 18 | 17 | 16 | 22 | 7 | 9 | 11 | 35 | 36 | 45 | 5 | 7 | 14 | 21 | 11 | 18 | 15 | 16 | 11 | 16 | 15 | 19 | 14 | 26 |
| Netherlands | 52 | 53 | 47 | 68 | 80 | 78 | 39 | 28 | -83 | 13 | 94 | 104 | 34 | 29 | 46 | 49 | 45 | 51 | 58 | 48 | 33 | 31 | 34 | 39 | 112 | 131 |
| Norway | 58 | 55 | -43 | -47 | 60 | 63 | 25 | 26 | 37 | 29 | 70 | 68 | 42 | 37 | 24 | 27 | 48 | 48 | 20 | 25 | 21 | 22 | 10 | 14 | 79 | 84 |
| Portugal | 29 | 38 | 30 | 28 | 36 | 49 | 10 | 15 | 17 | 13 | 54 | 75 | 28 | 40 | 22 | 29 | 30 | 28 | 11 | 21 | 19 | 26 | 16 | 24 | 31 | 42 |
| Spain | 17 | 21 | 23 | 21 | 22 | 30 | 8 | 9 | 18 | 26 | 27 | 37 | 13 | 14 | 14 | 21 | 18 | 23 | 14 | 18 | 14 | 17 | 10 | 17 | 22 | 39 |
| Sweden | 37 | 39 | 50 | 42 | 50 | 57 | 27 | 30 | 69 | 24 | 42 | 53 | 22 | 22 | 23 | 30 | 39 | 41 | 9 | 15 | 13 | 16 | 14 | 25 | 84 | 103 |
| United Kingdom | 24 | 27 | 18 | 27 | 25 | 26 | 18 | 19 | 13 | 8 | 43 | 50 | 14 | 18 | 25 | 30 | 37 | 39 | 29 | 31 | 18 | 18 | 19 | 22 | 45 | 68 |
| EU[5] (excl. intra-EU trade) | 9 | 12 | 13 | 14 | 8 | 12 | 5 | 7 | 9 | 18 | 19 | 24 | 4 | 7 | 10 | 14 | 14 | 21 | 9 | 12 | 5 | 6 | 6 | 8 | 21 | 36 |
| EU[5] (incl. intra-EU trade) | 23 | 27 | 24 | 26 | 27 | 32 | 15 | 17 | 18 | 28 | 40 | 48 | 13 | 16 | 23 | 29 | 27 | 35 | 20 | 22 | 17 | 20 | 17 | 21 | 41 | 57 |
| OECD[6] | 15 | 18 | 15 | 16 | 19 | 22 | 11 | 14 | 13 | 17 | 20 | 27 | 9 | 12 | 16 | 21 | 19 | 29 | 15 | 18 | 10 | 11 | 12 | 14 | 32 | 49 |

1. Imports as a percentage of domestic demand (estimated as production minus exports plus imports). Values greater than 100 can occur when exports exceed production because of the inclusion of re-exports - products that are imported and then re-exported without any further transformation.
2. Medical, precision and optical instruments is included in Manufacturing, n.e.c. and recycling.
3. Railroad equipment and transport equipment, n.e.c. is included in Motor vehicles.
4. Aircraft and spacecraft is included in Railroad equipment and transport equipment, n.e.c.
5. European Union includes Austria, Denmark, Finland, France, Germany, Italy, Netherlands, Portugal, Spain, Sweden and United Kingdom.
6. Calculated with the above fifteen countries.

*Sources:* OECD, STAN Indicators and Bilateral Trade Database, May 2005.

Table E.6 **Share of affiliates under foreign control in manufacturing employment and turnover**[1]

| | Share of affiliates | | | | | | Average annual growth rate 1997-02 | Share of affiliates | | | | | | Average annual growth rate 1997-02 |
|---|---|---|---|---|---|---|---|---|---|---|---|---|---|---|
| | 1997 | 1998 | 1999 | 2000 | 2001 | 2002 | | 1997 | 1998 | 1999 | 2000 | 2001 | 2002 | |
| Canada | .. | .. | .. | .. | .. | .. | .. | 49.6 | 50.3 | 51.4 | 50.0 | 51.9 | 51.0 | 1.8 |
| United States | 11.2 | 12.1 | 12.1 | 12.6 | 12.0 | 12.8 | 2.0 | 17.6 | 21.1 | 22.2 | 23.2 | 23.7 | 20.3 | 3.6 |
| Australia | .. | .. | .. | 22.7 | .. | .. | | .. | .. | .. | .. | .. | .. | |
| Japan[2] | .. | .. | .. | .. | .. | .. | .. | 1.6 | 1.8 | 2.5 | 2.5 | 2.6 | .. | 11.7 |
| Austria[2] | 18.7 | .. | .. | 19.6 | 18.0 | .. | -1.2 | 26.3 | 26.1 | .. | 27.1 | 24.5 | .. | 2.8 |
| Belgium | 19.1 | .. | .. | .. | .. | 32.3 | 8.7 | 47.5 | .. | .. | .. | .. | 57.2 | 2.4 |
| Czech Republic | 10.7 | 13.2 | 16.2 | 24.7 | 28.9 | 30.3 | 20.9 | 17.8 | 21.7 | 27.1 | 39.2 | 43.3 | 45.5 | 25.6 |
| Denmark | .. | .. | 10.2 | .. | .. | .. | .. | .. | .. | 12.0 | .. | .. | .. | .. |
| Finland | 12.4 | 13.8 | 15.9 | 15.9 | 17.2 | 17.4 | 8.2 | 13.7 | 14.3 | 16.2 | 14.4 | 16.2 | 16.3 | 10.0 |
| France[2] | 27.4 | 27.8 | 28.5 | 30.1 | 30.8 | .. | 6.0 | 32.0 | 31.7 | 33.6 | 35.0 | 35.9 | .. | 9.7 |
| Germany[2] | 6.7 | 6.0 | 6.2 | 6.0 | 5.8 | 16.6 | -3.8 | 12.5 | 10.8 | 10.1 | 9.4 | 8.3 | 24.4 | -6.0 |
| Hungary | 41.2 | 45.0 | 46.5 | 44.5 | 45.2 | 43.6 | 1.4 | 66.1 | 70.1 | 73.0 | 64.7 | 72.5 | 71.6 | 11.7 |
| Ireland[2] | 47.8 | 47.5 | 49.1 | 48.1 | 49.2 | .. | 1.7 | 69.2 | 72.3 | 75.9 | 78.2 | 79.5 | .. | 16.1 |
| Italy | .. | .. | .. | .. | 10.9 | .. | .. | .. | .. | .. | .. | 22.3 | .. | .. |
| Luxembourg[3] | 42.7 | 46.3 | 41.4 | .. | .. | .. | -0.1 | 49.4 | 52.4 | 52.9 | .. | .. | .. | 7.0 |
| Netherlands[2] | 19.7 | 21.9 | 18.9 | 18.3 | 21.0 | .. | 2.8 | 30.4 | 32.1 | 30.8 | 24.4 | 35.3 | .. | 6.7 |
| Norway | 14.2 | 17.4 | 19.9 | 21.4 | 23.1 | 22.2 | 7.6 | 19.9 | 23.9 | 27.5 | 28.1 | 29.7 | 28.6 | 8.8 |
| Poland | 12.5 | 14.8 | 18.6 | 20.9 | 21.9 | 24.1 | 7.6 | 19.4 | 26.1 | 33.8 | 34.7 | 35.2 | 38.9 | 18.9 |
| Portugal[2] | 8.3 | 8.8 | 8.9 | 10.1 | 8.6 | .. | 0.5 | 15.4 | 16.4 | 15.9 | 17.4 | 15.9 | .. | -0.9 |
| Spain | .. | .. | 16.5 | 16.8 | 16.4 | .. | .. | .. | .. | 29.9 | 29.7 | 28.5 | .. | .. |
| Sweden[2] | 19.0 | 21.1 | 24.1 | 29.1 | 32.7 | .. | 15.0 | 19.6 | 21.9 | 29.0 | 33.4 | 39.3 | .. | 22.9 |
| Turkey[2] | 5.3 | 5.5 | 5.4 | 5.7 | 7.0 | .. | 3.4 | 12.3 | 11.6 | 12.5 | 14.0 | 14.7 | .. | 6.8 |
| United Kingdom[3] | 17.8 | .. | 20.4 | .. | .. | .. | 4.5 | 31.4 | .. | 36.1 | .. | .. | .. | 13.7 |

1. Production instead of turnover for Canada and Ireland. National currency, 1995 prices.
2. 1997-2001.
3. 1995-1999.

*Source*: OECD, AFA and FATS databases, May 2005.

StatLink: *http://dx.doi.org/10.1787/107778074102*

Table E.12 **Technology balance of payments**

| | Million USD | | | | | | As a percentage of GDP | | | | | | Receipts/payments ratio (%) | |
|---|---|---|---|---|---|---|---|---|---|---|---|---|---|---|
| | Receipts | | Payments | | Balance | | Receipts | | Payments | | Balance | | | |
| | 1993 | 2003 | 1993 | 2003 | 1993 | 2003 | 1993 | 2003 | 1993 | 2003 | 1993 | 2003 | 1993 | 2003 |
| Canada[1] | 989.1 | 2 033.6 | 872.1 | 1 050.4 | 117.1 | 983.2 | 0.18 | 0.29 | 0.16 | 0.15 | 0.0 | 0.1 | 113 | 194 |
| Mexico | 96.9 | 54.0 | 501.9 | 608.1 | - 405.0 | - 554.1 | 0.02 | 0.01 | 0.12 | 0.10 | - 0.1 | - 0.1 | 19 | 9 |
| United States | 21 695.0 | 48 227.0 | 5 032.0 | 20 049.0 | 16 663.0 | 28 178.0 | 0.33 | 0.44 | 0.08 | 0.18 | 0.3 | 0.3 | 431 | 241 |
| Australia[2,3] | 199.7 | 103.0 | 370.0 | 224.9 | - 170.3 | - 121.9 | 0.06 | 0.03 | 0.12 | 0.06 | - 0.1 | 0.0 | 54 | 46 |
| Japan | 3 600.4 | 13 043.6 | 3 264.2 | 4 862.8 | 336.2 | 8 180.8 | 0.08 | 0.30 | 0.07 | 0.11 | 0.0 | 0.2 | 110 | 268 |
| Korea | .. | 816.4 | .. | 3 237.3 | .. | -2 420.9 | .. | 0.13 | .. | 0.53 | .. | - 0.4 | .. | 25 |
| New Zealand[4] | 20.0 | 7.9 | 7.0 | 3.7 | 13.0 | 4.2 | 0.05 | 0.01 | 0.02 | 0.01 | 0.0 | 0.0 | 285 | 214 |
| Austria | 1 055.6 | 2 548.5 | 1 433.1 | 2 712.2 | - 377.5 | - 163.7 | 0.57 | 1.01 | 0.77 | 1.07 | - 0.2 | - 0.1 | 74 | 94 |
| Belgium[6] | 2 498.8 | 5 872.5 | 2 705.1 | 4 757.3 | - 206.3 | 1 115.1 | 1.16 | 1.95 | 1.25 | 1.58 | - 0.1 | 0.4 | 92 | 123 |
| Czech Republic | .. | 187.9 | .. | 548.8 | .. | - 360.8 | .. | 0.22 | .. | 0.64 | .. | - 0.4 | .. | 34 |
| Denmark[4] | .. | 1 657.4 | .. | 1 055.3 | .. | 602.1 | .. | 0.96 | .. | 0.61 | .. | 0.3 | .. | 157 |
| Finland[6] | 89.5 | 1 728.0 | 326.7 | 1 476.3 | - 237.3 | 251.7 | 0.10 | 1.07 | 0.38 | 0.92 | - 0.3 | 0.2 | 27 | 117 |
| France | 1 816.9 | 5 188.5 | 2 551.6 | 3 233.6 | - 734.6 | 1 954.9 | 0.14 | 0.30 | 0.20 | 0.18 | - 0.1 | 0.1 | 71 | 160 |
| Germany | 7 236.7 | 21 958.2 | 10 291.1 | 23 095.9 | - 3 054.4 | -1 137.7 | 0.37 | 0.91 | 0.53 | 0.96 | - 0.2 | 0.0 | 70 | 95 |
| Greece | .. | .. | .. | .. | .. | .. | .. | .. | .. | .. | .. | .. | .. | .. |
| Hungary[4] | .. | 216.1 | .. | 503.7 | .. | - 287.6 | .. | 0.45 | .. | 1.05 | .. | - 0.6 | .. | 43 |
| Iceland | .. | .. | .. | .. | .. | .. | .. | .. | .. | .. | .. | .. | .. | .. |
| Ireland | 66.3 | 205.4 | 1 390.7 | 16 115.1 | - 1 324.4 | -15 909.7 | 0.13 | 0.14 | 2.77 | 10.59 | - 2.6 | - 10.5 | 5 | 1 |
| Italy | 2 666.7 | 3 108.4 | 3 505.5 | 3 794.6 | - 838.9 | - 686.2 | 0.27 | 0.21 | 0.35 | 0.26 | - 0.1 | 0.0 | 76 | 82 |
| Luxembourg | .. | 117.4 | .. | 105.0 | .. | 12.4 | .. | 0.43 | .. | 0.39 | .. | 0.0 | .. | 112 |
| Netherlands[2] | 6 208.0 | .. | 6 139.1 | .. | 68.9 | .. | 1.86 | .. | 1.84 | .. | 0.0 | .. | 101 | .. |
| Norway | 356.1 | 1 501.3 | 673.4 | 1 297.3 | - 317.3 | 204.0 | 0.30 | 0.68 | 0.58 | 0.59 | - 0.3 | 0.1 | 53 | 116 |
| Poland[5] | 132.5 | 136.0 | 134.7 | 813.4 | - 2.2 | - 677.4 | 0.13 | 0.08 | 0.13 | 0.49 | - 0.0 | - 0.4 | 98 | 17 |
| Portugal | 127.2 | 454.9 | 380.3 | 737.0 | - 253.1 | - 282.2 | 0.15 | 0.31 | 0.44 | 0.50 | - 0.3 | - 0.2 | 33 | 62 |
| Slovak Republic[1] | .. | 30.4 | .. | 64.9 | .. | - 34.4 | .. | 0.15 | .. | 0.31 | .. | - 0.2 | .. | 47 |
| Spain[3] | 32.7 | 190.4 | 668.0 | 1 025.6 | - 635.3 | - 835.2 | 0.01 | 0.03 | 0.13 | 0.17 | - 0.1 | - 0.1 | 5 | 19 |
| Sweden | 456.9 | .. | 49.9 | .. | 407.0 | .. | .. | .. | .. | .. | .. | .. | 916 | .. |
| Switzerland | 2 322.1 | 4 553.1 | 861.3 | 4 792.1 | 1 460.8 | - 239.0 | 0.96 | 1.42 | 0.36 | 1.49 | 0.6 | - 0.1 | 270 | 95 |
| Turkey | .. | .. | .. | .. | .. | .. | .. | .. | .. | .. | .. | .. | .. | .. |
| United Kingdom[6] | 2 956.5 | 22 513.1 | 2 649.2 | 9 567.0 | 307.3 | 12 946.1 | 0.31 | 1.25 | 0.28 | 0.53 | 0.0 | 0.7 | 112 | 235 |
| European Union[7] | 23 916.9 | 74 701.4 | 31 113.4 | 79 228.5 | - 7 196.5 | -4 527.1 | 0.35 | 0.74 | 0.45 | 0.78 | - 0.1 | 0.0 | 77 | 94 |
| OECD Total[7,8] | 53 206.8 | 145 930.0 | 43 596.3 | 115 489.5 | 9 610.5 | 30 440.6 | 0.27 | 0.51 | 0.22 | 0.40 | 0.0 | 0.1 | 122 | 126 |

1. 2001 instead of 2003.
2. 1992 instead of 1993.
3. 1998 instead of 2003.
4. 1999 instead of 2003.
5. 1994 instead of 1993; 2000 instead of 2003.
6. Break in series between the two years shown.
7. Including intra-zone flows. Excluding Czech Republic, Denmark, Greece, Hungary, Poland and the Slovak Republic. Data partially estimated.
8. Excluding Iceland and Turkey.

*Source:* OECD, TBP database, May 2005.

StatLink: *http://dx.doi.org/10.1787/827124084858*

Table F.5 **Share of value added in total gross value added[1], current prices**
Percentages

| | | Technology and knowledge-based industries | | | | | | | |
|---|---|---|---|---|---|---|---|---|---|
| | | High technology manufactures | Medium-high technology manufactures | Post and telecommunications services | Finance and insurance services | Business activities (excluding real estate activities)[2] | Total with 'market' sevices | Education and health | Total |
| | *ISIC Rev.3* | *2423, 30, 32, 33, 353* | *24 less 2423, 29, 31, 34, 352, 359* | *64* | *65-67* | *71-74* | | *80, 85* | |
| Canada | 2001 | 1.5 | 4.8 | 2.8 | 7.3 | 7.3 | 23.8 | 11.0 | 34.7 |
| Mexico | 2002 | 2.1 | 4.8 | 1.7 | 3.5 | 6.9 | 19.0 | 10.2 | 29.1 |
| United States | 2002 | 2.8 | 3.4 | 3.1 | 8.0 | 13.1 | 30.5 | 12.6 | 43.1 |
| Australia | 2001/02 | *3.2* [3,4] | → | 3.0 | 7.6 | 11.6 | 25.4 | 11.4 | 36.7 |
| Japan | 2002 | 3.1 | 6.0 | 1.6 | 7.0 | 7.9 | 25.6 | .. | .. |
| Korea | 2002 | 6.2 | 7.6 | 3.0 | 9.1 | 5.3 | 31.2 | 8.3 | 39.5 |
| New Zealand | 2001/02 | *3.1* [3,4] | → | 3.0 | 5.8 | 9.0 | 20.8 | 9.4 | 30.2 |
| Austria | 2002 | 1.9 | 5.6 | 2.2 | 5.6 | 9.0 | 24.3 | 10.0 | 34.3 |
| Belgium | 2002 | 2.2 | 5.5 | 2.5 | 5.6 | 12.3 | 28.1 | 13.5 | 41.6 |
| Czech Republic | 2002 | *10.2* [3,4] | → | .. | 3.5 | .. | .. | 7.8 | .. |
| Denmark | 2002 | 2.5 | 3.9 | 2.1 | 5.2 | 8.0 | 21.6 | 15.8 | 37.4 |
| Finland | 2002 | 5.6 | 4.6 | 3.6 | 3.7 | 6.9 | 24.3 | 13.0 | 37.3 |
| France | 2002 | 2.4 | 5.0 | 2.1 | 4.8 | 13.7 | 28.0 | 11.8 | 39.8 |
| Germany | 2002 | 2.4 | 9.6 | 2.6 | 3.9 | 13.6 | 32.1 | 10.7 | 42.8 |
| Greece | 2002 | 0.7 | 1.2 | 3.1 | 5.1 | 3.5 | 13.5 | 10.3 | 23.8 |
| Hungary | 2002 | 2.9 | 6.7 | 3.6 | 3.8 | 9.0 | 26.0 | 10.3 | 36.3 |
| Iceland | 2002 | 1.0 | 1.0 | 2.2 | 7.0 | 6.5 | 17.8 | 14.8 | 32.6 |
| Ireland | 2002 | 7.5 | 13.3 | 3.1 | 5.1 | 8.7 | 37.7 | 10.0 | 47.8 |
| Italy | 2002 | 1.9 | 5.0 | 2.2 | 5.8 | 9.9 | 24.8 | 9.8 | 34.6 |
| Luxembourg | 2002 | *1.6* [3,4] | → | .. | 28.5 | 8.1 | 38.1 [5] | 7.4 | 45.5 [5] |
| Netherlands | 2002 | 1.5 | 3.4 | 2.7 | 6.3 | 12.4 | 26.2 | 12.7 | 38.9 |
| Norway | 2002 | 0.8 | 2.2 | 2.1 | 3.4 | 7.0 | 15.6 | 13.7 | 29.3 |
| Poland | 2000 | 1.4 | 4.1 | .. | 2.3 | .. | .. | 8.8 | .. |
| Portugal | 2001 | 0.8 | 2.5 | 2.9 | 6.0 | 6.5 | 18.7 | 13.4 | 32.0 |
| Slovak Republic | 2002 | *7.9* [3,4] | → | .. | 3.6 | .. | .. | 6.9 | .. |
| Spain | 2002 | 1.0 | 4.4 | 2.7 | 5.4 | 6.5 | 19.9 | 10.1 | 30.1 |
| Sweden | 2002 | 3.0 | 6.5 | 2.5 | 3.6 | 10.4 | 26.1 | 16.1 | 42.1 |
| Switzerland | 2002 | *10.5* [3,4] | → | 2.9 | 13.6 | 9.3 | 36.3 | 6.2 | 42.5 |
| United Kingdom | 2002 | 2.5 | 3.6 | 3.0 | 6.4 | 13.1 | 28.7 | 12.1 | 40.7 |
| European Union | 2002 | 2.2 | 5.6 | 2.6 | 5.1 | 11.1 | 26.7 | 11.2 | 37.8 |
| Total OECD[6] | 2002 | 2.6 | 4.8 | 2.7 | 6.7 | 11.0 | 27.7 | .. | .. |

1. Value added measured at basic prices except for United States and Japan for which data are estimated at factor costs.
2. Business services includes renting of machinery and equipment (ISIC 71); computer-related services (ISIC 72); research and development (ISIC 73); and other services (ISIC 74) such as legal, accounting, market research and management consultancy activities, architectural, engineering and other technical activities.
3. Includes medium-high technology manufactures.
4. Includes "Shipbuilding" (ISIC 351).
5. Not including "Post and telecommunications" (ISIC 64).
6. OECD estimates do not include Turkey.

*Sources:* OECD: *STAN database*, 2005; *National Accounts of OECD countries Vol. II*, 2005; Secretariat estimates.

StatLink: *http://dx.doi.org/10.1787/801208256208*

Table F.6 **Share of value added in total gross value added[1], current prices**
Percentages

| | | Aggregate sectors | | | | | | | | |
|---|---|---|---|---|---|---|---|---|---|---|
| | | Agriculture, hunting, forestry and fishing | Mining and quarrying | Total manufacturing | Electricity, gas and water | Construction | Wholesale and retail trade; hotels and restaurants | Transport, storage and communication | Finance, insurance, real estate and business services | Community, social and personal services |
| | *ISIC Rev. 3* | *01-05* | *10-14* | *15-37* | *40-41* | *45* | *50-55* | *60-64* | *65-74* | *75-99* |
| Canada | 2001 | 2.2 | 5.7 | 18.3 | 2.9 | 5.3 | 13.6 | 7.0 | 25.4 | 19.6 |
| Mexico | 2002 | 3.8 | 1.3 | 18.4 | 1.4 | 5.0 | 19.7 | 10.5 | 19.9 | 19.9 |
| United States | 2002 | 1.0 | 0.9 | 14.5 | 1.8 | 4.8 | 13.7 | 6.1 | 32.0 | 25.2 |
| Australia | 2001/2002[2] | 3.8 | 5.3 | 11.7 | 2.5 | 6.2 | 13.5 | 8.2 | 28.8 | 20.1 |
| Japan[3] | 2002 | 1.3 | 0.1 | 18.1 | 3.7 | 6.7 | 12.8 | 6.0 | 28.4 | 22.9 |
| Korea | 2002 | 4.1 | 0.3 | 26.9 | 2.6 | 8.6 | 10.8 | 7.5 | 21.9 | 17.3 |
| New Zealand | 2001/2002[4] | 9.2 | 1.2 | 16.1 | 2.5 | 4.4 | 15.4 | 7.1 | 26.8 | 17.3 |
| Austria | 2002 | 2.0 | 0.5 | 20.1 | 2.4 | 7.4 | 17.6 | 7.3 | 22.7 | 20.0 |
| Belgium | 2002 | 1.2 | 0.1 | 18.2 | 2.5 | 4.8 | 13.8 | 6.8 | 28.1 | 24.4 |
| Czech Republic | 2002 | 3.1 | 1.4 | 25.5 | 4.3 | 6.6 | 14.4 | 11.1 | 17.4 | 16.2 |
| Denmark | 2002 | 2.4 | 2.6 | 15.6 | 2.2 | 5.0 | 13.5 | 7.7 | 24.3 | 26.6 |
| Finland | 2002 | 3.5 | 0.3 | 23.4 | 2.0 | 5.4 | 11.6 | 10.7 | 21.5 | 21.6 |
| France | 2002 | 2.6 | 0.2 | 17.6 | 1.9 | 4.9 | 12.7 | 6.3 | 30.3 | 23.6 |
| Germany | 2002 | 1.1 | 0.3 | 22.3 | 1.8 | 4.5 | 11.9 | 6.1 | 30.2 | 21.8 |
| Greece | 2002 | 7.0 | 0.7 | 11.5 | 1.8 | 8.1 | 20.2 | 8.6 | 20.8 | 21.2 |
| Hungary | 2002 | 3.7 | 0.2 | 21.7 | 3.0 | 5.3 | 13.2 | 8.2 | 21.5 | 23.2 |
| Iceland | 2002 | 9.3 | 0.1 | 12.3 | 3.8 | 7.5 | 12.5 | 8.2 | 21.4 | 24.9 |
| Ireland | 2002 | 2.7 | 0.5 | 31.8 | 1.2 | 8.1 | 12.5 | 5.5 | 21.8 | 15.8 |
| Italy | 2002 | 2.6 | 0.4 | 19.5 | 2.2 | 5.0 | 16.4 | 7.2 | 27.0 | 19.7 |
| Luxembourg | 2002 | 0.6 | 0.1 | 9.5 | 1.2 | 6.0 | 11.5 | 9.5 | 46.1 | 15.6 |
| Netherlands | 2002 | 2.5 | 2.6 | 14.7 | 1.7 | 5.9 | 14.8 | 7.2 | 26.4 | 24.1 |
| Norway | 2002 | 1.7 | 19.4 | 10.8 | 2.5 | 4.5 | 10.7 | 9.1 | 19.0 | 22.3 |
| Poland | 2002 | 3.2 | 2.3 | 17.6 | 4.0 | 6.6 | 22.5 | 7.9 | 15.2 | 20.8 |
| Portugal | 2002 | 3.6 | 0.3 | 16.8 | 2.6 | 7.6 | 17.3 | 6.6 | 19.0 | 26.3 |
| Slovak Republic | 2002 | 4.4 | 0.7 | 21.8 | 3.3 | 5.3 | 15.4 | 10.9 | 20.0 | 18.3 |
| Spain | 2002 | 1.3 | 0.2 | 19.0 | 2.4 | 5.5 | 15.4 | 6.1 | 31.2 | 19.0 |
| Sweden | 2002 | 3.2 | 0.4 | 16.7 | 2.1 | 9.2 | 19.1 | 8.7 | 20.0 | 20.4 |
| Switzerland | 2002 | 1.8 | 0.2 | 20.3 | 2.6 | 4.4 | 12.0 | 8.2 | 24.9 | 25.6 |
| Turkey | 2002 | 11.7 | 1.1 | 20.6 | 3.7 | 4.1 | 20.2 | 15.3 | 8.9 | 14.3 |
| United Kingdom | 2002 | 0.9 | 2.4 | 15.2 | 1.7 | 5.7 | 15.2 | 7.7 | 29.2 | 22.0 |
| European Union | 2002 | 2.2 | 0.9 | 18.6 | 2.1 | 5.7 | 14.8 | 7.2 | 26.7 | 21.8 |
| Total OECD | 2002 | 2.0 | 1.1 | 17.2 | 2.2 | 5.5 | 14.2 | 6.9 | 28.1 | 22.7 |

1. Value added measured at basic prices except for Japan and United States for which value added is measured at factor costs; and Turkey for which value added is measured at producer's prices.
2. Fiscal year 1st July 2001 to 30th June 2002.
3. For Japan, "Hotels and restaurants" (ISIC 55) is included in "Community, social and personal services" (ISIC 75-99).
4. Fiscal year 1st April 2001 to 31st March 2002.

*Sources:* OECD, *STAN database,* 2005; *National Accounts of OECD countries Vol. II,* 2005.

StatLink: *http://dx.doi.org/10.1787/148820633541*

Table F.7 **Manufacturing trade[1] by industry, total OECD[2]**

| | | Share in total manufacturing[3] | | | | | | | | | | Average annual growth | | | |
|---|---|---|---|---|---|---|---|---|---|---|---|---|---|---|---|
| | *ISIC Rev.3* | 1994 | 1995 | 1996 | 1997 | 1998 | 1999 | 2000 | 2001 | 2002 | 2003 | 1994-1998 | 1998-2002 | 2002-2003 | 1994-2003 |
| **High-technology industries** | | **21.2** | **21.5** | **21.9** | **23.0** | **24.0** | **25.3** | **27.1** | **26.3** | **25.6** | **24.8** | **9.8** | **4.6** | **10.5** | **7.6** |
| Aircraft and spacecraft | 353 | 2.6 | 2.2 | 2.4 | 2.8 | 3.3 | 3.3 | 3.2 | 3.6 | 3.4 | 3.0 | 12.5 | 3.5 | 0.7 | 7.2 |
| Pharmaceuticals | 2423 | 2.2 | 2.2 | 2.3 | 2.4 | 2.7 | 2.8 | 2.7 | 3.4 | 4.1 | 4.3 | 12.0 | 13.7 | 18.6 | 13.5 |
| Office, accounting and computing machinery | 30 | 5.6 | 5.8 | 5.9 | 6.2 | 6.3 | 6.5 | 6.7 | 6.2 | 5.7 | 5.4 | 9.8 | 0.4 | 8.6 | 5.4 |
| Radio, TV and communciations equipment | 32 | 7.3 | 7.9 | 7.7 | 8.0 | 8.1 | 8.9 | 10.6 | 9.1 | 8.5 | 8.1 | 9.3 | 4.1 | 9.0 | 6.9 |
| Medical, precision and optical instruments | 33 | 3.6 | 3.5 | 3.6 | 3.7 | 3.7 | 3.8 | 3.9 | 4.0 | 4.0 | 4.1 | 7.4 | 5.1 | 15.6 | 7.3 |
| **Medium-high-technology industries** | | **38.6** | **38.7** | **39.1** | **38.8** | **38.9** | **38.8** | **37.7** | **38.1** | **38.8** | **39.2** | **7.1** | **2.8** | **14.5** | **6.0** |
| Electrical machinery and apparatus, n.e.c. | 31 | 4.4 | 4.6 | 4.7 | 4.7 | 4.8 | 4.9 | 4.9 | 4.8 | 4.6 | 4.6 | 8.6 | 2.2 | 12.6 | 6.2 |
| Motor vehicles, trailers and semi-trailers | 34 | 13.2 | 12.8 | 13.1 | 13.2 | 13.7 | 14.2 | 13.5 | 13.7 | 14.5 | 14.5 | 7.7 | 4.4 | 13.4 | 6.9 |
| Chemicals excluding pharmaceuticals | 24 excl. 2423 | 9.3 | 9.7 | 9.4 | 9.3 | 9.0 | 8.8 | 8.7 | 8.8 | 9.0 | 9.3 | 5.8 | 3.0 | 17.1 | 5.8 |
| Railroad equipment and transport equipment, n.e.c. | 352 + 359 | 0.7 | 0.6 | 0.6 | 0.5 | 0.6 | 0.6 | 0.6 | 0.6 | 0.6 | 0.6 | 4.7 | 2.1 | 17.6 | 5.0 |
| Machinery and equipment, n.e.c. | 29 | 11.0 | 11.1 | 11.4 | 11.1 | 10.9 | 10.4 | 10.1 | 10.1 | 10.0 | 10.1 | 6.8 | 0.7 | 14.4 | 4.9 |
| **Medium-low-technology industries** | | **16.0** | **16.3** | **15.9** | **15.7** | **15.2** | **14.5** | **15.0** | **14.9** | **14.8** | **15.3** | **5.6** | **2.2** | **17.0** | **5.3** |
| Building and repairing of ships and boats | 351 | 0.7 | 0.6 | 0.6 | 0.6 | 0.6 | 0.6 | 0.6 | 0.6 | 0.7 | 0.7 | 5.3 | 4.9 | 17.1 | 6.4 |
| Rubber and plastics products | 25 | 2.8 | 2.8 | 2.8 | 2.8 | 2.9 | 2.9 | 2.7 | 2.8 | 2.9 | 3.0 | 7.6 | 3.1 | 16.3 | 6.6 |
| Coke, refined petroleum products and nuclear fuel | 23 | 2.2 | 1.9 | 2.3 | 2.2 | 1.7 | 1.9 | 2.7 | 2.5 | 2.4 | 2.7 | 0.0 | 11.9 | 23.7 | 8.0 |
| Other non-metallic mineral products | 26 | 1.7 | 1.7 | 1.6 | 1.6 | 1.6 | 1.5 | 1.4 | 1.5 | 1.5 | 1.5 | 4.8 | 1.6 | 13.8 | 4.3 |
| Basic metals | 27 | 6.0 | 6.6 | 5.9 | 5.8 | 5.8 | 4.9 | 5.1 | 4.9 | 4.7 | 4.9 | 5.9 | -2.2 | 16.8 | 3.5 |
| Fabricated metal products | 28 | 2.7 | 2.7 | 2.7 | 2.7 | 2.7 | 2.7 | 2.6 | 2.6 | 2.6 | 2.7 | 7.4 | 2.2 | 13.5 | 5.7 |
| **Low-technology industries** | | **24.2** | **23.4** | **23.0** | **22.4** | **21.9** | **21.4** | **20.2** | **20.7** | **20.9** | **20.7** | **4.3** | **1.8** | **12.3** | **4.1** |
| Manufacturing, n.e.c.; Recycling | 36-37 | 3.4 | 3.3 | 3.3 | 3.4 | 3.4 | 3.5 | 3.4 | 3.5 | 3.6 | 3.4 | 6.4 | 4.4 | 9.3 | 5.8 |
| Pulp, paper, paper products, printing and publishing | 21-22 | 3.8 | 4.2 | 3.8 | 3.6 | 3.5 | 3.5 | 3.4 | 3.3 | 3.3 | 3.3 | 4.9 | 1.2 | 12.7 | 4.1 |
| Food products, beverages and tobacco | 15-16 | 7.5 | 7.1 | 7.1 | 6.7 | 6.5 | 6.2 | 5.6 | 6.0 | 6.0 | 6.1 | 3.1 | 1.2 | 15.6 | 3.6 |
| Textiles, textile products, leather and footwear | 17-19 | 7.9 | 7.4 | 7.5 | 7.4 | 7.2 | 7.0 | 6.6 | 6.8 | 6.8 | 6.6 | 4.7 | 1.3 | 10.8 | 3.9 |
| Wood and products of wood and cork | 20 | 1.5 | 1.4 | 1.4 | 1.4 | 1.3 | 1.3 | 1.2 | 1.2 | 1.2 | 1.2 | 2.2 | 1.5 | 12.1 | 3.0 |
| **Total manufacturing** | **15-37** | **100.0** | **100.0** | **100.0** | **100.0** | **100.0** | **100.0** | **100.0** | **100.0** | **100.0** | **100.0** | **6.8** | **2.9** | **13.4** | **5.8** |

1. Average value of exports and imports.
2. Total OECD excludes Luxembourg and Slovak Republic.
3. Total may not add to 100% because of residual category.

*Source:* OECD, STAN Indicators database, March 2005.

StatLink: *http://dx.doi.org/10.1787/338567830054*

Table F.8 **Export shares**[1]

| | Total manufacturing | | High-technology industries | | | | | | | | | | | | Medium-high-technology industries | | | | | | | | | | | | | |
|---|---|---|---|---|---|---|---|---|---|---|---|---|---|---|---|---|---|---|---|---|---|---|---|---|---|---|---|---|
| | | | Total | | Aircraft and spacecraft | | Pharmaceuticals | | Office, accounting and computing machinery | | Radio, television and communication equipment | | Medical, precision and optical instruments | | Total | | Electrical machinery and apparatus, n.e.c. | | Motor vehicles, trailers and semi-trailers | | Chemicals excluding pharmaceuticals | | Railroad equipment and transport equipment, n.e.c. | | Machinery and equipment, n.e.c. | |
| | 1994 | 2003 | 1994 | 2003 | 1994 | 2003 | 1994 | 2003 | 1994 | 2003 | 1994 | 2003 | 1994 | 2003 | 1994 | 2003 | 1994 | 2003 | 1994 | 2003 | 1994 | 2003 | 1994 | 2003 | 1994 | 2003 |
| Canada | 100.0 | 100.0 | 10.3 | 12.1 | 2.4 | 4.6 | 0.4 | 1.2 | 2.9 | 1.5 | 3.4 | 3.3 | 1.1 | 1.5 | 45.5 | 43.8 | 1.8 | 2.1 | 30.8 | 28.0 | 6.1 | 6.3 | 0.7 | 0.3 | 6.1 | 7.1 |
| Mexico | 100.0 | 100.0 | 24.0 | 28.4 | 0.8 | 0.4 | 0.7 | 0.9 | 4.5 | 9.4 | 15.8 | 13.7 | 2.3 | 4.1 | 49.4 | 46.9 | 15.8 | 14.4 | 20.8 | 21.3 | 6.2 | 3.7 | 0.1 | 0.2 | 6.6 | 7.3 |
| United States | 100.0 | 100.0 | 32.9 | 35.8 | 8.1 | 7.8 | 1.6 | 3.2 | 7.8 | 6.3 | 10.1 | 11.5 | 5.4 | 7.0 | 39.5 | 38.9 | 4.6 | 4.6 | 11.4 | 11.1 | 10.2 | 11.2 | 0.4 | 0.4 | 12.9 | 11.4 |
| Australia | 100.0 | 100.0 | 12.0 | 11.8 | 1.7 | 1.4 | 1.9 | 3.7 | 4.2 | 2.2 | 2.2 | 1.7 | 2.0 | 2.9 | 16.9 | 18.9 | 2.3 | 1.8 | 3.7 | 7.1 | 5.1 | 4.8 | 0.1 | 0.3 | 5.6 | 4.9 |
| Japan | 100.0 | 100.0 | 31.2 | 28.9 | 0.2 | 0.5 | 0.6 | 0.9 | 9.1 | 5.4 | 16.5 | 16.0 | 4.8 | 6.2 | 51.1 | 54.2 | 6.1 | 5.8 | 21.8 | 23.5 | 7.0 | 8.9 | 1.5 | 1.4 | 14.6 | 14.5 |
| Korea | 100.0 | 100.0 | 28.0 | 36.1 | 0.8 | 0.3 | 0.4 | 0.4 | 3.8 | 9.4 | 21.6 | 24.4 | 1.4 | 1.6 | 26.0 | 32.2 | 4.6 | 2.9 | 6.9 | 12.0 | 8.0 | 9.3 | 0.2 | 0.2 | 6.3 | 7.8 |
| New Zealand | 100.0 | 100.0 | 2.3 | 5.4 | 0.1 | 0.8 | 0.4 | 0.9 | 0.1 | 0.7 | 0.8 | 1.2 | 0.9 | 1.8 | 12.4 | 13.4 | 1.5 | 2.2 | 0.5 | 1.2 | 6.1 | 4.7 | 0.0 | 0.1 | 4.2 | 5.2 |
| Austria | 100.0 | 100.0 | 10.1 | 14.9 | 0.3 | 1.6 | 2.6 | 4.0 | 1.1 | 1.8 | 3.9 | 5.0 | 2.3 | 2.5 | 41.4 | 40.7 | 7.8 | 6.0 | 11.2 | 13.3 | 5.8 | 5.4 | 1.0 | 1.8 | 15.7 | 14.2 |
| Belgium | 100.0 | 100.0 | 9.3 | 19.4 | 0.4 | 0.4 | 3.0 | 12.1 | 1.4 | 2.3 | 3.2 | 2.8 | 1.3 | 1.8 | 42.7 | 42.1 | 2.4 | 2.4 | 18.6 | 15.3 | 15.0 | 17.4 | 0.4 | 0.5 | 6.3 | 6.5 |
| Czech Republic | 100.0 | 100.0 | 4.8 | 14.7 | 0.0 | 0.4 | 1.3 | 0.8 | 0.9 | 6.6 | 1.5 | 5.2 | 1.0 | 1.7 | 36.0 | 44.7 | 3.8 | 9.2 | 8.9 | 16.8 | 10.3 | 4.7 | 1.6 | 1.0 | 11.4 | 13.0 |
| Denmark | 100.0 | 100.0 | 14.7 | 21.5 | 0.0 | 0.0 | 4.6 | 9.4 | 2.7 | 2.5 | 3.4 | 5.2 | 4.1 | 4.4 | 26.1 | 29.1 | 3.4 | 5.9 | 2.2 | 3.5 | 5.5 | 5.3 | 0.8 | 0.7 | 14.2 | 13.7 |
| Finland | 100.0 | 100.0 | 13.3 | 24.0 | 0.1 | 0.2 | 0.8 | 1.2 | 3.0 | 0.7 | 7.3 | 19.0 | 2.1 | 2.9 | 25.3 | 24.5 | 5.1 | 4.6 | 3.6 | 3.1 | 5.4 | 5.4 | 0.2 | 0.1 | 11.1 | 11.3 |
| France | 100.0 | 100.0 | 18.8 | 22.5 | 6.3 | 6.6 | 2.8 | 5.8 | 3.1 | 2.1 | 3.9 | 4.8 | 2.8 | 3.3 | 40.6 | 42.1 | 4.6 | 4.5 | 13.4 | 16.3 | 12.3 | 11.5 | 0.8 | 0.5 | 9.5 | 9.2 |
| Germany | 100.0 | 100.0 | 15.4 | 19.1 | 2.5 | 3.4 | 2.5 | 3.6 | 2.5 | 2.8 | 4.0 | 5.1 | 3.9 | 4.3 | 52.6 | 52.5 | 5.5 | 5.3 | 18.1 | 22.1 | 11.6 | 9.7 | 0.7 | 0.6 | 16.9 | 14.9 |
| Greece | 100.0 | 100.0 | 3.7 | 12.5 | 1.0 | 2.8 | 1.0 | 5.4 | 0.3 | 0.6 | 0.9 | 2.4 | 0.6 | 1.2 | 10.6 | 16.5 | 2.1 | 2.4 | 1.0 | 1.5 | 4.3 | 7.6 | 0.1 | 0.2 | 3.0 | 4.8 |
| Hungary | 100.0 | 100.0 | 12.2 | 32.1 | 2.9 | 0.1 | 3.1 | 2.2 | 0.3 | 7.3 | 4.5 | 20.4 | 1.4 | 2.2 | 29.6 | 40.5 | 7.6 | 9.3 | 5.7 | 18.3 | 8.7 | 4.5 | 0.3 | 0.4 | 7.2 | 8.0 |
| Iceland | 100.0 | 100.0 | 2.1 | 5.1 | 1.8 | 0.0 | 0.0 | 3.0 | 0.0 | 0.0 | 0.0 | 0.1 | 0.3 | 2.0 | 1.3 | 3.5 | 0.1 | 0.0 | 0.0 | 0.1 | 0.1 | 0.8 | 0.0 | 0.0 | 1.1 | 2.5 |
| Ireland | 100.0 | 100.0 | 36.6 | 53.6 | 0.6 | 0.4 | 8.1 | 20.4 | 19.6 | 19.2 | 4.8 | 6.0 | 3.5 | 7.8 | 23.1 | 30.3 | 3.2 | 2.0 | 0.6 | 0.4 | 15.2 | 25.8 | 0.0 | 0.1 | 4.0 | 2.0 |
| Italy | 100.0 | 100.0 | 10.0 | 11.0 | 1.3 | 1.2 | 1.9 | 3.9 | 2.4 | 1.0 | 2.4 | 2.5 | 2.1 | 2.5 | 37.6 | 39.8 | 3.5 | 3.5 | 7.7 | 8.5 | 5.3 | 5.9 | 1.0 | 1.0 | 20.1 | 21.0 |
| Netherlands | 100.0 | 100.0 | 19.9 | 31.1 | 1.3 | 0.7 | 2.5 | 4.0 | 8.3 | 13.4 | 4.5 | 7.4 | 3.2 | 5.5 | 29.7 | 29.5 | 2.8 | 2.7 | 4.1 | 4.7 | 15.4 | 15.3 | 0.4 | 0.4 | 7.2 | 6.4 |
| Norway | 100.0 | 100.0 | 8.4 | 11.2 | 0.5 | 2.3 | 1.9 | 2.5 | 1.8 | 1.2 | 2.1 | 2.5 | 2.1 | 2.7 | 25.2 | 27.5 | 2.4 | 2.7 | 2.4 | 2.7 | 13.4 | 12.5 | 0.2 | 0.2 | 6.8 | 9.4 |
| Poland | 100.0 | 100.0 | 4.1 | 6.6 | 0.3 | 0.3 | 1.6 | 0.6 | 0.2 | 0.2 | 1.3 | 4.4 | 0.7 | 1.0 | 22.3 | 35.7 | 3.9 | 6.5 | 5.3 | 15.0 | 6.5 | 5.7 | 0.5 | 0.9 | 6.2 | 7.7 |
| Portugal | 100.0 | 100.0 | 6.9 | 11.8 | 0.6 | 1.1 | 0.6 | 1.2 | 0.3 | 1.8 | 4.4 | 6.5 | 1.0 | 1.2 | 21.8 | 30.9 | 6.3 | 5.3 | 6.3 | 14.8 | 4.6 | 4.6 | 0.4 | 0.4 | 4.3 | 5.8 |
| Slovak Republic | .. | 100.0 | .. | 5.7 | .. | 0.1 | .. | 0.7 | .. | 1.5 | .. | 2.6 | .. | 0.8 | .. | 49.2 | .. | 6.4 | .. | 28.6 | .. | 4.8 | .. | 1.0 | .. | 8.3 |
| Spain | 100.0 | 100.0 | 9.9 | 10.8 | 2.2 | 1.6 | 1.7 | 3.3 | 1.7 | 1.1 | 2.9 | 3.5 | 1.3 | 1.4 | 46.1 | 47.0 | 3.8 | 3.6 | 26.8 | 26.6 | 7.3 | 8.8 | 0.7 | 0.9 | 7.6 | 7.0 |
| Sweden | 100.0 | 100.0 | 18.9 | 22.0 | 1.1 | 1.2 | 4.5 | 6.9 | 1.5 | 1.3 | 8.5 | 8.9 | 3.4 | 3.6 | 36.4 | 38.4 | 3.8 | 4.0 | 13.9 | 14.9 | 4.8 | 5.3 | 0.3 | 0.4 | 13.5 | 13.8 |
| Switzerland | 100.0 | 100.0 | 28.2 | 39.0 | 0.4 | 1.8 | 10.7 | 19.8 | 1.1 | 0.7 | 1.7 | 1.5 | 14.4 | 15.3 | 43.0 | 36.9 | 5.3 | 4.9 | 1.2 | 1.3 | 15.4 | 13.7 | 0.5 | 0.4 | 20.6 | 16.7 |
| Turkey | 100.0 | 100.0 | 2.5 | 6.5 | 0.3 | 1.2 | 0.5 | 0.5 | 0.1 | 0.1 | 1.4 | 4.4 | 0.2 | 0.3 | 14.9 | 25.5 | 2.7 | 2.8 | 3.2 | 12.3 | 5.7 | 3.1 | 0.1 | 0.2 | 3.3 | 7.2 |
| United Kingdom | 100.0 | 100.0 | 27.7 | 34.7 | 5.2 | 10.7 | 3.8 | 6.9 | 7.9 | 5.5 | 6.8 | 7.4 | 4.0 | 4.3 | 36.9 | 36.6 | 3.9 | 3.8 | 9.3 | 11.3 | 11.8 | 11.6 | 0.5 | 0.2 | 11.4 | 9.7 |
| European Union[2] | 100.0 | 100.0 | 16.3 | 21.9 | 2.6 | 3.2 | 2.8 | 5.6 | 3.7 | 4.0 | 4.2 | 5.6 | 3.0 | 3.5 | 40.7 | 41.7 | 4.3 | 4.3 | 12.6 | 14.8 | 10.6 | 10.5 | 0.6 | 0.6 | 12.6 | 11.5 |
| Total OECD[2] | 100.0 | 100.0 | 21.4 | 24.9 | 3.0 | 3.4 | 2.2 | 4.4 | 5.0 | 4.6 | 7.5 | 8.2 | 3.7 | 4.3 | 41.3 | 41.7 | 4.7 | 4.6 | 14.0 | 15.3 | 9.7 | 9.9 | 0.7 | 0.6 | 12.3 | 11.3 |

.. Not available.

1. Share of industries in total manufacturing exports.
2. Excluding Luxembourg and Slovak Republic.

*Source:* OECD, STAN Indicators database, March 2005.

StatLink: *http://dx.doi.org/10.1787/578506031531*

Table F.8 **Export shares**[1] *(cont.)*

| | Medium-low-technology industries | | | | | | | | | | | | Low-technology industries | | | | | | | | | | | |
|---|---|---|---|---|---|---|---|---|---|---|---|---|---|---|---|---|---|---|---|---|---|---|---|---|
| | Total | | Coke, refined petroleum products and nuclear fuel | | Rubber and plastic products | | Other non-metallic mineral products | | Building and repairing of ships and boats | | Basic metals and fabricated metal products | | Total | | Manufacturing, n.e.c. and recycling | | Wood and products of wood and cork | | Pulp, paper, paper products, printing and publishing | | Food products, beverages and tobacco | | Textiles, textile products, leather and footwear | |
| | 1994 | 2003 | 1994 | 2003 | 1994 | 2003 | 1994 | 2003 | 1994 | 2003 | 1994 | 2003 | 1994 | 2003 | 1994 | 2003 | 1994 | 2003 | 1994 | 2003 | 1994 | 2003 | 1994 | 2003 |
| Canada | 17.3 | 18.3 | 2.6 | 4.1 | 2.5 | 3.6 | 1.0 | 1.0 | 0.3 | 0.3 | 11.1 | 9.4 | 26.9 | 25.7 | 2.2 | 3.2 | 8.0 | 5.9 | 10.8 | 8.4 | 4.7 | 6.1 | 1.4 | 2.1 |
| Mexico | 11.7 | 9.4 | 1.1 | 1.1 | 2.4 | 2.0 | 1.9 | 1.4 | 0.0 | 0.1 | 6.3 | 4.8 | 14.8 | 15.3 | 3.7 | 3.8 | 0.7 | 0.2 | 1.2 | 1.0 | 3.6 | 3.2 | 5.7 | 7.0 |
| United States | 10.5 | 10.9 | 1.5 | 1.7 | 2.4 | 2.9 | 0.9 | 1.0 | 0.3 | 0.2 | 5.4 | 5.1 | 17.1 | 14.4 | 2.5 | 2.8 | 1.1 | 0.6 | 4.0 | 3.3 | 6.6 | 4.8 | 2.9 | 2.9 |
| Australia | 36.4 | 36.9 | 3.9 | 5.0 | 1.1 | 1.1 | 0.8 | 0.6 | 0.8 | 0.9 | 29.8 | 29.4 | 34.8 | 32.4 | 1.5 | 1.9 | 1.6 | 1.7 | 1.6 | 2.0 | 23.6 | 22.7 | 6.4 | 4.1 |
| Japan | 12.4 | 11.8 | 0.6 | 0.3 | 1.1 | 1.3 | 1.3 | 1.2 | 3.0 | 2.2 | 6.4 | 6.9 | 5.4 | 5.1 | 2.3 | 2.5 | 0.0 | 0.0 | 0.8 | 0.7 | 0.5 | 0.5 | 1.8 | 1.4 |
| Korea | 19.9 | 20.3 | 1.8 | 3.5 | 2.7 | 2.4 | 0.7 | 0.5 | 5.2 | 5.8 | 9.6 | 8.1 | 26.1 | 11.4 | 2.3 | 1.4 | 0.1 | 0.0 | 1.0 | 1.2 | 1.9 | 1.2 | 20.7 | 7.7 |
| New Zealand | 12.3 | 11.7 | 0.4 | 0.1 | 1.7 | 1.9 | 0.4 | 0.4 | 0.4 | 1.7 | 9.4 | 7.6 | 73.0 | 69.6 | 1.0 | 1.0 | 5.8 | 6.1 | 5.2 | 3.4 | 51.1 | 51.0 | 9.9 | 8.0 |
| Austria | 22.1 | 18.3 | 0.5 | 0.5 | 5.2 | 3.8 | 3.2 | 2.1 | 0.0 | 0.3 | 13.3 | 11.5 | 26.4 | 26.2 | 3.6 | 3.8 | 4.0 | 3.7 | 7.7 | 7.1 | 3.2 | 5.7 | 7.8 | 5.9 |
| Belgium | 20.2 | 16.9 | 3.4 | 4.1 | 3.4 | 3.1 | 2.5 | 1.7 | 0.1 | 0.0 | 10.9 | 8.0 | 27.8 | 21.6 | 5.6 | 3.8 | 1.0 | 0.9 | 3.0 | 2.7 | 10.5 | 7.9 | 7.7 | 6.3 |
| Czech Republic | 31.1 | 22.8 | 2.2 | 1.1 | 3.0 | 5.2 | 7.4 | 4.3 | 0.1 | 0.0 | 18.4 | 12.2 | 28.1 | 17.7 | 4.4 | 4.0 | 3.4 | 1.6 | 3.1 | 3.7 | 6.4 | 2.9 | 10.8 | 5.6 |
| Denmark | 15.4 | 13.1 | 1.6 | 1.8 | 3.5 | 3.7 | 1.8 | 1.3 | 2.8 | 0.9 | 5.7 | 5.4 | 43.9 | 36.3 | 5.8 | 5.0 | 2.0 | 1.4 | 2.9 | 2.4 | 26.9 | 20.4 | 6.2 | 7.1 |
| Finland | 18.9 | 21.1 | 2.2 | 3.5 | 2.1 | 2.1 | 1.3 | 1.3 | 1.8 | 3.5 | 11.5 | 10.7 | 42.4 | 30.4 | 1.6 | 1.0 | 8.2 | 5.4 | 27.5 | 20.6 | 2.7 | 1.9 | 2.4 | 1.5 |
| France | 16.2 | 15.3 | 1.7 | 2.2 | 3.4 | 3.3 | 2.2 | 1.6 | 0.3 | 0.9 | 8.6 | 7.3 | 24.4 | 20.2 | 2.1 | 1.9 | 0.7 | 0.6 | 3.3 | 2.9 | 12.1 | 9.5 | 6.3 | 5.3 |
| Germany | 15.5 | 14.6 | 1.0 | 1.5 | 3.4 | 3.6 | 1.7 | 1.4 | 0.4 | 0.4 | 8.9 | 7.7 | 16.5 | 13.8 | 2.1 | 1.9 | 0.5 | 0.7 | 3.5 | 3.4 | 5.0 | 4.2 | 5.3 | 3.7 |
| Greece | 33.1 | 29.2 | 12.6 | 8.0 | 2.2 | 3.2 | 6.1 | 2.9 | 0.4 | 0.4 | 11.9 | 14.6 | 52.7 | 41.8 | 1.2 | 1.3 | 0.8 | 0.5 | 1.2 | 2.2 | 20.8 | 15.8 | 28.7 | 22.2 |
| Hungary | 18.7 | 11.0 | 3.7 | 1.6 | 2.7 | 2.9 | 2.4 | 1.4 | 0.0 | 0.0 | 9.9 | 5.1 | 39.4 | 16.4 | 2.3 | 2.4 | 1.6 | 0.9 | 1.8 | 1.6 | 17.1 | 5.3 | 16.6 | 6.1 |
| Iceland | 15.6 | 25.4 | 0.1 | 0.3 | 0.3 | 0.5 | 0.1 | 0.1 | 1.5 | 0.9 | 13.7 | 23.7 | 81.0 | 66.0 | 0.0 | 0.0 | 0.0 | 0.0 | 0.2 | 0.3 | 79.3 | 64.4 | 1.5 | 1.2 |
| Ireland | 5.8 | 2.6 | 0.4 | 0.2 | 1.9 | 0.8 | 0.9 | 0.5 | 0.1 | 0.0 | 2.6 | 1.1 | 34.6 | 13.5 | 1.3 | 0.5 | 0.4 | 0.4 | 7.7 | 3.3 | 21.8 | 8.4 | 3.4 | 0.9 |
| Italy | 18.8 | 19.0 | 1.6 | 2.2 | 3.6 | 3.9 | 4.2 | 3.5 | 0.4 | 1.0 | 8.9 | 8.5 | 33.7 | 30.2 | 7.1 | 6.0 | 0.6 | 0.5 | 2.3 | 2.4 | 5.3 | 5.8 | 18.4 | 15.4 |
| Netherlands | 18.8 | 16.1 | 6.1 | 6.5 | 3.3 | 2.6 | 1.2 | 0.8 | 0.5 | 0.6 | 7.6 | 5.7 | 31.7 | 23.4 | 1.7 | 1.4 | 0.7 | 0.3 | 4.2 | 3.5 | 20.3 | 14.4 | 4.9 | 3.8 |
| Norway | 40.9 | 41.1 | 9.9 | 12.6 | 1.4 | 1.2 | 0.9 | 0.8 | 8.4 | 6.9 | 20.3 | 19.7 | 25.5 | 20.2 | 1.7 | 1.9 | 2.1 | 1.2 | 7.7 | 5.7 | 12.3 | 10.2 | 1.7 | 1.2 |
| Poland | 33.2 | 26.6 | 2.6 | 2.1 | 2.0 | 4.8 | 3.4 | 2.7 | 5.1 | 5.1 | 20.0 | 11.9 | 40.4 | 31.1 | 6.6 | 8.3 | 4.6 | 3.4 | 2.0 | 4.2 | 10.7 | 7.4 | 16.6 | 7.9 |
| Portugal | 14.5 | 15.6 | 3.9 | 2.2 | 1.8 | 3.6 | 4.9 | 3.8 | 0.3 | 0.2 | 3.7 | 5.8 | 56.8 | 41.8 | 2.4 | 3.2 | 5.3 | 4.5 | 5.8 | 5.1 | 6.7 | 6.7 | 36.7 | 22.3 |
| Slovak Republic | .. | 25.6 | .. | 4.4 | .. | 4.2 | .. | 2.5 | .. | 0.2 | .. | 14.2 | .. | 19.6 | .. | 4.5 | .. | 1.7 | .. | 3.9 | .. | 2.5 | .. | 6.9 |
| Spain | 20.8 | 19.0 | 2.3 | 2.8 | 3.5 | 3.6 | 4.2 | 3.5 | 0.9 | 1.2 | 10.1 | 7.9 | 23.2 | 23.2 | 2.2 | 2.3 | 0.8 | 0.8 | 3.1 | 3.3 | 9.5 | 9.7 | 7.5 | 7.2 |
| Sweden | 19.6 | 17.3 | 2.6 | 3.2 | 2.9 | 2.6 | 1.1 | 0.9 | 1.3 | 0.5 | 11.8 | 10.2 | 25.1 | 22.4 | 2.2 | 2.2 | 5.4 | 3.7 | 13.4 | 11.4 | 2.2 | 2.8 | 1.9 | 2.2 |
| Switzerland | 11.7 | 11.1 | 0.1 | 0.3 | 2.8 | 2.7 | 1.0 | 0.8 | 0.0 | 0.0 | 7.7 | 7.3 | 17.1 | 13.0 | 6.1 | 4.2 | 0.5 | 0.5 | 3.1 | 2.8 | 3.2 | 2.6 | 4.4 | 2.9 |
| Turkey | 24.7 | 22.9 | 1.5 | 2.2 | 2.2 | 3.3 | 3.7 | 4.3 | 0.4 | 1.0 | 16.9 | 12.2 | 57.9 | 45.0 | 0.9 | 2.9 | 0.4 | 0.3 | 1.0 | 1.0 | 11.4 | 5.9 | 44.3 | 34.9 |
| United Kingdom | 14.7 | 12.8 | 2.4 | 3.2 | 2.9 | 2.6 | 1.4 | 1.1 | 0.4 | 0.3 | 7.6 | 5.6 | 19.2 | 15.2 | 2.7 | 2.3 | 0.2 | 0.2 | 4.0 | 3.4 | 7.0 | 5.6 | 5.4 | 3.7 |
| European Union[2] | 17.3 | 15.8 | 2.2 | 2.6 | 3.3 | 3.3 | 2.3 | 1.8 | 0.5 | 0.7 | 9.0 | 7.5 | 25.5 | 20.6 | 3.2 | 2.8 | 1.1 | 1.0 | 4.4 | 3.9 | 9.0 | 7.1 | 7.8 | 5.9 |
| Total OECD[2] | 15.7 | 15.1 | 1.8 | 2.3 | 2.7 | 2.9 | 1.7 | 1.5 | 1.0 | 1.0 | 8.4 | 7.4 | 21.5 | 18.2 | 2.9 | 2.7 | 1.3 | 1.0 | 3.9 | 3.4 | 7.1 | 5.9 | 6.4 | 5.1 |

.. Not available.

1. Share of industries in total manufacturing exports.
2. Excluding Luxembourg and Slovak Republic.

*Source:* OECD, STAN Indicators database, March 2005.

Table F.9 **Contribution to the manufacturing trade balance**[1]

| | **Total manufacturing** | | **High-technology industries** | | | | | | | | | | | | **Medium-high-technology industries** | | | | | | | | | | | |
|---|---|---|---|---|---|---|---|---|---|---|---|---|---|---|---|---|---|---|---|---|---|---|---|---|---|---|
| | | | **Total** | | Aircraft and spacecraft | | Pharmaceuticals | | Office, accounting and computing machinery | | Radio, television and communication equipment | | Medical, precision and optical instruments | | **Total** | | Electrical machinery and apparatus, n.e.c. | | Motor vehicles, trailers and semi-trailers | | Chemicals excluding pharmaceuticals | | Railroad equipment and transport equipment, n.e.c. | | Machinery and equipment, n.e.c. | |
| | 1994 | 2003 | 1994 | 2003 | 1994 | 2003 | 1994 | 2003 | 1994 | 2003 | 1994 | 2003 | 1994 | 2003 | 1994 | 2003 | 1994 | 2003 | 1994 | 2003 | 1994 | 2003 | 1994 | 2003 | 1994 | 2003 |
| Canada | 0.0 | 0.0 | -4.5 | -3.5 | 0.5 | 1.1 | -0.5 | -1.0 | -1.4 | -1.5 | -1.8 | -1.1 | -1.2 | -1.1 | -2.2 | -2.6 | -1.6 | -1.2 | 3.1 | 2.1 | -0.6 | -0.9 | 0.1 | -0.2 | -3.3 | -2.4 |
| Mexico | 0.0 | 0.0 | 1.5 | 2.0 | -0.1 | 0.1 | -0.3 | -0.4 | 0.5 | 1.5 | 1.7 | 0.4 | -0.5 | 0.4 | 5.6 | 2.8 | 3.2 | 2.6 | 7.6 | 4.3 | -1.4 | -2.7 | -0.2 | -0.1 | -3.6 | -1.3 |
| United States | 0.0 | 0.0 | 3.5 | 4.5 | 3.0 | 2.6 | 0.3 | -0.1 | -0.5 | -0.6 | -0.3 | 1.1 | 1.1 | 1.4 | 1.6 | 1.4 | 0.1 | 0.0 | -2.9 | -2.6 | 2.5 | 2.4 | -0.1 | -0.1 | 2.1 | 1.7 |
| Australia | 0.0 | 0.0 | -5.6 | -6.5 | -0.3 | -1.2 | -0.4 | -0.6 | -1.9 | -1.8 | -1.7 | -2.3 | -1.2 | -0.6 | -11.0 | -9.1 | -1.0 | -0.8 | -4.3 | -3.3 | -1.5 | -1.1 | -0.3 | -0.3 | -4.0 | -3.6 |
| Japan | 0.0 | 0.0 | 4.7 | -0.8 | -0.9 | -0.9 | -0.9 | -0.8 | 2.0 | -1.5 | 4.3 | 2.3 | 0.3 | 0.2 | 14.1 | 15.1 | 1.4 | 0.6 | 7.8 | 9.2 | 0.0 | 0.6 | 0.5 | 0.5 | 4.5 | 4.2 |
| Korea | 0.0 | 0.0 | 1.4 | 1.9 | -1.3 | -0.2 | -0.2 | -0.4 | 0.3 | 2.6 | 4.7 | 2.0 | -2.1 | -2.2 | -5.2 | 0.5 | 0.4 | -1.7 | 2.1 | 4.6 | -2.0 | -1.0 | -0.1 | 0.0 | -5.6 | -1.5 |
| New Zealand | 0.0 | 0.0 | -9.9 | -7.1 | -2.3 | -1.2 | -1.4 | -1.0 | -2.8 | -2.3 | -2.1 | -1.9 | -1.2 | -0.8 | -13.7 | -13.5 | -0.9 | -0.5 | -6.0 | -7.4 | -2.3 | -2.4 | -0.2 | -0.3 | -4.3 | -3.0 |
| Austria | 0.0 | 0.0 | -2.6 | -1.6 | -0.1 | -0.3 | -0.1 | 0.2 | -1.3 | -0.8 | -0.5 | -0.3 | -0.6 | -0.4 | 0.4 | 0.1 | 1.5 | 0.3 | -1.0 | -0.5 | -1.3 | -1.4 | 0.0 | 0.4 | 1.1 | 1.3 |
| Belgium | 0.0 | 0.0 | -1.0 | -1.2 | -0.1 | 0.0 | 0.1 | -0.2 | -0.5 | -0.5 | 0.0 | -0.3 | -0.5 | -0.3 | 0.6 | 0.6 | -0.2 | -0.2 | 1.6 | -0.2 | 0.6 | 1.6 | -0.1 | -0.1 | -1.2 | -0.4 |
| Czech Republic | 0.0 | 0.0 | -7.1 | -3.0 | 0.0 | -0.2 | -1.2 | -1.2 | -2.4 | 0.7 | -1.5 | -1.6 | -1.9 | -0.6 | -2.7 | 2.3 | -0.1 | 0.9 | 1.1 | 3.1 | -0.7 | -1.8 | 0.6 | 0.2 | -3.7 | 0.0 |
| Denmark | 0.0 | 0.0 | -0.8 | 1.3 | 0.0 | 0.0 | 1.1 | 2.9 | -1.7 | -1.6 | -0.6 | -0.8 | 0.6 | 0.7 | -3.5 | -1.5 | -0.1 | 0.8 | -3.1 | -1.9 | -2.0 | -1.3 | -0.2 | -0.5 | 1.8 | 1.4 |
| Finland | 0.0 | 0.0 | -4.4 | 0.1 | -0.6 | -0.2 | -1.0 | -1.3 | -1.5 | -1.8 | -0.8 | 3.5 | -0.5 | 0.0 | -6.8 | -7.4 | -0.4 | -0.8 | -2.0 | -3.8 | -3.3 | -2.2 | -0.2 | -0.2 | -0.9 | -0.5 |
| France | 0.0 | 0.0 | -0.3 | 0.4 | 1.3 | 1.4 | 0.2 | 0.6 | -1.1 | -1.3 | -0.4 | -0.2 | -0.3 | -0.2 | 2.2 | 2.2 | 0.6 | 0.3 | 1.1 | 1.6 | 0.7 | 0.5 | -0.2 | -0.1 | 0.0 | -0.2 |
| Germany | 0.0 | 0.0 | -2.3 | -3.1 | -0.5 | -0.3 | 0.3 | -0.4 | -1.5 | -1.7 | -1.0 | -1.1 | 0.4 | 0.4 | 9.6 | 7.4 | 0.4 | -0.1 | 3.5 | 3.9 | 1.5 | 0.5 | 0.0 | 0.0 | 4.3 | 3.0 |
| Greece | 0.0 | 0.0 | -4.1 | -2.3 | 0.0 | -0.2 | -1.1 | -0.2 | -0.7 | -0.6 | -1.3 | -0.7 | -0.9 | -0.6 | -9.1 | -5.0 | -0.2 | 0.0 | -3.1 | -3.0 | -2.7 | -0.5 | -0.3 | -0.3 | -2.9 | -1.3 |
| Hungary | 0.0 | 0.0 | -2.0 | 2.2 | 1.3 | 0.0 | -0.3 | -0.3 | -1.6 | 1.3 | -0.5 | 1.3 | -0.8 | -0.1 | -4.4 | -0.2 | 1.5 | 1.0 | -1.6 | 2.5 | -1.5 | -1.3 | 0.0 | -0.1 | -2.8 | -2.3 |
| Iceland | 0.0 | 0.0 | -5.9 | -4.7 | 0.3 | -0.5 | -1.3 | -0.3 | -1.7 | -1.8 | -1.9 | -1.7 | -1.3 | -0.4 | -12.8 | -14.8 | -2.6 | -3.0 | -3.0 | -4.9 | -3.2 | -2.8 | -0.1 | -0.1 | -4.0 | -4.0 |
| Ireland | 0.0 | 0.0 | 1.8 | 5.5 | -0.5 | -0.9 | 2.0 | 6.6 | 2.2 | 0.3 | -2.3 | -1.5 | 0.4 | 1.1 | -3.1 | 1.4 | -0.6 | -1.0 | -2.5 | -2.8 | 2.0 | 7.5 | -0.2 | -0.1 | -2.0 | -2.3 |
| Italy | 0.0 | 0.0 | -3.5 | -3.6 | -0.2 | -0.1 | -0.4 | -0.4 | -0.7 | -1.2 | -1.5 | -1.3 | -0.7 | -0.5 | 0.8 | -0.1 | 0.1 | 0.1 | -1.4 | -3.3 | -4.0 | -2.9 | 0.2 | 0.1 | 6.0 | 5.9 |
| Netherlands | 0.0 | 0.0 | -1.1 | -1.7 | -0.4 | -0.4 | -0.2 | -0.1 | -0.5 | -0.6 | -0.1 | -0.9 | 0.1 | 0.2 | -1.4 | -0.2 | -0.3 | -0.4 | -2.1 | -1.6 | 1.6 | 2.2 | -0.2 | -0.2 | -0.4 | -0.2 |
| Norway | 0.0 | 0.0 | -3.4 | -3.1 | -0.4 | 0.4 | 0.0 | -0.3 | -1.4 | -1.9 | -1.1 | -1.1 | -0.5 | -0.3 | -4.2 | -3.6 | -0.9 | -0.8 | -2.8 | -3.6 | 2.8 | 2.7 | -0.3 | -0.5 | -3.1 | -1.4 |
| Poland | 0.0 | 0.0 | -5.3 | -4.4 | 0.0 | 0.0 | -1.4 | -1.8 | -1.5 | -1.3 | -1.4 | -0.8 | -1.1 | -0.5 | -8.2 | -2.9 | -0.1 | 1.0 | -0.6 | 1.1 | -3.0 | -2.7 | 0.0 | 0.2 | -4.5 | -2.6 |
| Portugal | 0.0 | 0.0 | -3.5 | -3.1 | -0.5 | -0.1 | -0.9 | -1.5 | -1.2 | -0.5 | -0.2 | -0.3 | -0.7 | -0.7 | -9.2 | -2.8 | 1.0 | 0.7 | -4.9 | 0.2 | -2.6 | -2.2 | -0.2 | -0.1 | -2.5 | -1.4 |
| Slovak Republic | 0.0 | 0.0 | .. | -4.4 | .. | -0.2 | .. | -1.2 | .. | -0.5 | .. | -1.4 | .. | -1.1 | .. | 1.7 | .. | -0.4 | .. | 4.9 | .. | -1.3 | .. | 0.1 | .. | -1.5 |
| Spain | 0.0 | 0.0 | -3.4 | -3.1 | 0.2 | 0.2 | -0.5 | -0.7 | -1.0 | -1.0 | -0.8 | -0.7 | -1.1 | -0.8 | 1.5 | 1.2 | -0.1 | -0.2 | 4.7 | 3.1 | -2.2 | -0.5 | 0.1 | 0.1 | -0.9 | -1.3 |
| Sweden | 0.0 | 0.0 | -0.6 | 0.6 | 0.0 | -0.1 | 1.1 | 1.9 | -2.1 | -1.7 | 0.8 | 0.6 | -0.4 | 0.0 | -0.5 | -0.4 | -1.0 | -0.6 | 2.2 | 0.7 | -2.4 | -1.6 | -0.1 | -0.1 | 0.8 | 1.3 |
| Switzerland | 0.0 | 0.0 | 4.7 | 6.7 | -0.3 | -0.1 | 3.1 | 4.4 | -2.1 | -1.9 | -1.0 | -1.1 | 5.0 | 5.4 | 4.3 | 1.6 | 0.7 | 0.6 | -3.9 | -3.4 | 2.4 | 1.1 | -0.1 | -0.2 | 5.3 | 3.7 |
| Turkey | 0.0 | 0.0 | -7.2 | -3.8 | -2.1 | 0.4 | -0.9 | -1.8 | -1.1 | -1.0 | -1.3 | -0.4 | -1.9 | -1.1 | -15.9 | -9.0 | -0.9 | -0.4 | -1.2 | 0.7 | -5.8 | -5.8 | -0.3 | -0.1 | -7.6 | -3.5 |
| United Kingdom | 0.0 | 0.0 | 1.9 | 2.5 | 0.8 | 1.3 | 0.9 | 1.2 | 0.0 | -0.6 | -0.1 | 0.2 | 0.4 | 0.4 | 0.9 | 1.3 | 0.0 | 0.2 | -1.6 | -1.5 | 1.4 | 1.9 | -0.2 | -0.1 | 1.2 | 0.9 |
| European Union | 0.0 | 0.0 | -1.4 | -1.0 | 0.1 | 0.1 | 0.2 | 0.3 | -0.9 | -1.0 | -0.6 | -0.5 | -0.1 | 0.1 | 2.5 | 2.3 | 0.2 | 0.0 | 0.6 | 0.4 | 0.0 | 0.5 | -0.1 | -0.1 | 1.8 | 1.4 |
| Total OECD[2] | 0.0 | 0.0 | 0.1 | 0.0 | 0.4 | 0.5 | 0.1 | 0.1 | -0.6 | -1.0 | 0.0 | 0.0 | 0.2 | 0.4 | 3.1 | 2.7 | 0.2 | 0.1 | 0.8 | 0.6 | 0.5 | 0.7 | 0.0 | 0.0 | 1.6 | 1.3 |

.. Not available.

1. Observed trade balance of industry minus theoretical trade balance, expressed in hundreds of manufacturing trade (see box in text).
2. Total OECD excludes Czech Republic, Korea, Luxembourg and Slovak Republic.

*Source:* OECD, STAN Indicators database, March 2005.

StatLink: *http://dx.doi.org/10.1787/875777248642*

Table F.9 **Contribution to the manufacturing trade balance**[1] *(cont.)*

| | Medium-low-technology industries | | | | | | | | | | | | | | Low-technology industries | | | | | | | | | | | | | |
|---|---|---|---|---|---|---|---|---|---|---|---|---|---|---|---|---|---|---|---|---|---|---|---|---|---|---|---|---|
| | Total | | Coke, refined petroleum products and nuclear fuel | | Rubber and plastic products | | Other non-metallic mineral products | | Building and repairing of ships and boats | | Basic metals | | Fabricated metal products, except machinery and equipment | | Total | | Manufacturing, n.e.c. and recycling | | Wood and products of wood and cork | | Pulp, paper, paper products, printing and publishing | | Food products, beverages and tobacco | | Textiles, textile products, leather and footwear | |
| | 1994 | 2003 | 1994 | 2003 | 1994 | 2003 | 1994 | 2003 | 1994 | 2003 | 1994 | 2003 | 1994 | 2003 | 1994 | 2003 | 1994 | 2003 | 1994 | 2003 | 1994 | 2003 | 1994 | 2003 | 1994 | 2003 |
| Canada | 1.9 | 2.1 | 0.8 | 1.4 | -0.4 | 0.0 | -0.3 | -0.2 | 0.1 | 0.0 | 2.3 | 1.4 | -0.6 | -0.4 | 4.9 | 4.0 | -0.5 | -0.2 | 3.6 | 2.5 | 3.4 | 2.3 | 0.1 | 0.6 | -1.7 | -1.2 |
| Mexico | -4.0 | -4.4 | -0.4 | -0.5 | -1.8 | -2.2 | 0.2 | 0.1 | 0.0 | 0.0 | -0.5 | -0.9 | -1.4 | -0.9 | -3.1 | -0.4 | 0.5 | 0.9 | -0.1 | -0.2 | -1.8 | -1.0 | -1.3 | -0.6 | -0.4 | 0.4 |
| United States | -1.4 | -0.9 | -0.5 | -0.7 | 0.1 | 0.2 | -0.2 | -0.2 | 0.1 | 0.0 | -0.9 | -0.1 | 0.0 | -0.1 | -3.7 | -5.0 | -1.6 | -1.9 | -0.4 | -0.5 | 0.7 | 0.5 | 1.3 | 0.3 | -3.8 | -3.3 |
| Australia | 10.5 | 9.7 | 1.1 | 1.0 | -1.3 | -1.1 | -0.4 | -0.4 | 0.3 | 0.3 | 11.1 | 10.4 | -0.3 | -0.6 | 6.1 | 5.9 | -0.7 | -0.9 | 0.1 | 0.3 | -1.7 | -0.7 | 8.9 | 8.0 | -0.5 | -0.9 |
| Japan | -1.3 | -0.8 | -1.8 | -2.4 | 0.3 | 0.4 | 0.1 | 0.0 | 1.3 | 1.0 | -1.3 | 0.2 | 0.2 | -0.1 | -17.6 | -13.5 | -1.7 | -1.4 | -2.2 | -1.4 | -0.8 | -0.5 | -7.9 | -5.5 | -5.1 | -4.6 |
| Korea | -1.0 | -0.9 | -1.5 | -1.0 | 0.7 | 0.4 | -0.4 | -0.6 | 1.7 | 2.6 | -2.1 | -2.4 | 0.5 | 0.1 | 4.7 | -1.4 | 0.5 | 0.0 | -0.8 | -0.4 | -0.6 | -0.4 | -1.7 | -1.8 | 7.4 | 1.1 |
| New Zealand | -1.5 | -2.4 | -0.6 | -1.9 | -1.0 | -0.8 | -0.6 | -0.7 | -0.1 | 0.5 | 1.2 | 0.9 | -0.4 | -0.3 | 25.1 | 23.0 | -0.7 | -1.1 | 2.7 | 2.8 | -0.3 | -0.9 | 22.3 | 21.6 | 1.1 | 0.7 |
| Austria | 1.7 | -0.3 | -0.4 | -1.2 | 0.7 | -0.1 | 0.4 | 0.1 | 0.0 | 0.0 | 0.7 | 0.8 | 0.5 | 0.1 | 0.5 | 1.8 | -0.3 | 0.1 | 1.1 | 1.2 | 1.4 | 1.4 | -0.5 | 0.2 | -1.3 | -1.1 |
| Belgium | 1.0 | 0.6 | 0.2 | 0.2 | -0.2 | 0.0 | 0.3 | 0.2 | 0.0 | 0.0 | 1.0 | 0.5 | -0.3 | -0.2 | -0.6 | -0.1 | -0.1 | -0.2 | -0.2 | 0.0 | -0.6 | -0.4 | 0.5 | 0.3 | -0.1 | 0.2 |
| Czech Republic | 5.6 | 0.2 | -0.2 | -0.6 | -0.6 | -0.5 | 2.5 | 1.0 | 0.1 | 0.0 | 2.3 | -0.8 | 1.5 | 1.0 | 4.2 | 0.6 | 0.8 | 0.9 | 1.4 | 0.4 | -0.7 | -0.2 | -0.2 | -0.6 | 2.9 | 0.0 |
| Denmark | -1.8 | -2.8 | -0.5 | -0.3 | -0.2 | 0.1 | 0.1 | -0.3 | 1.0 | -0.7 | -2.2 | -1.4 | 0.0 | -0.1 | 6.0 | 3.1 | 1.5 | 0.8 | -0.5 | -0.6 | -1.4 | -1.0 | 8.0 | 4.8 | -1.6 | -0.9 |
| Finland | -0.2 | 1.5 | -0.8 | -0.1 | -0.7 | -0.5 | -0.2 | -0.1 | 0.8 | 1.4 | 0.6 | 1.0 | 0.0 | -0.2 | 11.3 | 5.8 | -0.2 | -0.7 | 3.6 | 2.1 | 11.6 | 8.3 | -1.1 | -1.9 | -2.5 | -2.1 |
| France | -0.5 | -0.6 | -0.6 | -0.4 | 0.0 | -0.1 | 0.1 | -0.1 | 0.1 | 0.3 | -0.2 | -0.1 | 0.0 | -0.2 | -1.3 | -2.0 | -0.5 | -0.7 | -0.1 | -0.2 | -0.6 | -0.5 | 1.3 | 0.9 | -1.4 | -1.5 |
| Germany | -1.0 | -0.3 | -0.6 | -0.3 | 0.1 | 0.3 | -0.2 | 0.0 | 0.2 | 0.0 | -0.6 | -0.5 | 0.1 | 0.2 | -6.2 | -3.9 | -0.6 | -0.6 | -0.6 | -0.1 | -0.2 | -0.1 | -1.4 | -1.0 | -3.4 | -2.1 |
| Greece | 5.5 | 1.5 | 3.9 | 1.4 | -0.3 | 0.3 | 1.6 | 0.5 | -1.2 | -3.3 | 1.8 | 2.5 | -0.4 | 0.2 | 7.6 | 5.8 | -0.7 | -0.4 | -0.3 | -0.3 | -1.2 | -0.5 | 2.4 | 1.9 | 7.3 | 5.0 |
| Hungary | -0.2 | -2.7 | 0.0 | 0.1 | -0.3 | -0.8 | 0.1 | -0.3 | 0.0 | 0.0 | 0.3 | -0.9 | -0.3 | -0.8 | 6.5 | 0.7 | -0.3 | 0.3 | 0.2 | -0.1 | -1.5 | -0.8 | 5.5 | 1.2 | 2.6 | 0.0 |
| Iceland | -6.1 | -0.2 | -4.1 | -3.7 | -2.0 | -1.6 | -0.9 | -0.8 | -1.3 | -0.2 | 4.2 | 8.3 | -2.0 | -2.2 | 24.8 | 19.8 | -2.0 | -2.0 | -1.3 | -1.1 | -2.8 | -1.8 | 34.7 | 27.1 | -3.8 | -2.5 |
| Ireland | -3.6 | -4.3 | -1.0 | -1.3 | -0.8 | -0.9 | -0.3 | -0.4 | 0.0 | 0.0 | -1.0 | -0.8 | -0.5 | -0.8 | 4.9 | -2.6 | -0.2 | -0.8 | -0.4 | -0.4 | 1.4 | 0.0 | 6.1 | 0.4 | -1.9 | -1.8 |
| Italy | -0.3 | 0.9 | -0.6 | 0.0 | 0.5 | 0.7 | 1.3 | 1.1 | 0.2 | 0.1 | -2.8 | -2.1 | 1.2 | 1.2 | 2.9 | 2.8 | 2.6 | 2.0 | -0.6 | -0.5 | -0.7 | -0.4 | -3.0 | -1.1 | 4.6 | 2.9 |
| Netherlands | 1.0 | 0.7 | 1.9 | 1.3 | -0.3 | -0.2 | -0.3 | -0.2 | 0.2 | 0.2 | -0.4 | -0.2 | -0.1 | -0.2 | 1.6 | 1.2 | -0.6 | -0.5 | -0.7 | -0.4 | -0.4 | 0.0 | 4.8 | 2.9 | -1.6 | -0.8 |
| Norway | 6.7 | 8.5 | 3.8 | 4.9 | -1.0 | -1.1 | -0.3 | -0.5 | 1.8 | 1.8 | 3.8 | 4.5 | -1.4 | -1.1 | 0.9 | -1.9 | -0.8 | -1.3 | 0.1 | -0.5 | 1.4 | 0.7 | 3.6 | 2.1 | -3.3 | -2.9 |
| Poland | 7.7 | 1.5 | 0.1 | -0.1 | -1.4 | -0.3 | 0.5 | 0.3 | 2.5 | 1.1 | 5.2 | -0.2 | 0.8 | 0.7 | 5.9 | 5.8 | 2.1 | 3.1 | 2.0 | 1.2 | -1.5 | 0.0 | 1.0 | 1.5 | 2.2 | 0.0 |
| Portugal | -0.4 | -1.0 | 0.9 | -0.3 | -0.7 | 0.0 | 1.7 | 0.9 | -0.1 | 0.0 | -2.4 | -1.9 | 0.2 | 0.3 | 13.1 | 6.9 | 0.1 | 0.3 | 2.2 | 1.7 | 1.2 | 0.7 | -2.2 | -1.8 | 11.8 | 6.0 |
| Slovak Republic | .. | 2.3 | .. | 1.3 | .. | -1.1 | .. | 0.2 | .. | 0.0 | .. | 2.4 | .. | -0.6 | .. | 0.4 | .. | 1.0 | .. | 0.4 | .. | 0.3 | .. | -0.9 | .. | -0.4 |
| Spain | 2.7 | 1.3 | 0.0 | -0.1 | 0.1 | 0.2 | 1.4 | 1.0 | 0.3 | 0.3 | 0.9 | -0.3 | 0.0 | 0.2 | -0.8 | 0.6 | -0.1 | -0.1 | -0.2 | -0.2 | -0.5 | 0.1 | -0.5 | 0.8 | 0.4 | 0.0 |
| Sweden | -0.4 | -1.2 | -0.4 | -0.3 | -0.5 | -0.6 | -0.4 | -0.3 | 0.3 | -0.3 | 0.4 | 0.1 | 0.1 | 0.1 | 1.5 | 1.0 | -0.4 | -0.5 | 2.2 | 1.2 | 4.8 | 4.1 | -2.1 | -2.0 | -3.0 | -1.8 |
| Switzerland | -2.6 | -2.8 | -1.1 | -1.3 | -0.4 | -0.2 | -0.6 | -0.5 | 0.0 | 0.0 | -0.8 | -0.8 | 0.3 | 0.0 | -6.4 | -5.6 | -0.9 | -1.0 | -0.5 | -0.3 | -1.2 | -1.0 | -0.9 | -1.1 | -2.9 | -2.2 |
| Turkey | 2.5 | -2.4 | -0.9 | -1.3 | 0.2 | -2.1 | 1.3 | 1.7 | -0.6 | 0.4 | 2.8 | -1.8 | -0.2 | 0.7 | 20.6 | 15.2 | 0.0 | 0.9 | 0.0 | 0.0 | -0.9 | -0.8 | 2.7 | 1.5 | 18.7 | 13.7 |
| United Kingdom | 0.5 | 0.6 | 0.5 | 0.7 | 0.0 | -0.1 | 0.1 | -0.1 | 0.2 | 0.1 | -0.4 | 0.0 | 0.1 | -0.1 | -3.6 | -4.7 | -0.4 | -0.9 | -0.8 | -0.5 | -0.5 | -0.2 | -0.7 | -0.9 | -1.3 | -2.1 |
| European Union | 0.0 | -0.1 | -0.1 | 0.0 | 0.0 | 0.1 | 0.2 | 0.1 | 0.2 | 0.0 | -0.5 | -0.3 | 0.2 | 0.1 | -1.2 | -1.3 | 0.0 | -0.3 | -0.2 | -0.1 | 0.0 | 0.1 | -0.1 | -0.1 | -0.9 | -0.9 |
| Total OECD[2] | -0.2 | -0.2 | -0.3 | -0.3 | -0.1 | -0.1 | 0.1 | 0.0 | 0.3 | 0.2 | -0.2 | 0.0 | 0.0 | 0.0 | -3.0 | -2.4 | -0.6 | -0.7 | -0.3 | -0.2 | 0.1 | 0.2 | -0.4 | -0.1 | -1.9 | -1.6 |

.. Not available.

1. Observed trade balance of industry minus theoretical trade balance, expressed in hundreds of manufacturing trade (see box in text).
2. Total OECD excludes Czech Republic, Korea, Luxembourg and Slovak Republic.

*Source:* OECD, STAN Indicators databases, March 2005.

OECD PUBLICATIONS, 2, rue André-Pascal, 75775 PARIS CEDEX 16
PRINTED IN FRANCE
(92 2005 07 1 P) ISBN 92-64-01055-6 – No. 54077 2005